**DO NOT REMOVE
CARDS FROM POCKET**

DEREGULATING
WALL STREET

WILEY PROFESSIONAL BANKING AND FINANCE SERIES

EDWARD I. ALTMAN, Editor

THE STOCK MARKET, 4TH EDITION
Richard J. Teweles and Edward S. Bradley

TAX SHELTERED FINANCING THROUGH THE R & D LIMITED
PARTNERSHIP
James K. La Fleur

CORPORATE FINANCIAL DISTRESS: A COMPLETE GUIDE TO
PREDICTING, AVOIDING, AND DEALING WITH BANKRUPTCY
Edward I. Altman

CREDIT ANALYSIS: A COMPLETE GUIDE
Roger H. Hale

CURRENT ASSET MANAGEMENT: CASH, CREDIT, AND INVENTORY
Jarl G. Kallberg and Kenneth Parkinson

HANDBOOK FOR BANKING STRATEGY
Richard C. Aspinwall and Robert A. Eisenbeis

THE BANKING JUNGLE: HOW TO SURVIVE AND PROSPER IN A
BUSINESS TURNED TOPSY TURVY
Paul S. Nadler and Richard B. Miller

ELECTRONIC BANKING
Allen H. Lipis, Thomas R. Marschall, and Jan H. Linker

BUSINESS OPPORTUNITIES FROM CORPORATE BANKRUPTCIES
Rees Morrison

DEREGULATING WALL STREET: COMMERCIAL BANK PENETRATION
OF THE CORPORATE SECURITIES MARKET
Ingo Walter

Deregulating Wall Street

Commercial Bank Penetration of the Corporate Securities Market

INGO WALTER, EDITOR

A Wiley-Interscience Publication

JOHN WILEY & SONS

New   York   •   Chichester   •   Brisbane   •   Toronto   •   Singapore

Library of Congress Cataloging in Publication Data:
Main entry under title:

Deregulating Wall Street.

    (Wiley professional banking and finance series, ISSN 0733-8945)
    "A Wiley-Interscience publication."
    Includes index.
    1. Investment banking—United States. 2. Banks and banking—United States. 3. Wall Street.
I. Walter, Ingo.
HG4930.5.D46   1985   332.1'754'0973   85-5321
ISBN 0-471-81713-9

Printed in the United States of America

10 9 8 7 6 5 4 3 2 1

CONTRIBUTORS

Vincent P. Carosso is the William R. Kenan Professor of History at New York University.

Mark J. Flannery is Associate Professor of Finance at the School of Business Administration, University of North Carolina at Chapel Hill.

Stephen J. Friedman is a partner in the law firm of Debevoise & Plimpton, New York.

Ian H. Giddy is Visiting Associate Professor of Finance and International Business at the Graduate School of Business Administration, New York University.

Edward J. Kelly III is a lawyer based in Washington, D.C.

Thomas F. Huertas is Vice President, Citibank, N.A., New York.

Richard M. Levich is Associate Professor of Finance and Chairman, International Business, at the Graduate School of Business Administration, New York University.

James L. Pierce is Professor of Economics at the University of California, Berkeley.

Thomas A. Pugel is Associate Professor of Economics and International Business at the Graduate School of Business Administration, New York University.

Anthony Saunders is Associate Professor of Finance at the Graduate School of Business Administration, New York University.

Ingo Walter is Professor of Economics and Finance and Chairman of Finance at the Graduate School of Business Administration, New York University.

Lawrence J. White is Professor of Economics at the Graduate School of Business Administration, New York University.

SERIES PREFACE

The worlds of banking and finance have changed dramatically during the past few years, and no doubt this turbulence will continue through the 1980s. We have established the Wiley Professional Banking and Finance Series to aid in characterizing this dynamic environment and to further the understanding of the emerging structures, issues, and content for the professional financial community.

We envision three types of book in this series. First, we are commissioning distinguished experts in a broad range of fields to assemble a number of authorities to write specific primers on related topics. For example, some of the early handbook-type volumes in the series concentrate on the Stock Market, Investment Banking, and Financial Depository Institutions. A second type of book attempts to combine text material with appropriate empirical and case studies written by practitioners in relevant fields. An early example is a forthcoming volume on The Management of Cash and Other Short-Term Assets. Finally, we are encouraging definitive, authoritative works on specialized subjects for practitioners and theorists.

It is a distinct pleasure and honor for me to assist John Wiley & Sons, Inc. in this important endeavor. In addition to banking and financial practitioners, we think business students and faculty will benefit from this series. Most of all, though, we hope this series will become a primary source in the 1980s for the members of the professional financial community to refer to theories and data and to integrate important aspects of the central changes in our financial world.

EDWARD I. ALTMAN

Professor of Finance
New York University,
Schools of Business

PREFACE

More than 50 years ago a wedge was driven into the market for corporate financial services in the United States—the Glass-Steagall Act. Since that time, commercial banks and their affiliates have been barred from underwriting and dealing in corporate securities and from certain other activities which have been the exclusive preserve of the investment banking industry. Investment banks, in turn, have been barred from commercial banking activities. The origins of this separation lie in the political and economic events of the 1920s and early 1930s. It has dominated the manner in which financial services have been supplied to corporations ever since.

Much has changed since the Glass-Steagall Act became law, both in the fabric of financial regulation and in the structure of the American capital markets and the national economy. It seems appropriate, therefore, to reexamine the separation of commercial and investment banking from an economic point of view. Was the Glass-Steagall Act warranted under the circumstances of the time? Has the nation gained or lost from its enactment over the past half century? What are the economic implications of any deregulation of corporate finance that may be undertaken to extend the deregulation that has already occurred in the remainder of the financial services industry?

This volume is intended to address these questions from a predominantly economic point of view. The authors were asked to assess each of the major issues in a balanced manner, from the standpoint of the national interest—specifically, with reference to the soundness of the nation's financial system and to how well that system serves national needs with respect to economic efficiency and growth. The authors were asked, moreover, to evaluate the various dimensions of the problem in an academically defensible manner and yet to format their arguments in relatively nontechnical terms in order to make them accessible to noneconomists. None of this is easy; the problems are often highly complex, and the issue as a whole is highly charged, both economically and politically.

This book is the outgrowth of studies commissioned by J. P. Morgan & Co. Incorporated in 1983 as background for internal analyses of these issues. We are grateful to J. P. Morgan & Co. for allowing the authors to make use of the commissioned research in the preparation of this book. A conference on the project was held on November 30, 1984 under the auspices of the Salomon Brothers Center for the Study of Financial Institutions at New York University. The comments by Stephen J. Friedman, Vincent P. Carosso, and Thomas F. Huertas are products of that conference.

The individual authors are solely responsible for the content and conclusions of each chapter and are writing in their personal and private capacities. The authors also wish to thank Franklin Edwards, Anthony Santomero, Arthur Stonehill, Ithzak Swary, Gregory Udell, and Robert Eisenbeis. Edward Payen and William Prado assisted in preparing the manuscript for publication.

INGO WALTER

New York, New York
March 1985

CONTENTS

1 Introduction and Overview

INGO WALTER

Adam Smith would have been delighted. Information and transactions costs are falling. New competitors are entering the financial services field while others seek exit or combine with viable players as elegantly as possible. New financial products are introduced almost daily, their number and variety limited only by the human imagination. Artificial barriers to competition, some of which have been in place for decades, are being subjected to steady erosion. Competitors bid actively for human as well as financial resources, even as product, process, applications, management, and marketing technologies evolve faster than ever before. An environment of vigorous competition, based at its core on Adam Smith's concept of competitive advantage and specialization, is delivering enormous benefits in the prices and qualities of products made available to customers of all kinds.

This is where the financial services industry in the United States appears to be heading today—in what is probably the most exciting competitive environment to be found anywhere in the world. An archaic system of over 14,500 commercial banks is fast becoming streamlined, as major retail-oriented competitors spread geographically, and regional as well as local institutions plot defensive and collaborative strategies. Disintermediated financial flows link ultimate savers and ultimate investors, large and small, directly via the capital markets even as financial intermediaries scramble to enhance value-added in order to retain in some form their traditional role. Commercial banks are active in the government bond markets, in private placements, in financial advisory work, and in various other dimensions of investment banking. Investment banks, brokerage firms, insurance companies, retailers, and even manufacturing firms are developing lines of financial services where each believes there is a profitable market niche. Banks, meanwhile, are pressing on the real estate business, insurance, and even international trade. Traditional "industry" lines are blurring, even as "activity" lines remain as sharp as ever.

The results? If the process is permitted to work itself out, a far more efficient national financial system will eventually evolve, where excess profits ultimately disappear, transactions costs are driven to a bare minimum, information becomes much more readily available, the basis for rational decision making improves, and only the fittest competitors are able to prosper for very long. The process of financial allocation

1

in the national economy will improve materially, and the gap between what the ultimate saver receives and what the ultimate investor has to pay for funds will be narrowed to the finest possible margin. Perhaps even more important, the new American financial system will improve availability of resources to new and emerging industries, strip away resources from declining and uncompetitive sectors and firms sooner, quite possibly enhance the underlying incentives to save and to invest, accelerate technological change, bolster the ability to shift risk (perhaps arguably), absorb economic and financial shocks with less social damage, and generally support the process of sustainable economic growth.

The United States in recent years has been accused of lagging in many dimensions of economic performance compared with major rivals elsewhere in the world. It certainly is a leader with respect to financial reform and in the design of a system that will serve the nation well in the decades ahead.

It is perhaps in the American tradition that much of the dynamism giving shape to the new financial system is the product of free enterprise—individual firms seeking out new markets with new and improved products at lower cost. Government planning has played a negligible role, and private decisions largely determine both the pace and the direction of change. Yet finance has traditionally been a regulated industry, and so regulatory reform must eventually validate and consolidate the kinds of market-driven changes that are rapidly evolving.

Banking and finance comprise a highly sensitive sector. Fractional reserve banking has inherent risk elements, as does maturity mismatching in asset and liability management. So (despite careful diversification in asset deployment) do exposures incurred in lending activities. The very role of financial intermediation involves the assumption of risks. Moreover, fraud, misrepresentation, financial collapse, predatory behavior, self-dealing, bubbles, busts, and shocks have afflicted the American financial system over the centuries, as they have elsewhere in the world. Problems that afflict an individual institution may have serious consequences for those most directly involved, but may also damage those doing business with that institution in good faith, and may even damage the entire fabric of the national financial and economic system. These are what economists like to call "negative externalities"—costs that are imposed on the rest of society as a result of the private pursuit of profit in a particular line of economic activity.

To cope with this problem, the United States has established a number of institutions to form a set of safeguards that are robust enough to contain external damage triggered by crises in the financial sector, yet do not materially impair the creative forces of private enterprise. Deposit insurance limits erosion of confidence by banking customers. An official lender of last resort is put in place to inject liquidity to individual institutions in trouble (e.g., via the central bank's discount window) and to the financial system as a whole (via open market operations and changes in reserve requirements).

Along with institutional safeguards comes regulation to further support the safety and soundness of the financial system. The apparatus is familiar—reserve requirements, bank examination, maximum lending limits, securities regulation, separation of commercial banking from certain securities business, activity limitations on mutual savings banks and savings and loan institutions, and interest rate ceilings have been the traditional techniques.

Other countries use different kinds of safeguard structures, but the need for them is universally recognized. Indeed, some use bank nationalization to "socialize" both the risks and the returns, and not coincidentally to achieve a direct government role in credit allocation.

The problem with regulation and control is that it invariably erodes the *efficiency* of the system. All of the aforementioned regulatory and supervisory elements have the potential of displacing financial resource allocation from that which is most efficiently driven by the free interplay of market forces. This is as true of reserve requirements as it is of interest-rate ceilings on deposits. Thus the combination of a financial safeguard and regulation results in an erosion of financial efficiency. Greater security is never free; there is always a price to be paid. Here we are buying increased safety with respect to the national financial system and paying for it in the form of reduced financial market efficiency—a logical tradeoff. Is the existing arrangement in any sense optimal? Are we paying too high a price for the increased financial stability we are purchasing? Surely the United States would regard bank nationalization as an extortionate price to pay for any prospective increased financial safety that it would create. Is the price too high under the existing system as well?

Some answers have been provided in the current climate of financial deregulation, which has been broadly aimed at improving financial market efficiency without material sacrifices in system safety—improving the efficiency/safety tradeoff. Interest-rate ceilings on deposits have been largely lifted. Lending limits have been liberalized. New kinds of assets and sources of funding have been permitted to a variety of financial institutions. Futures and options markets have developed. At the same time, deposit insurance, for example, has remained as an essential component of the safeguard structure, with the benefits being passed through to ultimate borrowers and lenders, even as changes are underway to align premiums to individual institutions' losses and to eliminate free-riders. In fact, although the private sector's dynamism is driving for enhanced financial efficiency, thoughtful public policy is striving to ensure that this is not achieved at the risk of an unacceptable erosion of safety—and at the same time is reexamining existing structures in terms of their social and economic cost-effectiveness.

PLAN OF THE BOOK

This volume focuses on a single major aspect of the evolution of finance in the United States—the continued exclusion of affiliates of commercial banks from the origination, underwriting, and dealing in corporate securities. Originally put in place as a reaction to perceived problems of system safety associated with the securities activities of commercial banks, the corporate securities business has been reserved for the investment banking industry for over 50 years. Together with deposit insurance, securities regulation, and other needed reforms, this separation was intended as an integral and necessary component of the new system. But was it really necessary? Did the United States unnecessarily sacrifice substantial financial efficiency for a marginal gain in system safety—or perhaps none at all? Did we in fact pay far too much for little or no additional security? This is the essential focus of the chapters that follow.

We begin with a broad overview of the appropriate role of banks in the modern economy, which addresses these questions within the overall context of financial evolution. This includes the question of bank ''uniqueness'' in an institutional sense. We go on to trace the history of the separation of banking and securities activities, both from a legislative perspective and in relation to the setting in economic history in which it occurred. Next, we evaluate the gains, in terms of financial efficiency, that could be expected from deregulation, by permitting separate affiliates of commercial banks to underwrite and deal in corporate securities. Clearly, if there are no gains, it is difficult to justify deregulation. The prospective gains, in turn, have to be set off against prospective risks associated with deregulation. These include the risk attributes of the securities industry itself, its implications for the safety and soundness of the banking system, and potential conflicts of interest that may arise within firms whose affiliates are engaged in both commercial banking and in the securities business. Finally, we draw some lessons from the international capital markets, specifically the Eurobond market, where the same institutions engage in commercial and investment banking in a largely unregulated environment, contributing to a high degree of financial efficiency without apparent cost in terms of the system's safety and stability.

THE APPROPRIATE ROLE OF BANKS IN THE FINANCIAL SYSTEM

In Chapter 2, James L. Pierce concludes that it is desirable to expand the activities of bank holding companies to include the underwriting of corporate securities, as well as other financial services.

The major portion of the chapter is devoted to a criticism of the ''bank separateness'' school of regulation, whose tenets have been summarized in a 1983 essay by E. Gerald Corrigan. In that essay, Corrigan argues that banks (including thrifts) have the following unique functions that warrant restricting their ''other'' activities: (1) They offer transactions accounts, (2) they are the backup source of liquidity for all other institutions, and (3) they serve as the transmission belt for monetary policy. A distinction is drawn here between bank issuance of transactions accounts and their role in the money-transfer function. Professor Pierce argues that transactions accounts are no longer unique to banks, and that it is the Federal Reserve (rather than the banks) which is the ultimate source of backup liquidity, and that banks are not the sole component of the monetary policy ''transmission belt.'' More important, even if one grants the dubious proposition that banks are ''unique'' in the three functions specified by Corrigan, these roles are not threatened by allowing banking organizations to underwrite corporate securities and to engage in other financial-services activities.

At the core of the arguments of the bank separateness school is the belief that inappropriate activities and improper banking practices produced banking collapses in the nineteenth century and the massive financial collapse of the early 1930s. This assertion is not correct, according to Professor Pierce. Financial panics and banking collapses were produced by the inherent instability of the private fractional-reserve banking system that prevailed at the time. The introduction of federal deposit insurance and the restructuring of the Federal Reserve into an effective central bank in the 1930s provided the foundation for a stable financial system. Professor Pierce argues that these reforms, not those that restricted bank financial-services activities, have produced financial stability in the United States. The Glass-Steagall provisions of the 1933 Banking Act and related statutes cannot assure financial stability in the absence of deposit insurance and an effective central bank. They are a burdensome fifth wheel in the presence of these federal programs.

There is clearly a need to regulate banks in order to protect the insurance fund and to ease the burden on the Federal Reserve System. There is also a need to regulate all financial institutions, including banks, to guard against financial abuses. But the Glass-Steagall provisions and other statutes that restrict bank financial activities are not needed to meet these needs. They are met in other provisions of the law.

The Glass-Steagall Act, and other statutory provisions that have sought to restrict the financial-services activities of banks or their affiliates, have encouraged the entrance of unregulated financial conglomerates into banking. They have also been anticompetitive, according to Professor Pierce. Allowing banking organizations to have powers to underwrite corporate securities and to provide other financial services will not threaten the stability of the financial system, it will not prevent banks from acting as the Federal Reserve's agents for providing liquidity to the economy, and it will not affect monetary policy. It will encourage competition among financial-services firms, and it will encourage innovation.

Professor Pierce concludes in Chapter 2 with a brief proposal to expand the financial-services activities of banking organizations. He suggests that the underwriting of corporate securities and other financial services be conducted through separately capitalized subsidiaries of bank holding companies. To guard against the possibility of undue financial concentration, only de novo or "foothold" acquisitions of securities and other financial-services affiliates would be allowed, with the same treatment for the entrance of securities and other firms into banking.

THE HISTORICAL BACKGROUND

Chapters 3 and 4 focus on the history of the Glass-Steagall Act, prohibiting banks or their affiliates from engaging in corporate securities underwriting and dealing, as well as the economic and political environment that spawned it. In Chapter 3, Edward J. Kelly III carefully traces the legislative history of the Act. In Chapter 4, Mark J. Flannery supplies an economic evaluation of what happened and why.

The Glass-Steagall Act consists of four provisions of the Banking Act of 1933 which was probably the most substantial piece of financial legislation to emerge from the Great Depression. One of the Act's major provisions mandated a virtually complete separation of investment banking from deposit-taking activities. The Act thus eliminated most commercial banking involvement in securities underwriting, which had reached substantial levels by the late 1920s.

The Glass-Steagall Act's sponsors strongly believed that investment banking activities threatened the safety and soundness of the nation's commercial banks. Contrary to today's conventional wisdom, however, it appears that their concerns did not reflect an assessment about the riskiness of underwriting, per se. Instead, the "real bills doctrine" equated sound bank management with an asset portfolio confined to short-term, self-liquidating loans. Senator Carter Glass and other critics of the U.S. banking practice feared that bank involvement in securities underwriting had (directly and indirectly) led banks to increase their holdings of long-term investments. With most liabilities payable on demand, such asset management practices could expose banks to potentially serious liquidity or interest rate risks.

Kelly and Flannery argue that banks did in fact increase their holdings of long-term securities during the 1920s, probably because the demand for short-term corporate loans (viewed in a flow sense) declined substantially. But there is little evidence that the quality of bank securities holdings was responsible for the numerous bank failures of 1930–1933. Rather, the Federal Reserve System's unwillingness to provide liquidity to a banking system beset by depositor runs was largely responsible for the rash of bank failures that occurred at the time. Under the (macroeconomic and monetary policy) circumstances, many banks would have failed even if they had held no long-term bonds at all. Furthermore, there is no convincing evidence that bank securities activities somehow caused the Great Depression.

Reevaluation of the historical events preceding passage of the Glass-Steagall Act indicates that they bear little relation to contemporary securities markets. Most financial abuses from the 1920s would be effectively prevented by modern security markets regulation. Moreover, most of the questionable transactions that appeared to have occurred between banks and their securities affiliates would be deemed illegal under present-day laws and regulations. The desirability of permitting bank securities affiliates in the present regulatory environment should be assessed in terms that bank holding company regulation has now made familiar: Would such an activity provide sufficient net benefits to the public? The question cannot be answered by reference to the experience of the 1920s. Neither is there substantial evidence that the Glass-Steagall Act was a necessary component of the financial reforms of the 1930s. As such, the United States may have paid a price in terms of lost financial efficiency without a commensurate gain in financial stability.

THE COMPETITIVE DIMENSION

In Chapter 5, Thomas A. Pugel and Lawrence J. White use the structure-conduct-performance model of industrial organization to analyze the market for corporate securities underwriting, and to assess the likely effects of entry by commercial bank affiliates upon this market structure and performance. They conclude that the entry of commercial bank affiliates would increase competition in underwriting, leading to lower fees and better service for security issuers.

The market for underwriting the securities of large (e.g., Fortune 1000) companies is moderately concentrated, with the leading four underwriters together accounting for 40–50% of underwritings. The effective market may be even more concentrated, however, because of the specialization patterns that appear to exist among investment banking firms and the differing needs of various issuers. Small and medium-size issuers may face a more restricted set of providers of services; if these issuers cannot attract the attention of one or more of the leading (usually, New York-based) underwriters, they may only have a choice among a handful of local (regional) broker-dealers. The effective concentration facing these issuers may be quite high.

Barriers to entry consist of the necessity to develop a network of contacts and distributional outlets, to establish a reputation and prestige (customer loyalty), and the need to attract skilled personnel—plus the glaring barrier of Glass-Steagall's prohibition on commercial bank entry.

The service (or package of services) provided by underwriters is a complicated one. Customers (issuers) may have a difficult time judging quality in making pricing comparisons among underwriters. But many of the customers are large corporations that have (or are acquiring) the financial expertise to make their own judgments in a competitive marketplace.

Fees seem to be related to cost factors in the industry, but some fees appear to have been unduly stable over long periods of time. And issuers who attract more competition to their issues appear to gain lower underwriting fees (as indicated both by the empirical work done for this study by the authors and by the experience under Rule 415). These latter pieces of evidence indicate that competition in parts of the underwriting industry today is not as vigorous as it might be. Further, the industry has a consistent tendency to underprice new issues—to the loss and detriment of issuers.

Finally, profits in the securities industry generally have been healthy, but specific information about the profitability of underwriting is not available.

The evidence from the competitive structure, behavior, and performance of the underwriting industry—plus the inferences that can be drawn from the evidence concerning commercial bank affiliates' presence in the underwriting of general obligation bonds of state and local governments—indicates that entry into corporate securities underwriting and dealing by commercial bank affiliates would likely have beneficial effects in the form of lower fees and better service for issuers. The problems that are sometimes suggested as drawbacks to commercial bank entry—predatory behavior, tying, conflicts of interest, threats to safety and soundness of banks, or the creation of unfair competition—do not appear to Professors Pugel and White to be likely or serious.

RISKS ASSOCIATED WITH SECURITIES UNDERWRITING

In Chapter 6, Professor Ian H. Giddy examines the risks related to the business of equities underwriting in the United States. He describes in some detail the underwriting process and its decomposition into several more or less discrete functions. The return associated with securities underwriting, in the form of a "spread" between the price received by the issuer and the actual selling price of the securities involved, compensates the underwriters for their exposure to risk, for distribution services, and for the various costs incurred in the process.

Risk in the underwriting of corporate securities arises when an underwriting syndicate agrees to purchase a block of securities from the issuer at one price and to resell it to the public at another price, the offer price. The offer price sets an upper limit to the underwriter's revenues. But the underwriter who is unable to sell at the offer price, perhaps because of changes in market conditions, may be forced to hold the securities or sell at a loss.

Professor Giddy argues that this lopsided risk differs in degree, but not in character, from the risk of making a commercial loan. A key difference between commercial banking and securities underwriting lies in the way risk is limited. In lending, containment of risk is accomplished by careful credit analysis and portfolio diversification, encompassing a time period that is relatively long. In underwriting, risk-mitigation involves maintaining an extremely short underwriting period, as well as the use of various hedging options that have become available.

An empirical analysis of over 2500 U.S. equity issues during the period 1976–1983 indicates that net losses, defined as instances where the price paid by the underwriters apparently exceeded the price received, occurred in a very small proportion of cases.

Although there are risks inherent in equity underwriting, a conclusion that may be drawn from Giddy's analysis is that even maximum losses have been tolerable for firms in the industry, and that the associated risks are quite manageable. Despite the lack of good market price data for debt issues, the empirical evidence suggests a comparable conclusion for corporate bond underwriting.

Professor Giddy's interpretation of his results is that securities underwriting is not inherently riskier than commercial lending. Historically, losses have remained at a tolerable level and compare favorably with other risks inherent in banking and the financial services industry generally. Indeed, by adding an activity whose returns are not perfectly correlated with returns from other financial services, the addition of securities underwriting will tend to reduce (through greater diversification) the riskiness of the enterprise as a whole.

Moreover, the study suggests, the riskiness of holding particular financial assets depends not only on how volatile they are, but also on how liquid they are. The assets purchased in equity and bond underwriting *are* riskier than those purchased in commercial lending. Yet investment bankers are able to hold the magnitude of losses to a small percentage by reducing the holding period to a very small time interval. This is because there is a sufficiently liquid market that the securities can be marked-to-market, and they can be sold before their value has deteriorated seriously. In contrast, a major source of commercial bank risk lies in the time lag associated with the valuation and liquidation of consumer and commercial loans.

SECURITIES ACTIVITIES AND BANK SAFETY AND SOUNDNESS

Given the role of banks as important institutions in a nation's financial and economic system, they have long been the object of safety and soundness concerns. Given the nature of their linkage to depositors, borrowers, and other financial institutions—and particularly their alleged position at the core of the transactions (payments) system—there is a continuing concern that bank failure(s) could trigger significant social costs which extend far beyond the individual institution in difficulty. Whether banks or their holding companies are permitted to extend their range of activities into corporate securities underwriting and dealing, however structured, will therefore depend on the absence of materially adverse effects on institutional safety and soundness.

In Chapter 7, Anthony Saunders examines this issue from an economic perspective with respect to the involvement of bank holding companies, through separately capitalized affiliates, in the origination, underwriting, and dealing in corporate securities within the U.S. capital market.

Professor Saunders concludes that the risks posed by bank affiliate involvement in domestic securities business for the safety and soundness of the banking system are rather limited. Even if a securities affiliate were to sustain serious losses, a variety of economic incentives and institutional constraints exist to insulate the bank effectively. Indeed, it is argued on the basis of empirical evidence that securities activities by bank holding companies might represent effective diversification, and thus actually serve to enhance the safety and soundness of banks in the national economy—as suggested in the empirical analysis in the previous chapter by Ian Giddy.

Further insights into this question can be gained by assessing the results of capital market studies that focus on "efficient markets" and investor's risk perceptions as reflected in equity prices and returns. The evidence from these studies suggests, for instance, that the legislative containment of bank holding company activities in 1970 had no statistically significant effect in changing investors' perceptions regarding bank holding company exposure to risk. Conversely, regulatory denials on the part of the Fed of applications for extension of activities by bank holding companies served to increase investors' perceptions of exposure to risk in the period immediately following. The evidence using market models thus supports the earlier findings and suggests that involvement of bank holding companies, through affiliates, in securities activities may ameliorate the degree of risk associated with these institutions (and enhance the safety and soundness attributes of banks) through market and geographic diversification.

On both conceptual and empirical grounds, then, Saunders' analysis shows no likely material impairment—and indeed some potential for enhancing the safety and stability of the banking system—as a result of the involvement by commercial bank affiliates in corporate securities underwriting and dealing.

THE PROBLEM OF CONFLICTS OF INTEREST

In addition to the safety and soundness concerns related to the participation by affiliates of bank holding companies in corporate securities activities, there is the issue of potential conflicts of interest, which in turn raises questions about the appropriate structure of external surveillance and regulatory mechanisms. Are the potential conflicts of interest indeed serious from the standpoint of economic analysis? If they are found to be relatively minor or easily manageable within existing institutional structures, they should not stand in the way of the benefits of financial deregulation.

In Chapter 8, Anthony Saunders explores the economic underpinnings of nine conflicts found in the literature opposing modifications to the Glass-Steagall Act. In each case, the nature of the potential conflict is briefly explained, as are the conditions under which it might in fact be exploited and lead to social or economic difficulties. Specific factors that, on the other hand, serve to limit the significance of several of these potential conflicts are also discussed.

The core of the chapter is an evaluation of the economic incentives and disincentives that will tend to determine whether such conflicts are in fact exploited. Incentives that may favor exploitation include managerial behavior which is at variance with the fundamental long-run profit-maximizing interests of the holding company and its shareholders. However, various institutional and market factors such as the nature of bonus or profit-sharing schemes, as well as the competitive nature of the market for corporate control and bank products and services, are important in containing these incentives.

Other factors working against exploitation of potential conflicts are discusssed in considerable detail, focusing on the value of the holding company as a going concern to its shareholders. This value includes the imbedded market value of its reputation (or goodwill). Also of importance is the role of the bond-rating agencies and the examination (or surveillance) activities of supervisory and regulatory institutions.

Saunders' main conclusion is that the profitability of exploiting conflicts of interest is dependent on the competitive nature of the markets in which the bank and its securities affiliate interact, and the degree of information available to participants in those markets. In particular, if markets are highly (and increasingly) competitive and the quality and speed of dissemination of information available to customers about the behavior of sellers are good, then it is unlikely that conflicts could be consistently and profitably exploited. Because financial markets are becoming more competitive as a result of deregulation, and information is often quickly and efficiently disseminated, it can be argued that the potential for persistent conflict exploitation is rather low and declining.

Saunders concludes that, on balance, the economic incentives bearing on bank holding companies and their affiliates are such that the persistent and extensive exploitation of potential conflict situations is unlikely. Thus the benefits of restricting bank holding company expansion into securities activities, in terms of preventing conflicts of interest, appear to be rather small indeed compared to the costs incurred by society in the form of reduced financial efficiency and contribution to economic growth.

In Chapter 9, Edward J. Kelly III discusses the legal and regulatory constraints that are intended to prevent the exploitation of conflicts of interest. Whereas the analysis by Saunders evaluates the economic incentives and disincentives for conflict exploitation, Kelly is concerned with the external constraints. He finds them to be very robust indeed, so that they complement the overall economic disincentives and in some sense represent a backup system of constraints to impede the persistent exploitation of conflicts of interest involving securities activities by affiliates of commercial banks.

LESSONS FROM THE INTERNATIONAL CAPITAL MARKET

In the discussions concerning participation by securities affiliates of U.S. commercial bank holding companies in corporate financial services, it is often forgotten that this participation has existed for decades in the Eurobond market and for far longer in national capital markets abroad. Indeed, U.S. commercial bank affiliates are major, innovative, and successful participants in the Eurobond market and—where they are permitted to do so—in foreign securities markets as well. It is therefore appropriate to examine the behavior of these markets, and to ascertain what lessons, if any, they hold for financial deregulation in the United States.

The evidence presented in Chapter 10 by Richard M. Levich suggests that the Eurobond market has indeed "succeeded" in the sense that the market can survive without artificial support and continues to fulfill the very real demands of both borrowers and lenders. In the early years, the market enjoyed "protection" because of U.S. domestic policies that pushed borrowers offshore. Demand for Eurobond issues has fluctuated through time with both exchange rate and interest rate expectations. Underwriters took protective measures—for example, to deal with AAA clients to minimize credit risks; to adequately spread underwriting risks among multiple firms; to set transaction costs high enough to provide an adequate cushion; and to establish "gray markets" to minimize the price risk of unsold securities.

Levich's analysis suggests that if the United States allows commercial banking and investment banking activities to take place within the context of a single holding company, the result will *not* be a system of "universal banks" that resembles those existing in Europe. This is because concentration in the banking industry is, and is likely to remain, far less in the United States than in Europe, the linkages between corporations and banks are weaker in the United States than in Europe, and the thrust of government regulation is vastly dissimilar.

Evidence from the Eurobond market strongly suggests that, within its essentially unregulated environment with no artificial barriers to entry, underwriters do indeed behave prudently. They have organized a market, providing substantial benefits to both borrowers and lenders, without incurring substantial risks. The evidence offers strong reason to believe that U.S. commercial bank affiliates could similarly behave prudently in competition with the traditional U.S. investment banking houses, without undermining the basic safety and stability of the system. Regulation and supervision of commercial bank-related corporate securities underwriting and dealing activities would establish minimum capital requirements, adequate disclosure of information, and sufficient separation from commercial banking operations. The increased competition would in all likelihood result in significant net benefits to the economy at a minimal increase in risk to society.

CONCLUSIONS

This volume essentially represents an exercise in cost-benefit analysis applied to a specific policy issue—the prospective entry of bank holding company affiliates into corporate securities acivities in the United States after more than 50 years of separation. This presupposes, of course, that investment banks and other firms engaged in financial services would be equally free to enter commercial banking through separately structured affiliates.

The *benefits* are largely associated with improved allocational efficiency in the national capital market to the benefit of both borrowers and lenders, as well as enhanced real output and income. They are also associated with intensified innovation in financial products and processes, and perhaps accelerated rates of growth in capital formation. And there is the increasing international integration of capital markets, wherein domestic deregulation could significantly benefit U.S. firms in their competitive positioning around the world. The potential benefits are thus static and dynamic, national and international in scope.

The potential *costs* are related to possible threats to the safety and soundness of the banking system, conflicts of interest, as well as possible impairment to the effectiveness of the capital-allocation process in the United States. The economic analysis contained in this volume suggests that these risks are limited, and are certainly constrained by the existing structure of securities and banking regulation. Possible regulatory gaps could be easily closed with appropriate legislation.

The analysis is undertaken in as balanced a manner as possible, largely viewed from an economic perspective with reference to the national interest. The issues under discussion here involve high stakes. It will be up to the political mechanism to decide what is indeed in the national interest. The analysis contained in this volume suggests that the benefits of deregulation do appear to outweigh the costs significantly, and that the nation should proceed with the task that lies ahead.

2 On the Expansion of Banking Powers

JAMES L. PIERCE

Considerable controversy has developed in recent years concerning whether banks should be allowed to offer an expanded menu of financial services. Recent developments, including the acquisition of banking powers by thrift institutions, the move of nonbanking firms into banking areas, and the introduction of new activities by banks have sparked the debate. Proponents of expanding bank financial-services activities argue that economic forces, rather than government regulation, should determine the financial services that banks provide. Opponents argue that expanding banking powers to include the underwriting of corporate securities, the provision of general insurance and mutual funds, and other financial services is undesirable because it could threaten the safety and soundness of the banking system. This chapter contributes to the debate by addressing three issues. It examines the current role of banks, it evaluates the benefits and costs of expanding banking powers, and it endorses an approach to deregulation that allows enhanced powers for banking organizations while assuring the safety and soundness of the banking system.

This chapter stresses several propositions. First, the Glass-Steagall provisions of the Banking Act of 1933 did not prohibit banks from engaging in many types of securities activities. The Glass-Steagall provisions only prohibited banks from direct underwriting and dealing in corporate securities and most types of municipal revenue bonds and banks from offering mutual funds.[1] Second, the composition of bank liabilities and assets have changed dramatically since the 1930s. Banks no longer depend upon transactions accounts as their primary source of funds, and their lending is spread over a large number of areas and maturities.[2] Third, the stability of the monetary system is now assured by federal deposit insurance and an effective central bank. Fourth, provisions of the securities acts, the Federal Reserve Act, and the Bank Holding Company Act prevent the self-dealing, abuses from conflicts of interest, and other problems that arose prior to the mid-1930s.

It is crucial to keep these propositions in mind if there is to be a fruitful discussion of the implications of expanding the powers of banking organizations. If these propositions are forgotten or omitted, it is all too easy to fall into the trap of arguing that expanding bank powers will return the banking system to the world of the 1920s and early 1930s. This cannot occur.

THE CURRENT ROLE OF BANKS

In evaluating the desirability of allowing banks expanded powers, it is important to appreciate the powers that they currently possess. It is equally important to appreciate the contributions that both government regulation and economic forces have made which affect the role of banks in the economy.

Efforts to regulate bank activities began in the early nineteenth century, and the evolution to the current regulatory structure was largely completed by the mid-1930s. This structure is intended to assure the ''safety and soundness'' of banks and to prevent banks from engaging in undesirable practices. Law and regulation have sought to define the role of banks in the economy by restricting the activities in which they engage. This has meant that bank activities often have been determined not by economic forces and natural specialization, but by government *fiat*.

The govermment prohibits banks from engaging in commercial activities such as retail trade and manufacturing in an effort to separate banking from other areas of the economy,[3] and banks are also excluded from certain kinds of financial activities. The separation of banking from these financial activities is far from absolute, however.[4] Banking organizations are prohibited from engaging in certain kinds of securities activities, such as underwriting and dealing in corporate securities, and from offering general forms of insurance and mutual funds. Banking organizations are allowed to hold certain corporate securities for their own accounts; to aid in the private placement of corporate securities; to act as agent for customers in purchasing and selling securities of all kinds; to underwrite and deal in general obligation municipal securities; to deal in U.S. government securities; to underwrite and deal overseas in corporate securities; to engage in trust activities, including the packing of ''mutual funds'' for trust customers; to deal in foreign exchange, financial futures, and bullion; and to offer credit life insurance. Despite the substantial powers that banking organizations possess, existing prohibitions limit the ability of the banking industry to offer a full range of financial services to the public.

Banks currently have considerable flexibility in the liabilities they can issue. In fact, by providing federal deposit insurance, the government has granted a considerable competitive advantage to banks and other depository institutions over other financial organizations.[5] Until recently, commerical banks had the exclusive right to offer transactions accounts, but the monopoly has disappeared because thrift institutions can offer NOW accounts and under certain circumstances demand deposit accounts. The ability of banks to exploit the competitive advantage of federally insured accounts was limited by interest rate ceilings that were imposed during the 1930s in a misguided attempt to protect the ''safety and soundness'' of banks. Many of these ceilings have been eliminated, but the prohibition against paying interest on demand deposit accounts remains.

Restrictions on bank activities have not prevented a quiet revolution in bank portfolio composition from occurring over the last 30 years, which has remained largely unnoticed by the proponents of forced specialization. For example, in 1952 approximately 70% of commercial bank assets were supported by demand deposit accounts. By the end of 1982 only 24% of bank assets were supported by transactions accounts of any kind. Banks now issue liabilities in virtually all facets of the money and capital markets. They offer negotiable CDs with denominations in excess of the insured amount, and they offer Eurodollar liabilities, repurchase agreements (RPs), and subordinated debt. Bank holding companies and nonbank affiliates issue commercial paper and other debt instruments. The asset side of bank balance sheets has also experienced remarkable change. In 1952, banks held only 35% of their assets as loans and related assets. By the end of 1982, the figure stood at 70%. The nature of bank lending and related activities has also changed dramatically.[6] Banks have gone from being short-term lenders to business to providing business loans over a wide spectrum of maturities. There also has been a remarkable rise in consumer and mortgage lending by banks and their affiliates. As a final example, banks and their holding company affiliates have become a substantial force in the leasing business.

Over the last decade, a combination of improved technology, high interest rates, and regulatory constraints has accelerated the change in the role of banks and it has blurred the distinction between banking and other financial activities. With the advent of high-speed and increasingly inexpensive data processing systems, the costs of financial transactions have fallen markedly in recent years.[7] Aided by the revolution in data processing, communications, and accounting systems—and sparked by high and variable interest rates—banks *and* other institutions now offer a host of attractive services to the public. For example, banks offer highly automated cash-management systems that allow businesses to economize on demand deposit account balances. Similarly, the securities industry developed money market mutual funds that offer high return, liquid assets to the public through which third-party payments can be made.

These developments broke down the barrier between banking and other financial activities. Nonbank financial institutions can offer demand depositlike accounts to the public at market interest rates without the regulatory impediments faced by banks. This led to the demise of most interest rate ceilings (except the prohibition against paying interest on demand deposit accounts), but it did not stem the tide of securities and other firms entering the "banking" business. These "nonbanking" firms now operate full-service financial centers in which insurance, full securities services, mutual funds, real estate, and conventional "banking" are offered under one roof. Through the acquisition of thrift institutions and "nonbank banks," which offer insured accounts, these financial conglomerates can, and do, engage in a wider range of activities than conventional commercial banks.

Banks have been resourceful in rising to the competitive challenge under the existing regulatory structure. For example, they offer discount brokerage services, they rent space in their offices to insurance companies, and they have moved to operate their own "nonbank banks."[8] Desite these innovations, banks are still unable to offer as large a menu of financial services as nonbank financial conglomerates.

Many banks are experiencing competitive pressures from the securities, insurance, and commercial firms that have entered banking through the back door. Furthermore, faced with high-cost distribution networks that are the legacy of Regulation Q and the prohibition against paying interest on demand deposit balances, many banks are seeking new sources of revenue provided by activities from which they are currently prohibited, such as underwriting corporate securities, operating mutual funds, and offering general insurance services. Many bankers are asking the natural question: "If securities and insurance firms can enter banking, why prohibit banks from entering the securities and insurance business?"

This question and attempts to obtain legislative changes have provoked a response by nonbanking competitors and many regulators that it is not socially desirable for banks to enter new lines of activity. The concerns and criticisms voiced by these groups are largely an appeal for the continuation of the restrictions on bank securities and insurance activities of the Glass-Steagall and Bank Holding Company Acts. It is argued that banks can continue to perform their proper role in the economy only if the restrictions on bank activities specified in these acts are left in place.

In attempting to determine the "proper" role of banking, it is important to bear in mind that government regulation has inhibited the evolution of banking, but it has not stopped it. The role of banks today is radically different from what it was a few decades ago. This has occurred without the financial disruptions and credit abuses that characterized the American financial scene prior to the mid-1930s.[9] These developments suggest that it is possible to have changes in the role of banks without returning to the situation that existed prior to the mid-1930s.

THE BANK-SEPARATENESS SCHOOL

Much has been written about the need to limit bank activities. An informative analysis of why bank activities should be restricted is provided by E. Gerald Corrigan in his article "Are Banks Special?"[10] Corrigan argues that banks (defined to include all types of depository institutions) enjoy a unique and crucial role in the economy that warrants restricting their "nonbanking" activities. He lists three unique roles of banks: they offer transactions accounts, they are the backup source of liquidity for all other institutions, and they are the transmission belt for monetary policy. He concludes that these three functions require that limits be placed on banking powers, and on the ownership and control of banks. Corrigan argues that separating banking from nonbank financial activities assures both the "safety and soundness" of the banking system, and the impartiality of bank credit decisions.

Note that for Corrigan's conclusion to be correct, two conditions must be met. Banks must be unique in performing the three essential functions *and* those functions must be threatened by allowing banks to engage in new activities. It is argued below that neither condition is met in reality. Banks are not unique in such functions as offering transactions accounts or acting as backup sources of liquidity. Furthermore, the importance that banks enjoy as backup sources of liquidity and as the transmission belt of monetary policy is largely a consequence of law and regulation and not of any basic economic forces. More important, even if one concedes the proposition that banks (including thrifts) have the three unique functions listed by Corrigan, allowing them to engage in new financial-services activities will have no significant effect on their ability to perfor:n these functions.

Before turning to these issues, however, it is important to stress that the analysis which follows uses Corrigan's essay as its focal point because it states the case for restricting bank activities relatively systematically and completely. It represents a view that has substantial support within the Federal Reserve System, among certain members of Congress, and within the popular press. The comments that follow are not so much a criticism of Corrigan's article as they are of the "bank-separateness" school it represents.

ARE BANKS UNIQUE?

The first step in the analysis is to address the issue of bank uniqueness. It will be argued later that this issue is something of a red herring because allowing banks to provide new financial services will not imperil their provision of existing services. It makes no difference, therefore, whether they are unique or not. It is still useful, however, to discuss bank uniqueness because it is an important element in the argument of Corrigan and other members of the bank-separateness school.

The Role of Banks in the Monetary and Payments Systems

Banks offer transactions accounts whose balances are payable on demand, at par, in the form of cash, or payments to third parties. These characteristics make transactions accounts the principal component of the nation's stock of money.[11]

Until recently, banks were unique in the provision of transactions accounts, but now thrift institutions also offer these accounts. It might appear that this problem can be solved by following Corrigan and including thrifts in the definition of banks. In some respects this is a reasonable approach, but it trades one problem for another. Thrift institutions are not bound by the Glass-Steagall provisions of the Banking Act of 1933 or by the Bank Holding Company Act which restrict bank activities and bank ownership. Thrifts can, and do, engage in many of the activities that the bank-separateness school would prohibit for banks. If "banks" are unique in the provision of transactions accounts, then presumably all banks should be treated alike by law and regulation in terms of providing other services.[12]

Even if thrifts are included in the definition of banks, they still are not unique because money market mutual funds also offer transactions accounts by teaming up with agent banks for check writing and wire transfers. Corrigan and others argue that these accounts are different from those issued by banks (depository institutions) because the accounts are not insured and, therefore, payment at par is not guaranteed.[13] Deposit insurance does make the transactions account liabilities of money funds different from those of commercial banks and thrifts. It should be noted, however, that payment at par is not a property of banking per se, but of a governmental policy to insure the liabilities of depository institutions and not of money market funds. Furthermore, the bank-separateness school is engaging in hairsplitting when arguing that payment at par makes banks unique. Money market mutual funds back their liabilities with short-term assets in major companies, including banks. These liquid and safe assets allow the money funds to compete successfully with banks by effectively providing payment at par.[14]

The provision of transactions accounts by money market mutual funds is not an insignificant issue because the liabilities of these mutual funds are quantitatively important. They currently equal nearly 50% of total transactions accounts at depository institutions. This gives an indication of the extent to which money market funds have eliminated the uniqueness of banks. Furthermore, ''nonbank banks'' controlled by financial conglomerates offer insured transactions accounts. It is unrealistic to argue that banks and other conventional depository institutions have a unique role because only they offer transactions accounts.

Banks (including thrifts) do have a unique role in the nation's payment system. They, together with the Federal Reserve, handle the payments and settlements for third-party payments using transactions accounts. This role is also played by ''nonbank banks'' controlled by financial conglomerates, however, and these payments activities are functionally separate and distinct from the actual provision of transactions accounts.[15] Furthermore, this unique role is produced by governmental *fiat* that excludes others from the payments system, and not by any economic forces. In principle, the power to handle payments and settlements could be extended to other firms. As matters stand, however, banks and ''nonbank banks'' play a unique, technical (agent's) role that is crucial to the nation's payment system. It is argued later in this chapter that there is nothing in the proposed expansion of banking powers which would threaten this low-risk role for banks and ''nonbank banks.''

Banks as the Transmission Belt for Monetary Policy

Members of the bank-separateness school assert that banks require special regulatory treatment because they are the transmission belt of monetary policy. Although this is not the place to discuss the arcane issue of whether banks are essential to monetary policy, it should be noted that the nonuniqueness of banks in the transmission of monetary policy has been demonstrated repeatedly by monetary economists.[16] For the sake of simplicity, however, it will be agreed that under the current institutional and regulatory structure, the banking system plays an important role in transmitting changes in monetary policy to the rest of the economy. This still leaves the question: ''So what?'' All that the transmission-belt function requires is that the banking system exists, not that bank activities in securities, insurance, and other markets be restricted. It is unrealistic to believe that without these restrictions, the banking system would collapse and the Federal Reserve would lose its transmission belt.

The Federal Reserve uses open market operations, reserve requirements, and the discount window to affect the quantity of money, credit, and interest rates in the economy with the ultimate objective of affecting national output, employment, and prices. It is useful to examine the effect of each of these policy instruments to determine whether there is any fundamental and unique role that banks play in connecting changes in these instruments to changes in the objectives of policy.

Open market operations involve purchases and sales of U.S. government securities by the Federal Reserve. Purchases of securities by the Fed increase the nation's monetary base (currency and reserves of depository institutions), which increases the quantity of money and credit in the economy.[17] Sales of securities reduce the monetary base which produces declines in the quantity of money and credit. Banks are an important element in the process by which open market operations affect money and credit, as are money market mutual funds and other financial institutions.[18]

Banks (and thrifts) are unique because they are required by law to hold idle reserves against their transactions account and nonpersonal time account liabilities.[19] This uniqueness is produced by law and not by any economic forces. Although monetary policy functions quite well in many countries without imposing substantial cash reserve requirements, Federal Reserve officials have argued forcefully that they are essential for U.S. monetary policy. It would be unfortunate if financial deregulation and restructuring turned on this issue. There is nothing in the proposals to expand the powers of banking organizations that would prevent the Fed from continuing to impose reserve requirements on the transactions accounts and nonpersonal time account liabilities of depository institutions. Thus this element of the transmissions belt is unaffected by financial deregulation. Although a case can be made for extending reserve requirements to the liabilities of money market mutual funds and any other transactions' accountlike devices, this issue is separate and distinct from the question of expanding the powers of banks. It does illustrate, however, that there is nothing inherently unique about reserve requirements for banks.

The third instrument of monetary policy involves the discount window. The monetary base increases when the Federal Reserve extends credit through the discount window, and the monetary base declines when credit extensions decline. Changes in these credit extensions have much the same effect on the quantity of money and credit as do open market operations. As a practical matter, the Federal Reserve uses open market operations as its primary means of affecting the quantity of money and credit. It uses the discount window to provide funds to institutions that are encountering liquidity problems which cannot be solved easily by selling assets or borrowing funds in private markets. The availability of funds from the discount window is administered, or rationed, by the Fed to prevent institutions from using this source of funds for normal business purposes.[20]

Only banks and other depository institutions against which reserve requirements can be assessed are allowed to use the discount window. Other institutions have access only in the event of a national emergency. This gives banks and thrifts a unique status, but it is a matter of law and regulation not of any economic forces.

The access of banks and thrifts to the discount window suggests that if these institutions were subjected to increased liquidity problems, their use of the discount window would rise. If the admission of banks into new areas and the more free access of financial conglomerates to banking were to increase bank risk and weaken public confidence in banks, an increased number of banks might be subjected to large deposit outflows. To the extent that these outflows could not be offset by increased interbank borrowing, the affected banks would have to turn to the discount window. In this situation, there would be increased fluctuations in borrowing from the discount window and the average amount of borrowing would rise.

Although it is unlikely that these events would occur, if they did, they would not significantly reduce the efficacy of monetary policy. The Fed engages in open market operations to offset any undersired changes in the quantity of reserves produced by changes in borrowing at the discount window. If borrowing rises, the Federal Reserve sells an equal amount of securities in the open market. These open market sales reduce total reserves in the system by the amount that discount window borrowing increases total reserve. After the smoke has cleared, total reserves and the quantity of money and credit remain unchanged.[21] When borrowing at the discount window falls, the Fed purchases securities in the open market, which expands reserves to offset the decline from reduced use of the discount window. Again the quantity of reserves, money, and credit are unaffected.

These procedures have been used in the past, such as with the large swing in borrowed reserves associated with the failure of Franklin National Bank in 1974, and are now being used to handle the borrowing from the discount window by Continental Illinois. There is no reason to believe that the possibility of greater fluctuations and a higher average level of borrowed reserves would significantly reduce the efficacy of monetary policy. Furthermore, it is unlikely that this change in the use of the discount window would occur at all.

Banks as the Backup Source of Liquidity

There is an additional role of the discount window, whose potential increased use might be a source of concern for the bank-separateness school. Corrigan and others assert that the banking system is the backup source of liquidity for other institutions. If deregulation were to produce greater banking instability, this function could be disturbed. Although members of the bank-separateness school overstate the role of private banks as the source of backup liquidity relative to other financial institutions such as insurance and commercial credit companies, the role is important. What they fail to mention, however, is that banks alone cannot provide the liquidity. Consider a financial crisis in the commercial paper market such as occurred with the failure of the Penn Central. During such a crisis, many highly solvent corporations find it difficult (if not impossible) to borrow in the commercial paper market. They draw on their lines of credit from banks. But by itself, the banking system cannot supply the funds. There are virtually no excess reserves in the banking system, so no money and credit expansion is available from that source. Banks can "create" additional money and credit only to the extent they have additional reserves. A bank's only recourse is to turn to the CD and other markets for funds. This represents a reshuffling of money-market credit rather than any net increase. In the absence of Federal Reserve support, there is little reason to believe that during a financial crisis banks will be any more successful in raising funds in the money markets than their large corporate customers.

During a financial crisis, the Federal Reserve opens the discount window to banks so that they can obtain funds to honor their credit commitments.[22] Federal Reserve support of banks through access to the discount window provides assurance that funds will be available to banks to repay maturing CDs. This allows banks to raise funds in the CD market even when the money market is not available to many of their large corporate customers. It also limits the extent to which banks must actually use the discount window. It is the Federal Reserve *not* private banks that is the ultimate source of backup liquidity to other institutions. It uses banks as the conduit, but they cannot provide the liquidity by themselves. Banks can "create" money and credit only if the Fed provides the reserves.

The Federal Reserve's role as the lender of last resort, and the economy's ultimate source of liquidity, is crucial to the stability of the financial system. Even in the unlikely event that banking deregulation would somehow reduce stability in other financial markets, the banking system would continue to play its role by serving as agent for the Federal Reserve's provision of liquidity. As long as the Fed does its job in providing liquidity during financial crises, there will be a banking system.

The arguments of the bank-separateness school are not compelling. They overstate their case by arguing that banks are unique because they offer transactions accounts, act as the transmission belt for policy, and as the backup source of liquidity. Banks and other depository institutions are unique because they have cash reserve requirements and special access to the discount window. Reserve requirements could be imposed on other types of institutions such as money market funds, or reserve requirements could be eliminated for depository institutions. In either case, monetary policy would remain intact. Furthermore, the discount window could be made available to nonbanking firms such as insurance companies and other financial institutions who could then serve as the Fed's agents for providing liquidity. In principle, the Fed could lend directly to whoever needs assistance; it is not necessary to use intermediaries. Thus the special features of banks are the result of law and regulation and not of any fundamental economic forces. Finally, and more important, reducing or eliminating the separateness of banks from securities underwriting and other financial-services activities would not affect the important role that they currently play.

ASSURING STABILITY OF THE BANKING SYSTEM

Banks' monetary and payments functions do give them an important role in the economy. Few would disagree with the assertion that maintenance of the nation's monetary and payments systems is an appropriate objective of public policy. Where disagreements arise is in how best to achieve this objective.

Members of the bank-separateness school argue that an essential element in achieving stable monetary and payments systems is to assure the safety and soundness of the individual banks in the banking system. It is argued, at least implicitly, that if individual banks are not allowed to fail, or at least only allowed to fail gracefully through government-arranged mergers or government guarantees to uninsured depositors, the public will always have faith in banks and the system will remain sound. Efforts to produce stability by this means are made at the cost of inefficiency and anticompetitive practices. It is argued below that it is unnecessary to protect each and every bank from failure in order to preserve the stability of the monetary and payments systems.

In order to analyze the issues involved, it is crucial to distinguish the safety of an individual bank from that of the banking system. A basic fallacy in the argument of the bank-separateness school is the assertion that regulatory restrictions can preclude bank runs and financial panics. Prior to the financial reforms of the 1930s that established federal deposit insurance and restructured the Federal Reserve into an effective central bank, the banking system was inherently unstable. This instability was not the result of weak regulation and supervision of banks, although there were many weak and poorly supervised banks; rather it was a consequence of private, fractional-reserve banking. Under a fractional system, which exists in a stable form today, banks accept deposits that are payable on demand. To meet these demands, banks hold only a fraction of their deposit liabilities as cash reserves and liquid assets. The remainder is lent out.

If the system is running smoothly, there are no large currency drains or substantial increases in bank demand for cash reserves. In this situation, the relatively small amount of cash and liquid assets is sufficient to meet withdrawals. Customer withdrawals tend to be offset by deposits by other customers, so the net drain on cash and liquid assets is small. Furthermore, if one bank has large net withdrawals, the funds are usually deposited in other banks. This means that banks losing funds can borrow from banks gaining funds.[23] It also has a ready market for its sales of securities and other liquid assets because banks gaining funds are purchasing these assets. The banking system can, and does, handle large net withdrawals from individual banks provided that the public deposits the funds in other banks.[24]

The situation is different when the public makes withdrawals of cash rather than shifting funds from one bank to another. In this case, one bank's deposit drain is not offset by deposit inflows at other banks.[25] Massive currency drains occur during financial panics. The public loses faith in banks and attempts to make cash withdrawals. In a fractional-reserve system, bank holdings of cash are far less than their deposit liabilities. Each bank attempts to meet its withdrawals by drawing down cash, selling assets, borrowing from other banks, and refusing to renew loans. Despite these efforts there is not enough cash to meet withdrawal demands.[26] During a general panic, banks hoard their cash in the expectation of currency drains rather than lending it to other banks. There are massive sales of securities and other assets by banks, which reduce asset values. Banks also stop lending. These reactions produce a decline in business activity, increased unemployment, and a rise in bankruptcy. Some of the loans on banks' books become worthless. Thus not only are banks unable to meet all demands for cash withdrawals, they are also forced into insolvency as the value of their assets falls below the value of their liabilities.

Note that it is the public's flight to currency that causes the banking collapse. A prudently managed bank can find itself cash deficient and insolvent as a consequence of the financial panic. A bank that under normal circumstance has adequate cash, capital, and good loans becomes a bank with no cash, bad loans, and no capital.

Also note that the public and banks act rationally during a collapse. Once the public becomes fearful of the safety of its deposit balances, it is rational and prudent to withdraw currency as quickly as possible before the bank goes under. Under these circumstances, it is rational and prudent for banks to hoard cash, sell assets, and curtail their lending. The combined effect is to produce a financial and economic collapse. The instability of the system is the result of private fractional-reserve banking, not of bank mismanagement or abusive practices. Flights to currency (specie) caused banking and financial collapse because prior to the mid-1930s there was no effective central bank to provide the currency and offset the drains on bank reserves.[27]

The huge losses that are experienced by depositors, borrowers, financial institutions, and the economy in general indicate the importance of eliminating financial panics and banking collapses. Attempts were made during the nineteenth and early twentieth centuries to eliminate financial panics by regulating the activities of banks.[28] It was believed that if banks could be made to operate safely and prudently, they would not experience losses and the public would retain its faith in banks.[29] This would forestall runs on banks. There was some validity to this proposition in that news of banking irregularities, large banking losses, and so on, could, in principle, trigger a general run on banks. Many banks were managed prudently and well, but a few bad apples could, under the appropriate circumstances, spoil the whole barrel. It is important to note, however, that there is little evidence that news of banking problems triggered panics.[30] For example, the rate of banking failures was relatively high during the 1920s and earlier periods, but this did not trigger a general run on banks. Some special event such as a war scare, a flight of gold, or a stock market collapse was required to set off a run on banks. Evidence of poor banking practices may have contributed, but it was not the primary factor.

A private, fractional-reserve banking system cannot guarantee stability, no matter what regulatory restrictions are imposed. In the absence of appropriate governmental stabilization policies, the only way that the private banking system can be assured of stability is either to require banks to hold 100% of their deposit liabilities as cash or to have a perfect maturity match between their deposit liabilities and government securities. Although these measures would produce stability, they mean that banks would cease to function as extenders of credit to the private sector. Banks would cease to be banks. They would be depositories that process payments transactions.

The instability of the private, fractional-reserve banking system was eliminated by two fundamental reforms of the 1930s. Neither of these reforms had any connection with the Glass-Steagall provisions or other restrictions on bank activities. First, the introduction of federal deposit insurance eliminated the incentives for small depositors to withdraw their money (currency) from the bank when they feared bank failures. The government guaranteed that their money was safe.[31] Second, the Federal Reserve was reorganized into a true central bank with authority and clear responsibility for meeting currency drains and for providing liquidity to the financial system. These two reforms converted the fractional-reserve system from instability to stability by eliminating an important source of currency drains and by providing a source of currency and other liquidity. There have been no economic panics and financial collapses since.[32] In today's world, turmoil in securities and other markets, and failure of individual banks do not bring the banking system down like a house of cards.[33]

If these federal programs make the banking system stable, why are banks regulated? There are two basic reasons. With federal insurance and Federal Reserve sup-

port activities, smaller depositors are insured and large depositers are largely protected. Under these circumstances, there is relatively little depositor policing of
bank risk taking. Risk has been shifted from depositors to the federal government.[34]
In order to protect the insurance fund and to avoid massive Federal Reserve bailouts,
government regulation limits bank risk taking. This is accomplished through loan
limits, capital requirements, and other devices in the regulators' bag of tools.[35]

The second reason for bank regulation is to reduce or eliminate financial abuse.
Thus bank activities are monitored and controlled to handle potential problems of
self-dealing, conflict of interest, tied-sales, and so on. Note that these regulatory
activities are no different from those applied to other sellers of financial services, and
indeed little different from the activities of the Food and Drug Administration or the
Federal Aviation Administration.

Unfortunately, members of the bank-separateness school got carried away in their
zeal for banking "reform." It became a cornerstone of the school that virtually all
bank failures were to be avoided.[36] This was accomplished by laws and regulations
designed to protect bankers from themselves.[37] The consequence was over-regula-
tion, which produces considerable waste and inefficiency.

In the turmoil of the early 1930s it was understandable, but unfortunate, that the
government sought to treat the symptom and not the disease of bank failures through
the Glass-Steagall provisions of the Banking Act of 1933 and other laws that sought
to make banks "safe." With the banking collapse of the early 1930s, thousands of
banks appeared to have been poorly managed. They held huge quantities of bad loans
and worthless securities. This led reformers to the conclusion that banks could not
be trusted. After all, look at the mess that banks were in. The solution seemed obvious.
Banks must be forced to make safe investment and loan decisions, they must be excluded from the corporate securities industry, and they must be prevented from engaging in "destructive competition."[38]

The attempt to protect bankers from themselves led to a rash of anticompetitive
legislation in the 1930s. For example, the prohibition of interest on demand deposit
accounts, and interest rate ceilings for savings and time accounts were imposed to
end the supposed "destructive competition" among banks.[39] Furthermore, many activities of banks were disallowed on the grounds that bankers would abuse the priv-
ilege.

Economic reality finally caught up with the restrictions favored by the bank-separateness school when the public demanded services that banks were not supposed
to provide. Competitive pressures from unregulated money market mutual funds
forced the end of Regulation Q ceilings. Similarly, RPs and other devices have allowed banks, in effect, to pay interest on many demand deposit accounts. Furthermore, branching restrictions have been circumvented for wholesale banking, and
some significanct breaches are occurring in retail banking. Finally, and perhaps most
importantly, the economic incentives to provide the public what it wants in financial
services became so great that nonbanking firms have found ways to enter banking
through the back door.

There has been a great waste of resources and talent as market participants have
sought ways to circumvent the regulatory restrictions imposed by the bank-separate-

ness school.[40] Ironically, attempts to impose arbitrary restrictions on bank activities have forced banking activities into the less-regulated world of the financial conglomerates.

THE ROLE OF PUBLIC POLICY IN INFLUENCING THE FUTURE ROLE OF BANKS

In influencing the future role of banks, public policy should control bank risk to ensure the smooth functioning of the nation's monetary and financial systems while promoting economic efficiency and progress by encouraging competition among banking organizations and between banking organizations and other financial institutions. Effective public policy balances these two considerations. A desirable balance can be achieved only if policymakers appreciate the sources of risk in various activities and how the risks of individual activities interact to produce the aggregate risk for a bank. Policymakers must also appreciate the difference between the risk of an individual institution and the risk for the entire financial system.

It is essential to stress at the outset that the discussion of the future role of banks assumes the continuation of their provision and processing of transactions accounts, and their role as conduits for monetary policy. Under existing institutional arrangements, these "core" functions are essential to the nation's monetary and payments system and therefore must be retained.

After this point is made, however, many questions remain. Transactions accounts are no longer the major source of funds for banks. Banks have already entered a large number of markets. These activities have not endangered the monetary and payments system, so why new activities cause problems?[41] Lowered transactions costs and other advances have allowed financial conglomerates to offer many financial services under one roof. What are the potential public benefits and costs of allowing banking organizations to operate these financial centers, and of allowing nonbanks to enter the banking business more freely?

In evaluating the desirability of allowing new activities for banking organizations, it is necessary to examine the social benefits and costs that are involved. A new activity has social benefits if it offers greater convenience to the public, lowers the costs of providing financial services, and increases competition among the providers of financial services. A new activity is socially costly if it raises bank risk, provides the possibility of financial abuse, or increases financial concentration.

Let us first examine the benefits and costs of attempting to maintain the status quo, that is, of not changing existing law and regulation. There appear to be two benefits from this approach. First, fears concerning additions to bank risk, conflicts of interest, self-dealing, tied sales, and so on, coming from new activities can be put to rest if new activities are not allowed. Second, regulators have substantial experience in dealing with banking as we currently know it. By not expanding allowable activities, regulators can continue to operate as they have in the past.

There are potential costs, however, of maintaining the status quo. First, sufficient economic incentives exist to virtually guarantee that there will be a continued expansion of nonbanking firms into banking areas. The convenience provided to the public by one-stop financial centers[42] and the economies of scale and of scope that are available make financial "conglomeration" highly attactive to many nonbanking firms.[43] Thus the role of financial conglomerates will gain in importance. In this case, attempts to maintain tight control over bank activities are likely to result in less regulatory control as traditional banking services are performed by "nonbanking" firms. The status quo may not prove to be as comfortable or static as it might first appear.

A second potential cost of favoring the status quo involves the likely response of banks to competitive pressure. Using large amounts of resources and talent, the banking industry may continue to find ways to circumvent existing laws and regulations. This raises bank costs and is inefficient. Alternatively, banks may have reached the limits of creative circumvention and will be unable to expand their activities. If this occurs, costs will be incurred in futile attempts, and nonbanking firms will tend to displace banks over time. Aside from the potential costs of this displacement that have been mentioned, there also will be a decline in competition as banking organiations become less important. Furthermore, the competitive disadvantage of banking organizations could induce them to bear more risk in an attempt to maintain earnings. It appears that the benefits of maintaining the status quo are less than the potential social cost.

Now let us examine the potential social benefits and costs of expanding allowable bank activities. The primary benefits of allowing banks to enter new financial-services areas involve greater public convenience, reduced cost of providing financial services, and increased competition within the financial sector.[44] Entry of new firms and strong competition are the hallmarks of a market economy. Allowing banks to underwrite and deal in corporate securities, offer general insurance, mutual funds, and other services will expand competition in these areas.

The potential costs of allowing banking organizations to expand their activities involve possible increase in risk and possible infringement on the impartial extension of credit by banks. Without adequate safeguards, there is also the risk of huge financial conglomerates developing if the largest banks are permitted to merge with the largest securities, insurance, and other financial-services firms.

In analyzing the impact of new activities on bank risk, it is simplistic and deceptive to look at each potential activity as though it provides a net addition to risk. First, one must ask of the new activity: "risky compared to what?" Available evidence suggests that new activities such as underwriting corporate securities, general insurance underwriting, and mutual fund operations are actually less risky than conventional lending activities of banks.[45]

Furthermore, it is not the risk of a particular activity that is crucial, but rather the impact of the addition of the activity to the risk of the entire banking enterprise and the banking system. It is well known that diversification can reduce risk. If the returns on new activities are not perfectly (positively) correlated with the returns on old activities, total bank risk can be reduced by adding new activities. A good example of the diversification principle is provided by securities underwriting. Available evidence indicates that the returns to securities firms are negatively correlated with the returns to banking in general.[46] This means that, on average, when returns to banking are relatively low, the returns to securities activities are relatively high, and vice versa. Thus a banking organization can actually reduce its total risk by combining the underwriting of corporate securities with its other activities.

Even if new activities were pursued through a bank itself or a bank subsidiary, total risk to a bank would likely fall. Both current practice and proposed legislation indicate, however, that new financial-services activities would be operated through nonbank subsidiaries of bank holding companies rather than through the bank itself. This tends to insulate the bank to an important degree from the fortunes of the affiliates. It is interesting to note, however, that to the extent that the bank is insulated from its nonbank affiliates, the benefits of diversification may be lost to the bank. The stockholders of the holding company experience less risk because of diversification, but the bank may not.[47]

It appears that allowing banking organizations to offer a wider range of financial services can provide a higher return for given risk, or a lower risk for a given return.[48] This is presumably why they are seeking entry into these activities.

The second potential cost of allowing banking organizations to engage in new activities involves the possibility that the new activities may interfere with the impartial extension of credit by banks by creating conflicts of interest and possibilities for self-dealing. Furthermore, the new activities might produce increased financial concentration and disturb the execution of banks' fiduciary responsibilities. If there were compelling reasons for believing that these undesirable effects would occur, then their negative social value might outweigh any potential benefits.

This is not the place for a detailed discussion of all these issues.[49] A few comments are in order, however. Many of the concerns about potential abuses by banks, should they enter new lines of activity, seem to assume implicitly that we are back in the unregulated world of the 1920s. The feared abuses from conflicts of interest, self-dealing, tied sales, and loss of fiduciary responsibilities are illegal, thanks to the securities acts and banking laws that were passed in the 1930s and later. Holding company subsidiaries and banks are covered by these laws. Those who oppose entry of banking organizations into new activities on the grounds of financial and credit abuse should demonstrate how the practices could develop under existing law. If, in fact, it is possible to demonstrate the possibility, then it appears that the proper remedy lies in strengthening the law, not in excluding banking organizations from new financial activities.[50]

It is frequently asserted by members of the bank-separateness school that it is impossible to separate totally the fortunes of a bank from its holding company affiliates. This is probably true in a formal sense, but very substantial insulation exists. Insulation is provided by corporate separateness, by Section 23A of the Federal Reserve Act that limits transactions between the bank and holding company affiliates, and by other provisions of law. It is important to note the Garn-St Germain Act of 1982 strengthened Section 23A of the Federal Reserve Act to cover transactions between banks and REITs or similar entities that were previously excluded. This eliminates an important source of financial abuse for bank holding companies. Furthermore, regulatory procedures have been strengthened to guard against the kinds of bank-holding company abuses that occurred in the cases of Hamilton Bankshares and problems facing Beverly Hills Bancorp.[51] Contrary to the opinion of some observers,[52] substantial separation can and does exist between the activities of banks and their holding company affiliates. If the provisions of Section 23A or regulatory procedures are not deemed adequate, then strengthening should be recommended.[53] Furthermore, efforts to impose greater corporate separateness can also have a significant role.[54] It should be noted that the purpose of these steps is to keep bank risk under reasonable control, not to eliminate it. Bank risk exists for commercial lending and other activities; there is no good reason to attempt to eliminate it totally for the activities of financial-services affiliates.

The problem of potential financial concentration must also be faced. There appears to be a public consensus that levels of concentration experienced in many other industries are not acceptable for banking. This suggests that more stringent standards are necessary than just enforcement of the antitrust statutes. The legitimate fears concerning financial concentration can be put to rest by allowing only de novo operations or "foothold" acquisitions. This eliminates the possibility of the largest banks acquiring the largest securities or insurance firms, or vice versa.[55]

A PROPOSAL FOR FINANCIAL REFORM

The proposal that follows is designed to achieve the benefits of allowing banking organizations to enter into new financial activities, while assuring that the traditional functions of banking organizations are retained and that anticompetitive practices are avoided.

Any serious proposal to grant banking organizations additional powers must offer assurances that banks will continue to operate in a manner which protects the monetary and payments systems. This requires that transactions accounts continue to be insured and that banks continue to be regulated to avoid undue risk taking. Thus as far as banks are concerned there would be no change in the regulatory environment.

Furthermore, reserve requirements, access to the discount window and to other Federal Reserve services would not change. Thus there is nothing in the following proposal that has any particular implications for monetary policy. The issue of whether reserve requirements and banks' special access to the discount window are necessary for the successful pursuit of monetary policy is important, but it is separate and distinct from the issue of allowing new activities for banking organizations. Similarly, the question of whether insurance coverage and reserve requirements should be extended to money market mutual funds that offer the functional equivalent of transactions accounts is important, but it also is separate and distinct from the issue of increasing the powers of banking organizations.[56]

The proposal itself provides no new powers to banks. The increased powers go instead to affiliates of bank holding companies. These separate corporate entities would have authority to underwrite, broker, and deal in corporate securities and municipal revenue bonds. They could also underwrite and sell general insurance and offer other financial services such as mutual funds. This allows banking organizations to enter into the securities, insurance, and other financial-services business; and it allows firms in these businesses directly into banking.

In the interest of having a controlled evolution of the financial-services industry, it may be wise to retain the historic separation of "banking" from "commerce." Thus a bank holding company could not have commercial affiliates. The bank holding company would be allowed into new financial-services activities, but nothing else. This raises problems for unitary S&L holding companies which have commercial affiliates, because S&Ls are the functional equivalents of banking affiliates. If the national policy is to retain the separation of banking and commerce, this loophole should be closed and orderly divestiture required. If this remedy is not followed, logic indicates that the separation of banking and commerce is not national policy, and bank holding companies should be empowered to have commercial affiliates.[57]

Authority of the banking regulators would extend only to the banks in a holding company and to bank subsidiaries. The Federal Reserve would retain its crucial powers under Section 23A of the Federal Reserve Act and would have power to require whatever reports from the holding company and its affiliates that are required to enforce the law. Nonbank affiliates and their holding companies would, of course, be covered by the legal and regulatory protections that require disclosure, and disallow self-dealing, tied sales, and other activities. Nonbank affiliates would not have government protection against failure. Funds invested with these affiliates would be at risk.

Financial-services affiliates of holding companies would have to be started de novo or be the result of "foothold" acquisitions. Similar restrictions would apply to acquisition of banks by financial-services firms. It probably would be desirable for the Federal Reserve to police these moves into new business.

In addition, enabling legislation should strive to maximize corporate separateness within elements of the bank holding company. For example, significant separation of boards of directors and employees could be required.

There appear to be no compelling reasons why the conventional banking business cannot coexist with corporate securities underwriting and other financial-services activities within a bank holding company. The trick is to have sufficient safeguards in the system. The solution is not to try to turn back the clock and to resist the powers of economic change and evolution. With adequate safeguards, the conventional banking system will remain sound while allowing financial innovation and heightened competition to go forward. The public retains its insured deposits, the Federal Reserve retains control over monetary policy, whereas the general public benefits from a more competitive financial-services industry.

NOTES

[1]The Garn-St Germain Act of 1982 amended the Bank Holding Company Act to explicitly prohibit banks and their holding company affilliates from engaging in general insurance activities. This is a fundamental change in the Holding Company Act because it sets the precedent of a "laundry list" of disallowed activities.

[2]These changes have accelerated in recent years as technological advances have produced a blurring of the distinction between banks and other financial intermediaries. The role of technical change is discussed later.

[3]The Export Trading Act has breached to some extent the wall between banking and commerce.

[4]At this point, no distinction is made between a bank and its holding company or its holding company affiliates.

[5]The large shift of funds by the public from money market mutual funds and other investments to the new insured money market deposit accounts authorized by the Garn-St Germain Act is evidence of the importance of insurance to the public.

[6]See Rosenblum and Pavel, "Financial Services in Transition: The Effects of Nonbank Competitors." Federal Reserve Bank of Chicago, 1984, for details.

[7]For a discussion of the technological developments and their effects, see Donald Hester, "Innovations and Monetary Control," *Brookings Papers on Economic Activity,* Vol. 1, 1981; Edward Kane, "Strategic Planning in a World of Deregulation and Rapid Technological Change." Ohio State University Working Paper, August 1983; and Almarin Phillips, "Changing Technology and Future Financial Activity." University of Pennsylvania Working Paper, May 1983.

[8]At this writing, the status of acquisition of "nonbank banks" formations by commercial banks is unclear. A moratorium on such acquisitions has expired, but no new acquisitions have been authorized. Furthermore, bills have been introduced in Congress to prohibit the formation of such banks.

[9]The increase in the number of bank failures in recent years and the problems encountered by Continental Illinois could be used as evidence that this is not the case. These issues are discussed later.

[10]Gerald E. Corrigan, "Are Banks Special?" Federal Reserve Bank of Minneapolis, *Annual Report,* 1982, pp. 1–24.

[11]About two-thirds of the money stock (M1) is transactions accounts, the remainder is currency, coin, and traveler's checks.

[12]Corrigan does not appear to recommend that thrift institutions be subjected to the restrictions of the Glass-Steagall Act or the Bank Holding Company Act.

[13]Here we are not talking about payment at par that is provided by the Federal Reserve as part of its check clearing activities, but rather the payment at par that comes for guaranteeing the nominal value (price) of an asset.

[14]It is not productive to enter the rather sterile debate over whether balances at money market mutual funds are "really" money. The Federal Reserve excludes these balances from its narrowly defined money stock, M1, but includes the balances in its broader definitions. The important point is that money market mutual funds offer highly liquid assets to the public which can be used to make third-party payments. This means that depository institutions are no longer unique in the provision of such assets to the public.

[15]One reason for a financial conglomerate to acquire a "nonbank bank" is to allow it to process the transactions account activities of its money fund rather than rely on an agent bank.

[16]For example, see Karl Brunner and Allan Meltzer, "An Aggregative Theory for a Closed Economy," in J. Stein (ed.), *Monetarism* (Amsterdam: Elsevier North-Holland, 1976); John Gurley and Edward Shaw, *Money in a Theory of Finance.* (Washington, D.C.: The Brookings Institution, 1960); James Tobin, "Commercial Banks as Creators of Money," in Dean Carson (ed.), *Banking and Monetary Studies.* (Homewood, Ill.: Irwin, 1963); and Lyle Gramley and Samuel Chase, "Time Deposits in Monetary Analysis," *Federal Reserve Bulletin,* 51 (October 1956), pp. 1380–1406.

[17]Open market operations are also used to offset any undesired effect on the monetary base arising from such factors as fluctuations in Federal Reserve float.

[18]For a detailed discussion of the role of depository institutions and of other financial firms in affecting the quantity of money and credit in the economy, see James Pierce, *Monetary and Financial Economics.* New York: Wiley, 1984.

[19]See Tobin, "Commercial Banks as Creators of Money," pp. 417–441 for a more complete discussion.

[20]This explains why the discount rate can be substantially below market interest rates, whereas borrowing from the discount window remains relatively small.

[21]There is no evidence that changes in the mix between borrowed and nonborrowed reserves have any significant effect on money, credit, or interest rates.

[22]Any undesired affect on the monetary base is offset by open market operations.

[23]The interbank (federal funds) market is a highly effective vehicle for channeling funds from surplus to

deficit banks. The existence of this market is the major reason why banks hold only a relatively small amount of liquid assets. Contrary to the assertion of the bank-separateness school, small holdings of liquid assets are not necessarily an indication of bank weakness when there is a federal funds market.

[24]The funds could be deposited overseas. This does not cause problems because U.S. banks have access to funds offshore.

[25]If banks suddenly increase their holdings of cash reserves relative to their deposit liabilities, funds also drain from the system. For simplicity, we stress the role of the public's currency drains.

[26]Here we are discussing a banking panic where a central bank does not provide the needed currency and bank reserves. This situation existed in the United States until the mid-1930s.

[27]For a discussion of the sad performance of the Federal Reserve during the financial collapse of the early 1930s, see Milton Friedman and Anna Schwartz, *A Monetary History of the United States, 1867–1960.* Princeton, N.J.: Princeton University Press, 1971.

[28]For a brief history of these efforts, see Pierce, *Monetary and Financial Economics.*

[29]It is also important that other large players do not collapse. Thus insurance companies and others came to be regulated to guard their assets and to assure that they could meet their obligations.

[30]For a detailed discussion of banking panics, see Friedman and Schwartz, *A Monetary History.*

[31]The regulators have provided implicit guarantees to large depositors in some instances, such as for Franklin National and explicit guarantees in the case of Continental Illinois.

[32]The government has taken some extraordinary steps in some cases, however.

[33]Failure of an individual bank can cause disruption for its customers, although this is rarely a problem because of mergers. These disruptions are unfortunate, but they are probably no more painful than the consequences of the failure of a railroad, airline, or farm equipment manufacturer. Most important, failure of an individual bank, or even a number of banks, does not spell doom for the banking system. Furthermore, the possibility of failure is important for disciplining bank management.

[34]For detailed discussions of the role of deposit insurance and of regulation in general, see George Benston (ed.), *Financial Services: The Changing Institutions and Government Policy.* (Englewood Cliffs, N.J.; Prentice-Hall, 1983); John Karaken and Neil Wallace, "Deposit Insurance and Bank Regulation: A Partial Equilibrium Exposition," *Journal of Business* (July 1978); and Sherman Maisel (ed.) *Risk and Capital Adequacy in Commercial Banks,* National Bureau of Economic Research. (Chicago: University of Chicago Press, 1981).

[35]It has been proposed that variable insurance premiums and capital requirements be used as methods of limiting risk. These are simply different means to the same end. Note that the more effective risk-reducing measures become, the smaller the incentive for large depositors to apply market discipline. For a discussion of some of these issues, see Tim Campbell and Paul Horvitz, "Reform of the Deposit Insurance System: An Appraisal of the FHLBB and FDIC Studies," *Contemporary Policy Issue,* Western Economic Association, May 1984.

[36]Bank failures embarrass regulators, and they go to considerable lengths to avoid them. Their chagrin is often reinforced by Congressional criticism when failures occur.

[37]As explained in a later footnote, the problems of Continental Illinois were not the result of deregulation.

[38]Such disparate sources as Friedman and Schwartz, *A Monetary History;* John Kenneth Galbraith, *The Great Crash.* (Boston: Houghton Mifflin, 1955); and *Economic Report of the President,* 1984. (Washington, D.C.: The Brookings Institution, 1960), all confirm that the banking collapse was not caused by poor management, improper securities transactions, or "destructive competition."

[39]It appears that the prohibition against paying interest on demand deposits was a quid pro quo for deposit insurance. See A. Gibson "Deposit Insurance in the United States: Evaluation and Reform," *Journal of Financial and Quantitative Analysis* (March 1972).

[40]For a discussion of how regulation produces circumvention, which produces regulation, see Kane, "Strategic Planning."

[41]It would be a mistake to view the problems of Continental Illinois as a reason for opposing the expansion of bank activities. That bank did not encounter difficulties as the result of deregulation or of nonbank activities. It is almost exclusively a wholesale bank and was largely unaffected by deregulation of interest

rates for consumer deposit accounts. Continental Illinois does illustrate that banks can take on too much risk in their conventional lending activities. Allowing a wholesale bank such as Continential Illinois into securities and other activities could reduce its risk.

[42]See Veronica Bennett, "Consumer Demand for Product Deregulation," *Economic Review*, Federal Reserve Bank of Atlanta (May 1984).

[43]For a different view of the profitability of nonbank financial conglomerates, see William Ford, "Banking's New Competition: Myths and Realities," *Economic Review*, Federal Reserve Bank of Atlanta (January 1983).

[44]See Bennett, "Consumer Demand;" Samuel Hayes et al., *Competition in the Investment Banking Industry*. (Cambridge, Mass.: Harvard University Press, 1983); Thomas Pugel and Lawrence White, "An Analysis of the Competitive Effects of Allowing Commercial Banks to Underwrite Corporate Securities"; Anthony Saunders, "An Economic Perspective on Bank Uniqueness and Corporate Securities Activities." Graduate School of Business Administration, New York University, January 1984; Samuel Hayes, "Investment Banking: Commercial Bank Inroads," *Economic Review*, Federal Reserve Bank of Atlanta, May 1984; and William Silber, *Municipal Revenue Bond Costs and Bank Underwriting: A Survey of the Evidence*. Salomon Brothers Center, Graduate School of Business Administration, New York University, Monograph No. 1979-3.

[45]See Saunders, "An Economic Perspective"; Arnold Heggestad, "Riskiness of Investments in Nonbank Activities by Bank Holding Companies," *Journal of Economics and Banking* (1975), pp. 219–223; and Robert Eisenbeis, "How Should Bank Holding Companies Be Regulated?" *Economic Review*, Federal Reserve Bank of Atlanta, January 1983.

[46]Heggestad "Riskiness of Investments," pp. 219–223; and Robert Eisenbeis, "Risk Considerations in Deregulating Bank Activities," *Economic Review*, Federal Reserve Bank of Atlanta, May 1984.

[47]The holding company could pass these benefits on to the bank by sending earnings "downstream." It is not clear how often this would occur, but if the bank is in trouble, but viable, it is rational for the holding company to support it.

[48]Even if risk does increase, the probability of bank failure need not rise if the mean return to the bank also increases.

[49]See Anthony Saunders "Conflicts of Interest: The Case of Commercial Banks and Their Corporate Securities Activities." Graduate School of Business Administration, New York University, April 1984.

[50]This may come at the cost of some increase in regulation, however.

[51]For a discussion of these two cases as well as of the REITs, see Joseph Sinkey, *Problem and Failed Institutions in the Commercial Banking Industry*. Greenwich, Conn.: JIA Press, 1979.

[52]For example, see Eisenbeis, "How Should Bank Holding Companies Be Regulated?"

[53]The desirability of strengthening laws and procedures must be weighed against increased cost of regulation, however.

[54]For details, see Samuel Chase and D. Waage, "Corporate Separateness as a Tool of Bank Regulation," Washington, D.C.: Samuel Chase, 1983.

[55]This is particularly important because the securities industry is highly concentrated.

[56]It is possible to disregard the issue of insurance because nonbank subsidiaries would offer money market mutual funds. These funds would not be insured and the public would be so informed. There is a great need, however, for public policy to address the whole issue of insurance.

[57]As mentioned earlier, the Export Trading Company Act already has breached the gap between banking and commerce.

REFERENCES

Bennett, Veronica. "Consumer Demand for Product Deregulation," *Economic Review*, Federal Reserve Bank of Atlanta, May 1984.

Benston, George (ed.). *Financial Services: The Changing Institutions and Government Policy,* Englewood Cliffs, N.J.: Prentice-Hall, 1983.

Brunner, Karl, and Allan Meltzer. "An Aggregate Theory for a Closed Economy," in J. Stein (ed.),
Monetarism. Amsterdam: Elsevier North-Holland, 1976.

Campbell, Tim, and Paul Horvitz. "Reform of the Deposit Insurance System: An Appraisal of the FHLBB
and FDIC Studies," *Contemporary Policy Issue,* Western Economic Association, May 1984.

Chase, Samuel, and D. Waage. "Corporate Separateness as a Tool of Bank Regulation." Washington,
D.C.: Samuel Chase, 1983.

Corrigan, E. Gerald. "Are Banks Special?" Federal Reserve Bank of Minneapolis, *Annual Report,* 1982,
pp. 1–24.

Economic Report of the President, 1984. Washington, D.C.: U.S. Government Printing Office.

Eisenbeis, Robert, "How Should Bank Holding Companies Be Regulated?" *Economic Review.* Federal
Reserve Bank of Atlanta, January 1983.

———, "Risk Considerations in Deregulating Bank Activities," *Economic Review.* Federal Reserve
Bank of Atlanta, May 1984. Ford, William, "Banking's New Competition: Myths and Realities,"
Economic Review. Federal Reserve Bank of Atlanta January 1983.

Friedman, Milton, and Anna Schwartz. *A Monetary History of the United States, 1867–1960.* Princeton,
N.J.: Princeton University Press, 1971.

Galbraith, John Kenneth. *The Great Crash.* Boston: Houghton Mifflin, 1955.

Gibson, A., "Deposit Insurance in the United States: Evaluation and Reform," *Journal of Financial and
Quantitative Analysis* (March 1972).

Gramley, Lyle, and Samuel Chase. "Time Deposits in Monetary Analysis," *Federal Reserve Bulletin,*
51 (October 1956), pp. 1380–1406.

Gurley, John, and Edward Shaw, *Money in a Theory of Finance.* Washington, D.C.: The Brookings Institution, 1960.

Hayes, Samuel, A. Michael Spence, and David Marks. *Competition in the Investment Banking Industry.*
Cambridge, Mass.: Harvard University Press, 1983.

Hayes, Samuel. "Investment Banking: Commercial Bank Inroads," *Economic Review,* Federal Reserve
Bank of Atlanta, May 1984.

Heggestad, Arnold. "Riskiness of Investments in Nonbank Activities by Bank Holding Companies,"
Journal of Economics and Business (June 1975), pp. 219–223.

Hester, Donald. "Innovations and Monetary Control," *Brookings Papers on Economic Activity,* 1, 1981.

Kane, Edward. "Strategic Planning in a World of Deregulation and Rapid Technological Change." Ohio
State University Working Paper, August 1983.

Karaken, John, and Neil Wallace. "Deposit Insurance and Bank Regulation: A Partial Equilibrium Exposition," *Journal of Business* (July 1978).

Maisel, Sherman (ed.), *Risk and Capital Adequacy in Commercial Banks.* National Bureau of Economic
Research, Chicago: University of Chicago Press, 1981.

Phillips, Almarin. "Changing Technology and Future Financial Activity," University of Pennsylvania
Working Paper, May 1983.

Pierce, James. *Monetary and Financial Economics.* New York: Wiley, 1984.

Pugel, Thomas, and Lawrence White. "An Analysis of the Competitive Effects of Allowing Commercial
Banks to Underwrite Corporate Securities," Chapter 5 in this book.

Rosenblum, Harvey, and Christine Pavel. "Financial Services in Transition: The Effects of Nonbank
Competitors." Federal Reserve Bank of Chicago, 1984.

Saunders, Anthony. "An Economic Perspective on Bank Uniqueness and Corporate Securities Activities." Graduate School of Business Administration, New York University, January 1984.

———. "Conflicts of Interest: The Case of Commercial Banks and Their Corporate Securities Underwriting Affiliates." Graduate School of Business Administration, New York University, April 1984.

Silber, William. *Municipal Revenue Bond Costs and Bank Underwriting: A Survey of the Evidence*. Salomon Brothers Center, Graduate School of Business Adminsitration, New York University, Monograph No. 1979-3.

Sinkey, Joseph. *Problem and Failed Institutions in the Commercial Banking Industry*. Greenwich, Conn.: JIA Press, 1979.

Tobin, James. "Commercial Banks as Creators of Money," in Dean Carson (ed.), *Banking and Monetary Studies*. Homewood, Il.: Irwin, 1963.

Comment

STEPHEN J. FRIEDMAN

This book focuses largely on whether changes ought to take place in the laws governing bank securities activities, and the kind of risks that would attend those changes. That is a commendable exercise, especially in light of the lack of depth in grappling with the real issues that accompanies most discussions of this question. I am sure that the reader is familiar with Keynes's comment that "practical men, who believe themselves to be quite exempt from any intellectual influence, are usually the slaves of some defunct economist. Madmen in authority, who hear voices in the air, are distilling their frenzy from academic scribblers of a few years back."

The fact is, of course, that the roots of the idea that banks ought not to be involved in the securities markets go back to the mid-nineteenth century English thought. That notion was born in a very different world, and it makes sense to examine the continuing validity of its underlying assumptions.

Although my own views lie on the side of expanding the power of banks to engage in securities activities, my purpose here is not polemical. It is simply to share the thought that, whatever one's views about the way things "ought" to be, events are in the driver's seat, and the history of change in the financial markets teaches that the current trends are ineluctable. We are, in fact, wasting precious time debating "whether," when our energies should be devoted to "how."

My conclusions are simple. *First,* the Glass-Steagall Act has lost its moral force, a victim of the ambiguities that hedged its original drafting and changes that have taken place since that time. *Second,* as a consequence, the current state of financial regulatory policy is not in equilibrium. If movement is inevitable, and if history teaches the rarity of Congressional retrenchment, the most likely scenario is for further ad hoc changes. Then when everything has happened, the Congress will come along and do its job.

As background, let me spend a moment on the nature of legislative change in the regulation of financial markets. It is probably something for which we should all be thankful, but financial regulation does not occupy the thoughts of many members of Congress. What is it that persuades the Congress to act? There are three kinds of things that tend to draw its attention away from the two-year election cycle and the delights of foreign policy; they are disaster, scandal, and the need to tidy up from time to time.

We are all familiar with the function of disaster as an engine of change. The Great Crash in 1929 and subsequent events gave rise to five major pieces of securities legislation stretching from the Securities Act of 1933 to the Investment Company Act of 1940. The collapse of the banking system in 1933 produced a similar legislative response—which included the creation of a whole new kind of financial institution, federally chartered savings and loans. Twenty years earlier, a series of banking crises culminating in the panic of 1907 had produced the Federal Reserve Act of 1913. Today the travails of Continental Illinois and other banks may portend another round of legislation addressed to the fundamental questions of banking.

Scandal has also been a force for change, and there is no handier contemporary example than the legislation in 1979 which grew out of the inquiries into Bert Lance's banking activities.

What I have called the tidying-up response is really the ratification of change that has already occurred. There is a rampant misconception in human affairs that if we do nothing, then nothing will change. That perfectly silly notion is at the root of procrastination in our private lives and in the Congress. Dean Acheson is said to have had three boxes on his desk instead of the usual two: an "in" box, an "out" box, and one that bore the label "too hard." Redrawing the lines of the financial markets is plainly too hard, both substantively and politically. Unable to decide, Congress has failed to act, even in the face of the most extreme provocation, such as the interstate manifestation of the nonbank bank. But the world has not stood still, only Congress.

Recent history has many examples of similar behavior in financial regulation. Brokerage commission rates were fixed by the New York Stock Exchange until 1975. For years the Congress and the SEC did nothing in spite of an institutionalization of savings that made the fixed rates a joke. By the time fixed rates received a legal burial, they had been long eroded by noncash competition and institutional membership on regional securities exchanges. Those events were not a very efficient way of deregulating rates, and official action was necessary to eliminate the high transaction costs involved in circumventing the legal rules.

The deregulation of deposit interest rates provides a similar case study. First NOW accounts were necessary to replace the proliferation of bill-payer accounts, automatic transfer accounts, and their Rube Goldberg relations. Then deregulation of passbook and time deposits was made a reality by the clear and present danger of the money market funds and the looming threat of small-denomination taxable and tax-free commercial paper. Again, market rates of interest were in fact available to all but the smallest depositors. Congress simply acted to eliminate the inefficiencies and, in the case of the money market funds, the real threat to the deposit base.

What had been prohibited in form had been permitted in fact. And the Congress was just tidying up. Changes in the marketplace, strong consumer response to new services, and regulatory acquiescence had all coalesced to draw the fangs of the deposit interest rate controls. The prohibitions became overwhelmed by the exceptions, and it no longer made sense to outlaw conduct that was permitted in so many other forms. Regulation Q had no moral authority.

How did that state of affairs come about? It arose from a change in economic conditions—the rise of inflationary interest rate cycles—pushing market participants into new paths; from the incredible responsiveness and innovativeness of free markets; from the delegation of legislative responsibility to the regulators; and from the reluctance of the regulators to stand in the way of what the firms they were regulating thought was necessary for their survival.

What is it that causes bankers and regulators to ignore what seemed to be the original intent of the Congress? If Congressional intent is to be respected, it must be manifested in clear legislative statements which rest on a basis of principle that permits lawyers and judges to apply the law to a constantly shifting state of facts. If the principles are clear, then each individual decision reenforces the legislative mandate. If the principles are not clearly embodied, if the prohibitions are twisted to accommodate practical problems, and if the process of application becomes one of balancing competing interests, then the process changes completely. When the issue becomes whether the new animal in the zoo looks more like a horse (which is permitted) or a zebra (which is not), the possibilities for manipulation multiply rapidly.

In my judgment, exactly those conditions exist today in the area of bank securities activities. First, there has been a major shift in the economic ground rules that once separated the market in which banks operated from the public securities markets. The prototypical bank on which Senator Glass built his concept of the banking system raised funds from a consumer deposit base made secure by the existence of the Federal Reserve and the system of deposit insurance. For major banks today, however, purchased funds account for 60–70% of their deposit base. Those funds are uninsured, highly volatile, and quite expensive because they must be sought in the international capital markets, the most competitive markets the world has ever known. As the Continental Illinois experience demonstrates, the existence of the Federal Reserve was not enough to keep those funds in a bank which is perceived to be in trouble. Even an unprecedented "blank check" issued to all depositors could not completely stem the outflow.

Senator Glass's perfect bank made short-term, "self-liquidating" loans. Today's banks commonly lend in what was once perceived to be the middle of the maturity spectrum—6–10 years—but what is now in fact near the upper end for corporate debt.

The short maturities of the assets and liabilities of Senator Glass's hypothetical bank insulated it from interest rate fluctuations. In today's world, everything conspires in the opposite direction. Longer maturities on both sides of the balance sheet, combined with the massive level of investment and trading in government securities, all conducted against the backdrop of the enormous volatility of interest rates since the mid-1960s, have made the management of market risk in the fixed income market a full-time job.

What are the consequences of these developments? First, the market risk of interest rate movements that is so much a part of underwriting and dealing in corporate securities is already a fixture in the everyday life of a major bank—as a borrower, a lender, an investor, and an underwiter and dealer in Treasury securities, government-obligations, and bank-eligible revenue bonds. Second, the significantly higher risks that these changes import into the traditional business of banking have significantly changed the relative risks of commercial and investment banking. A lender puts its money at the risk of the solvency of the borrower for the full period of the loan; the underwriter does so for only a short time. The market risk in trading corporate securities is not different from the market risk in trading government securities. The issuer-specific credit risk is also present in term lending to the same degree as in publicly traded bonds, but there is less liquidity in bank loans.

Second, the markets in which major banks operate is becoming significantly ''securitized.'' The banks raise money by issuing negotiable certificates of deposit. Many banks make loans by purchasing participations in loans in a manner that does not differ much from what an insurance company does when it purchases a publicly traded bond. And the process of originating participations bears some resemblance to underwriting. That is not to say that banks have entered the public securities markets for corporate securities; it is simply that what were once two very different markets are now very close together. The ill-fated rationale of the Federal Reserve Board in the Bankers Trust commercial paper case is testament to that growing together.

Third, the development of international capital markets has made banking tremendously competitive, reducing spreads to extremely low levels, especially in view of the increased risk in the banking system. That development has driven banks to seek greater fee income—it is profitable and considerably less risky. For institutions that are legally confined to rendering financial services, the only place to turn is the securities business. The underwriting, trading, investing, and analytical skills that bankers have developed in bank-eligible activities are all transferable, more or less directly, to securities activities which have been reserved to securities firms.

Here we must ask why the regulators have not been leaning over backwards to protect the safety and soundness of the banking system from new risks and to preserve the historic separation between commercial and investment banking. The answer is that there is no historic separation—only specific prohibitions—and that they have correctly perceived that there are not significant incremental risks in securities activities; the major risks to the banking system are from banking, not securities activities, and it is hard to take seriously the enumeration of risks and subtle hazards which dot judicial opinions when the regulators know that precisely those risks are undertaken by banks every day in connection with bank-eligible activities—and are dealt with by the regulators.

If we examine the source of the problems of the larger troubled banks over the past 10 or 15 years, it is largely lending (real estate, energy, and developing countries) and the large losses that can be piled up in a short time in trading government bonds and currencies in a volatile market that have gotten banks into trouble. In contrast, the sources of contention—sponsoring mutual funds, underwriting the relatively small remaining proportion of nonbank eligible revenue bonds, and even underwriting the corporate debt securities that banks are already permitted to own as investments—seem to present very little incremental risk.

What of the ''subtle hazards'' to which the Supreme Court is so fond of referring?

One can only say that, hazards they may be, and subtle they may be, but they are also present in many activities which are clearly permitted to banks—especially the underwriting of bank-eligible revenue bonds. If the dangers are amenable to regulation rather than prohibition there, why should it be any different with corporate debt securities? Or even equities?

The plain fact is that it is very hard to get excited about any of these dangers—unless you are a competitor whose ox is being gored. The Glass-Steagall Act, as it stands today, draws no clear lines, rests on no consistent principles, and is, in fact, merely a remnant of another time.

Is it possible to seriously suppose that the Congress will turn back the clock to draw clear lines of separation and enunciate consistent principles? It is hard to find an example of such a step.

If Congress will not turn back the clock, will it or the regulators freeze the status quo? Does it make sense to say that banks can underwrite housing revenue bonds on the same basis as investment banks but not commercial paper? Or public power revenue bonds? Do the present tortured rules on advising but not sponsoring mutual funds make sense? If the views of the Washington, D.C. district court rather than the Northern California district court prevail in the commingled IRA case, is it conceivable that banks will continue to be prohibited from commingling nonfiduciary funds? If the new FDIC regulations stand and state nonmenber banks are permitted to underwrite corporate equities, will it be long before a Delaware or a South Dakota provides the necessary power? And if state nonmembers have the power, doesn't the late nineteenth–early twentieth century experience with exactly the same pattern teach us where the law for national banks will go? What will the Fed say when the first major state-chartered bank leaves the Federal Reserve System to avoid the Glass-Steagall Act and to take advantage of accommodating state law and FDIC regulations? The centrifugal forces are too great. Of course, we live and work in the short run. But not that short a run.

The loss of moral force in the law regulating financial markets is not a trivial matter. As practice departs farther from principle, it becomes more difficult for both regulators and lawyers to tell bankers what is permissible and what is not. That encourages responses based on narrow self-interest. Examples verging on lawlessness are all around us. Some banks openly advertise their distribution of mutual fund shares, for which they are paid a soliciting dealer's commmision—as "agent" for their customers. Senator Garn tells the Comptroller of the Currency not to act on nonbank banks—even though the Congress has not proved able to act to close the loophole. The Fed tries to close the same loophole through indefensible definitions of statutory terms like *commercial loans,* and is rebuffed in the courts. No one who cares about a society under law can be happy with these events.

Finally, let me again revert to deposit interest rate controls for an analogy. For years, beginning at least with the Hunt Commission report in the 1970s, proposals were made for an orderly phase-out of deposit interest rate controls in order to give thrifts an opportunity to object. When it came, the phase-out was relatively abrupt, and the adjustment not as orderly as one would have liked.

We must pay much more attention to the nuts and bolts of how bank securities activities will be regulated. There is a somewhat simplistic view at large that all regulatory problems can be solved by putting bank securities activities in separate affiliates and regulating them ''equally.'' I will tell you that is not that simple. While holding company subsidiaries are separate from the bank on paper, in fact the two are often closely intertwined. That poses difficult regulatory issues that require careful thought.

If we continue to debate whether we should permit what seems inevitable, we may lose a precious opportunity to shape the final outcome.

3 Legislative History of the Glass-Steagall Act

EDWARD J. KELLY III

Securities market abuses of the 1920s ultimately precipitated several major pieces of financial legislation, including the Glass-Steagall provisions of the Bankruptcy Act of 1933.[1] Adopted in response to the stock market crash, the ensuing depression, and the banking crisis that had culminated in the declaration of a national bank holiday in March 1933, the Act, among other things, provided for federal deposit insurance, strengthened the Federal Reserve System, and expanded branch banking. It also included four provisions that mandated a substantial separation of commercial and investment banking. These provisions have come to be commonly referred to as the Glass-Steagall Act.[2] Section 16[3] restricts the securities activities of national banks, most notably by prohibiting them from underwriting corporate securities. Section 20[4] of the Act supports the thrust of Section 16 by prohibiting member banks from being affiliated with any entity "engaged principally in the issue, flotation, underwriting, public sale, or distribution at wholesale or retail or through syndicate participation of stocks, bonds, debentures, notes, or other securities. . . ."[5] Section 32[6] generally prohibits officer, director, or employee interlocks between member banks and individuals or entities "primarily engaged" in activities similar to those described in Section 20. Finally, Section 21[7] makes it unlawful for any person or organization "engaged" in activities similar to those specified in Section 20 to engage "at the same time to any extent whatever" in the business of deposit banking.[8]

As a technical matter, the legislative history of the Glass-Steagall Act extends only from its introduction as a bill at the beginning of the Seventy-third Congress in March 1933 to its enactment into law in June of that year. It is important to recognize, however, that the substance of the Act was the subject of considerable, and virtually uninterrupted, congressional attention beginning in early 1931, with some significant legislative developments dating back to 1929. Senator Carter Glass of Virginia, an influential member of the Senate Committee on Banking and Currency, introduced in June 1930 the first bill to which the origins of the Glass-Steagall Act can be traced. This bill was succeeded by several revised versions in 1932 and 1933. One version of it actually passed the Senate in January 1933, during the lame-duck session of the Seventy-second Congress. As the depression deepened and the bank failures which had plagued the country since the early 1920s ripened into a full-blown crisis in March 1933, a consensus developed that something had to be done to reform the banking structure. Senator Glass stood ready with proposals that had been in various stages of development for three years and with a theory of banking practice that had some historical legitimacy, even if it had lost its relevance and vitality years before. Glass wanted to separate commercial and investment banking, and the abuses Congress believed were associated with banks' securities activities and the damaged reputation of the financial community provided him with an opportunity to achieve his objective.

BACKGROUND

In considering the legislative history of the Glass-Steagall Act, it is important to review, at least briefly, the history of banking regulation in this country. Historically, commercial and investment banking activities were viewed as inherently incompatible.[9] Commercial banks, which operated mainly with depositors' funds, were expected to confine themselves to making "short-term, self-liquidating loans to finance goods in the process of production and commercial transactions."[10] The provision of long-term capital to corporations by commercial banks was regarded as dangerous business.[11] The theoretical basis of these views was the "real bills" doctrine.[12] This doctrine held that if banks engaged only in the types of transactions described above "the expansion of the bank money [would] be in proportion to any extension in trade that [might] take place or to 'the needs of trade,' and that, when trade contract[ed], bank loans [would] be correspondingly paid off."[13] A closely associated doctrine held that "if only commercial loans [were] made, the currency [would] have a desirable elasticity and the banks [would] at all times be in a liquid position."[14] Because of the influence of these theories, national banks operated for years under a legal regime that restricted their ability to underwrite, or to deal in, investment securities.[15] Even after the Comptroller of the Currency eased these restrictions at the turn of the century, national banks were prohibited from underwriting, or dealing in, corporate stocks.[16]

The restrictive features of federal regulation made it difficult for national banks to compete effectively with private bankers and with state-chartered banks and trust companies that did not operate under similar constraints.[17] In response to these conditions, national banks began to create state-chartered affiliates that could underwrite and deal in corporate securities.[18] Although this development elicited unfavorable congressional comment as early as 1913,[19] neither Congress nor the Comptroller took steps to reverse the trend toward more substantial bank involvement in securities activities.

The securities activities of national banks increased markedly during World War I when the banks played an important role in the marketing of government war bonds.[20] The war bond program had two important effects: It enabled the banks to develop an efficient distribution network for securities, and it made the public more receptive to purchasing securities.[21]

Although the Comptroller at times expressed concern over the securities activities of national banks,[22] such activities continued during the early 1920s.[23] Later, the Comptroller's attitude toward national bank participation in the securities markets began to change.[24] To some extent, this change in attitude was not a matter of choice. National bank participation in securities underwriting had become a fact of economic life and any attempt to limit these activities would have resulted in defections to the state systems.[25] The Comptroller's adoption of this new attitude culminated in passage of the McFadden Act in 1927.[26] This legislation ''reaffirmed'' national banks' authority to underwrite certain investment securities and was designed to prevent any further erosion of the national banking system.[27] McFadden was carefully drafted to ''reaffirm'' national banks' authority to underwrite certain investment securities. The Comptroller initially allowed only bond underwriting, but later approved underwriting of certain equity issues as well.[28]

CONGRESS' CONSIDERATION OF THE GLASS-STEAGALL ACT

Congress' Reaction to the Crash

The stock market crash in October 1929 set the stage for the reimposition of restrictions on the securities activities of commercial banks.[29] There was considerable sentiment that banks' participation in speculative activities had contributed to the crash. In May 1929, five months prior to the crash, Senator King had introduced Senate Resolution 71.[30] This resolution authorized the Senate Committee on Banking and Currency to investigate the Federal Reserve System, with particular attention to banks' involvement in speculative securities activities either through the extension of credit to support such activities or through securities affiliates.[31] In his first annual message to Congress in December 1929, President Hoover recommended that Congress consider the separation of commercial and investment banking as part of a larger study of the entire financial system.[32]

In April 1930, the Senate Committee on Banking and Currency reported to the full Senate a modified version of Senate Resolution 71, which authorized a ''complete survey'' of the national and Federal Reserve banking systems.[33] The Senate approved the resolution in May 1930.[34] Shortly thereafter, in June, Senator Glass introduced a bill, S. 4723,[35] to which the origins of the Glass-Steagall Act can be traced. Glass described the bill as ''merely a tentative measure to which I hope to direct the Senate inquiry into the banking system.''[36] Although the bill bore little resemblance to the legislation that ultimately became the Glass-Steagall Act, it did contain a provision somewhat similar to Section 16.[37] The bill also provided for the regulation of securities affiliates by requiring member banks to file reports on each of their affiliates with the federal regulatory authorities. The term *affiliate* was defined broadly to include, among other things, a ''finance company, securities company, investment trust, or other similar institution'' controlled directly or indirectly by a bank ''or by the shareholders thereof who own or control a majority of the stock of such bank.''[38]

A Vulnerable Banking System

An increasing number of bank failures provided further impetus for congressional action in the banking field. During the years 1921–1929, there had been about 5500 bank failures.[39] Eighty-two percent of the failed banks had been small, state-chartered, rural institutions.[40] But these failures reflected basic flaws in the nation's banking structure. The nation had too many small rural banks that were inadequately supervised, poorly managed, and undercapitalized. Of the banks that failed, 39% had capital of less than $25,000, and 88% had capital of less than $100,000.[41] Seventy-nine percent of the banks that failed during the period had been located in communities with less than 2500 inhabitants, with 39% having been located in towns with less than 500 people.[42] Many of these banks had suffered from the depressed state of staple agriculture.[43] They also had been the victims of improved transportation, most notably the auto, which had put larger, more efficient banks within easy reach of many of their former customers.[44]

Even after the wave of failures during the 1920s, there were still 24,912 separately incorporated unit banks scattered across the country in June 1929.[45] Of these banks, 72% had capital of less than $100,000.[46] It requires little imagination to anticipate the devastating effects of a significant economic downturn on a banking structure that was so fundamentally flawed. Moreover, as the smaller banks failed, it was only a matter of time before larger, more sound banks were likely to feel the pressure, particularly from a loss of depositor confidence.

As one might expect in light of the factors discussed above, the number of bank failures increased substantially during 1930. Although there had been about 650 bank failures in 1929,[47] there was no banking panic immediately following the crash.[48] In late 1930, however, a crisis began to develop. In November 1930, there was a rash of bank failures in Missouri, Indiana, Illinois, Iowa, Arkansas, and North Carolina,[49] with a total of 256 banks failing during the month.[50] Another 352 banks failed in December 1930,[51] bringing the total for the year to about 1350.[52] The failure of the Bank of United States in December 1930, had a particularly adverse effect on depositor confidence.[53] The failure, involving deposits of more than $200 million, was the largest in history at that time.[54] Moreover, many people thought that the bank had a special, official status.[55] The seeds of a full-blown panic, precipitated by a loss of public confidence in the banking system, had been planted.

The failure of the Bank of United States was significant for another reason. Apparently, there was a widespread perception that the bank's securities activities, conducted through a system of affiliates, had been seriously implicated in its failure.[56] In 1931, a subcommittee of the Senate Committee on Banking and Currency stated that

[t]he significance of bank security affiliates and their operations was known to the public in only a most general way, until the failure of the Bank of United States in December

1930, clearly indicated the disastrous results that could follow upon a flagrant abuse of this device, such as took place in that case.[57]

The subcommittee later observed:

Activities of affiliates in supporting a bank's own stock or in holding real estate have both been the source of substantial loss in individual cases. Taken as a whole, however, it would appear that the security affiliates of the banks studied in connection with the committee's questionnaire ordinarily engaged in such activities to a moderate extent only. It is well to remember, however, that it was precisely this type of activity, and especially the first mentioned, which brought on the disastrous collapse of the Bank of United States . . . and contributed to several large bank failures elsewhere.[58]

It is clear that the officers of the Bank of United States abused the affiliate system and used affiliates to conduct their personal, and highly speculative, business ventures.[59] It is equally clear, however, that the abuses involved in that case provided little support for restricting banks' securities activities by separating commercial and investment banking. It appears that the affiliates of the Bank of United States were involved in the securities business only to the extent that they were used by the bank's officers to trade in the bank's own stock and to engage in other manipulative activities.[60] One commentator has pointed out that the affiliates of the Bank of United States had been formed to handle the affairs and "illicit promotions" of the bank's officers.[61] He suggests, however, that when the press attributed the bank's failure to abuse of the affiliate system, "the public and many politicians became suspicious of the activities of all commercial bank affiliates."[62] He goes on to state that "when the continued existence of the entire affiliate system was threatened, the close relationship between the two banking functions that had grown up within that system automatically became vulnerable."[63] In politics, the perception is often more important than the underlying reality.

Senate Resolution 71 Hearings

Against this background, a subcommittee of the Senate Committee on Banking and Currency in early 1931 conducted the first major hearings on the subjects ultimately covered by the Glass-Steagall Act.[64] The subcommittee was created under the authority granted by Senate Resolution 71, which, as noted,[65] the Senate had passed in May 1930. The subcommittee was chaired by Senator Glass,[66] who was very much a traditionalist in the area of banking practices. He had been a principal architect of the Federal Reserve Act,[67] which was based on the English system "with the idea of banking liquidity as its controlling motive."[68] In this regard, the Act "was drawn for two purposes: the first that of absolutely preventing the use of bank reserves in speculative lines; the other that of making sure that the loans of the reserve banks were always liquid and based on actual transactions in business."[69]

During the Brokers' Loans Hearings in 1928, Glass stated that the framers of the Federal Reserve Act thought "we should have a system that would meet the requirements of legitimate industry and commerce, and not a system that would lend itself to what many of us regard as an unproductive operation of stock and commodity gambling.''[70] It is clear that Glass had been concerned with commercial banks' involvement in the securities markets for some time. Glass not only thought commercial banks' securities activities were inconsistent with sound banking practice, but also regarded the banks' use of Federal Reserve credit to support them as a perversion of the Federal Reserve Act.[71] In fact, Glass later identified these activities as a major cause of the depression.[72]

Under Glass' direction, the subcommittee explored the banks' role in the events leading to the stock market crash and to the increasing number of bank failures. In this regard, the hearings focused on banks' participation in ''speculative'' securities activities through the extension of credit to support such activities, through investment practices, and through securities affiliates.[73] In an appendix to the hearings, the subcommittee suggested that

> [t]he experience of the past 10 years lends spectacular confirmation to the view that the more intensive participation by commercial banks in the capital market exaggerates financial and business fluctuations and undermines the stability of the economic organization of the country.[74]

In a section of the appendix devoted to securities affiliates, the subcommittee stated that such affiliates were engaged in a variety of activities, ranging from acting as a real estate holding company to underwriting securities.[75]

Referring generally to securities affiliates, the subcommittee identified a number of ways in which the operations of such an affiliate could affect adversely the position of a bank:

> (1) The security affiliate may borrow money from the parent bank. . . .[76]
>
> (2) The affiliate may sell securities to the bank or another of its affiliates under repurchase agreements, or vice versa.
>
> (3) The bank is closely connected in the public mind with its affiliates, and should the latter suffer large losses it is practically unthinkable that they would be allowed to fail. Instead, the bank would normally support it by additional loans or other aid, thus becoming more deeply involved itself. The knowledge that the affiliate has suffered large losses may in itself be sufficient to cause unfavorable rumors, however unjustified, to spread about the bank.
>
> (4) The bank, to relieve the affiliate of excess holdings, may purchase securities from it . . .
>
> (5) The bank may lend much more freely to customers on issues sponsored by the security affiliate, in order to facilitate their distribution, than it would otherwise do. Also, it may prove more difficult to insist upon the maintenance of adequate margins on these security loans than on other such advances, in view of the fact that customers are encouraged to make loans by the bank's own affiliate.

(6) The good will of the bank with its depositors may be adversely affected to a serious degree when the latter suffer substantial losses on security issues purchased from the affiliate. Because of the tendency of the selling organization of the affiliate to consider the bank's depositors as its preferred list of sales prospects, this condition may become an important handicap to a bank during a major period of security market deflation.

(7) Operations by the affiliate in the market for the bank's own stock may cause undesirably wide fluctuations in the latter. Also, efforts made in some cases to push the sale of the bank's stock through the affiliate to depositors of the institution hurts the position of the bank when its shares suffer a major market decline subsequently.

(8) Wide variations in the net asset value, earning power, and dividend-paying ability of security affiliates tend to make bank stock price fluctuations much greater than would otherwise be the case.

(9) The existence of the affiliates may induce the bank to make unwise commitments, in the knowledge that in case of need they can be shifted to the affiliates, and thus be removed from the bank's condition statement.

(10) Knowing its access to the resources of the bank in case of need, security affiliates in their turn may tend to assume various commitments less cautiously than do private investment banking houses.

(11) In the case of a trust company or a bank with a trust department, the possession of a security affiliate may adversely affect the independence with which fiduciary activities are exercised.[77]

Continued Deterioration of the Banking System

No immediate action was taken in response to these hearings. The banking situation, however, continued to deteriorate throughout 1931. After a lull in early 1931, a "spate of runs began in March . . . and reached a high point in June, attacking the Midwest, Pennsylvania, and New York in particular, intensifying with the collapse of the major European central banks."[78] The situation was aggravated further by England's abandonment of the gold standard in September.[79] In view of steadily eroding depositor confidence, banks moved to achieve greater liquidity so that they could meet renewed runs. One commentator has stated that "by the end of 1931, bankers had called in loans, converted to cash, and pursued deflationary policies to the point where they felt themselves caught in the relentless economizing."[80] There were 2290 bank failures during 1931.[81]

Renewed Congressional Activity

In January 1932, Senator Glass introduced S. 3215.[82] This bill was much more extensive and severe in its treatment of commercial banks' securities activities than S. 4723, the bill Glass had introduced in mid-1930.[83] S. 3215 was designed to separate securities affiliates from commercial banks.[84] It also contained provisions similar to those that became Sections 16 and 32 of the Glass-Steagall Act.[85] Moreover, S. 3215 included a provision that can be viewed as a forerunner of Section 21 of the Glass-Steagall Act.[86] That provision prohibited any "corporation engaged in commerce as defined in this Act" from depositing its funds "with any individual, private banker, or banking association or trust company, except banking associations incorporated under the laws of the United States or some of the States or Territories thereof."[87]

Professor Willis, who, as noted,[88] had served as special counsel to the Senate Resolution 71 subcommittee, later suggested that this provision was designed primarily to prevent "the siphoning off of deposits in incorporated banks into private institutions which would, as in the past, feed them into stock exchange loans."[89] It is noteworthy that the Pujo Committee had stated:

> Interstate corporations should not be permitted to deposit their funds with unsupervised, unregulated, private bankers who do not disclose their resources or liabilities, who keep no reserve and are free to invest their depositors' money as they see fit.[90]

Moreover, at the Senate Resolution 71 hearings, the New York Superintendent of Banks had submitted a report to the subcommittee that had been filed with the Governor of New York, which recommended legislation to require private bankers to discontinue accepting deposits and to liquidate their deposit liabilities.[91]

The financial community was adamantly opposed to S. 3215. Two commentators have stated that "[b]ankers' associations, individual financiers and chambers of commerce joined in condemning [S. 3215] as a vicious bill and an insuperable bar to economic recovery."[92] The press reported that the Treasury Department also was opposed to the bill and that there was sentiment in support of conducting hearings on the legislation.[93] In early February, Glass made a speech on the Senate floor about the banking community's opposition to his bill.[94]

Senator Glass revised S. 3215 and introduced a new bill, S. 4115, in March 1932.[95] S. 4115 reflected the thrust of S. 3215,[96] but did not contain some provisions of the earlier bill, including the section identified above as a predecessor of Section 21 of the Glass-Steagall Act.

Hearings on S. 4115

In late March 1932, the Senate Committee on Banking and Currency held hearings on S. 4115.[97] At the hearings, representatives of the banking community objected to the bill on the ground that it was extremely deflationary.[98] In addition, the Federal Reserve Bank of New York characterized as "unwise" the provisions calling for a divorce of "the banking system and the capital market."[99] Governor George L. Harrison stated that these provisions would "disturb the mechanism of the capital market, the free functioning of which is now so important to a recovery from existing business conditions."[100]

Eugene Meyer testified for the Federal Reserve Board.[101] He stated that "affiliations between member banks and security companies have contributed to undesirable banking developments.''[102] But Meyer went on to state:

> There are difficulties . . . in the way of accomplishing a complete divorce of member banks from their affiliates arising from the fact that a law intended for that purpose is likely to be susceptible of evasion or else to apply to many cases to which it is not intended to apply. Therefore, the board is not prepared at this time to make a definite recommendation, but submits, for the consideration of the Committee on Banking and Currency, a [provision] which is designed to provide for the divorce of security affiliates from member banks after three years. . . .[103]

Meyer explained the tentative nature of the Board's proposal by citing "the absence of full information on the subject."[104] He stated that the Board had discussed the idea of deferring the separation issue pending further study.[105] Meyer noted that

> [the Board did not feel], in the absence of more definite information, any too great confidence in any recommendation that [it] or anyone else could make. But this is a suggestion for your consideration, which was the best we could evolve in the board with the assistance of our experts.[106]

Senate's Consideration of S. 4412

Following the hearings, Glass again revised his bill and introduced S. 4412 on April 18, 1932.[107] S. 4412 was reported by the Committee to the full Senate on the same day.[108] This bill, as reported, included the new section suggested by Governor Meyer.[109] The report accompanying S. 4412 offered the following assessment of the condition of member banks:

> The outstanding development in the commercial banking system during the prepanic period was the appearance of excessive security loans, and of overinvestment in securities of all kinds. The effects of this situation in changing the whole character of the banking problem can hardly be overemphasized. National banks were never intended to undertake investment banking business on a large scale, but the whole tenor of legislation and administrative rulings concerning them has been away from recognition of such a growth in the direction of investment banking, as legitimate. Nevertheless it has continued; and a very fruitful cause of bank failures, especially within the past two years, has been the fact that the funds of various institutions have been so extensively "tied up" in long-term investments. The growth of the investment portfolio of the bank itself has been greatly emphasized in importance by the organization of allied or affiliated companies under State laws, through which ever more extensive advances and investments in the security market could be made.[110]

The report was very critical of securities affiliates. It stated:

> There seems to be no doubt anywhere that a large factor in the overdevelopment of security loans, and in the dangerous use of the resources of bank depositors for the

purpose of making speculative profits and incurring the danger of hazardous losses, has been furnished by perversions of the national banking and State banking laws, and that, as a result, machinery has been created which tends towards danger in several directions.

(a) The greatest of such dangers is seen in the growth of ''bank affiliates'' which devote themselves in many cases to perilous underwriting operations, stock speculation, and maintaining a market for the banks' own stock often largely with the resources of the parent bank. This situation was never contemplated by the national banking act, and it would, therefore, appear that the affiliate system calls for the establishment of some legislative provisions designed to deal with the situation. It has been suggested from many quarters that the affiliate system be simply ''abolished.'' This suggestion has much authority behind it, but, in addition to the manifest difficulty of enforcement, owing to the existence of well-known subterfuges to maintain control, there remains the question whether it would be of much real service so long as State legislation permits the growth of affiliates in connection with State banks and trust companies. The committee has, therefore, determined to present proposed legislation aimed at the following objects:

(1) To separate as far as possible national and member banks from affiliates of all kinds.

(2) To limit the amount of advances or loans which can be obtained by affiliates from the parent institutions with which they are connected.

(3) To install a satisfactory examination of affiliates, working simultaneously with the present system of examination applicable to the parent banks.[111]

S. 4412 was debated on the Senate floor in May 1932. During the debate, Senator Glass mentioned the banking community's continued opposition to the separation of securities affiliates from commercial banks,[112] but suggested that

[t]he committee ascertained in a more or less definite way—we think quite a definite way—that one of the greatest contributions to the unprecedented disaster which has caused this almost incurable depression was made by these bank affiliates.[113]

Glass stated that the affiliates ''sent out their high-pressure salesman and literally filled the bank portfolios of this country with these investment securities.''[114] At one point he asserted that

the great banks in the money centers choked the portfolios of their correspondent banks from Maine to California with utterly worthless investment securities, nearly eight billions of them being the investment securities tottering South American republics and other foreign countries.[115]

Senator Walcott, who was a member of the Senate Committee on Banking and Currency, stressed that the affiliates were engaged in speculative activities ''quite contrary to legitimate commercial banking.''[116] Walcott also attributed the unprecedented level of bank failures to the purchase by small correspondent banks of ''the very securities that the larger banks have forced upon them.''[117] Senator Bulkley, who had been asked by Glass to address the provisions of the bill relating to securities affiliates and investment banking, described the bill as a prophylactic measure designed ''to protect the operations of the banking system itself, and to protect the depositors and customers of the banks. . . .''[118] To this end, the bill prohibited national and state member banks from carrying on the investment security business either directly, or through affiliates.[119] Bulkley cited a range of problems arising from banks' relationships with securities affiliates.[120] The problems discussed by Bulkley were similar to those reviewed by the subcommittee in the Appendix to the Senate Resolution 71 hearings.[121] The thrust of Bulkley's comments is perhaps best captured by the following statement:

> [T]he banker who has nothing to sell to his depositors is much better qualified to advise disinterestedly and to regard diligently the safety of depositors than the banker who uses the list of depositors in his savings department to distribute circulars concerning the advantages of this, that, or the other investment on which the bank is to receive an originating profit or an underwriting profit or a distribution profit or a trading profit or any combination of such profits.[122]

Although Glass tried repeatedly to persuade the Senate to take final action on S. 4412, the Senate did not act before the end of the session.[123]

The election of President Roosevelt in November 1932 provided additional momentum for the adoption of Glass' proposals. Although the Democratic Party platform had not specifically endorsed Glass' bill, it had called for the separation of securities affiliates from commercial banks and for further restrictions on the use of the Federal Reserve facilities for speculative purposes.[124] The President-elect also had endorsed such action during the campaign.[125] Armed with this new support, Glass finally persuaded the Senate to act on S. 4412 in January 1933, during the lame-duck session of the Seventy-second Congress. Following a filibuster by Senator Long prompted by his opposition to the bill's branch banking provisions,[126] the Senate passed S. 4412 by a vote of 54 to 9 on January 25, 1933.[127]

Glass' statements during the debate were similar to those he had made in June. He stated, among other things, that he wanted ''to make it impossible hereafter to have the portfolios of commercial banks filled with useless speculative securities, so that when stringency comes upon the country these banks may not respond to the requirements of commerce.''[128] Glass suggested that this was the problem ''with the country today, and it is because the bill would avert a repetition of that disaster that intense and bitter opposition has been organized against it.''[129] Glass was willing, however, to accede to the still-vital opposition on the part of the banking community to the extent that he agreed to amendments to delay the effect of the legislation, and in particular to increase from three to five years the period for separation of securities affiliates from commercial banks.[130] Despite the overwhelming vote in the Senate, Glass was thwarted again when the House failed to act on Section 4412 before the end of the Seventy-second Congress.[131]

Important Events in Early 1933

Stock Exchange Practices Hearings. In the early months of 1933, several events helped Glass considerably in his efforts to secure enactment of his proposals. First,

the Pecora hearings on stock exchange practices focused public attention on objec-
tionable financial practices[132] and, in particular, on the abuses involved in the relationship between National City Bank and its securities affiliate, the National City
Company. The hearings revealed, among other things, that National City Bank and
its affiliate repeatedly had failed to disclose material facts to investors; the affiliate
had engaged in high-pressure sales tactics; the affiliate had traded in the stock of the
bank and participated in a range of manipulative activities; the bank had provided the
affiliate with customers; and the bank had used the affiliate to relieve the bank of bad
loans to the detriment of shareholders.[133]

The Banking Crisis.   The high incidence of bank failures that had plagued the nation for years finally gave rise to a full-blown panic in late 1932 and early 1933. This
panic culminated in President Roosevelt's declaration of a bank holiday in March
1933.[134]

During 1932, about 1450 banks had failed.[135] The majority of failures still had
been occurring among small banks. For the year ending October 31, 1932, 84.5% of
the banks that had failed had been institutions with capital of less than $100,000.[136]
The rash of failures among small banks, however, had begun to put pressure on the
larger ones. The surviving banks' efforts to achieve greater liquidity had only aggravated the situation, because as they had converted assets into cash the market value
of their remaining assets had become further depressed. The situation had been further
aggravated by the general economic downturn that had hit the country. Between 1929
and 1933, "net national product fell by more than one-half in current prices, more
than one-third in constant prices, and more than one-third in monthly wholesale
prices."[137] By the end of 1932, banking systems in some states had begun to fail
entirely.[138]

These developments quickly led to a total erosion of depositor confidence[139]
which, in turn, led to hoarding and to renewed runs on existing banks. The public's
currency holdings increased about 16% between the end of 1932 and February
1933.[140] Moreover, as two commentators have pointed out, "any runs on banks for
whatever reason became to some extent self-justifying, whatever the quality of assets
held by banks."[141] In January 1933, 237 banks failed, followed by 148 failures in
February.[142] These numbers, however, do not reflect the increasing number of states
that had been forced to declare bank holidays. Iowa, Louisiana, and, most important,
Michigan, had declared bank holidays by mid-February.[143] These developments put
intense pressure on the New York banks, which were faced not only with demands
for cash from their local depositors, but also with withdrawals by the interior banks.[144]
By early March, holidays had been declared in about half the states, including New
York and Illinois.[145] Although President Roosevelt's declaration of a national bank
holiday and Congress' enactment of emergency banking legislation in early March
stabilized the situation and permitted the reopening of most of the surviving banks,[146]
a consensus had developed regarding the need for reform of the banking structure.

Aldrich's Announcement.   Finally, Winthrop Aldrich, the new chairman of the
Chase National Bank, announced in March that he supported a separation of com-

mercial and investment banking and that the Chase would sever its investment affiliate.[147] In making his announcement, Aldrich commended the National City Bank for its recent decision to drop its securities affiliate, and went on to propose several major reforms designed to effect a separation of commercial and investment banking.[148] Among these proposals was one to prohibit private bankers from receiving deposits unless they agreed to submit to the same regulation and disclosure requirements as commercial banks.[149] Aldrich suggested that "no corporation or partnership dealing in securities should be permitted to take deposits even under regulation."[150]

One commentator has suggested that the combination of the Pecora hearings and Aldrich's announcement broke the back of the banking community's opposition to the Glass legislation.[151] She notes that other bankers followed Aldrich's lead and that after the spring of 1933 there was no real opposition to separating commercial and investment banking.[152] In this regard, it is also noteworthy that in March 1933,

> [m]any . . . affiliates were . . . in process of liquidation, or had been previously dissolved, either because final passage of the Glass bill was anticipated or because banks welcomed the opportunity to rid themselves of affiliates which they had thought necessary or highly desirable during the twenties.[153]

The investment banking business had dropped off substantially, and "no one was prepared to predict how soon, if ever again, this commercial banking sideline might be able to pay its own way."[154]

The Glass-Steagall Act Becomes Law

At the beginning of the Seventy-third Congress in March 1933, Glass introduced S. 245, which largely reflected the changes that had been made in S. 4412 during the Senate debate in January.[155] In May, S. 245 was replaced by S. 1631.[156] S. 1631 included for the first time a section basically identical to Section 21 of the Glass-Steagall Act.[157] The introduction of the bill also marked the reappearance of a section very similar to Section 32.[158] At this point, provisions substantially similar to all four sections of the Glass-Steagall Act were included in the bill.[159]

The Senate Committee on Banking and Currency reported S. 1631 to the full Senate on May 15, 1933.[160] The report accompanying the bill was similar to the one that had accompanied S. 4412, and, in fact, contained some language identical to language in the earlier report.[161]

The Senate debated S. 1631 in late May 1933. The statements of the bill's proponents were not much different from the ones they had made on prior occasions. At one point, for example, Senator Glass stated:

> [T]hese affiliates, I repeat, were the most unscrupulous contributors, next to the debauch of the New York Stock Exchange, to the financial catastrophe which visited this country and was mainly responsible for the depression under which we have been suffering since. They ought to be separated, and they ought speedily to be separated, from the parent banks; and in this bill we have done that.[162]

The debate, however, is noteworthy in several respects. For the first time, Glass discussed the provision that was to become Section 21 of the Glass-Steagall Act. Glass described this provision as "rather controversial" and stated that he had included it "in the original so-called 'Glass bill.' "[163] He said that the provision had been eliminated in succeeding drafts in response to "the bitter hostility of the large private banking interests of the country," which Glass feared might be sufficient to kill the bill.[164] Glass noted, however, that in this bill "the large private banks, whose principal business is an investment business," were prohibited "from receiving deposits."[165] Later, Senator Bulkley fought off an amendment to Section 21 on the ground that it "would materially change one of the most important principles in the bill."[166] In this regard, both Bulkley and Glass described the provision as "vital."[167] Finally, Bulkley offered an amendment to change the words "engaged principally" which then appeared in Section 21 to "engaged."[168] Bulkley stated:

> It has become apparent that at least some of the great investment houses are engaged in so many forms of business that there is some doubt as to whether the investment business is the principal one. Therefore this word must be eliminated in order to make sure that we will accomplish a separation of . . . investment and deposit banking.[169]

The amendment was adopted[170] and the Senate later passed the bill without a record vote.[171]

Following the House-Senate conference on the legislation, which for present purposes basically resulted in adoption of the Senate bill,[172] the Senate and House both approved the conference report on June 13.[173] The legislation was signed into law on June 16, 1933.[174]

CONCLUSION

The legislative history of the Glass-Steagall Act is the story of a theory carried along by events. Standing alone, Senator Glass' theory of sound banking practice was not sufficiently persuasive to secure enactment of the divorce provisions. The theory needed the support provided by the collapse of the banking system and the damaged reputation of the financial community. In the next chapter, Professor Flannery suggests that Congress misperceived the causes of the depression and the banking crisis and grossly overestimated the extent to which commercial banks' securities activities were responsible for these events. In this light, the wisdom of retaining the Glass-Steagall Act should be reviewed.

NOTES

[1]48 Stat. 162 (codified in scattered sections of 12 U.S.C.).

[2]See Natter, *The Glass-Steagall Act: Separation of Commercial and Investment Banking,* in, HOUSE COMM. ON BANKING, FINANCE, AND URBAN AFFAIRS, FORMATION AND POWERS OF NATIONAL BANKING

ASSOCIATIONS—A LEGAL PRIMER 4–9 (Comm. Print 98-4 1983); Clark and Saunders, *Judicial Interpretation of Glass-Steagall: The Need for Legislative Action,* 97 BANKING L. J. 721, 725 (1980).

[3]12 U.S.C. Section 24. Section 16 states in relevant part:

[A] national banking association . . . shall have power—To exercise by its board of directors or duly authorized officers or agents, subject to law, all such incidental powers as shall be necessary to carry on the business of banking; by discounting and negotiating promissory notes, drafts, bills of exchange, and other evidences of debt; by receiving deposits; by buying and selling exchange, coin and bullion; by loaning money on personal security; and by obtaining, issuing and circulating notes according to the provisions of this chapter. The business of dealing in securities and stock by the association shall be limited to purchasing and selling such securities and stock without recourse, solely upon the order, and for the account of customers, and in no case for its own account, and the association shall not underwrite any issue of securities or stock: Provided, That the association may purchase for its own account investment securities under such limitations and restrictions as the Comptroller of the Currency may by regulation prescribe. In no event shall the total amount of the investment securities of any one obligor or maker, held by the association for its own account, exceed at any time 10 per centum of its capital stock actually paid in and unimpaired and 10 per centum of its unimpaired surplus fund, except that this limitation shall not require any association to dispose of any securities lawfully held by it on August 23, 1935. As used in this section the term "investment securities" shall mean marketable obligations, evidencing indebtedness of any person, copartnership, association, or corporation in the form of bonds, notes and/or debentures commonly known as investment securities under such further definition of the term "investment securities" as may by regulation be prescribed by the Comptroller of the Currency. Except as hereinafter provided or otherwise permitted by law, nothing herein contained shall authorize the purchase by the association for its own account of any shares of stock of any corporation. The limitations and restrictions herein contained as to dealing in, underwriting and purchasing for its own account, investment securities shall not apply to obligations of the United States, or general obligations of any State or of any political subdivision thereof. . . .

Section 5(c) of the Banking Act of 1933 applied the restrictions of Section 16 to member banks. *See* 12 U.S.C. Section 335.

[4]12 U.S.C. Section 377. Section 20 states in relevant part:

After one year from June 16, 1933, no member bank shall be affiliated in any manner . . . with any corporation, association, business trust, or other similar organization engaged principally in the issue, flotation, underwriting, public sale, or distribution at wholesale or retail or through syndicate participation of stocks, bonds, debentures, notes, or other securities. . . .

[5]*Id.*

[6]12 U.S.C. Section 78. Section 32 states in relevant part:

No officer, director, or employee of any corporation or unincorporated association, no partner or employee of any partnership, and no individual, primarily engaged in the issue, flotation, underwriting, public sale, or distribution, at wholesale or retail, or through syndicate participation, of stocks, bonds, or other similar securities, shall serve the same time as an officer, director, or employee of any member bank except in limited classes of cases in which the Board of Governors of the Federal Reserve System may allow such service by general regulations when in the judgment of said Board it would not unduly influence the investment policies of such member bank or the advice it gives its customers regarding investments.

[7]12 U.S.C. Section 378. Section 21 states in relevant part:

After the expiration of one year after June 16, 1933, it shall be unlawful—(1) For any person, firm, corporation, association, business trust, or other similar organization, engaged in the business of issuing, underwriting, selling, or distributing, at wholesale or retail, or through syndicate participation, stocks, bonds, debentures, notes, or other securities, to engage at the same time to any extent whatever in the business of receiving deposits subject to check or to repayment upon presentation of a passbook, certificate of deposit, or other evidence of debt, or upon request of the depositor: Provided, That the provisions of this paragraph shall not prohibit national banks or State banks or trust companies (whether or not members of the Federal Reserve System) or other financial institutions or private bankers from dealing in, underwriting, purchasing, and selling investment securities, or issuing securities, to the extent permitted to national banking associations by the provisions of Section 24 of this title: Provided further, That nothing in this paragraph shall be construed as affecting in any way such right as any bank, banking association, savings bank, trust company, or other banking institution, may otherwise possess to sell, without recourse or agreement to repurchase, obligations evidencing loans on real estate. . . .

[8]The variations in wording among Section 20 ("engaged principally"), Section 21 ("engaged"), and Section 32 ("primarily engaged"), are significant. The Supreme Court has interpreted "primarily engaged" in Section 32 to mean "substantial." Board of Governors v. Agnew, 329 U.S. 441, 446 (1947). This is a more stringent standard for determining violations of the Act than that embodied in Section 20, *see id.,* at 447–448, but it is less stringent than the one embodied in Section 21. See Board of Governors, FRS v. Investment Company Inst., 450 U.S. 46, 60–61 n.26 (1981).

[9]*See* U.S. DEPARTMENT OF TREASURY, PUBLIC POLICY ASPECTS OF BANK SECURITIES ACTIVITIES 4 (1975) [hereinafter TREASURY PAPER]; Golembe Associates, *Commercial Banking and the Glass-Steagall Act* 20–21 (1982) (prepared for the American Bankers Association) [hereinafter *Golembe Paper*]; Peach, *The Security Affiliates of National Banks,* in, WALL STREET AND THE SECURITY MARKETS 111 (V. Carosso (ed.) 1975); Perkins, *The Divorce of Commercial and Investment Banking: A History,* 88 BANKING L. J. 483, 486 (1971). See also *Operation of the National and Federal Reserve Banking Systems: Hearings Pursuant to S. Res. 71 Before a Subcomm. of the Senate Comm. on Banking and Currency,* 71st Cong., 3d Sess. 999, 1030, 1052 (1931) [hereinafter *S. Res. 71 Hearings*]. This view was drawn largely from the English, as opposed to the German, system. See TREASURY PAPER, *supra,* at A-2; *Golembe Paper, supra,* at 20–21; Perkins, *supra,* at 485–486; M. NADLER AND J. BOGEN, THE BANKING CRISIS 36 (1933). During the Senate debate on the Glass bill in 1932, Senator Bulkley explicitly endorsed the English practice. *See* 75 CONG. REC. 9911 (daily ed. May 10, 1932) (statement of Sen. Bulkley).

[10]TREASURY PAPER, note 9 *supra,* at 4.

[11]*See* Peach, note 9 *supra,* at 111; Perkins, note 9 *supra,* at 485–486. *See also Stock Exchange Practices: Hearings Before the Senate Comm. on Banking and Currency on S. Res. 84 and S. Res. 56,* 73d Cong., 2d Sess. 3979 (statement of Winthrop W. Aldrich, President, Chase National Bank).

[12]*See Golembe Paper,* note 9 *supra,* at 21–22; Perkins, note 9 *supra,* at 501–502.

[13]*See* L. MINTS, A HISTORY OF BANKING THEORY 9 (1945). Mints suggests that "banking legislation has been too much controlled, in the United States at any rate, by the belief that a restriction of the banks to the making of loans for bona fide commercial purposes will automatically provide for all needed variations in the means of payment." *Id.,* at 5. He states: "This belief, which I have called the "real bills doctrine," is utterly subversive of any rational attack on the problem of monetary policy. If there is a central theme to what I have written, it is that this doctrine is unsound in all its aspects." *Id.*

[14]*Id.,* at 9.

[15]*See* TREASURY PAPER, note 9 *supra,* at A-2–A-3; Perkins, note 9 *supra,* at 486–490.

[16]*See* TREASURY PAPER, note 9 *supra,* at A-4–A5; Peach, note 9 *supra,* at 50–51.

[17]*See* TREASURY PAPER, note 9 *supra,* at A-4–A-5; Perkins, note 9 *supra,* at 486–490. The adherence to the English system broke down more quickly in the state banking systems due to the rise of the trust companies after the Civil War. In response to this development, state banks sought, and were granted, more liberal charters. *Id.*

   The *Golembe Paper* suggests that the English system never was followed strictly in this country either at the federal or the state level. *See Golembe Paper,* note 9 *supra,* at 23–26. Among other things, the paper points out that commercial banks have been involved from their inception in providing long-term credit to business and government. *Id.,* at 25–29. *See also* M. NADLER & J. BOGEN, note 9 *supra,* at 37.

   One commentator has pointed out that the English merchant banks combined depository, lending, brokerage, and investment functions, and were widely copied on the continent and in the United States. *See* Asher, "Glass-Steagall: A Fresh Look," *ABA Banking Journal* 62 (Feb. 1981). He suggests that Senator Glass and other proponents of the "English system" were "fooled" by the merchant banks' decision not to deal with the rising middle class. To fill the gap, "the British clearing banks came into existence." They took deposits and made loans to the general public. Eventually, they became larger than the merchant banks. The merchant banks, however, continued to take deposits from business and the wealthy, to make loans to these groups, and to engage in underwriting and brokerage activities. Asher states that "there was never a split in the British system between banking and investment—not in law, not in practice." *Id.*

[18]*See* TREASURY PAPER, note 9 *supra,* at A-5; Perkins, note 9 *supra,* at 486–490; Peach, note 9 *supra,* at 51–52, 59. The First National Bank in New York City organized the first securities affiliate on record in 1908. *See S. Res. 71 Hearings,* note 9 *supra,* at 1052. Perkins states that the First National Bank had been engaged in the securities business for many years prior to 1908. Perkins, note 9 *supra,* at 489. It formed an affiliate in response to the federal government's criticism of the bank's buying and selling of common stock. *Id.*

[19]H.R. REP. NO. 1593, 62d Cong., 3d Sess. 164 (1913) [hereinafter PUJO REPORT]. The Pujo Committee, which was created to investigate the concentration of control of money and credit, stated in its report:

> The national banks of the great cities are exceeding their charter powers in the character of the business they are conducting and from which their principal revenues are derived. They are acting as promoters, underwriters, and houses of issue for the securities of railroad and industrial corporations. Their activities have extended even into foreign countries and to highly speculative and undeveloped enterprises, through the thin disguise of the so-called security companies that are attached to them. . . . *Id.,* at 151.

The committee also stated:

> [We are] of opinion that national banks should not be permitted to become inseparably tied together with security holding companies in an identity of ownership and management. These holding companies have unlimited powers to buy and sell and speculative in stocks. It is unsafe for banks to be united with them in interest in management. The temptation would be great at times to use the bank's funds to finance the speculative operations of the holding company. *Id.,* at 155.

The committee went on to recommend that [t]he stockholders of a national bank should be expressly prohibited from becoming associated as stockholders in any other corporation under agreements or arrangements assuring that the stock of such other corporation shall always be owned by the same persons or substantially the same persons who own the stock of the bank or that the managements shall be substantially the same. *Id.,* at 164.

The Committee also recommended that

> [n]ational banks should be prohibited from directly or indirectly engaging in any promotion, guaranty, or underwriting, involving the purchase, sale, public offering, or issue, or other disposition of the securities of any corporation. *Id.*

[20]*See* TREASURY PAPER, note 9 *supra,* at A-6; Perkins, note 9 *supra,* at 491.

[21]*See* TREASURY PAPER, note 9 *supra,* at A-6; J. BROOKS, ONCE IN GOLCONDA 5 (1970); R. PATTERSON, THE GREAT BOOM AND PANIC 9 (1965); Perkins, note 9 *supra,* at 491. Perkins states that "[m]any banks and trust companies either expanded their bond departments or formed security affiliates to handle [the war bond] business." *Id.*

[22]*See S. Res. 71 Hearings,* note 9 *supra,* at 1067–1068 (citing 1920 ANNUAL REPORT OF THE COMPTROLLER OF THE CURRENCY); Peach, note 9 *supra,* at 148–150.

[23]*See* M. FRIEDMAN & A. SCHWARTZ, A MONETARY HISTORY OF THE UNITED STATES 1867–1960 240, 244–245 (1963).

[24]*See* TREASURY PAPER, note 9 *supra,* at A-8; Peach, note 9 *supra,* at 150. Perkins points out that during the war years "in an effort to strengthen the still experimental Federal Reserve System, state banks and trust companies were allowed to enter the new system without having to give up any of the corporate privileges granted to them by state law." Perkins, note 9 *supra,* at 491. Perkins states:

> The result of this decision by the Federal Reserve Board in Washington was to recognize formally the right of at least one class of member banks to engage in investment banking. Any national bank that had heretofore pondered the ultimate legality of the security affiliate system interpreted this move as a go-ahead signal to pursue profits in the investment banking field. [*Id.*]

[25]*See* TREASURY PAPER, note 9 *supra,* at A-8. *See also* M. FRIEDMAN & A. SCHWARTZ, note 23 *supra,* at 245; C. BREMER, AMERICAN BANK FAILURES 95–96 (1935). Apparently, the concern was not so much over the number of member banks, but rather over the comparison between the assets held by state and national banks. The assets of state banks were increasing, whereas those of national banks were declining. The Comptroller believed that this threatened the federal government's control over credit. *See* TREASURY PAPER, note 9 *supra,* at A-8.

[26]*See id.*

[27]*See id.; Golembe Paper,* note 9 *supra,* at 35; Peach, note 9 *supra,* at 150.

[28]*See* Perkins, note 9 *supra,* at 496. Although the Comptroller initially restricted the "approved list" under the McFadden Act to debt securities, he later expanded it to include equity securities. *Id.,* at 494 n.27. *See also* TREASURY PAPER, note 9 *supra,* at A-9.

[29]*See* V. CAROSSO, INVESTMENT BANKING IN AMERICA 368 (1970); TREASURY PAPER, note 9 *supra,* at A-16; Natter, note 2 *supra,* at 4–6; Peach, note 9 *supra,* at 14–15.

[30]S. Res. 71, 71st Cong., 1st Sess., 71 CONG. REC.1830 (daily ed. May 24, 1929).

[31]*Id.*

[32]*See* V. CAROSSO, note 29 *supra,* at 368.

[33]*See* S. REP. No. 493, 71st Cong., 2d Sess. (1930).

[34]72 CONG. REC. 8335 (daily ed. May 5, 1930).

[35]S. 4723, 71st Cong., 2d Sess., 72 CONG. REC. 10,973 (daily ed. June 17, 1930).

[36]72 CONG. REC. 10,973 (daily ed. June 17, 1930) (statement of Sen. Glass).

[37]S. 4723, note 35 *supra,* at sec. 2.

[38]*Id.,* at secs. 7, 9.

[39]*See* 77 CONG. REC. 3949 (daily ed. May 22 , 1933 (statement of Rep. Bacon); S. KENNEDY, THE BANKING CRISIS OF 1933 16 (1973); C. BREMER, note 25 *supra,* at 12; M. NADLER & J. BOGEN, note 9 *supra,* at 24; N.Y. Times, May 29, 1932, sec. 9, at 1.

[40]S. KENNEDY, note 39 *supra,* at 205.

[41]C. BREMER, note 25 *supra,* at 47.

[42]*Id.*

[43]*See* S. Res. 71 Hearings, note 9 *supra,* at 3–7 (statement of J. W. Pole, Comptroller of the Currency); S. KENNEDY, note 39 *supra,* at 16; M. FRIEDMAN & A. SCHWARTZ, note 23 *supra,* at 240, 249; C. BREMER, note 25 *supra,* at 57. During 1921–1929, "about 70 per cent of all bank failures . . . occurred in twelve agricultural states, of which 41 per consisted of banks situated in seven Western grain states." H. P. WILLIS & J. CHAPMAN, THE BANKING SITUATION 315 (1934). *See also* 77 CONG. REC. 3949 (daily ed. May 22, 1933) (statement of Rep. Bacon); 75 CONG. REC. 9897 (daily ed. May 10, 1932) (statement of Sen. Glass).

> "Two fundamental causes are at the root of the small bank failures—lack of diversity and necessarily lack of earning power. Most of the small banks are what may be termed, as I have stated, 1-crop or 1-enterprise banks. Where the loans of a bank are made to a community which depends on cotton, and cotton prices are low, or a crop fails, the bank is unable to stand the shock, and the amount of losses can not be absorbed, due to the lack of earnings, and it eventually fails. And so if it is in a tobacco community; so if it is in a coal-mining section.

[44]*See* S. Res. 71 Hearings, note 9 *supra,* at 7 (statement of J. W. Pole, Comptroller of the Currency); M. FRIEDMAN & A. SCHWARTZ, note 23 *supra,* at 240.

[45]M. NADLER & J. BOGEN, note 9 *supra,* at 35.

[46]*Id.*

[47]77 CONG. REC. 3949 (daily ed. May 22, 1933) (statement of Rep. Bacon); S. KENNEDY, note 39 *supra,* at 19.

[48]*Id.*

[49]*Id. See also* M. FRIEDMAN & A. SCHWARTZ, note 23 *supra,* at 308.

[50]*Id.*

[51]*Id.,* at 308–309.

[52]S. KENNEDY, note 39 *supra,* at 19; C. BREMER, note 25 *supra,* at 13.

[53]*See* M. FRIEDMAN & A. SCHWARTZ, note 23 *supra,* at 309–311; M. NADLER & J. BOGEN, note 9 *supra,* at 42. *See also* S. KENNEDY, note 9 *supra,* at 1–3.

[54]*See id.,* at 1; M. FRIEDMAN & A. SCHWARTZ, note 23 *supra,* at 309–311.

[55]*See id.,* at 310–311.

[56]*See e.g.,* Peach, note 9 *supra,* at 151.

[57]S. *Res. 71 Hearings,* note 9 *supra,* at 1054.

[58]*Id.,* at 1058.

[59]*See, e.g.,* P. TEMIN, DID MONETARY FORCES CAUSE THE GREAT DEPRESSION? 91–94 (1976); Perkins, note 9 *supra,* at 496–497; Werner, "Biggest Bank Failure," *Fortune* 62 (March 1933).

[60]*See, e.g.,* P. TEMIN, note 59 *supra,* at 91–94; Werner, note 59 *supra. See also* 75 CONG. REC. 9905 (daily ed. May 10, 1932) (statement of Sen. Walcott).

[61]Perkins, note 9 *supra,* at 497.

[62]*Id.*

[62]*Id.*

[64]S. *Res. 71 Hearings,* note 9 *supra.*

[65]*See* note 34 *supra* and accompanying text.

[66]S. *Res. 71 Hearings,* note 9 *supra,* at 1.

[67]*See* 75 CONG. REC. 9973 (daily ed. May 11, 1932) (statement of Sen. Norbeck); TREASURY PAPER, note 9 *supra,* at A-13.

[68]H. P. WILLIS & J. CHAPMAN, note 43 *supra,* at 32. *See also* S. *Res. 71 Hearings,* note 9 *supra,* at 50 (statement of Sen. Glass). M. FRIEDMAN & A. SCHWARTZ, note 23 *supra,* at 191; *The Chase Economic Bulletin,* vol. 12, no. 1, at 5 (Apr. 25, 1932). Professor Willis of Columbia was Glass' principal advisor on the Glass-Steagall Act and served as special counsel to the subcommittee. *See* S. *Res. 71 Hearings,* note 9 *supra,* at 1. Willis also had helped Glass to draft the Federal Reserve Act. *See* Perkins, note 9 *supra,* at 498. *See also* TREASURY PAPER, note 9 *supra,* at A-12–A-15; Peach, note 9 *supra,* at 151–152; Perkins, note 9 *supra,* at 497–505.

[69]*Brokers' Loans: Hearings Before the Senate Comm. on Banking and Currency on S. Res. 113,* 70th Cong., 1st Sess. 16 (1928) (statement of Dr. Henry Parker Willis) [hereinafter *Brokers' Loans Hearings*]. *See also* M. FRIEDMAN & A. SCHWARTZ, note 23 *supra,* at 191–192.

[70]*Brokers' Loans Hearings,* note 69 *supra,* at 53 (statement of Sen. Glass). *See also The Chase Economic Bulletin,* vol. 12, no. 1, at 5 (April 25, 1932).

[71]*See generally* TREASURY PAPER, note 9 *supra,* at A-12–A-15; Perkins, note 9 *supra,* at 497–505.

[72]*See* 75 CONG. REC. 9887 (daily ed. May 10, 1932) (statement of Sen. Glass). *See also* Perkins, note 9 *supra,* at 500.

[73]S. *Res. 71 Hearings,* note 9 *supra,* at 999. At one point early in the hearings Glass indicated the nature of his agenda when he stated:

> [W]hen we have had occasion to propose modifications of either the Federal Reserve Act or the National Banking Act it has seemed to me that instead of creating a national standard of sound banking which the State systems might be induced to follow, we have introduced into the national banking system some, if not many, of the abuses of the State systems, in order to enable national banks to compete with State banks. *Id.,* at 14.

It is noteworthy that Glass apparently had some doubts about the feasibility of separating securities affiliates from commercial banks. He stated: "Well I myself . . . rather question the feasibility maybe of abolishing [securities affiliates] because they have been permitted for so long to exist. It might create a confusion and embarrassment that would be worse than the evil itself." *Id.,* at 40. But Glass did say that if it were not possible to control securities affiliates, "[he] should be agreeable to prohibiting them." *Id.,* at 41.

[74]*Id.*, at 1001.

[75]*Id.*, at 1057. The subcommittee's discussion highlights the broad scope of the term *securities affiliate* as used by Congress during its consideration of the Glass-Steagall Act. The subcommittee stated that securities affiliates served as: (1) wholesalers of security issues; (2) retailers of securities; (3) holding and finance companies; (4) investment trusts (engaged in buying and selling securities acquired purely for investment or speculative purposes); (5) assets realization companies (used to take over from the parent bank loans and investments that proved to be doubtful or illiquid); (6) mediums for supporting the market for the bank's own stock; and (7) real estate holding companies. The subcommittee noted that "in most cases" the securities affiliates "exercised a combination of these functions, and in some instances they have exercised all of them." *Id.*

[76]*Id.*, at 1063. The subcommittee described this debtor-creditor relationship as "very prevalent," *id.*, and characterized it as "the most direct manner in which the affiliate may impair the liquidity of the bank. . . ." *Id.*, at 1064. In a succeeding subsection of the appendix, the subcommittee stated:

> The loan relationship as it exists between the bank and its affiliate differs from that prevailing with the general run of the bank's customers in an essential respect. When dealing with its affiliate, the bank is really dealing with itself, in view of the identity of ownership and management that is established. As a result, there tends to be a breaking down of those limitations on the extension of credit which the bank sets up in other cases to guard against the making of excessive or poorly-secured loans. *Id.*, at 1066.

[77]*Id.*, at 1063–1064.

[78]S. KENNEDY, note 39 *supra*, at 19.

[79]*See* R. PATTERSON, note 21 *supra*, at 190–93; M. NADLER & J. BOGEN, note 9 *supra*, at 70–71.

[80]S. KENNEDY, note 39 *supra*, at 20.

[81]S. REP. NO. 584, 72d Cong., 1st Sess. 6 (1932).

[82]S. 3215, 72d Cong., 1st Sess., 75 CONG. REC. 2403 (daily ed. Jan. 21, 1932).

[83]*See* notes 35–38 *supra* and accompanying text.

[84]S. 3215, note 82 *supra*, at Sections 20, 23, 24.

[85]*Id.*, at Sections 18, 21.

[86]*Id.*, at Section 33.

[87]*Id.*

[88]*See* note 68 *supra*.

[89]H. P. WILLIS & J. CHAPMAN, note 43 *supra*, at 82.

[90]PUJO REPORT, note 19 *supra*, at 164.

[91]*S. Res. 71 Hearings*, note 9 *supra*, at 271, 277 (statement of John A. Broderick, Superintendent of Banks, State of New York).

[92]M. NADLER & J. BOGEN, note 9 *supra*, at 53.

[93]*See* N.Y. Times, Jan. 27, 1932, at 1. *See also* N.Y. Times, Jan. 28, 1932, at 10; N.Y. Evening Post, Jan. 30, 1932, at 1.

[94]75 CONG. REC. 2999 (daily ed. Feb. 1, 1932) (statement of Sen. Glass).

[95]S. 4115, 72d Cong., 1st Sess., 75 CONG. REC. 6329 (daily ed. March 17, 1932).

[96]*Id.*, at Sections 17, 20.

[97]*See Operation of the National and Federal Reserve Banking Systems: Hearings on S. 4115 Before the Senate Comm. on Banking and Currency*, 72d Cong., 1st Sess. (1932) [hereinafter *S. 4115 Hearings*].

[98]*See, e.g., id.*, at 17–18 (statement of Allan M. Pope, President, Investment Bankers' Association of America); *id.*, at 59 (statement of Harry J. Haas, President, American Bankers' Association). At one point, Glass suggested that the bankers were testifying as part of an "organized protest." *Id.*, at 447. *See also* N.Y. Times, March 31, 1932, at 1.

[99]*S. 4115 Hearings*, note 97 *supra*, at 501 (Letter of George L. Harrison, Governor, Federal Reserve Bank of New York). Governor Harrison's letter had been unanimously approved by the directors of the Bank. *Id.*, at 499.

[100]*Id.*, at 501.

[101]*Id.*, at 357 (statement of Eugene Meyer, Governor, Federal Reserve Board).

[102]*Id.*, at 388.

[103]*Id.* The provision suggested by Meyer contained language virtually identical in major respects to the language that ultimately was included in Section 20 of the Glass-Steagall Act.

It is noteworthy that Meyer offered the Board's proposal as a substitute for Section 18 of S. 4115. *Id.* Section 18 of S. 4115 was similar to the provision that ultimately became Section 32 of the Glass-Steagall Act. Meyer stated that he was offering the substitute because Section 18 "would be capable of easy evasion and would become ineffective in many cases." *Id.*, at 387. He also criticized Section 18's prohibition of correspondent relationships between member banks and certain types of business entities as overly broad. *Id.*, at 387–388.

[104]*Id.*, at 388.

[105]*Id.*

[106]*Id.* In response to questions, Meyer later stated that "it is impossible to classify absolutely all affiliates that deal in securities as wicked and vicious." *Id.*, at 393.

[107]S. 4412, 72d Cong., 1st Sess., 75 CONG. REC. 8350 (daily ed. April 18, 1932).

[108]*Id. See also* S. REP. No. 584, 72d Cong., 1st Sess.

[109]S. 4412, note 107 *supra,* at Section 18. S. 4412, however, also reflected Meyer's suggestion that his proposal be substituted for Section 18 of S. 4115. As noted, *see* note 103 *supra,* Section 18 of S. 4115 was a predecessor of Section 32 of the Glass-Steagall Act. After this section was eliminated from S. 4412, a provision similar to Section 32 did not reappear until May 1933 when Glass introduced S. 1631. *See* S. 1631, 73d Cong., 1st Sess. sec. 31, 77 CONG. REC. 3109 (daily ed. May 10, 1933).

[110]S. REP. No. 584, 72d Cong., 1st Sess. 8 (1932).

[111]*Id.*, at 9–10.

[112]75 CONG. REC. 9888, 9898 (daily ed. May 10, 1932) (statement of Sen. Glass).

[113]*Id.*, at 9887 (daily ed. May 10, 1932) (statement of Sen. Glass).

[114]*Id.*

[115]*Id.*, at 9883 (daily ed. May 10, 1932) (statement of Sen. Glass).

[116]*Id.*, at 9906 (daily ed. May 10, 1932) (statement of Sen. Walcott).

[117]*Id. See also id.*, at 9911 (daily ed. May 10, 1932) (statement of Sen. Bulkley).

[118]*Id.*, at 9909, 9912, 9914 (daily ed. May 10, 1932) (statement of Sen. Bulkley).

[119]*Id.*, at 9913 (daily ed. May 10, 1932) (statement of Sen. Bulkley).

[120]*Id.*, at 9911–9913 (daily ed. May 10, 1932) (statement of Sen. Bulkley).

[121]*See S. Res. 71 Hearings,* note 9 *supra,* at 1063–1064; notes 76–77 *supra* and accompanying text.

[122]*See* 75 CONG. REC. 9912 (daily ed. May 10, 1932) (statement of Sen. Bulkley).

[123]*See* Perkins, note 9 *supra,* at 518. Perkins suggests that the Republican leadership wanted to avoid "agitation" on banking issues just before a national campaign. *Id.*

[124]*See* 76 CONG. REC. 1940 (daily ed. Jan. 17, 1933) (statement of Sen. Glass); V. CAROSSO, note 29 *supra,* at 370.

[125]*See* 76 CONG. REC. 1940 (daily ed. Jan. 17, 1933) (statement of Sen. Glass). *See also, id.*, at 1407 (daily ed. Jan. 9, 1933) (statement of Sen. Glass).

[126]*See, e.g., id.*, at 1452 (daily ed. Jan. 10, 1933) (statement of Sen. Long); *id.*, at 2208 (daily ed. Jan. 21, 1933) (statement of Sen. Glass). *See also* S. KENNEDY, note 39 *supra,* at 73, 207–208; M. NADLER & J. BOGEN, note 9 *supra,* at 54.

[127]76 CONG. REC. 2517 (daily ed. Jan. 25, 1933).

[128]*Id.*, at 2000 (daily ed. Jan. 18, 1933) (statement of Sen. Glass).

[129]*Id. See also* N.Y. Times, Dec. 22, 1932, at 27; N.Y. Times, Jan. 11, 1933, at 27.

[130]76 CONG. REC. 2407–2408 (daily ed. Jan. 24, 1933). *See also id.*, at 2408 (daily ed. Jan. 24, 1933) (statement of Sen. Glass).

[131]*See* S. KENNEDY, note 39 *supra*, at 73–74; H. P. WILLIS AND J. CHAPMAN, note 43 *supra*, at 98; Perkins, note 9 *supra*, at 521. One commentator has suggested that the House was initially reluctant to act on the bill because President-elect Roosevelt still had problems with it. In particular

> Roosevelt believed the Glass proposals did not go far enough; he wanted protection on investors against fictitious or bad securities, segregation of savings from commercial deposits, revision of the liquidating corporation clause to permit immediate reopening of failed banks, and branch banking limited to no more than a countrywide basis. S. KENNEDY, note 39 *supra*, at 73.

When the House finally considered the bill, "debate bogged down over the guarantee of bank deposits." *Id.*, at 74.

[132]*See generally Stock Exchange Practices: Hearings Before a Subcomm. of the Senate Comm. on Banking and Currency on S. Res. 84 and S. Res. 239,* 72d Cong., 2d Sess. (1933).

[133]*See* F. PECORA, WALL STREET UNDER OATH 70–123 (1939). *See also* V. CAROSSO, note 29 *supra*, at 330. *See generally* S. KENNEDY, note 39 *supra*, at 111–119. There appears to be a consensus among the commentators that the Pecora hearings were a significant factor in the passage of the Glass-Steagall Act. *See, e.g.,* TREASURY PAPER, note 9 *supra*, at A-23; S. KENNEDY, note 39 *supra*, at 212; V. CAROSSO, note 29 *supra*, at 330; H. P. WILLIS & J. CHAPMAN, note 43 *supra*, at 101–102; M. NADLER & J. BOGEN, note 9 *supra*, at 44; Karmel, *Glass Steagall: Some Critical Reflections,* 97 BANKING L. J. 631, 637 (1980); Perkins, note 9 *supra*, at 522.

[134]*See* TREASURY PAPER, note 9 *supra*, at A-22; S. KENNEDY, note 39 *supra*, at 158–159; 204; R. PATTERSON, note 21 *supra*, at 197; M. NADLER & J. BOGEN, note 9 *supra*, at 146.

[135]*See* S. REP. NO. 77, 73d Cong., 1st Sess. 6 (1933).

[136]M. NADLER & J. BOGEN, note 9 *supra*, at 35.

[137]S. KENNEDY, note 39 *supra*, at 18–19.

[138]*See id.*, at 63–64; M. FRIEDMAN & A. SCHWARTZ, note 23 *supra*, at 325.

[139]Two commentators have suggested that "the growth of postal savings deposits from 1929 to 1933 is one measure of the spread of distrust of banks." *Id.*, at 308 n.8. In November 1914, postal savings deposits totaled $57 million. By August 1929 they had grown by only $100 million. In October 1930, they stood at $190 million. Between then and March 1933 they increased to $1.1 billion *Id. See also* J.F.T. O'CONNOR, BANKS UNDER ROOSEVELT 24 (1938).

[140]*See* M. FRIEDMAN & A. SCHWARTZ, note 23 *supra*, at 326.

[141]*Id.*, at 355.

[142]S. REP. NO. 77, 73d Cong., 1st Sess. 6 (1933).

[143]*See* M. FRIEDMAN & A. SCHWARTZ, note 23 *supra*, at 325.

[144]*See* S. KENNEDY, note 39 *supra*, at 144, 149–150; M. FRIEDMAN & A. SCHWARTZ, note 23 *supra*, at 326; M. NADLER & J. BOGEN, note 9 *supra*, at 141, 153. Between February 1 and March 1, the interior banks withdrew $760 million in balances they held with New York banks. M. FRIEDMAN & A. SCHWARTZ, note 23 *supra*, at 326.

[145]*See id.*, at 325; S. KENNEDY, note 39 *supra*, at 144–145, 155 n.9.

[146]*See id.*, at 203. *See generally* C. COLT & N. KEITH, 28 DAYS (1933); C. BREMER, note 25 *supra*, at 18–19. The emergency banking legislation, among other things, granted the President certain emergency banking and currency powers; provided for the appointment of conservators for certain national banks with impaired assets; permitted the Reconstruction Finance Corporation to buy preferred stock, capital notes, and debentures of banks; and provided for emergency issues of Federal Reserve Bank notes. *See* M. FRIEDMAN & A. SCHWARTZ, note 23 *supra*, at 421–422, 427 n.4.

[147]*See* Wall St. Journal, Mar. 10, 1933, at 8; N.Y. Times, March 9, 1933, at 1. *See also Stock Exchange Practices: Hearings Before the Senate Comm. On Banking and Currency on S. Res. 84 and S. Res. 56,* 73d Cong., 2d Sess. 3977 (statement of Winthrop W. Aldrich, President, Chase National Bank) [hereinafter *Stock Exchange Practices Hearings*].

[148]*See* Wall St. Journal, Mar. 10, 1933, at 8; N.Y. Times, March 9, 1933, at 1. The National City Bank had announced its plan to drop its affiliate the day before Aldrich's announcement. *See* Wall St. Journal, March 9, 1933, at 4; N.Y. Times, March 9, 1933, at 1.

[149]*See* Wall St. Journal, Mar. 10, 1933, at 8.

[150]*Id. See also Stock Exchange Practices Hearings,* note 147 *supra,* at 3979 (statement of Winthrop W. Aldrich, President, Chase National Bank).

[151]S. KENNEDY, note 39 *supra,* at 212–213. *See also* M. NADLER & J. BOGEN, note 9 *supra,* at 54.

[152]S. KENNEDY, note 39 *supra,* at 212–213. *See also* Wall St. Journal, Mar. 13, 1933, at 5 (President of bank in Cincinnati supports Aldrich); Wall St. Journal, Mar. 16, 1933, at 6 (President of bank in Cleveland supports Aldrich).

Aldrich's announcement did not meet with universal approval. Arthur Schlesinger offers the following description:

> In March [1933], Winthrop Aldrich, succeeding the unfortunate [Albert H.] Wiggin as head of the Chase, made an unexpected demand for the separation of commercial and investment banking. This represented, however, very much a minority view on Wall Street; Aldrich's action was interpreted as a Rockefeller assault on the House of Morgan; and for a time he achieved almost the dignity of a traitor to his class. W. C. Potter of the Guaranty Trust characterized his proposals as "quite the most disastrous" he had "ever heard from a member of the financial community"; and J. P. Morgan himself predicted that separation of deposit and investment banking would have the most dire effects on his firm's future ability to supply capital "for the development of the country."
> [A. SCHLESINGER, THE AGE OF ROOSEVELT: THE COMING OF THE NEW DEAL 434–435 (1958).]

As Schlesinger notes, Aldrich's announcement probably was directed at the House of Morgan. See S. KENNEDY, note 39 *supra,* at 212–213; N.Y. Times, March 9, 1933, at 1; Wall St. Journal, March 10, 1933, at 8.

[153]Peach, note 9 *supra,* at 158.

[154]Perkins, note 9 *supra,* at 522.

[155]S. 245, 73d Cong., 1st Sess., 77 CONG. REC. 196 (daily ed. Mar. 11, 1933).

[156]S. 1631, 73d Cong., 1st Sess., 77 CONG. REC. 3109 (daily ed. May 10, 1933).

[157]*Id.,* at Section 21. It appears that Winthrop Aldrich was largely responsible for the inclusion of Section 21 in S. 1631. The section was consistent with some of the proposals Aldrich had made in March. *See* notes 148–150 and accompanying text. Moreover, in a biography of Aldrich, A. M. Johnson credits Aldrich with drafting the section of the Glass bill "prohibiting firms dealing in securities from accepting deposits," and states that Glass later acknowledged Aldrich's contribution. *See* A. JOHNSON, WINTHROP W. ALDRICH 156 (1968). This is true. When Aldrich testified at the Stock Exchange Practices Hearings in late 1933, Glass confirmed that he had met with him to discuss the Glass-Steagall Act. During the course of a discussion with Glass at these hearings, Aldrich took credit for drafting Section 21. *See Stock Exchange Practices Hearings,* note 147 *supra,* at 4016, 4032 (statement of Sen. Glass) (colloquy between Sen. Glass and Winthrop W. Aldrich). *See also* Wall St. Journal, May 11, 1933, at 1.

In view of certain elements of Aldrich's announcement in March 1933, *see* notes 148–150 and accompanying text; note 152 *supra;* S. KENNEDY, note 39 *supra,* at 212–213, it is likely that Section 21 was drafted with J. P. Morgan in mind. *See also* J. BROOKS, note 21 *supra,* at 149, 211; 8 ST. JOHN'S L. REV. 193, 195–196 (1933).

As noted, *see* notes 90–91 accompanying text, provisions similar to section 21 had been in existence for years.

[158]S. 1631, note 156 *supra,* at Section 31.

[159]*Id.,* at Sections 16, 20, 21, and 31.

[160]*See* S. REP. NO. 77, 73d Cong., 1st Sess. (1933).

[161]*Compare id.,* at 8–10 *with* S. REP. NO. 584, 72d Cong., 1st Sess. 8–10 (1932).

[162]77 CONG. REC. 3726 (daily ed. May 19, 1933) (statement of Sen. Glass).

[163]*Id.,* at 3730 (daily ed. May 19, 1933) (statement of Sen. Glass).

[164]*Id.*

[165]*Id.*

[166]*Id.,* at 4178–80 (daily ed. May 25, 1933); *id.,* at 4179 (daily ed. May 25, 1933) (statement of Sen. Bulkley). The thrust of the amendment to Section 21 offered by Senator Tydings was not clear and his

description of it was very confused. *See id.,* at 4178–79 (daily ed. May 25, 1933) (statement of Sen. Tydings). He appears to have had some concern about the constitutionality of Section 21. *Id.* Senator Glass assured him that the provision was constitutional. In this regard, Glass ackowledged that he was not a lawyer, but stated that he had "been supplied with a document . . . at least an inch thick, which gave our committee opinion after opinion, of inferior, superior, supreme Federal courts, in justification of the authority which we here try to assert." *Id.,* at 4179 (daily ed. May 25, 1933) (statement of Sen. Glass).

[167]*Id.,* at 4179 (daily ed. May 25, 1933) (statement of Sen. Bulkley); *id.,* at 4180 (daily ed. May 25, 1933) (statement of Sen. Glass).

[168]*Id.,* at 4180 (daily ed. May 25, 1933) (statement of Sen. Bulkley). For the later significance of this amendment, see note 8 *supra.*

[169]77 Cong. Rec. 4180 (daily ed. May 25, 1933) (statement of Sen. Bulkley).

[170]*Id.* (daily ed. May 25, 1933).

[171]*Id.,* at 4182 (daily ed. May 25, 1933). As a technical matter, the Senate agreed to Glass' motion to substitute the provisions of S. 1631 for the House-passed version of the bill, *see id.,* at 4181–82 (daily ed. May 25, 1933), and then passed H.R. 5661. *Id.,* at 4182 (daily ed. May 25, 1933).

    The House had passed H.R. 5661 by a vote of 262 to 19 on May 23, 1933. *See id.,* at 4058 (daily ed. May 23, 1933). This chapter focuses on activities in the Senate because the House, at least with respect to the provisions of interest here, basically followed the Senate's lead. *See e.g., id.,* at 3835 (daily ed. May 23, 1933) (statement of Rep. Steagall). The principal force behind the legislation was Senator Glass. Moreover, the debates on the legislation in the House were very similar to those in the Senate. *See, e.g., id.* ("The purpose of the regulatory provisions of this bill is to call back to the service of agriculture and commerce and industry the bank credit and the bank service designed by the framers of the Federal Reserve Act.") ("The purpose [of the bill] is to strengthen the banking structure, . . . to provide more effective regulation and supervision to eliminate dangerous and unsound practices, and to confine banks of deposit to legitimate functions and to separate them from affiliates or other organizations which have brought discredit and loss of public confidence.").

[172]*See id.,* at 5861 (daily ed. June 13, 1933) (statement of Sen. Glass); *id.,* at 5892 (daily ed. June 13, 1933) (statement of Rep. Steagall).

[173]*See id.,* at 5863 (daily ed. June 13, 1933) (Senate); *id.,* at 5898 (daily ed. June 13, 1933) (House).

[174]It is noteworthy that the drafters of the Glass-Steagall Act may have thought that it would have a broader scope than it has today. Other provisions of the Banking Act of 1933 would have required all banks "availing themselves of the permanent insurance provision of the bill" to become "members of the Federal Reserve Banking system." *Id.,* at 5861 (daily ed. June 13, 1933) (statement of Sen. Glass). *See also id.,* at 5896 (daily ed. June 13, 1933) (statement of Rep. Luce); *Stock Exchange Practices Hearings,* note 147 *supra,* at 4034 (statement of Sen. Glass); 8 St. John's L. Rev. 193, 195 (1933).

REFERENCES

Brokers' Loans: Hearings Before the Senate Comm. on Banking and Currency on S. Res. 113, 70th Cong., 1st Sess. (1928).

C. Bremer, American Bank Failures (1935).

J. Brooks, Once in Golconda (1970).

V. Carosso, Investment Banking in America (1970).

Clark and Saunders, *Judicial Interpretation of Glass-Steagall: The Need for Legislative Action,* 97 Banking L. J. 721 (1980).

C. Colt & N. Keith, 28 Days (1933).

M. Friedman & A. Schwartz, A Monetary History of the United States 1867–1960 (1963).

H.R. Rep. No. 1593, 62d Cong., 3d Sess. (1913).

A. JOHNSON, WINTHROP W. ALDRICH (1968).

Karmel, *Glass-Steagall: Some Critical Reflections,* 97 BANKING L. J. 631 (1980).

S. KENNEDY, THE BANKING CRISIS of 1933 (1973).

L. MINTS, A HISTORY OF BANKING THEORY (1945).

M. NADLER & J. BOGEN, THE BANKING CRISIS (1933).

J.F.T. O'CONNOR, BANKS UNDER ROOSEVELT (1938).

Operation of the National and Federal Reserve Banking Systems: Hearings Pursuant to S. Res. 71 Before a Subcomm. of the Senate Comm. on Banking and Currency, 71st Cong., 3d Sess. (1931).

Operation of the National and Federal Reserve Banking Systems: Hearings on S. 4115 Before the Senate Comm. on Banking and Currency, 72d Cong., 1st Sess. (1932).

R. PATTERSON, THE GREAT BOOM AND PANIC (1965).

Peach, *The Security Affiliates of National Banks,* in WALL STREET AND THE SECURITY MARKETS (V. Carosso ed. 1975).

F. PECORA, WALL STREET UNDER OATH (1939).

Perkins, *The Divorce of Commercial and Investment Banking: A History,* 88 BANKING L. J. 483 (1971).

S. REP. No. 584, 72d Cong., 1st Sess. (1932).

S. REP. No. 77, 73d Cong., 1st Sess. (1933).

A. SCHLESINGER, THE AGE OF ROOSEVELT: THE COMING OF THE NEW DEAL (1958).

Stock Exchange Practices: Hearings Before a Subcomm. of the Senate Comm. on Banking and Currency on S. Res. 84 and S. Res. 239, 72d Cong., 2d Sess. (1933).

Stock Exchange Practices: Hearings Before the Senate Comm. on Banking and Currency on S. Res. 84 and S. Res. 56, 73d Cong., 2d Sess. (1933).

P. TEMIN, DID MONETARY FORCES CAUSE THE GREAT DEPRESSION? (1976).

U.S. DEPARTMENT OF TREASURY, PUBLIC POLICY ASPECTS OF BANK SECURITIES ACTIVITIES (1975).

H. P. WILLIS & J. CHAPMAN, THE BANKING SITUATION (1934).

4 An Economic Evaluation of Bank Securities Activities before 1933

MARK J. FLANNERY

Securities market abuses of the 1920s ultimately precipitated several major pieces of financial legislation, including Glass-Steagall provisions of the Banking Act of 1933. One of the Act's provisions mandated a complete separation of commercial bank deposit-taking from investment banking activities. Legislators and financial critics, led by Senator Carter Glass of the Senate Committee on Banking and Currency, believed that bank securities activities in the 1920s had substantially contributed to the bank failures of 1930–1933 and perhaps to the Great Depression as well. The Glass-Steagall Act was thus a response to what Glass and others considered an unsound combination of disparate types of financial activity.

During the past decade there have been a series of efforts to loosen or eliminate the strictures Glass-Steagall imposed on commercial banks. Much of the debate surrounding these efforts has appealed—explicitly or implicitly—to the pre-1933 experience for evidence that commercial bank involvement in securities underwriting is inherently dangerous to society and to the banks involved. This chapter reexamines the historical evidence on bank securities activities in the 1920s, focusing in particular on the existence of evidence relevant to the question of whether commercial banks *today* should be strictly excluded from investment banking activities.

COMMERCIAL BANK INVESTMENT BANKING ACTIVITIES PRIOR TO 1933

Significant commercial bank involvement in underwriting securities predated the 1920s, with some state-chartered commercial banks heavily involved in underwriting securities from the beginning of the twentieth century. During World War I, many banks participated heavily in distributing government bonds (the "Liberty Loans") to finance World War I. This had two notable subsequent effects on the banking industry. First, the Liberty Loans were widely held for patriotic reasons, and thereby accustomed individual investors to the idea of buying open market securities. Second, many banks received their first experience with underwriting securities while distributing Liberty Loan bonds. Prior to the McFadden Act (1927), national banks were prohibited from underwriting securities, although some banks were in fact distributing securities through their bond departments.[1] McFadden was carefully drafted to "reaffirm" national banks' authority to underwrite certain investment securities. The Comptroller initially allowed only bond underwriting, but later approved underwriting of certain equity issues as well.

The banking system experienced a relatively large decline in loan demand during the 1920s, which accelerated banks' involvement with marketable securities. Loans and discounts as a proportion of total assets declined for New York City banks from 54.88% at year-end 1920 to 49.84% in December 1925. By December 31, 1929, loans accounted for only 43.74% of New York City bank assets. The corresponding proportions for all member banks were 56.86% in 1920, 53.73% in 1925, and 53.54% in 1929. This reduction in loan demand reflected two primary forces at work.[2] First, in the bullish securities market of 1920s, corporations issued large net amounts of public securities which replaced bank loans on corporate balance sheets. In other words, the demand for traditional types of corporate bank loans fell, especially during the first half of the decade. Even with no change in the stock of investable funds available, therefore, bankers would have been driven to find new outlets for their funds. In addition, however, the Federal Reserve generally pursued an easy money policy until approximately 1928, partly in an effort to help stabilize the value of European currencies. This afforded U.S. banks a relatively large growth in deposits, which further reinforced their tendency to increase their investment securities portfolios.

Bank underwriting activities grew quite naturally out of their increased purchases of marketable securities for their own accounts. As their own holdings expanded, bank bond departments developed an expertise in evaluating numerous types of corporate liabilities. It was a natural progression, then, for banks to recommend specific purchases to their customers and correspondents, and finally to underwrite the securities directly. By 1929, 459 U.S. banks (out of approximately 27,000) were underwriting securities through their bond departments or some other part of the bank. An additional 132 banks originated securities through a separate firm in some way affiliated with the bank.[3]

National banks and some state-chartered banks were limited in their ability to underwrite securities within the bank itself. For example, the McFadden Act initially prevented national banks from originating any type of stocks. Many banks therefore formed affiliated firms to undertake their securities business. An affiliate could take several forms, but two were most common and influential. Peach[4] provides additional details. First, the affiliate could be established as a separately incorporated subsidiary of the bank itself. By procuring a general corporate charter for the subsidiary, the bank could thus engage indirectly in a wide range of nonbanking business, including securities underwriting and distribution. The second prominent means of establishing an affiliated securities corporation involved chartering a separate corporation that was capitalized with the proceeds of a "special dividend" paid to bank shareholders. The bank and the securities firm were thus unrelated legal entities that happened to be owned by the same shareholders. In some cases, stocks of the bank and its affiliate were printed on opposite sides of the same piece of paper, ensuring that the two firms' owners would be identical.

Whichever corporate form the securities affiliate took, interlocking directorates and overlapping officers were common. Although each securities firm was allegedly an independent entity, the public could quite justifiably identify it closely with its affiliated commercial bank.[5] In many instances, the public was encouraged to do just that. Kennedy,[6] for example, observes that "Commercial and investment banking were virtually the same at National City, as at Chase and many other of the nation's largest banks."

The banks' underwriting activities tended to differ from traditional investment banking in two ways. First, they underwrote almost no equities.[7] Second, bank affiliates relied heavily on retail sales of underwritten securities, whereas the private investment banks generally engaged in wholesale distributions to relatively sophisticated purchasers. Perkins describes this dimension of bank securities activities:

> The creation of an investment banking structure with many retail outlets was a sharp divergence from the traditional wholesale approach to security distribution followed by the older private banking houses like J. P. Morgan & Co. and Kuhn, Loeb & Co. A network of branch offices with a large force of security salesmen was established either through merger with local and national brokerage firms or by natural growth. Innovative leadership in the investment banking field was rapidly being assumed by the expanding commercial banking community.[8]

This method of doing business resulted in rapid bank expansion: Banks and their affiliates originated 45.5% of all new bond issues in 1929, which was their peak year in this regard, up from only 22% in 1927.[9] In short, bank securities activities grew quickly during the 1920s and became very prominent by decade's end.

In many ways, the combination of a commercial bank and its investment affiliate resembled a modern bank holding company. The crucial difference was that securities affiliates were entirely unregulated in the 1920s. There was no legal distinction between a separately capitalized securities affiliate and any other bank customer, leaving bankers free to undertake virtually any desired transaction with their own affiliates regardless of the potential effect on the bank's welfare.[10]

For a number of years before 1933, Senator Glass and others had lamented the growing involvement of commercial banks in investment banking. However, there had been little public support for a complete separation of the two lines of business and much opposition to the idea from bankers. A subcommittee of the Senate Banking and Currency Committee held hearings in early 1933 on stock exchange practices that became a watershed in Glass' drive to divorce investment banking from deposit-taking in the United States. The subcommittee's counsel, Ferdinand Pecora, carefully documented a number of insider dealings and fraudulent activities undertaken by National City Bank and its securities affiliate, the National City Corporation.[11] Publicity surrounding National City Bank chairman Charles Mitchell's testimony generated a widespread and intense public reaction. Bankers came to be viewed as venal, selfish, and perhaps responsible for the depression. These so-called Pecora hearings played a significant role in the adoption of the divorce provisions as a prominent element of the Banking Act of 1933.

Today, the question that naturally presents itself is whether the 1920s' experience with bank involvement in investment banking provides any useful perspective on the appropriateness of the Glass-Steagall Act's restrictions in the 1980s. The next two sections consider this question in some detail.

THE PUBLIC INTEREST IN CURTAILING BANKS' SECURITIES AFFILIATES IN 1933

The potential public policy problems associated with bank involvement in securities underwriting and financing can be summarized under three broad categories.

1.   Banks' securities affiliates were involved in fraudulent activities at the expense of the general public and, sometimes, of their parent bank's shareholders and depositors.
2.   Large banks' investment banking activities may have endangered other, smaller banks due to the close ties that characterize correspondent banking relationships.
3.   Banks' investment banking activities may have somehow threatened their own safety and soundness.

Each of these general categories is discussed separately.

Did Bank Securities Affiliates Act Fraudulently?

The Senate hearings on stock exchange practices clearly reveal that bank securities underwriting was at least occasionally characterized by fraud, misrepresentation, and malfeasance at the firms whose principals gave testimony. Two further questions present themselves. First, were bank securities affiliates alone in these abuses? The answer here, also supported by the Senate hearings is clearly "no." The bank-related abuses that did occur in no way reflected any peculiar characteristics of the banking industry. H. Parker Willis, writing in the wake of the well-publicized hearings, denied that bankers deserved any special blame for the depression:

> Probably the most convincing defense of the conduct of our banking community—any of the speculators and businessmen who have figured in a minor way in the recent investigations—is simply that they afford a fairly genuine picture not merely of business ideals but of the rank and file of American standards and ethics of business. The men investigated have followed their own lights and the lights of the community in which they were residents. [12]

J. K. Galbraith provides a similar assessment of American business ethics at the time:

> The fact was that American enterprise in the twenties had opened its hospitable arms to
> an exceptional number of promoters, grafters, swindlers, imposters, and frauds. This,
> in the long history of such activities, was a kind of flood tide of corporate larceny.[13]

Although a variety of questionable activities had been undertaken in securities markets during the 1920s, it must be remembered that financial activities were virtually
unregulated by modern standards. Furthermore, the securities market abuses that occurred were certainly not confined to bank-related underwriters.

Congress sought to remedy the 1920s' financial market abuses via the Securities
Act of 1933 and the Securities Exchange Act of 1934. This legislation was designed
to prevent a number of abuses, including insider dealings, stock pools, and fraudulent
prospectuses. These problems involved unfair behavior by informed powerful traders, but they generally had nothing to do specifically with bank underwriting activities.

A second relevant question is whether the activities of National City, Chase and
the other banks involved in the hearings on stock exchange practices were representative of the industry at large. Willis, for example, felt that there was "no evidence" on the question whether securities market abuses were widespread:

> A fair examination of the facts disclosed by the Senate investigation leaves the feeling
> that but few persons relatively, have been examined, and that these, while often "prom-
> inent" are not in themselves representative of either banking or business. We must,
> accordingly, reject entirely the notion that—so far as these inquiries show—there has
> been a revelation of demonstrated crookedness on the part of American finance, trade
> and banking at large. There has been nothing of the sort. The showing has related to a
> few carefully selected personalities, which *may or may not be representative of specific
> conditions.*[14]

It thus remains an unanswered question how widespread were the activities identified
and publicized by the Pecora hearings.

There remains the question of whether commercial banks had inherently greater
or more difficult conflicts of interest in underwriting securities than did private investment bankers. If so, restrictive legislation alone might be insufficient to protect
the public from work securities abuses. However, this question was never explored
in depth in the debates or testimony preceding passage of the Glass-Steagall Act.
Although it may be a legitimate subject of inquiry (see chapters 6 and 7 by Giddy and
Saunders), it is not a question about which we have any significant historical information.

Did Bank Securities Activities Harm Correspondent Banks?

Senator Glass was convinced that large banks' sale of securities to smaller banks was
responsible for many bank failures following the 1929 stock market crash. Glass

asserted that bank securities affiliates "sent out their high-pressure salesmen and literally filled the bank portfolios of this country with their investment securities."[15] He further claimed that "great banks in the money centers choked the portfolios of their correspondent banks from Maine to California with utterly worthless investment securities."[16] In short, he believed that because large *banks* were offering securities for sale, other bankers purchased more securities or lower-quality securities than they otherwise would have.

Table 4.1 shows that small member banks' overall holdings of investment securities did not in fact rise sharply during the 1920s. Small "Country" banks' marketable securities rose from 25.38% of total assets in 1920 to 27.28% in 1929. More striking is the fact that the *composition* of small banks' investments shifted away from U.S. government bonds and toward the "other bonds, stocks, and securities" categories. This fact reflects developments in the corporate sector, where corporations were issuing marketable securities to replace bank debt. Whether these latter investments were substantially more risky than the loans and government bonds they replaced cannot be answered unambiguously with available data, but the question will be discussed in the section "The Effect of Security Holdings on Bank Soundness," as is the relationship between securities investments and bank soundness.

The essential question here is whether the participation of banks as security underwriters in the 1920s had any effect on the banking system's security holdings.[17] As noted above, the banking system was relatively flush with investible funds because of the reduced corporate loan demand and the Fed's easy-money policies during the 1920s. Banks needed to purchase some sort of asset with these funds, and marketable corporate securities were in growing supply. In short, a natural bank demand for marketable debt developed during the 1920s, and it is likely that private investment bankers would gladly have sold into the commercial banking system in the absence of bank securities affiliates. Market forces are too strong for such a profit opportunity *not* to have been exploited during the 1920s. If bank securities affiliates had not been in operation, the banking system would likely have bought similar amounts and similar quality bonds from other purveyors.

Were Investment Banking Activities a Threat to the Affiliated Bank?

Numerous commentators of the time considered the comingling of investment banking activities with commercial banking to be fundamentally unsound for the banks involved. Most of their statements are relatively vague about *why* such a connection is dangerous, although vagueness did not reduce their conviction. For example:

> That the combination of investment and commercial banks has been a major cause of bank failure has been fully recognized in the Banking Act of 1933, which contains . . . provisions designed to separate these two types of banking and to prevent the undue use of commercial bank funds for speculative purposes."[18]

> One of the greatest contributors to the unprecedented disaster which has caused this almost incurable depression was made by these banks [securities] affiliates.[19]

Table 4.1 Securities Holdings of Member Banks as a Proportion of Total Asset, 1920–1933 (Selected Dates)

	NYC Banks			"Country" Banks			All Member Banks		
	U.S. Government Bonds	Other Bonds, Stocks, and Securities	Loans and Discounts	U.S. Government Bonds	Other Bonds, Stocks, and Securities	Loans and Discounts	U.S. Government Bonds	Other Bonds, Stocks, and Securities	Loans and Discounts
19/29/20	6.86%	7.64%	54.88%	11.87%	13.51%	56.88%	8.85%	10.78%	56.86%
12/31/25	8.82%	7.19%	49.84%	9.19%	17.94%	53.70%	9.08%	12.46%	53.73%
10/4/29	7.77%	6.42%	49.85%	8.23%	19.31%	55.78%	8.50%	12.11%	55.31%
12/31/29	7.84%	6.90%	47.09%	7.78%	19.50%	54.91%	7.91%	12.12%	53.54%
12/30/33	24.80%	12.38%	36.25%	16.17%	20.78%	40.59%	21.41%	15.15%	37.88%

There are three general reasons why securities underwriting and distribution (whether conducted via an affiliate or within the bank itself) might endanger the bank.[20]

1.   Underwriting may be a risky and dangerous business per se. If so, the bank's profits and capital could be threatened (directly or indirectly) by a large enough underwriting loss, which would then expose depositors to loss as well. Whether investment banking is an excessively risky activity for commercial banking firms certainly deserves serious study. In particular, the determination of "excessive" riskiness should be undertaken in the context of the modern Bank Holding Company Act and *its* criteria for appropriate bank-related activities. (See chapter 6, by Giddy.) In the current regulatory environment, bank holding company legislation and regulation occupies a prominent place. By contrast, security affiliates of the 1920s were completely unregulated in their dealings with affiliated banks. Because the banking structure and regulatory environment were so different, the experience of 1929–1933 can provide no real evidence that investment banking cannot safely be combined with commercial banking activities today.

2.   Bank affiliates' securities activities may have led banks to increase the proportion of bonds held in their portfolios, or to reduce the quality of those bonds. Numerous writers complained about the banks' increased holdings of long-term securities during the 1920s, which was considered unsound banking practice. The justification for this assessment lay in the "real bills doctrine," which held that banks should invest primarily in short-term, self-liquidating loans. Because most bank liabilities were payable on demand, long-term investments (*regardless* of their credit quality) were thought to expose the bank to unacceptable liquidity risks: Faced with a large deposit outflow, the bank could not be certain of liquidating its long-term bonds at their face value.

It is this concern for bank liquidity that generated much of the historical concern with bank investment activities, and not necessarily a concern for credit quality per se. This liquidity interpretation of bank asset deterioration is clearly supported by several of the contributions to Willis and Chapman. After lamenting the banks' increased purchases of long-term securities during the 1920s, one writer noted a mitigating factor:

> The changes elsewhere reviewed in the character of the deposit liabilities of banks, tending as they have to increase the percentage of deposits with a slow turnover (time deposits), in some measure accounts and furnishes defense for the increase in long-term assets.[21]

That is, longer deposit maturities could justify greater commitment of bank funds to investments in order to balance the overall asset/liability portfolio.[22] (The author's lament continues, however, with the comment that the increase in bank time deposits was insufficient to justify their increased security positions during the 1920s.) Willis himself shows no concern for the credit quality of bank investments when he says:

> The banks, moreover, have suffered and are still suffering from asset deterioration. . . . Today, it is the result of the effort of the government to force its bonds and short-term notes upon the banks.[23]

Throughout their tome, many comments of this nature clearly indicate that the concern over "declining bank asset quality" is essentially a criticism of bank liquidity management.

The illiquidity danger posed by banks holding substantial long-term securities would be especially severe if bankers purchased low-quality bonds whose market value would presumably decline differentially in the event of a liquidity scare or "panic." For reasons discussed in the section on "The Effect of Security Holdings on Bank Soundness," however, it is unlikely that these investment portfolios can reasonably be held responsible for the widespread bank failures of 1930–1933.

3. Securities activities might lead a bank to undertake more (uncompensated) risks in its loan portfolio for the benefit of the combined (bank plus securities affiliate) corporation. The contemporary literature was rife with statements or allegations that a banker would lend on preferential (i.e., nonrisk-adjusted) terms to customers purchasing securities from his or her securities affiliate; lend to an issuing corporation to "tide it over" until the securities could be sold; purchase extensive amounts of unsold (and therefore presumably overpriced) securities underwritten by the affiliate; and so forth. There was a strong feeling that bankers were making too many loans collateralized by securities. Bankers thereby acquired a (residual) interest in long-term asset values. The drawbacks to such security-based loans were similar to the liquidity and maturity-mismatch problems associated with a bank's outright purchase of securities for its own account. If a deposit outflow occurred when the market turned down, the bank might be unable to meet cash demands without incurring large losses on its asset portfolio.

Despite such concerns, the possibility that banks actually did themselves serious harm via their securities activities must be considered remote. William F. Upshaw, writing in the Federal Reserve Bank of Richmond's *Monthly Review,* concludes that:

> In reality, most banks that had securities affiliates survived the holocaust of bank failures from 1930 through 1933, although the affiliates sustained substantial losses in a number of cases. After an extensive investment by the Senate Subcommittee, only the Bank of United States was singled out as an example of failure caused by the relationship of the bank and its securities affiliate.[24]

(It is important to remember that the failure of the Bank of United States was mostly due to fraud, which happened to be perpetrated via affiliated firms.) Friedman and Schwartz[25] further contend that the relative slowness with which bank failures occurred as the economy moved into recession indicates that "if there was any deterioration at all in the *ex ante* quality of loans and investments of banks, it must have been minor, to judge from the slowness with which it manifested itself."[26]

Summary

The public interest in limiting or controlling bank securities underwriting in 1933 derived from two distinct concerns: for the security-purchasing public, and for bank safety and soundness. The former had little to do with *bank* securities activities in particular, but was rather a reaction to widely publicized (and perhaps widespread) abuses in the securities market in general. The Securities Act of 1933 and the Securities Exchange Act of 1934 addressed and largely remedied many of these problems. The Banking Act of 1933 also addressed some financial abuses of the 1920s, by imposing restrictions on insider loan dealings at banks and by limiting transactions among banks and their affiliates. Whether bank security activities per se warrant special attention is an issue that must be addressed in the context of the present day's regulatory environment.

The historical concern about the effect of securities activities on bank soundness involved a set of questions currently discussed under the heading "asset/liability balance" more than the safety of investment banking activities per se. These latter issues are discussed at length in the following section.

THE EFFECT OF SECURITY HOLDINGS ON BANK SOUNDNESS

It is commonplace to observe that many U.S. commercial banks failed during the prosperous 1920s, but the pace and proportion of failures increased markedly as economic activity declined after 1929. Table 4.2 presents details. The extraordinary number of bank failures during the period 1930–1933 caused considerable (and understandable) consternation among depositors, shareholders, regulators, and legislators.

In seeking an explanation for these failures, commentators have sometimes declared bank securities activities a primary cause. Most notable about these comments, however, is their focus *not* on banks securities underwriting, but rather on the substantial involvement of commercial banks in holding long-term assets for their own accounts. Bank soundness had long been identified, at least in theory, with steadfast adherence to the "real bills doctrine" which stipulated that banks should finance the economy's legitimate "needs of trade." This was considered equivalent to holding primarily short-term, self-liquidating bills of commerce—working capital loans secured by or tied to goods-in-process inventories.

The real bills doctrine had several dimensions, but the one most germane to banks' securities activities in the 1920s was this prescription for bank soundness. Most banks' deposit liabilities were payable on demand. To defend themselves against possible deposit outflows, therefore, prudent bankers would hold assets that were short-term and highly liquid. *Liquid* here means readily marketable at a stable price. Long-term bonds were recognized as marketable, though there was always the chance that their market value would fall below par. In 1933, this possibility loomed large in analysts' minds. In Willis and Chapman, for example, one author writes that during the 1920s, "changes in corporate financing influenced our banking system to effect a major change in the character of its assets from a predominance of *liquid* commercial paper to a type of asset based on *non-liquid securities*."[27] Note that the author's concern here focused on the liquidity of bank portfolios rather than bank underwriting activities per se.

A modern analogy to this issue is the concern over interest-rate risk exposure and gap management. Many current analysts argue that prudence requires a bank to as-

Table 4.2 Bank Suspensions, 1921–1933

	Number of Failed Banks	Deposits of Failed Banks (thousands)	Number of Failed Banks as a Percentage of All Banks	Deposits of Failed Banks as a Percentage of All Bank Deposits
1921	506	$ 172,806	1.16%	0.619%
1922	366	$ 91,182	1.15%	0.300%
1923	646	$ 149,601	2.10%	0.462%
1924	775	$ 210,150	2.58%	0.609%
1925	617	$ 166,937	2.08%	0.440%
1926	975	$ 260,153	3.28%	0.661%
1927	669	$ 199,332	2.39%	0.491%
1928	498	$ 142,386	1.84%	0.338%
1929	659	$ 230,643	2.47%	0.543%
1930	1350	$ 837,096	5.29%	2.01%
1931	2293	$1,690,232	9.87%[a]	4.42%
1932	1453	$ 706,187	6.94%[a]	2.43%
1933	4000	$3,596,708	20.53%[a]	14.23%

Data: Columns 1, 2, 4: Milton Friedman and Anna J. Schwartz, *A Monetary History of the United States, 1957–1960.* Princeton: Princeton University Press, 1963, Tables 16 and A-1. Column 3: Walter E. Spahr "Bank Failures in the United States," *American Economic Review* (March 1932), pp. 208–238, Table H.

[a] Estimates based on the assumption that no new bands were formed after January 1, 1930, with closings reducing the number of surviving banks in subsequent years.

semble assets whose maturity (duration, time-to-repricing) complements that of its liabilities. If maturity gaps are kept reasonably small, deposit withdrawals can be covered and market interest rate changes will not have ruinous effects on the bank's soundness.

Analysts writing in the midst of the depression had seen bank investment portfolios expand sharply during the 1920s, followed by a sharp fall in bond prices as the depression deepened. One measure of the severity of these bond value declines comes from Temin,[28] who reports that the differential between BAA-rated and AAA-rated bonds rose from 117 basis points in June 1929 to 300 basis points two years later. Bond ratings imply a constant degree of credit-worthiness. This increase in the yield differential probably reflects an increasing aversion to risk-taking among investors. This change in preferences would have had a substantial effect on bond values. For example, a 20-year BAA-rated bond that *remained rated* BAA would have lost approximately 15% of its market value in the two years following mid-1929.

More reflective of the decline in a bond portfolio's value, however, is Temin's calculation that an *unmanaged* bond portfolio's yield (i.e., the change in yield without controlling for the change in quality) would have risen 503 basis points (from 1.96% to 6.99% above the AAA-bond rate) between June 1929 and June 1931. This implies a decline of approximately 35% in the market value of an average 20-year bond.

Hindsight clearly indicates that bonds were a bad buy in 1929. Many banks with large bond holdings did in fact fail. Does this imply that bank securities investments were ''unsound'' on an ex ante basis? More important (for the present discussion) does it imply that bank-related underwriting activities were ''unsound''? It is crucial to distinguish here between ex ante risk—what could reasonably have been anticipated when the bonds were bought—and ex post results—what actually happened. Writing in 1955, Galbraith notes that:

> In fact, many of these [contemporary banking] practices were made ludicrous only by the Depression. Loans which would have been perfectly good were made perfectly foolish by the collapse of the borrower's prices or the markets for his goods or the value of the collateral he had posted. . . . A Depression such as that of 1929–32, were it to begin as this is written, would also be damaging to many currently impeccable banking reputations.[29]

Corporate bankruptcies and defaults rise in any recession, and the early 1930s witnessed one of the most severe economic contractions in U.S. history. Regardless of whether banks' ex ante bond investments had declined in quality during the 1920s, the depression caused a major reduction in bond values as the market's expected default rate rose.

A major cause of decline in bond quality was the fact that the price level fell sharply between 1929 and 1933. The domestic GNP deflator dropped 25%, while other measures of the price level dropped similarly.[30] A direct implication of this observation is that the real repayment burden of outstanding long-term bonds *rose* 25% in about three years.[31] This increase in real debt burden was greatest (in present value terms) for bonds with the longest remaining terms to maturity. In other words, corporations (or countries) with the longest term bonds outstanding would suffer the largest decline in market value and hence the highest probability of failure, other things being equal. The ability of corporations to bear such debt burdens would necessarily decline even if there had been no reduction in real demand for their output. But real GNP fell 29% over the same time period.

This combination of severe price deflation and the real economy's contraction made it inevitable that nominally denominated bonds would fall substantially in value as the depression progressed. Given the severe price-level shock that occurred in the early 1930s, long-term bond values inevitably fell more than shorter-term commercial loans did. This would be true almost regardless of the ex ante credit quality of bank loans and investments. Bank examination practices served to focus still further attention on the decline of banks' bond portfolio values. The decline in a bond portfolio's value was easy for examiners to quantify, because most bonds held by banks were traded in a market that provided timely valuations. By contrast, corporate and other loans were not revalued daily in an active market.

> So long as [loans] did not come due, they were likely to be carried on the books at face value; only actual defaults or postponements of payments would reduce the examiner's evaluation.[32]

Given the combination of their decline in value and the nature of bank examinations, it was only natural that bond holdings attracted considerable attention in the wake of a bank failure.

The question arises, therefore, whether proponents of the real bills doctrine were correct in assigning responsibility for the widespread bank failures to bank securities investments. Here the answer is a rather vigorous no. Although a large number of banks did fail during 1930–1933, the primary reasons seem to have been the banking industry's structure and the failure of monetary policy to deal with the situation as it developed, rather than the quality of bank bond portfolios.

Bank Failures and Banking Structure

The United States began the 1920s with an unusually large number of banks. Table 4.3 clearly indicates that the 1920 marked the apex of banking firms per capita in the twentieth century. This situation was described by Willis and Chapman:

> The rapid growth in the number of banks in the country between the middle eighties and 1920 resulted in part from a number of favorable economic factors and in part from the competition between State and national banking systems in the granting of charters.[33]

Many of these banks were located in small towns. They had very small amounts of equity capital, and their loan portfolios were poorly diversified. Such firms were subject to failure even when confronted with a relatively small shock. In addition, the soundness of many small banks was closely tied to the local agricultural scene, and the 1920s was a poor time for agriculture, which occupied 20% of the U.S. population.[34] A variety of events conspired to induce a major agricultural collapse in 1930, which necessarily affected the soundness of many rural banks.

The way commercial banks were chartered and regulated also contributed to the industry's weakened condition. Both the states and the federal government could charter new banks, and existing banks were generally free to switch charters if they felt one set of regulations was less burdensome than the other. As a consequence,

Table 4.3   Per Capita Banking Firms in the U.S., 1900–1935

	Number of Commercial Banks[a]	Population[b] (Continental U.S.)	Population Per Bank
1900	12,427	76.1 million	6126
1910	24,514	92.3 million	3764
1920	30,291	106.5 million	3517
1925	28,442	114.9 million	4039
1935	15,478	127.2 million	8220

[a]Source: Helen M. Burns, The American Banking Community and New Deal Banking Reforms, 1933–1935. Westport, Conn.: Greenwood Press, 1974.

[b]Source: Information drawn from Statistical Abstracts of the United States.

regulators were reluctant (or unable) to impose serious restrictions on their banks. This "competition in laxity" among supervisors did not foster effective control over bank safety and soundness. Willis summarized the situation as follows:

> While there can be no doubt that bank supervision in general is on a higher plane than it was 20 years ago, it is nevertheless a fact that dual control of banking has tended to keep down the standards of supervision as well as of banking law. . . . The inability of supervisors to make full and effective use of such powers that they have arises out of the fact that banks are able to avoid the supervision of one system by leaving it and entering the other.[35]

Finally, it appears that advances in communications and transportation during the 1920s rendered superfluous a number of small banks in remote areas. When transportation was difficult and expensive, the small local bank provided the only banking services available in some areas. With the advent of widespread automobile ownership, however, geographic isolation provided small bankers with less effective protection. Some small institutions were thus doomed to extinction, one way or another, regardless of what happened in the national company.[36]

With a large number of small, poorly supervised, undercapitalized banks in a changing competitive environment, any shock to the system would inevitably cause failures. The depression that began in mid-1929 deepened in 1930 and combined with the especially poor agricultural situation to overcome a large number of banks, most of which were very small.

> [A]lthough the bankers were not unusually foolish in 1929, the banking structure was inherently weak. The weakness was implicit in the large number of independent units. When one bank failed the assets of others were frozen while depositors elsewhere had a pregnant warning to go and ask for their money. Thus one failure lead to another failure and these spread with a domino effect. Even in the best of times local misfortune or isolated mismanagement could start a chain reaction. . . . When income employment and values fell as the result of a depression bank failures could quickly become epidemic. This happened after 1929. Again it would be hard to imagine a better arrangement for magnifying the effects of fear. The weak destroyed not only the other weak, but weakened the strong.[37]

> As agricultural prices fell and businesses failed, banks who financed agricultural trade and some aspects of industrial production found themselves under increasing pressure. The rate of bank failures jumped dramatically in the last quarter of 1930, scaring both depositors and banks and leading to an increase in the demand for currency and for excess reserves that continued throughout the Depression.[38]

A clear assessment emerges from this discussion that the banking structure was responsible for a large number of the depression's bank failures.

Bank Failures and the Failure of Monetary Policy

Given the foregoing situation, the failure of any one bank might induce the public to "panic" and "run" on other banks to obtain riskless currency in place of deposit claims whose risks were unknown—the problem of "contagion." Kennedy observed that:

> The closing of the Bank of United States [in November 1930] . . . showed up two fatal flaws of the American banking structure: first, a need for fundamental reform of bank organization, operation, and supervision; and second, the unique relation between credit and finance on the one hand, and *public confidence and fear* on the other.[39]

Modern discussions of bank runs[40] indicate that it is easier (and safer) for an individual to run on the bank than to determine if the bank is fundamentally sound. Because no bank can liquidate all of its assets quickly without substantial losses—no matter how well the bank is managed—a bank run can become a self-fulfilling prophecy of bank failure.

In the United States, the evidence indicates that "runs" were an important cause of bank failures in the early 1930s. When the admittedly troubled Bank of United States failed in late 1930, it set off a series of runs on other perfectly sound banks. Similarly, the Michigan banking holiday, declared in February 1933 to provide time to rescue Detroit's two large but troubled banks, was instrumental in causing deposit runs on other institutions.[41]

The most difficult situation for a fractional-reserve banking system to deal with arises when the public wishes to make substantial withdrawals from the system as a whole. No individual bank—regardless of its "soundness"—can immediately honor the claims of a large proportion of depositors for cash. The same is true for the banking system in general. The Federal Reserve system was designed to mitigate this problem for the banks: By lending through the discount window or by purchasing securities in the open market, the Fed can increase the amount of currency available to the banks and, therefore, to their customers. In the absence of such central bank action, however, there is simply too little currency available to satisfy both the public's demand and the banks' need for legal reserves. This is not a stable situation:

> Under such circumstances, any runs on banks for whatever reason became to some extent self-justifying, whatever the quality of assets held by banks. Banks had to dump their assets on the market, which inevitably forced a decline in the market value of those assets and hence of the remaining assets they held.[42]

In other words, as bankers scrambled for currency with which to pay off their depositors (or to convince their depositors that they *could be* paid off), they had nowhere to sell their marketable bonds except at a great discount. As bank bond portfolios fell in value, however, depositors became (justifiably) more prone to panic, which forced the banking system to unload still more bonds at ever-lower prices. Some extraordinary force was needed to break this cycle, and the Federal Reserve system had been designed to provide such a force.

Prior to the Fed's creation in 1913, the major bank clearing houses sometimes agreed to suspend the convertibility of their deposits into currency as a means of coping with depositor runs. It was believed that the Federal Reserve system would substitute its ability to serve as "lender of last resort" for the need to suspend bank deposits' convertibility.[43] Unfortunately, in the early 1930s the Fed failed to provide the banking system with liquidity via discount window advances or open market operations. Friedman and Schwartz are extremely critical of the Fed's inaction during the early 1930s.

> If deterioration of credit quality or bad banking was the trigger, which it may to some extent have been, the damaging bullet it discharged was the inability of the banking system to acquire additional high-powered money to meet the resulting demands of depositors for currency, without a multiple contraction of deposits. That inability was responsible alike for the extent and importance of bank failures and for the indirect effect bank failures had on the stock of money. In the absence of the provision of additional high-powered money, banks that suffered runs as a result of the initial failure of "bad" banks would not have been helped by holding solely U.S. government securities in addition to required reserves. If the composition of their assets did not stop the runs simply by its effect on depositors' confidence, the banks would still have had to dump their government securities on the market to acquire needed high-powered money, and many would have failed. Alternatively, the composition of assets held by banks would hardly have mattered if additional high-powered money had been available from whatever source to meet the demands of depositors for currency without requiring a multiple contraction of deposits and assets. The trigger would have discharged only a blank cartridge. The banks would have been under no necessity to dump their assets. There would have been no major decline in the market prices of the assets and no impairment in the capital accounts of banks. The failure of a few bad banks would not have caused the insolvency of many other banks any more than during the twenties when a large number of banks failed.[44]

To summarize, the real bills doctrine's concern for bank liquidity may have been appropriate prior to the Fed's creation. But the Fed was intended to use open market operations and its discount window to insulate the banking system from aggregate changes in the demand for currency versus bank deposits. The Federal Reserve system was thus a partial substitute for the "real bills" method of managing bank liquidity. Hindsight makes it clear that massive bank failures of 1930–1933 resulted in large measure from the Fed's failure to provide the economy with adequate liquidity. The extent and quality of bank holdings were secondary factors at best. Even a bank with 100% real bills in its portfolio would have been hard-pressed to survive a substantial run without assistance from the Fed's discount window.

Finally, it is important to emphasize that the preceding discussion of bank failures has contained no reference to bank underwriting activities. The banking system's problem in the early 1930s was that bank portfolios were not sufficiently liquid to accommodate widespread depositor runs. This problem is endemic to a fractional-reserve banking system, regardless of the quality of its assets.

DID BANK SECURITIES ACTIVITIES CAUSE THE DEPRESSION?

Many bank critics believed that "excessively speculative" bank securities activities somehow caused the depression. Following the Pecora hearings in early 1933, bank-

ers received considerable blame—at least in the popular press—for the economy's
sorry state. In a *Current History* article published in January 1934, Willis considered
the question "Are the Bankers to Blame?" and concluded in the negative. The preceding sections' analysis here has also argued that the depression's widespread bank
failures were not due to poor ex ante investment decisions by bankers. Rather, subsequent events—including Federal Reserve behavior—affected the banking system
in adverse but unforeseeable ways.

What, then, did cause the worst depression in modern U.S. history? Even today,
the evidence is unclear. The two most prominent hypotheses are:

1. The depression was a monetary phenomenon, one sympton of which was the
numerous bank failures.

2. A sharp, exogenous fall in aggregate demand initiated the economic downturn
in 1929, which later deepened as a result of monetary contraction. These alternative
views tend to agree that events after 1930 were largely the result of monetary forces
and the attendant, panic-induced bank failures. Bernanke[45] has added a further dimension to the effect of bank failures on the real economy. He argues (and presents
supporting empirical evidence) that the massive bank failures of 1930–1933 sharply
raised the cost of financial intermediation services to the nonbank sector. Because
bank credit was essential to so many firms, its sudden unavailability made continued
operations difficult, which induced layoffs and bankruptcies in unprecedented numbers. Despite their substantial agreement about post-1930 events, the hypotheses differ in their explanation for the initial economic downturn, which began prior to the
stock market crash in October. Monetary policy tightened in 1928 and remained relatively restrictive until the stock market crash. During this time, the Fed kept interest
rates high to limit securities market speculation. Friedman and Schwartz[46] claim that
this monetary restraint induced a recession that started in the early summer of 1929.
(For example, industrial production fell 12.3% between July and December 1929.)
A moderate recession ensued, comparable to that of 1921, and a tentative recovery
may have begun by early 1931.[47] However, the banking panics of late 1930 and March
1931 then generated a sharp rise in the public's desired currency-to-deposit ratio.
Without some offsetting Federal Reserve action, the results were widespread bank
failures (as discussed above) and a sharp drop in the money supply, which further
depressed the economy.

The alternative explanation for the initial economic downturn is Keynesian—an
exogenous decline in the demand for goods and services. Although many writers had
claimed the initial demand shock came from the investment sector, Temin's analysis
implies that aggregate demand fell in 1929–1930 because *consumption* fell.[48] Temin
argues further that the depression's first year was not viewed with unusual concern
by the people involved. For example, bond rating agencies downgraded a smaller
proportion of outstanding bonds during 1930 than they did in the recession years of
1921 or 1937.

Taken together with the evidence from the contemporary press, the data on agency ratings suggest the following hypothesis on expectations. People responded to the fall in

business activities and prices in 1930 in roughly the same way they reacted to the fall in 1921. They knew business was bad but they expected it to recover soon. It was only when business failed to show signs of recovery in the fall of 1930 that expectations changed. As far as one can see, it was the failure of business to pick up in the fall of 1930 rather than the decline of stock-market prices in 1929 that produced the change.[49]

In short, the depression may have begun in 1929 from monetary constraint or a Keynesian decline in consumption demand. In either case, the banking system's subsequent problems must be viewed as more an effect of the depression than its cause.

SUMMARY AND CONCLUSIONS

Banks rapidly expanded their participation in securities underwriting during the 1920s. By 1929 they handled nearly half of all new bonds and had become broad-based distributors of securities to the retail sector. The stock market crash of 1929 and the ensuing depression caused many securities to fall dramatically in value. This led some observers to conclude that bank participation in financing long-term investments was unsound and had *caused* the widespread bank failures of 1930–1933 and perhaps even the depression itself.

Empirical support for this contention is weak to nonexistent. Rather, the economic downturn that began in mid-1929 was followed by a major agricultural recession in 1930. A number of banks failed as a consequence, which caused serious banking panics and depositor runs at other institutions. Because the Federal Reserve failed to supply adequate liquidity at the time, the banking system was forced to meet withdrawals by selling marketable assets. Bond values plummeted, exacerbating the banks' problems. Had the Fed performed the role it was designed for, many sound but illiquid banks would have survived.

The question whether investment banking is a proper activity for commercial banking firms was raised prominently in the 1930s and recurs today. Several historical facts are relevant to the current policy debate.

1.   Most historical opposition to mixing investment and commercial banking reflected a concern about illiquidity or "maturity mismatch" effects. Although the Glass-Steagall Act prohibited bank involvement in securities underwriting and stock market loans, there are still no legislative restrictions on bank "overinvestment" in securities. Liquidity and portfolio quality are today central regulatory concerns, monitored through the bank examination process. By contrast, bank examination and supervision before 1933 was lax and (at least to some analysts of the time) incompetent.

2.   Bank securities affiliates may have undertaken their share of misrepresentations, frauds, and malfeasance, but they were no different in this respect than private investment bankers. The Securities Act of 1933 and the Securities Exchange Act of 1934 have largely eliminated such abuses from the capital markets.

3.   Securities affiliates were fashioned in a legislative and regulatory environment that was totally unprepared to cope with bank affiliates of any kind. Many dealings between banks and their affiliates in the 1920s would be entirely prohibited today.

It seems that the recent debate over bank involvement in securities underwriting must turn primarily on current facts. History provides no convincing evidence that the securities activities of commercial banks posed any unique problems in the 1920s. The desirability of bank securities affiliates in the present regulatory environment should be assessed in terms that bank holding company regulation has now made familiar: Would investment banking activities performed by commercial banking firms provide net benefits to the public? This question cannot be answered by reference to the experience of the 1920s.

NOTES

[1]Edwin J. Perkins, "The Divorce of Commercial and Investment Banking: A History," *The Banking Law Journal* **88,** No. 6 (June 1971), p. 494.

[2]See H. Parker Willis and John M. Chapman, *The Banking Situation*. (New York: Columbia University Press, 1934), near p. 615; Milton Friedman and Anna J. Schwartz, *A Monetary History of the United States, 1857–1960*. (Princeton: Princeton University Press, 1963); or Edwin J. Perkins, "The Divorce of Commercial and Investment Banking: A History," *The Banking Law Journal,* **88,** No. 6 (June 1971), pp. 483–528.

[3]Authorities differ in the numbers they give for this kind of banking activity. The numbers in the text are from Nelson W. Peach, *The Security Affiliates of National Banks*. (Baltimore, Md.: Johns Hopkins Press, 1941), p. 83.

[4]Nelson W. Peach, *The Security Affiliates of National Banks*. (Baltimore, Md.: The Johns Hopkins Press, 1941), chap. 3.

[5]The history of banks securities activities thus fits readily into Kane's framework of "regulation-circumvention-reregulation" within a "regulatory dialectic." (Some things apparently never change.) (See Edward J. Kane, "Accelerating Inflation, Technological Innovation and the Decreasing Effectiveness of Banking Regulation," Journal of Finance, **36** [May 1981], pp. 355–367.)

[6]Susan E. Kennedy, The Banking Crisis of 1933. (Lexington: University Press of Kentucky, 1973), p. 111.

[7]The National City Company, which was generally regarded as the most aggressive bank securities affiliate, sold *exclusively* bond issues between 1911 and 1926. In 1927 it handled two stock issues; in 1928, six; and in 1929, only two or three (Kennedy, "Banking Crisis," p. 113).

[8]Perkins, "Divorce of Commercial Banking," p. 492.

[9]See Kennedy, p. 113. These data are from Peach "Security Affiliates" p. 109, Table III.

[10]The Banking Act of 1933 has been described as "an important first attempt by the federal government to regulate bank holding companies." (Michael A. Jessee and Steven A. Seelig, *Bank Holding Companies and the Public Interest.* (Lexington, Mass.: D.C. Heath, 1977), p. 8. Congress also enacted Section 23A of the Federal Reserve Act in 1933, which limits the amount a bank can lend to any affiliated corporation and requires collateral on such loans (William Upshaw, "Bank Affiliates and Their Regulation," Federal Reserve Bank of Richmond *Monthly Review* (March–May 1973), p. 4

[11]See Kennedy, *The Banking Crisis of 1933,* chap. 5.

[12]H. Parker Willis was perhaps the most prominent academic expert of his day on U.S. banking. He had played a key advisory role in drafting the Federal Reserve Act, and was a principal advisor to Senator Glass in the years preceding passage of the Glass-Steagall Act. Willis' massive book with John Chapman *The Banking Situation*. (New York: Columbia University Press, 1934), was intended to summarize and document the condition of American banking up to and including the early depression years. See H. Parker Willis, "Are the Bankers to Blame?" *Current History* (January 1934), p. 393.

[13]John Kenneth Galbraith, *The Great Crash*. (Boston: Houghton Mifflin, 1955), p. 183.

[14]Willis, "Are the Bankers to Blame?" p. 386, emphasis added.

[15]75 *Congressional Record* (May 10, 1932), p. 9887.

[16]Ibid., p. 9883.

[17]It would be interesting and important to know what proportion of small banks bought their securities from other banks versus from private investment bankers. Unfortunately, that information is unavailable.

[18]C. D. Bremer, *American Bank Failures*. (New York: Columbia University Press, 1935), p. 124.

[19]C. Glass, 75 *Congressional Record*, p. 9887.

[20]A number of particular means by which a securities affiliate might harm its bank were detailed in 1931 by a Senate subcommittee chaired by Sen. Glass. Upshaw ("Bank Affiliates," p. 17), quotes extensively from the subcommittee Hearing record.

[21]H. Parker Willis and John M. Chapman, *The Banking Situation*. (New York: Columbia University Press, 1934), p. 631.

[22]Elsewhere Willis, "The Banking Act of 1933—An Appraisal," *American Economic Review* (March 1934b), pp. 101–110, makes the same point: "It is regrettable that the commercial banks of the nation should be buyers of investment securities at all; but since they are in the time-deposit business, perhaps such action is not to be avoided" (p. 106).

[23]Ibid., p. 911.

[24]William F. Upshaw, "Bank Affiliates and Their Regulation" (Parts I, II, III), Federal Reserve Bank of Richmond *Monthly Review* (March, April, May 1973), p. 17.

[25]Milton Friedman and Anna J. Schwartz, *A Monetary History of the United States, 1857–1960*. (Princeton: Princeton University Press, 1963).

[26]Ibid., p. 354.

[27]Willis and Chapman, *The Banking Situation*, p. 615, emphasis added.

[28]Peter Temin, *Did Monetary Forces Cause the Great Depression?* (New York: Norton, 1976), p. 117.

[29]Galbraith, *The Great Crash*, p. 184.

[30]Temin, *Monetary Forces*, p. 6.

[31]Bernanke ("Nonmonetary Effects,") reports that the ratio of total debt servicing costs to national income more than doubled during the depression, from 9% in 1929 to 19.8% in 1932–1933.

[32]Friedman and Schwartz, *Monetary History*, p. 356.

[33]Willis and Chapman, *The Banking Situation*, p. 197.

[34]Temin, *Monetary Forces*, p. 2.

[35]Willis and Chapman, *The Banking Situation*, p. 201.

[36]See Friedman and Schwartz, *Monetary History*, p. 249; and Willis and Chapman, *The Banking Situation*, chap. 14.

[37]Galbraith, *The Great Crash*, pp. 184–185.

[38]Temin, *Monetary Forces*, p. 2.

[39]Kennedy, *Banking Crisis of 1933*, p. 5, emphasis added.

[40]Douglas Diamond and Phillip H. Dybvig, "Bank Runs, Deposit Insurance, and Liquidity," *Journal of Political Economy*, **91** (June 1983), pp. 401–419.

[41]Kennedy, *Banking Crisis of 1933*, p. 96.

[42]Friedman and Schwartz, *Monetary History*, p. 355.

[43]Ben S. Bernanke, "Nonmonetary Effects of the Financial Crisis in the Great Depression," *American Economic Review* (June 1983), pp. 257–276.

[44]Friedman and Schwartz, *Monetary History*, pp. 356–357.

[45]Bernanke "Nonmonetary Effects."

[46]Friedman and Schwartz, *Monetary History*.

[47]Ibid., p. 313.

[48]Temin, *Monetary Forces*, p. 172.

[49]Ibid., p. 82.

REFERENCES

Bernanke, Ben S. "Nonmonetary Effects of the Financial Crisis in the Great Depression," *American Economic Review* (June 1983), pp. 257–276.

Bremer, C. D. *American Bank Failures*. New York: Columbia University Press, 1935.

Burns, Helen M. *The American Banking Community and New Deal Banking Reforms, 1933–1935*. Westport, Conn.: Greenwood Press, 1974.

Diamond, Douglas and Phillip H. Dybvig. "Bank Runs, Deposit Insurance, and Liquidity," *Journal of Political Economy*, **91** (June 1983), pp. 401–419.

Friedman, Milton, and Anna J. Schwartz. *A Monetary History of the United States, 1857–1960*. Princeton: Princeton University Press, 1963.

Galbraith, John Kenneth. *The Great Crash*. Boston: Houghton Mifflin 1955.

Herman, Edward S. *Conflicts of Interest: Commercial Bank Trust Departments*. New York: The Twentieth Century Fund, 1975.

Jessee, Michael A., and Steven A. Seelig. *Bank Holding Companies and the Public Interest*. Lexington, Mass.: D. C. Heath, 1977.

Kane, Edward J. "Accelerating Inflation, Technological Innovation and the Decreasing Effectiveness of Banking Regulation," *Journal of Finance*, 36 (May 1981) pp. 355–367.

Kennedy, Susan E. *The Banking Crisis of 1933*. Lexington: The University Press of Kentucky, 1973.

Peach, Nelson W. *The Security Affiliates of National Banks*. Baltimore, Md.: The Johns Hopkins Press, 1941.

Pecora, Ferdinand. *Wall Street Under Oath: The Story of our Modern Money Changers*. New York: Simon and Schuster, 1939.

Perkins, Edwin J. "The Divorce of Commercial and Investment Banking: A History," *The Banking Law Journal* **88**, No. 6, (June 1971), pp. 483–528.

Spahr, Walter E. "Bank Failures in the United States," *American Economic Review* (March 1932), pp. 208–238.

Temin, Peter. *Did Monetary Forces Cause the Great Depression?* New York: Norton, 1976.

Upshaw, William F. "Bank Affiliates and Their Regulation" (Parts I, II, III), Federal Reserve Bank of Richmond *Monthly Review* (March, April, May 1973), pp. 14–20, 3–9, 3–10.

Willis, H. Parker. "Are the Bankers to Blame?" *Current History* (January 1934a), pp. 385–393.

———— "The Banking Act of 1933—An Appraisal," *American Economic Review* (March 1934b), pp. 101–110.

———— and John M. Chapman. *The Banking Situation*. New York: Columbia University Press, 1934.

Comment

VINCENT P. CAROSSO

Chapters 3 and 4 make a compelling case for the need to review the continued separation of commercial and investment banking mandated by the Glass-Steagall Act of June 1933. Kelly does so by detailing the half-century-old law's convoluted history through Congress, and Flannery reaches the same conclusion by refuting the strongest argument used to press for the statute's approval. Neither chapter offers entirely new information. What each does, and in a most able manner, is to weigh carefully the evidence used to defend the law's divorcement provisions. The results of Kelly's and Flannery's findings underscore the fact that Glass-Steagall rests on dubious theory and flimsy evidence. Politics and the times, not the requirements of an improved banking system, dictated Glass-Steagall's passage; special interests, most notably the investment banking and securities industry, which originally had opposed the measure, have succeeded (until now) in keeping the statute in force but not in preventing its erosion.

Kelly's account of Glass-Steagall's origins and rationale rests on an impressive collection of sources and secondary literature. His chapter correctly focuses on the impact of the stock market crash, bank failures, and the deepening Depression in getting Congress to reimpose the institutional separation of commercial and investment banking that it had dropped only a half-dozen years earlier in the McFadden Act of February 1927. Mr. Kelly is also correct in citing the influence of the Pujo subcommittee's exaggerated and misleading charges on Glass-Steagall's divorcement provisions. My own view, which I set forth a decade ago in an article on the "money trust" controversy, is that the Pujo subcommittee's majority report had a more profound influence on shaping the New Deal's banking and securities statutes than is generally acknowledged.[1]

The connection between the House of Representative's "money trust" investigation of 1912–1913 and the Senate's hearings on stock exchange practices a generation later is more direct than Kelly suggests. Both inquiries were motivated by the same classic antimonopoly, anti–big business, anti–Wall Street fears and suspicions that have determined the shape of the nation's banking system from the time of Alexander Hamilton to the present day. Mr. Kelly's careful analysis of Glass-Steagall's progress through Congress clearly shows the extent to which prejudice, misinformation, and self-interest finally succeeded in accomplishing the separation of commercial and investment banking, which the Pujo subcommittee's majority report had recommended 20 years earlier. "The legislative history of the Glass-Steagall Act," Kelly concludes, "is the story of a theory carried along by events." And, I would add, sustained by old, widely held misconceptions about the banking business. Separation of commercial and investment banking, Glass-Steagall's framers argued, would promote economic stability and strengthen the financial system. Neither was accomplished; what Glass-Steagall did was to augment the federal government's regulatory controls over the banking system.[2]

Flannery's examination of the commercial banks' security underwritings in the 1920s provides still further evidence that Glass-Steagall's divorcement provisions were motivated by political rather than banking considerations. The charge, made popular by the Senate stock practices hearings, that the security operations of commercial banks and their affiliates were responsible for the "great crash" and the widespread bank failures that followed it, had little, if any, basis in fact. At no time did Ferdinand Pecora, the Senate subcommittee's publicity-wise counsel, prove that (in his words) "the catastrophic collapse of the entire banking structure of the country" stemmed from the banks' underwriting activities.[3] Nor was he any more successful in demonstrating that the volume and quality of the banks' securities investments were responsible for the more than 9000 bank failures that occurred between 1930 and 1933. The "primary reasons" for the suspensions, Flannery makes clear, "seem to have been the banking industry's structure and the failure of monetary policy to deal with the situation as it developed."

Pecora devoted no attention to either consideration. Nor did he make much of an effort to get the best information available on the nature and extent of the banks' bond holdings. He saw his duty differently. He was determined to expose the boom era's speculative practices, tie them to Wall Street's leaders, and show how they, acting as both commercial and investment bankers, had used their dual position to enrich themselves at the public and their own institution's expense. The examination of Charles Mitchell, National City Bank's chairman and the country's most prominent representative of the all-purpose banker, provided Pecora the occasion to accomplish his several purposes: to demolish the reputation of the chief of the nation's second largest bank and, through its affiliate, the National City Company, the world's largest seller of securities, which he also headed; to blame the financial crisis on the union of commercial and investment banking; and to charge, as the Pujo subcommittee's counsel had done before him, that the pervasive power and influence of Wall Street's leaders were responsible for the country's financial and economic plight. Pecora succeeded brilliantly in discrediting Mitchell personally and blasting the public image of several other respected bankers, but he failed to disclose any evidence that either the commercial banks' securities transactions or the private banks' deposit business was responsible for the financial debacle of the early 1930s. The fact that the Pecora probe, like the Pujo inquiry before it, was not the careful and impartial investigation that its defenders claimed it to be proved of little import. The disclosure of personal wrongdoing by some of the country's most eminent bankers, together with disturbing revelations of questionable practices by some prestigious securities firms, eased the way for widespread reform and regulation of the financial system, including the legal separation of commercial and investment banking. The severity of the banking crisis, as both papers convincingly show, more than any proven deficiencies in the banks' securities activities, accounted for Glass-Steagall's divorcement clauses. If the need for such a restriction was questionable 50 years ago, the benefits of continuing it today remain to be proven. *De jure* separation in the face of *de facto* reunification is not in the public interest. Kelly's and Flannery's chapters provide much needed and pertinent information on a too long neglected topic of fundamental importance.

NOTES

[1]Vincent P. Carosso, "The Wall Street Money Trust from Pujo through Medina," *The Business History Review,* **47** (Winter 1973), pp. 421–37.

[2]F. Ward McCarthy, Jr., "The Evolution of the Bank Regulatory Structure: A Reappraisal," *Economic Review,* **70** (March-April 1984), p. 18.

[3]Ferdinand Pecora, *Wall Street Under Oath: The Story of Our Modern Money Changers* (New York, 1939), p. 7.

5 An Analysis of the Competitive Effects of Allowing Commercial Bank Affiliates to Underwrite Corporate Securities

THOMAS A. PUGEL
LAWRENCE J. WHITE

The Glass-Steagall Act, which consists of four provisions of the Banking Act of 1933, requires the separation of commercial banking from investment banking. [1] The former activity is usually characterized as the taking of deposits and the making of commercial loans; the latter activity is usually characterized by dealing in and underwriting securities. Firms engaged in one area are not generally permitted also to engage in the other (although some exceptions are allowed).

This chapter will focus on the area of the underwriting of corporate securities. Specifically, we will be examining the nature of competition among underwriters and the likely effects on this competition that would result from a change in the Glass-Steagall Act to permit commercial bank affiliates to underwrite corporate securities. We conclude that the entry of commercial bank affiliates into corporate securities underwriting would increase competition in this area; the increased competition would likely lead to lower fees and better service for issuers, thus benefiting securities issuers and the American economy generally. We believe that small and medium-sized companies would be among the prime beneficiaries of this heightened competition.

*We would like to thank Ernest Bloch, Anthony Saunders, Thomas F. Huertas, Morris Mendelson, Howard H. Newman, Hans R. Stoll, and Ingo Walter for helpful suggestions and comments during the research for this study. We would also like to thank Linda Canina for her research assistance.

The General Case for Competition

The American polity has generally shown a preference for competition and open entry in the organization of its markets. The 94-year history of the antitrust laws and the recent trend toward the deregulation of previously regulated industries are indications of this preference for competition. This preference is not absolute, of course. A number of industries have been, and some continue to be, subject to economic regulation involving controls over prices, profits, and/or entry. (Many industries are also subject to health-safety-environment regulation involving controls over production processes, product design, and/or information requirements; such regulation is not directly at issue in the debate over the competitive effects of Glass-Steagall's prohibition on commercial bank entry into corporate securities underwriting.) But such economic regulation is usually seen as the exception in the American economy, rather than the rule.

Economic theory provides strong support for this preference for competition over restraint.[2] Competition among profit-seeking firms in a marketplace (as compared with regulatory restraints on competition) is likely to lead to lower prices, improved service, more choice of quality levels, more innovation, greater efficiency (lower costs) in production, and larger output. Firms that sell products (or services) at prices that buyers find attractive are likely to succeed; high-cost and inefficient firms are likely to fall by the wayside. Open entry into a market by new firms reinforces these effects, by keeping any existing groups of competitors ''honest'' and by allowing for the easy flow of new ideas, new efficiencies, and new ways of doing things. Efficient allocations of resources can more easily displace the inefficient, with beneficial consequences for buyers in the marketplace.

Although this statement of the benefits of competition and open entry has general validity, the limitations of the competitive process should also be recognized.[3] First, if an adequate number of competitors cannot be sustained in the market—either because the efficiencies of large size indicate that only one or a very few firms can adequately meet demand at lowest cost, or because predatory behavior by one or more firms has driven out others and barriers to entry are high—then the competition process is no longer assured. Monopoly (or oligopoly) behavior (i.e., the exercise of market power) is likely to replace it, with the probable effects of higher prices, lower output, and less assurance of adequate service or quality choice.

Second, if the participants (sellers or buyers) in the market generate ''externalities'' or spillovers (i.e., costs imposed on or benefits received by others, outside the context of the marketplace), then the competitive outcome need not be allocatively efficient; too much or too little of the product or service is produced, and too little effort is made to correct the ''externality.'' (Air and water pollution are familiar examples of ''negative externalities.'')

Third, incomplete information about marketplace conditions on the part of buyers and/or sellers can cause the competitive process to achieve unsatisfactory results. If buyers have incomplete information (e.g., about sellers' prices or the attributes of their products), the market power of some sellers may increase, and some goods or services (that buyers might buy if they had more information) may not be produced.[4]

If sellers have incomplete information (e.g., about market prices or about buyers' preferences), inappropriate quantities and/or types of goods and services may be produced.

These possible failings of the competitive process can, in specific instances, provide the justification for possible governmental actions or restrictions to correct them. But in none of the instances of "market failure" discussed above would a widespread limitation on entry (of the type created by the Glass-Steagall Act) be the best means of dealing with the problem. Further, the question of whether actual governmental actions provide actual net improvements in the workings of markets—in essence, whether imperfect governments can improve on imperfect markets—is an empirical question that cannot be answered by a priori theorizing. This study will offer empirical evidence that suggests that the entry of commercial bank affiliates into corporate securities underwriting would be beneficial for the competitive process in this area—that is, that the Glass-Steagall prohibition on entry does not represent sensible public policy.

The Structure-Behavior-Performance Model

Analyses of the competitive workings of markets have come to be known (within the economics profession) as the study of "industrial organization": the study of how industries (markets) are organized (structured) and of the competitive consequences that flow from that structure. One particularly useful analytical framework employed by industrial organization specialists for organizing information about markets and establishing causal relationships (so that predictions about actual behavior and outcomes can be made and tested against reality) is the "structure-behavior-performance" model.[5] By *structure* we mean the conditions present in a market (or industry) that are largely beyond the control of any single firm (such as the number and relative sizes of sellers, the conditions of entry into the market, the complexity and nature of the product, the number and sizes of buyers, etc.). By *behavior* we mean the activities of the firms in the market (such as pricing and innovation efforts). By *performance* we mean the outcomes in the market, as judged against some norms (such as prices that approximate the long-run marginal costs, including a competitive profit or rate of return on invested capital, of producing a good or service).

The structure-behavior-performance model predicts a causal relationship running from structure through behavior to performance. For example, comparisons between competition and monopoly involve a simple application of the structure-behavior-performance model: The structural condition of many sellers (rather than just one) with easy conditions of entry leads to the behavioral prediction of lower prices and greater output and to the performance outcome of prices that are likely to approximate long-run marginal costs (rather than to incorporate excess, or monopoly, profits). This model has been enriched with insights and hypotheses concerning oligopoly, so that predictions about markets with a few sellers (more than the single seller that characterizes pure monopoly, less than the many sellers that characterize pure competition) can be made and tested.

The causality of the structure-behavior-performance model need not run in only one direction. Over time, performance may affect behavior or structure as well. And there are differences within the economics profession as to the strength of the predictions that can be made from the model (and the policy conclusions that can be drawn from it).[6] Nevertheless, it is a serviceable, convenient framework for understanding the functioning of markets, and we shall rely on it extensively in our analysis of competition in the underwriting of corporate securities.

THE MARKET AND ITS CHARACTERISTICS

This study focuses on the market for the underwriting of publicly offered corporate securities. This section of the study defines and discusses the activities that comprise the provision of such underwriting services by investment banks, as well as closely related services that are often also provided by the banks. Several types of underwriting are defined and discussed. Government regulations that directly influence underwriting and secondary market trading are presented. Finally, the behavior of the corporate issuers of the securities is explored, by discussing the alternatives available in their efforts to raise new funds and the factors that influence a corporation's choice of a particular investment bank to underwrite its new issues. This section provides the background for subsequent sections that explore competition in underwriting and the likely impact of the entry of commercial bank affiliates.

The Market

Firms active in the securities industry are engaged in one or more of a number of activities, including underwriting, dealing, brokerage, and providing various kinds of financial advice. This study focuses on firms engaged in the underwriting of publicly offered corporate securities. This comparatively narrow focus can be justified on economic grounds, in that it appears to be an activity separable from the others and recognized as such by those active in the industry. The focus is also justified in that our study explores the competitive implications of removing legal barriers to the entry of commercial bank affiliates into this type of underwriting, through appropriate modifications of the Glass-Steagall Act.

Underwriting is generally considered to involve three major activities: origination, risk-bearing, and distribution. Origination involves decisions on the type (e.g., debt or equity), quantity, pricing, timing, and other features of the new securities issue. Management of the issue, especially in the determination of the method of distribution, is often considered part of the origination function. Risk-bearing involves the purchase by the investment bank of the issue at a fixed price, thus putting the investment bank at risk in terms of the eventual sale of the issue to the public. This risk-bearing is sometimes called underwriting (in the narrow sense of the term). Distribution involves selling the securities to the public. A distinction is usually made between sales to institutional buyers (who often purchase in large blocks) and sales to individuals through retail distribution.

Several activities of investment banks are closely related to the underwriting of corporate securities. Dealing and market-making are activities in which the investment banks buy and sell securities in the secondary markets, with a willingness to hold inventories of these securities for their own account. These activities are closely related to underwriting in that they can be used to stabilize the market price during the primary distribution and they encourage purchase of the primary issue by enhancing the liquidity of the secondary market. A second activity of investment banks that is closely related to underwriting is the provision of advice on corporate finance, including advice on capital structure and assistance in mergers and acquisitions. Often this kind of advice blends into the origination function. These two activities are sufficiently closely related to underwriting of corporate securities that they will necessarily play an important role in the discussion of competition in the market for underwriting services.[7]

Other related activities are of lesser interest. Pure brokerage involves the execution of a customer order to buy or sell securities, but the broker does not take a position. Brokering and dealing are related to underwriting in that they provide the ongoing volume of secondary market activities that permit investment banks to have resources in place for primary distribution. Brokerage itself is of lesser interest in this study, because commercial banks are permitted to offer brokerage services.[8]

Underwriting of government securities is another related activity. Commercial banks are currently permitted to underwrite certain government securities: general obligation bonds of states and localities; bonds issued for housing, university, or dormitory purposes; U.S. Government bonds; and the bonds of certain international organizations. Competition in this area of underwriting is not a focus of the study, although evidence from this area will be cited in the discussion of the likely impact of the entry of commercial bank affiliates into the corporate securities underwriting business.

Types of Underwriting

The process of underwriting corporate securities is not homogeneous. Key distinctions are usually made between negotiated and competitive-bid underwriting and between firm commitment and best efforts underwriting.

In a negotiated underwriting the issuer chooses a lead manager and normally selects the co-manager, as well as having a powerful voice in shaping the syndicate. In discussions with the issuer, the lead manager performs the origination function. The lead manager also puts together a syndicate, which may include co-managers, to spread the risk and to provide for distribution. The manager decides who the members of the syndicate will be and the size of the participation of each member. The function of lead manager entitles the manager to an additional fee and control over the syndicate, including running the books. The function also contributes to the reputation of the investment bank, which can improve its chances of acquiring business from other issuers, and requires close contact with the current issuer, developing a relationship that enhances the likelihood of repeat business.

In a competitive-bid underwriting the issuer frequently designs the issue, thus performing much of the origination function (either in-house or by contracting for these services). Investment banks then bid for the issue, vying to become the lead manager or one of the group of co-managers. Each bidder often has a potential syndicate largely in place, and in any case the winner generally forms a syndicate in order to spread the risk and distribute the issue. Public utilities are often required by federal or state regulators to issue securities through competitive bid underwriting.

Thus the key distinction between negotiated and competitive bid underwriting is in how the origination function is handled. There is also variation in how the risk-bearing aspect of underwriting is handled, and this leads to the distinction between firm commitment and best efforts underwriting.

The description of risk bearing offered so far is often called firm commitment underwriting, in which the syndicate purchases the issued securities at a fixed price and then attempts to distribute them to the public; this is, by far, the most common form of underwriting. An alternative is best efforts underwriting, in which the investment banks do not buy the securities, but rather only attempt to distribute them and transmit funds to the issuer as sold. The risk of an unsuccessful issue is thus shifted back to the issuer. Except for small, regional issues, best efforts underwriting today is of diminished importance.

Regulation

Two important federal laws mandate the regulation of investment banks and securities trading by the Securities and Exchange Commission. The Securities Act of 1933 requires the registration of new and certain secondary issues offered to the public and the disclosure of information relevant to the decisions of the public on whether or not to purchase the securities. The Act prohibits misrepresentation and fraud in the provision of this information. The Act affects investment banks in that they must apply due diligence to ascertain the truth and completeness of the information disclosed.

The Securities and Exchange Act of 1934 applies to secondary market trading. It requires the registration of exchanges, brokers, and dealers and provides for a substantial amount of self-regulation. The Act also requires ongoing disclosure of information by companies whose securities are publicly traded.

An important recent change in SEC regulation of new issues is the adoption of Rule 415, which first went into effect provisionally in March 1982 and is now permanent. Rule 415 streamlines the issue of new securities in several ways. First, a company can register all securities of a particular type of debt or equity that it reasonably expects to issue over the next two years, and these securities are put "on the shelf." While they are on the shelf, the requirements of disclosure are met by reference to the company's Securities and Exchange Act disclosure statements—for example, its 10-K and 10-Q filings. This streamlined procedure not only reduces paperwork, but also reduces the time spent awaiting clearance of the terms of a specific issue taken "off the shelf." The lag between the date on which the registration is first filed with the SEC and the date of the offering, which can be several weeks for a traditional filing, is reduced to several days (or less) for a 415 filing because the registration statement is already effective. All that remains to be done is to notify the SEC of the particular terms of securities taken "off the shelf."

Finally, it may be noted that the existence of these national regulations in part justifies the treatment of the "geographic" market for underwriting services as confined to the United States (or possibly, for some types of issues, to a region of the United States). As Chapter 10 shows, however, the Eurobond market represents a very real alternative for large, well-known companies.

The Large Investment Banking Firm

Underwriting of corporate securities, especially those of the larger corporations, is dominated by about 20–25 large investment banking firms. The large investment banks have differing characteristics, but most engage in a broad range of securities-related activities, including underwriting, brokering, dealing, advising, arbitraging, and speculating. The resources of investment banks are often employed in several functions almost simultaneously. This multiproduct activity results either in true joint costs, or at least in difficult problems of cost accounting (because of difficulties in profit attribution and arbitrary accounting procedures) for individual activities. Thus the profitability of a particular activity (e.g., underwriting) is difficult to determine with any precision.

An indication of the relative importance of different activities for the largest 21 investment banks can be obtained through a breakdown of their sources of revenue.[9] In 1981 these 21 firms had revenues of about $14 billion. Income from underwriting accounted for 7.4% of this revenue. Securities commissions accounted for 22.1%, whereas margin interest income accounted for 13.8%. Net gains on their trading accounts provided 24.9% of revenues. Other securities-related activities, including advisory services, accounted for 16.6%, with other sources accounting for the remainder (15.2%). Of course, these percentages vary from firm to firm. Generally, income from underwriting provides a small, but still important, share of total revenues to these firms.

The Issuers

In the market for underwriting services, the corporate issuers of the securities can be considered the "buyers" of the services (whereas the public is the ultimate buyer of the securities themselves). The issuers can be divided into subgroups in a variety of ways. One useful approach is to distinguish the larger corporations, including firms such as those in the Fortune 1000, from smaller corporations, many of which are regional firms. In any case, the decision of a corporation interested in raising funds can be viewed as involving two rather distinct steps: first, the method used to raise the funds and second, if a public underwriting is chosen, the investment bank (or banks, if there are co-managers) used to manage the underwriting. (An investment banker who has a continuing advisory relationship with the issuer may advise the issuer on the first step and then manage the issue.)

A company interested in obtaining additional funds has a number of alternatives to the issue of new securities, either debt or equity, through an underwritten public offering in the United States. The company instead could attempt a private placement of new securities, using an intermediary to locate purchasers. Such private placements are not subject to SEC regulations on publicly offered new issues. Investment banks assist in most private placements, but commercial banks are also permitted to act as intermediaries in private placements. In 1976, for example, commercial banks assisted in 94 private placement transactions, accounting for 11% of the number and 7.3% of the value of all private placements in that year.[10]

The company could attempt a direct sale of its issue. This approach includes rights or warrants offerings for common stock. Rights issues nevertheless involve intermediaries. Underwriters ''stand by'' to take up any unsubscribed shares at the end of the subscription period, and they buy warrants and sell stock during this period in order to smooth-out the distribution process. The issuer pays a fee for these services. Or the company could issue debt or equity securities abroad, in the Euro-securities markets.[11]

The company could also turn to other sources of funds that do not involve the issue of new securities. Most important of these sources are loans from commercial banks (domestic or overseas), as well as issuance of commercial paper. Retained earnings are also an important source of funds.

The existence of close, but clearly not perfect, substitutes implies some degree of price elasticity of demand for the services of underwriting publicly offered securities. Some authors believe this price elasticity is high, which would tend to limit the exercise of any market power by investment banks in this area.[12] Others suggest that issuers often use underwritten offerings even when other methods of raising funds are significantly less expensive, implying that other important factors enter the decision, so that the price elasticity need not be so high.[13]

If the company chooses to raise funds through the underwritten issue of publicly offered securities, the company still must choose the type of underwriting and the firm or firms that will manage the issue. If the issuer chooses underwriting through competitive bids, the choice of investment bank is based upon the bids received. In a negotiated underwriting, the issuer instead chooses an investment bank before the details of the issue, including price, are determined.

For a negotiated underwriting, then, factors other than price influence the choice of the managing investment bank. These other factors generally include the reputation of the investment bank, the quality of service offered, its capital base, and its distribution capabilities. Thus, the product (service) is differentiated. Investment banks differ in their areas of strength and weakness. Issuers differ in the qualities of investment banks desired. This leads to a matching of investment banks and issuers, in which issuers tend to choose investment banks that exhibit (or are reputed to have) the desired characteristics and capabilities.

Hayes, Spence, and Marks have studied this matching process in some depth.[14] They posited that issuers might be interested in one or more of the following characteristics of an investment bank: expertise in corporate finance; retail distribution capabilities; institutional distribution capabilities; expertise in their industry; general research capability; and capabilities in international corporate finance and international distribution. In their empirical analysis, they found that only two of these characteristics had significant power in explaining the pattern of client-bank matches existing in the late 1970s: expertise in corporate finance and industry expertise. The apparent lack of importance of the other characteristics appears plausible: for example, distribution capabilities are provided by the syndicate as a whole, not just by the managing bank.

The determinants of the matching process identified by Hayes et al. appear to be consistent with the importance of traditional ties and ongoing relationships that is often suggested by a major feature of competition in (negotiated) underwriting. But other evidence suggests that ongoing relationships, even if they were of major importance in the past, appear to be weakening. Hayes et al. found a rather substantial fluidity of client-bank affiliations during the 1970s, at least for the large clients that they studied. At the same time, they found that the largest two components of this fluidity, aside from clients' moving to no identifiable affiliation, were switches by clients among the largest few investment banks (the "special bracket" firms) or switches from other banks to these largest few investment banks. Hayes et al. also report some difficulty in identifying "who was with whom" in a substantial number of cases. Indeed, one of the major services publishing lists of these matches, *Institutional Investor,* stopped doing so after 1979, claiming that the increasing difficulty in determining these matches had rendered their listing of dubious value.

In part, the increasing fluidity may be the result of the clients' increasing in-house competence in corporate finance. The clients appear to be more interested in pursuing suggestions for innovative financing approaches and more willing to shop for innovations. It appears that this trend will be intensified with the growing use of Rule 415 to issue securities. These involve the issuer much more in the design and timing of new issues, reducing the extent of origination services provided by the investment bank. Many Rule 415 issues thus have more of the characteristics of competitive bidding or institutional block-trades.

The Special Role of Incomplete Information

The securities markets, and especially the markets for new securities, are ones of incomplete information. Potential investors have incomplete information about issuers; potential issuers have incomplete information about investors. Underwriters serve as an intermediary agent: They advise issuers on the nature of the investment market and the type, size, and price of issues that would best appeal to that market, and subsequently seek out those investors in order to sell the issue to them. As part of this last function, they simultaneously confirm to the investors that purchases of the issuer's securities are good investments.

Thus a large part of the underwriter's task is that of an information specialist: collecting information about investors (so as to advise issuers) and about issuers (so as to confirm to investors). To do this last task effectively the underwriter needs to acquire a large amount of information about the issuer. Geographical proximity of the underwriter to the issuer may make this process easier. Also, information about large companies (that are more likely to have multifaceted operations and to operate in multiple markets) may be more easily gathered by a larger underwriter (in addition to the larger underwriter's being better able to handle the larger issuer's more varied financial and advisory needs). And a continuing relationship between an underwriter and an issuer may make information collection and evaluation easier. These tendencies are consistent with the discussion above and our findings below.

Also, the constant change in market conditions and the unique nature of each securities flotation means that issuers, in addition to having incomplete information about the market generally, may have incomplete information about the underwriting services themselves (with judgments about the quality of performance being especially difficult). Under these circumstances, as was noted in the first section, the market power of the providers of the service (underwriting) may increase.

MARKET STRUCTURE

The structure of a market is comprised of those features that are relatively stable and largely beyond the control of any firm in the market. The features of most interest are those that have implications for the nature of competitive behavior and thus for the economic performance of the market. This section presents information on the most important elements of the structure of the market for the underwriting of publicly offered corporate securities. These elements include the level of concentration in the provision of underwriting services and trends in this concentration, the extent of turnover in the rankings of the leading firms over time, the extent to which the firms can be divided into competitive groups (with competition expected to be more intense among firms within the same group and less intense between firms in different groups), and the height of barriers to entry into the industry and barriers to mobility from one competitive group to another. One feature of the industry that is at least partly structural—the nature and extent of product differentiation—was discussed in the previous section. That discussion is extended here to consider the significance of the nature of the product and the nature of the buyers.

The increasing importance of securities offered under Rule 415 appears to be altering some of the structural features of and behavior in the market for underwriting services. This section concludes with an examination of the impact of Rule 415 on market structure.

Concentration

The number and size distribution of sellers is considered a key element of a market's structure, with major implications for competitive behavior and the performance of the market. Various measures of market concentration can be used to summarize the information on the number and size distribution of sellers, the most common measure being the concentration ratio: the share of the total market held by the largest firms.

The level of concentration is expected to influence competitive behavior because the smaller number of larger firms in a more concentrated market are likely to recognize their mutual interdependence; that is, they recognize that action by any one firm is likely to have a major impact on the other large firms, leading to competitive reactions by the others. The net result could be that all of the firms become less profitable. Because they are more fully aware of their mutual interdependence, firms in a more concentrated market are more likely to reach an understanding (even if only tacit) to restrain competition along some dimensions, especially competition in pricing. Such restraint then leads to higher prices and higher profits, at the expense of buyers of the goods or services involved. In turn, this outcome creates economic inefficiency, as output is restricted and buyers shift to less desirable substitutes or simply do without this type of good or service.

The level of concentration is also likely to influence the nature and intensity of nonprice competition—for example, the rate at which innovations are developed, introduced, and diffused through the market. The relationships in this area are complex and less well understood, and drawing conclusions on possible inefficiencies is difficult.

In relation to an activity such as underwriting, a high level of concentration could result in larger, more stable spreads. This would enhance the profit rates of the firms providing the service, but would also lead some potential issuers of securities to seek alternative (but otherwise less desirable) means of raising funds, or to forgo raising funds in the public markets. This would create static inefficiency in the allocation of resources, with too few resources devoted to providing underwriting services. It may also create more general dynamic inefficiencies, to the extent that the level and pattern of real investment (such as investment in plant and equipment) by potential issuers is affected. This dynamic inefficiency would then result in a lower rate of economic growth. Thus, there are important reasons for analyzing the level of concentration in the underwriting business.

Concentration: Levels and Trends.   The industry providing underwriting of publicly offered corporate securities is often viewed as a pyramid. A small number of firms provide much of the management function, suggesting that in origination a small number of companies have a large share of the business. The level of concentration is somewhat less for the underwriting functions of risk-bearing and distribution. Concentration is also lower in the related activities of dealing and brokerage.

The most typical measure of concentration in underwriting is the share of the dollar volume of new issues managed or co-managed by the largest investment banks. The management function, with its emphasis on origination services, is considered of special importance because of the client contact involved, the control of the syndicate, and the extra fees accruing to a manager. One problem in the presentation of concentration estimates is the manner in which credit or responsibility for an underwriting is to be allocated among the lead manager and co-managers, when there is more than one for that issue. The first set of concentration measures presented here allocates proportionate credit to each co-manager, following Miller,[15] who believes this to be the most reasonable method. (Other methods, including full credit to the lead manager, full credit to each co-manager, and proportionate credit with a bonus share to the lead manager, are sometimes used. These latter methods would give somewhat different impressions of concentration, but the differences are not major ones.)

Table 5.1 provides estimates of concentration in the underwriting of corporate securities, based on the dollar volume of issues (aggregating debt and equity) man-

**Table 5.1   Concentration in the Management of
Publicly Offered Corporate Securities, 1934–1983**

Period	Concentration Ratios			
	1 Firm	3 Firm	5 Firm	10 Firm
1983	19	42	57	79
1981	13	35	53	74
1978	11	31	46	70
1975	16	38	54	76
1960–1969	11	28	40	61
1952	15	40	51	71
1947–1949	24	52	60	74
1934–1938	25	43	53	69

Sources: 1983: *Investment Dealers' Digest*, January 10,
1984 and January 17, 1984. 1981, 1978, 1975, 1960–1969:
*Investment Dealers' Digest. Corporate Financing Direc-
tory*, various issues. 1952, 1947–1949, 1934–1938, Erwin
Miller, *Background and Structure of the Industry*, in Irwin
Friend et al., *Investment Banking and the New Issues Market*. Cleveland: World Publishing, 1967, Table 2.26.

Note: Proportionate credit given to co-managers.

aged or co-managed and giving proportionate credit to each co-manager. For recent years concentration levels in the industry are in the range that is considered moderate for manufacturing industries—with four-firm concentration levels (not actually shown in the table) in the range of 40–50%. This is barely on the threshold of the range in which concentration levels in manufacturing industries appear to result in an increased likelihood of mutual restraint of competitive behavior.[16] Furthermore, there appears to be no clear long-term trend in concentration over the entire period shown in the table. Rather, the data suggest that concentration was falling slowly from the mid-1930s to the 1960s and has been rising during the 1970s and into the 1980s.[17]

The trends during the 1970s have been explored in depth by Hayes et al.[18] They calculated four-firm, eight-firm and 15-firm concentration levels for the volume of new issues managed for each year during 1972–1977, giving full credit to each co-manager. They examined negotiated and competitive-bid underwriting separately and also examined debt and equity issues separately within each of the former categories. Table 5.2 presents simple averages of their concentration estimates for each category. These are not directly comparable with the data presented in Table 5.1, not only because full credit is given (rather than proportionate credit), but also because the "market universe" is limited to the top 25 underwriters (rather than the entire universe of underwriters). Nonetheless, these estimates confirm the conclusion that underwriting is moderately concentrated. Furthermore, competitive-bid underwriting is somewhat less concentrated than negotiated underwriting.[19] The larger investment banks have a greater share of negotiated underwriting, a finding consistent with the propositions that expertise in origination is rather concentrated in the larger banks and/or that reputation and ongoing client relationships favor the larger banks in negotiated underwriting. Concentration in debt and equity is very similar, although equity offerings exhibit slightly lower concentration.[20]

Hayes et al. then test statistically for the presence of significant time trends in concentration over this rather brief period. They use regression analysis and control for variations in the total volume of underwriting in each category from year to year. The effort is complicated by the fact that the concentration levels tend to vary noticeably from year to year, making the identification of a trend rather difficult. They conclude that concentration was rising in a statistically significant way for negotiated debt and negotiated equity offerings, with the rising trend for combined equity almost statistically significant. Concentration was falling in a statistically significant way for competitive debt, competitive equity, combined debt, and the combined total.

Hayes et al. also explore concentration trends, using data on gross spread revenues (management fees, fees for the underwriting guarantee, and selling concessions), for the period 1970–1977.[21] The limitation of their "market universe" to the top 25 firms is not nearly as appropriate here as it is for offerings managed, because smaller firms also obtain a significant portion of these fees.[22] Indeed, concentration in revenues is substantially lower than concentration in management. Nonetheless, in their analysis

Table 5.2   Concentration in Underwriting, Averages Over 1972–1977

	Concentration Ratios		
Type of Offering	4 Firm	8 Firm	15 Firm
Negotiated:			
Debt	47	70	90
Equity	44	68	89
Total	46	69	89
Competitive Bid:			
Debt	35	59	86
Equity	32	56	85
Total	33	57	86
Combined:			
Debt	40	64	89
Equity	39	63	87
Total	39	63	88

Source: Samuel L. Hayes, III, A. Michael Spence, and David Van Prang Marks. *Competition in the Investment Banking Industry*. Cambridge, Mass.: Harvard University Press, 1983, Tables 3, 4, and 5.

Note: Simple averages of annual concentration ratios. Full credit is given to each co-manager.

they conclude that concentration was rising significantly for combined debt and the combined total, although no trend was significant for combined equity.[23]

In putting all of this evidence together, Hayes et al. conclude that there was some trend toward rising concentration and this was strongest in the area of negotiated debt offerings. It could also be concluded that this evidence on trends in concentration is simply mixed.

Turnover Among the Leading Firms.   The ranking of the leading firms and the extent to which the ranking changes from year to year are also of interest in an analysis of industry competition. A number of researchers have posited that substantial turn-over in these rankings from year to year, based on substantial variability in market shares, is indicative of substantial competition, especially if the variability is not due to minor variations in product differentiation, such as annual model changes or ''new, improved'' products, or to mergers.[24] On the other hand, the rankings of market shares of firms in an entrenched oligopoly, with competition substantially con-strained, would tend to be stable from year to year, or to change only gradually. Thus, information on turnover among the leading firms is often used as a part of the analysis of competition in an industry, but its use is limited by certain conceptual difficulties or ambiguities (as suggested above) and by the lack of a criterion for determining what is or is not ''substantial'' turnover.

Table 5.3 shows the top 10 firms in underwriting, ranked from first to tenth based on the dollar volume of offerings managed, with full credit given to all co-managers, for each fifth year of the period 1950–1980. The table suggests neither complete stability nor very large turnover, but rather some amount of turnover and a notable staying power for a number of the largest firms. Of the top five firms in 1980, Merrill Lynch had been in the top five in every year shown except 1955, and First Boston and Morgan Stanley had each been in the top five in every year shown.[25] Salomon Brothers and Goldman Sachs, in contrast, moved into the top five only in the later years shown. Of the second five firms in 1980, Lehman Brothers and Blyth Eastman (formerly Blyth) were in the top 10 in every year shown, and Kidder Peabody in every year but one. Dean Witter and E. F. Hutton were not in the top 10 in any of the earlier years shown. In general there appears to be more turnover in the lower part of the ranking, and this would be confirmed if the analysis was extended to the eleventh through twentieth firms in these years.[26]

Thus, information on turnover in the rankings of the leading firms suggests that there is some fluidity of rankings at the top, but that several firms have managed to stay within the top group over rather long periods of time. This information by itself, however, is not sufficient to draw any strong conclusions about the extent and vigor of competition in underwriting.

Regional Broker-Dealers.   The discussion, thus far, has focused on the market shares of the leading (frequently, New York based) underwriters who cater mainly to the largest issuers in the country—roughly the Fortune 1000. For this group of large issuers, the relevant market for underwriting services is a national one.

Another group of underwriters is also worthy of note: the regional broker-dealers.

Table 5.3 The Top 10 Underwriting Firms, 1950–1980

1950	1955	1960	1965	1970	1975	1980
Halsey, Stuart	Morgan Stanley	First Boston	First Boston	First Boston	Merrill Lynch	Merrill Lynch
Morgan Stanley	First Boston	Halsey, Stuart	Lehman Bros.	Merrill Lynch	First Boston	Salomon Brothers
First Boston	Halsey, Stuart	Morgan Stanley	Blyth	Lehman Bros.	Salomon Bros.	First Boston
Merrill Lynch	Blyth	Lehman Bros.	Merrill Lynch	Salomon Bros.	Morgan Stanley	Morgan Stanley
Kidder Peabody	Glore, Forgan	Merrill Lynch	Morgan Stanley	Morgan Stanley	Goldman, Sachs	Goldman, Sachs
Blyth	Kuhn, Loeb	Blyth	White, Weld	Blyth	Blyth Eastman	Lehman Bros.
Lehman Bros.	White, Weld	White, Weld	Salomon Bros.	Halsey, Stuart	Lehman Bros.	Blyth Eastman
White, Weld	Lehman Bros.	Kidder Peabody	Kidder Peabody	Goldman Sachs	Halsey, Stuart	Kidder Peabody
Union Securities	Smith Barney	Kuhn, Loeb	Lazard Freres	Kidder Peabody	Kidder Peabody	Dean Witter
Stone & Webster	Alex Brown & Sons	Stone & Webster	Kuhn, Loeb	White, Weld	Smith Barney	E.F. Hutton

Source: Samuel L. Hayes, III, A. Michael Spence, and David Van Prang Marks. *Competition in the Investment Banking Industry.* Cambridge, Mass.: Harvard University Press, 1983.

Note: Rankings based on volume of offerings managed, with full credit given to all co-managers.

This is a group of smaller firms, located outside of New York, who tend to be the managing underwriters for small and medium-size issuers. According to an SEC-SBA study,[27] between 1972 and 1980 regional broker-dealers managed 79% of the initial public offerings of issuers. These regional broker-dealers also make markets in the securities of these smaller firms and frequently serve as part of the distribution syndicates for larger issues managed by the leading underwriters.

The number of regional broker-dealers who are prepared to act as a managing underwriter appears to be in the range of 200–250, and this number has been declining because of discontinuance of business and because of mergers among them. They are located in various cities across the United States and tend to focus on local issuers. Thus, from the prospect of a small or medium-sized company that (for the reasons discussed in the section on "The Special Role of Incomplete Information") cannot attract the attention of a leading nationally oriented underwriter, the effective market for underwriting services may be a local one, with the choice restricted to a handful of broker-dealers. Although published evidence is not available, the effective concentration ratios in these local markets are likely to be quite high.

Competitive Groups Within the Industry

Information on concentration levels and trends provides a picture of the relative sizes of firms in an industry. Analysts of industry competition also recognize that firms in an industry can often take rather different approaches in competing for the market. In many industries these differences can be classified into a limited number of viable strategic approaches, giving rise to groupings of firms, called strategic groups or competitive groups.

The concept of strategic groups assists an analysis of industry competition in several ways. First, a firm should recognize that it competes most directly with other firms in the same group, because they are all using a similar approach to the market. Second, groups compete with each other to varying degrees. Intergroup competition is likely to be greater if the groups are attempting to serve the same buyers, even though they take substantially different approaches in this effort. Intergroup rivalry is less intense if the groups are serving different buyer groups—in this case the situation approaches one in which the groups should be considered separate industries. In the case in which there is substantial customer overlap, the presence of different strategic groups is posited to be pro-competitive. Firms in different strategic groups find it more difficult to reach tacit understandings to restrain competition, because they do not share the same competitive strengths and weaknesses.[28]

There are several approaches to grouping firms in the investment banking industry. The two most common are (1) grouping firms by company trading functions, size, and location, used by the SEC and the Securities Industry Association; and (2) grouping firms into brackets, reflecting the pyramidal structure of underwriting syndicates.

The SEC grouping divides firms into large investment bank houses, national full-line firms, New York-based firms, New York Stock Exchange regional firms, and several other categories.[29] The firms in the first two groups, as of 1983, are shown

Table 5.4   SEC Groupings of Firms, 1983

Large Investment Banking Houses	National Full-Line Firms
Bear, Stearns	Prudential/Bache
Dillon Read	A. G. Becker
First Boston	Dean Witter
Goldman Sachs	Drexel Burnham Lambert
Kidder Peabody	A. G. Edwards & Sons
Lazard Freres	E. F. Hutton
Lehman Brothers, Kuhn Loeb	Merrill Lynch
Morgan Stanley	Paine Webber
Salomon Brothers	Shearson/American Express
Wertheim	Smith Barney
	Thompson McKinnon

in Table 5.4. The 10 large investment banking houses are characterized by an emphasis on large-scale underwriting and trading. The 11 national full-line firms are characterized by extensive networks of branch offices, with an emphasis on retail distribution and brokerage. (Two of these ceased to exist as independent firms in 1984.) These 21 firms have 70% of the total assets of all securities firms (numbering about 2,400) that do business with the public and belong to an organized exchange. For a number of purposes, such as the analysis of underwriting of securities offerings of national corporations, these 21 are often taken to be the entire ''industry'' or ''market universe.''

This SEC/SIA grouping provides some insights into competition in underwriting, especially in suggesting differences in retail distribution capabilities. In other ways, this method of grouping is less useful. For example, Merrill Lynch is difficult to place, given its substantial activities in large-scale underwriting and trading, in addition to its extensive retail distribution network.

The second approach to grouping underwriting firms is by their typical status in the syndicate, an approach giving rise to various ''brackets'' in the industry. Bracket standing depends upon the frequency with which the investment bank manages or co-manages a syndicate, the frequency with which it participates in others' syndicates, the size of its participations, and its general status and prestige. In the late 1970s five investment banks were accorded the top status in the special bracket (or bulge group): First Boston, Merrill Lynch, Morgan Stanley, Salomon Brothers, and Goldman Sachs. There has been some turnover in this group, as Dillon Read and Kuhn Loeb dropped out of this group during the early 1970s, whereas Goldman Sachs entered it.[30] These special-bracket firms are often lead managers, have strong corporate client bases, and (except for Morgan Stanley) are strong in distribution and market-making. The next group is the major bracket (15 firms in the late 1970s), followed by the major out-of-order, the mezzanine, and the submajor brackets.

Although this method does provide a way of placing firms in the industry into one of several rank categories, it has not provided much information beyond that found in the information on concentration.

A third approach to competitive groupings in the industry is that of Hayes et al., derived from their empirical analysis of affiliations between issuers and firms (discussed previously). It is based on the proposition that the competitive strengths of different investment banks vary, and thus specific banks are likely to attract (or to compete for) certain types of clients more than others. Based on their empirical analysis, Hayes et al. calculate the probability that each investment bank would attract each issuing firm in the sample as a client. (They intended to use the top 20 investment banks in the analysis, but two, Lazard Freres and Shearson, had to be excluded because of lack of data.) They then calculate the correlations among the sets of these probabilities for all possible pairs of the 18 investment banks. If the correlation is substantially positive, the two investment banks apparently compete closely for the same subsets of clients, and this pair of investment banks is considered part of the same competitive group.

Using this approach, Hayes et al. conclude that four competitive groups existed among these 18 banks, as shown in Table 5.5. Group 1 is mostly national full-line firms, with First Boston as a notable exception. These firms tend to be stronger among nonindustrial clients, especially those in retailing, transportation, and utilities. Their clients tend to be smaller and to have lower bond ratings, less institutionally held stock, and fewer sales outside the United States. These investment banks tend to have

Table 5.5   Competitive Groups in Underwriting, Based on the Analysis of Hayes, Spence, and Marks

Group 1	Group 3
Bache	Dillon Read
Bear Stearns	Drexel Burnham
E. F. Hutton	Goldman Sachs
First Boston	Lehman Brothers
Kidder Peabody	Morgan Stanley
Loeb Rhoades	Warburg
Paine Webber	
Smith Barney	
Group 2	Group 4
Merrill Lynch	Blyth Eastman
Salomon Brothers	Dean Witter

Source: Samuel L. Hayes, III, A. Michael Spence, and David Van Prang Marks. *Competition in the Investment Banking Industry.* Cambridge, Mass.: Harvard University Press, 1983, Chap. 6.

a smaller share of their representatives in institutional and foreign sales and also tend to have smaller staffs of corporate finance personnel. Group 3 includes mostly large investment banks. The characteristics of these institutions and their client bases tend to be the opposite of those of the firms in Group 1. Thus, for example, these firms are stronger in attracting industrial clients. Both firms in Group 2 have used their strengths in distribution to rise into special bracket status. The two firms in Group 4 are characterized by a strong West Coast presence as well as strength in retail distribution capabilities.

The analysis of Hayes et al. indicates that there are competitive groupings of firms within the underwriting business. For instance, firms in Groups 1 or 3, particularly, compete much more with other firms in the same group for client business than they do with firms in the other group. Nonetheless, Hayes et al. also point out that cross-group competition does exist. It is difficult to tell whether, on net, the existence of these competitive groupings makes competition overall more or less intense than it otherwise would be.

More generally, the results are consistent with the proposition that the larger, higher-quality clients tend to affiliate with the leading, particularly special bracket, firms. Banks whose strength is in retail distribution generally find it hard to lure these clients away.

Entry Barriers and Mobility Barriers

The height of barriers to entry, indicating how difficult it would be for a new firm to enter successfully into competition with firms already established, is of interest in an analysis of industry competition because it indicates the degree to which established firms may feel threatened by potential competition. Even if the established firms might agree (explicitly or implicitly) to restrain competition among themselves, the threat of entry (in the absence of entry barriers) tends to force the established firms to pursue pricing and other policies that approximate a highly competitive outcome. Deviations from the competitive outcome would attract entry and erode the agreement. As the height of entry barriers rises, this threat is reduced, permitting more scope for restraints of competition that, for example, raise profitability without attracting entry. Barriers to entry thus permit deviations from the competitive outcome to persist over longer periods of time. Barriers to mobility are similar to barriers to entry, but tend to protect firms in one strategic or competitive group in an industry from shifts into this group by firms established in other groups.

The height of entry barriers appears to vary by the type of securities activity pursued by the entrant.[31] Barriers are modest—entry is not difficult—in local retail brokerage and regional branch-network retail distribution. An entrant would need to commit a reasonable amount of capital and hire appropriate personnel, but these do not appear to present a serious barrier. Entry into institutional brokerage, block-trading, and market-making would require the commitment of more capital, but entry barriers are still relatively modest. The entrant would need to accept the higher risks associated with carrying inventories or securities. The entrant would also need to attract personnel who have or could develop contacts with institutional customers.

Thus, barriers to entry into securities distribution activities appear to be generally modest.

Barriers to entry (and barriers to mobility) into the origination function of underwriting and into the role of syndicate manager are considered to be substantially higher. Capital requirements may be somewhat higher, but the key aspects appear to be personnel and reputation. A client must believe that the firm has the abilities to design and price the issue—faith in the market judgment of the underwriter—and to form a syndicate and manage a successful distribution. Much depends on the quality of personnel, especially expertise and capabilities in corporate finance advising. People with this expertise are limited in number, and an entrant may have difficulty luring them away from the established firms and into the relatively risky participation in the entrant's efforts. The entrant also faces a marketing-based entry barrier, because the established firms already have a reputation and track record, whereas the entrant's capabilities are relatively untested. The existing firms also benefit from established contacts and client loyalty.

Thus, barriers to entry into the origination and management aspects of underwriting appear to be substantial. Evidence to support this proposition is available, but it is not extensive. Hayes et al. point to the fact that many of the national full-line firms have worked to expand their shares of origination by committing capital and hiring personnel. Most have made little progress, because they have had serious difficulties in attracting the best or prime customers away from the special bracket firms. Indirect evidence is also available, based on levels of concentration. Higher entry barriers tend to result in higher levels of concentration, although there are also other influences on concentration levels. It has already been noted that concentration levels are higher in management than in other activities in the securities industry, such as distribution or brokerage. This is consistent with the existence of higher barriers into origination and management.

The use and structure of syndicates might also enhance barriers to entry or mobility. The power of the syndicate manager to control the size of others' participations could be used to discipline firms that were competing too aggressively to attract business or were otherwise adversely affecting the status quo. Although this is an intriguing possibility, apparently it does not apply, because there is no evidence of the use of syndicate control to discipline firms that compete too aggressively. Rather, a firm's place in the syndicate is based largely on its capabilities and capacities, tempered by the fact that a firm is expected to participate in both "hot" and "less easily moved" new issues.

The most clear-cut barrier to entry into the securities industry is the Glass-Steagall Act. A commercial bank or an affiliate of a commercial bank cannot legally underwrite or deal in securities for its own account, except for: U.S. government securities; general obligation bonds of state and local governments; bonds issued for housing, university, or dormitory purposes; and the obligations of certain international organizations of which the United States is a member. Thus, commercial banks and their affiliates cannot engage in the underwriting of publicly offered corporate securities. One important set of potential entrants is thus excluded by law.

Nature of the Product and the Nature of the Buyers (Issuers)

An important component of market structure is the nature of the product. If the product (or service) is comparatively simple, with few facets or dimensions, firms in a concentrated industry may find it easier to reach an implicit understanding as to noncompetitive prices or behavior. If, instead, the product is complex, there are more dimensions on which a firm can compete, and monitoring of any understanding by industry members becomes very difficult, thereby increasing the likelihoood that an understanding would break down and more vigorous competition would occur.[32]

Complexity of the product, however, also has an opposite effect. Greater complexity makes comparison shopping by buyers more difficult; it raises transactions and information costs. With greater information costs on the part of buyers, individual sellers are less constrained by the competition of rivals and are freer to exercise market power. Greater complexity may mean higher prices (relative to costs), rather than lower prices.[33]

The nature of the buying side of a market (for underwriting services, this would be the issuers) is also important. If buyers are knowledgeable, purchase frequently, and can do comparison shopping, and if there are comparatively few buyers, so that each one's purchases are large compared with overall sales in the market and the "capture" of any one customer's purchases would have a very large impact on a seller's sales and profitability, competition among sellers is likely to be more vigorous.[34]

Underwriting services appear to be quite complex, involving many subjective judgments as to appropriate timing, issue size, issue price, interest rate and maturity (for debt), or the value of unique features of the securities offered; they involve largely one-of-a-kind transactions. It may be difficult for an issuer to make comparative judgments among underwriters, to comparison shop properly, or even (after the fact) to decide whether a particular underwriting was performed in a manner that was most advantageous to the issuer. On the other hand, most issuers among the Fortune 1000 should be large enough to have or to acquire in-house financial market expertise with respect to underwriting. As is discussed below, the changes wrought by Rule 415 have made it easier for large issuers to comparison shop. Unfortunately, smaller issuers remain unaided by Rule 415 and may not have the size to justify much in-house expertise. These smaller issuers thus may lack the capabilities to shop around extensively and to evaluate the quality of underwriting services offered or provided.

There are a large number of *potential* issuers, essentially all corporations in business in the United States. With a few possible exceptions, such as AT&T before divestiture or GMAC, the business of any one of these issuers is not large compared to the size of the total market or to the size of total underwritings done by the leading investment banks. Thus, the possible benefits of gaining any one issuer's business is not likely to encourage an underwriter to offer extraordinary terms in order to gain this business. Further, although issuers can readily discover the terms and spreads applied to other new issues, the "special" circumstances of every offering would probably allow underwriters to prevent special concessions to any one sizable issuer from becoming widespread. Thus, the structure of the buyer side of the market leaves the buyers (issuers) with normal bargaining power, based on their ability to shop around (which Rule 415 has enhanced for large issuers), but does not generally appear to give buyers the power to dictate terms nor necessarily to be able to break any tacit understanding that might be reached by underwriters to restrain competition over terms offered to issuers.

The Impact of Rule 415

Rule 415 permits a company to register with the SEC all the securities of a particular type that it reasonably expects to issue over the next two years. The issuer often designs the various issues without the assistance of an investment bank, leaving open the rate or price, timing of issue, and underwriter. The company can bring the issue "off the shelf" much more quickly than for a traditional new issue. This reduction in time greatly reduces the risk of being adversely affected by changes in the market while waiting for SEC approval; in the past such delays have, at times, even caused companies to cancel new issues because of shifts in the market.

When the company decides to pull an issue off the shelf for public offering, it can either negotiate with one investment bank as to pricing and underwriting the issue, or it can offer the issue for a type of competitive-bid underwriting. In either case, the investment bank or banks interested have a much shorter time period to reach decisions (often only a few hours) than would be the case with traditional underwriting. Pricing must be done quickly. There is little time to build a syndicate, implying that syndicates might tend to be smaller and more deals would be "internalized"—done without a syndicate. There is little time to scout buyer interest, suggesting more "bought deals," in which the underwriter takes the whole issue without any indications of buyer interest. The short time period also makes difficult the performance of "due diligence" on disclosure by the issuer. This tends to limit the use of Rule 415 to the larger, better known, publicly owned corporations, a limitation now formally mandated by the SEC.

Rule 415 thus has changed several important aspects of the process of underwriting, to the advantage of some investment banks and to the disadvantage of others. Investment banks posited to benefit are those that: (1) have the personnel with the expertise and skill to gauge the market and price new issues rapidly, as well as to manage the accelerated process; (2) have the capitalization that permits them to carry large blocks of new issues before the distribution is accomplished; and (3) have the in-house capabilities in distribution, especially to institutional investors that buy large blocks of the new issues. Investment banks that are disadvantaged include not only those potential issue managers that are short in the above characteristics, but also the firms that played a role in distribution in syndicates formed to underwrite issues in the traditional manner. In the latter group the regional investment banks may be especially affected, because they often do not become part of the smaller syndicates of Rule 415 issues, are unable to offer a sufficiently wide range of products to their securities-buying customers, and thus begin to lose the business of these customers.

Evidence on the operation of Rule 415 during its first 18 months or so supports many of these posited effects. During the period from March 1982, when Rule 415 went into effect, through June 1983, 33% of publicly offered new issues were brought to market under Rule 415—45% of new debt issues and 17% of new equity issues.[35] In calendar 1983 about 38% of new issues occurred under Rule 415.[36] The top five investment banks were lead managers for 66% of all new issues by dollar volume in 1982 and 57% in 1983. The top five investment banks were lead managers for 77% of Rule 415 new issues in 1982 and for 75% in the first half of 1983.[37] Thus, the larger, better capitalized "special bracket" investment banks appear to be able to gain a larger share of Rule 415 business. Salomon Brothers moved into the top spot in volume as a lead manager in 1983, based partly on its capabilities in institutional distribution of Rule 415 debt issues.[38]

In Rule 415 debt issues, investment banks bought the issues without consulting potential buyers in over half the cases, during the period of March 1982 through June 1983.[39] It has been suggested that underwriting of Rule 415 debt issues largely has the character of block trades, because the banks acquire the debt issue and then sell it in large chunks to institutional investors.

Several studies have been done comparing Rule 415 offerings with traditional offerings. A Salomon Brothers study of all debt and equity offerings managed or co-managed by one of the top 12 firms compared the 16 months prior to March 1982, before Rule 415 became effective, with the 16 months after. The study found that the managing underwriters committed to purchase 38% of the new debt issues before March 1982 and 63% after and 31% of the new equity issues before and 52% after.[40] The authors attribute these shifts largely to the impact of Rule 415.

Another study compared 11 Rule 415 equity issues by six corporations with six prior (traditional) equity issues by the same six corporations. The lead manager purchased an average of 11.6% of the six prior new issues, but took all of the new issues in five of the Rule 415 offerings and an average of 35.3% in the other six Rule 415 offerings. Sales to institutional investors averaged 42.7% for the six prior offerings and 61.5% for the 11 Rule 415 offerings. The study further used a sample of 33 regional underwriters to determine the impact of Rule 415 on them, using a matched sample of the six prior equity issues and six Rule 415 issues. An average of 21 of the regional firms had participated in the distribution of the prior six issues, whereas none participated in four of the six Rule 415 issues, and only five participated in the other two. These regional firms had underwritten an average of 12.9% of the prior issues and only 1.6% of the Rule 415 issues.[41] These comparisons are believed to be reflective of the general changes accompanying the adoption of Rule 415.

Thus, the adoption of Rule 415 is having a major impact on the market for securities underwriting services. It appears to be favoring the larger investment banks that have the capitalization, the willingness to bear the risk of carrying large inventories of new issues, the capabilities in institutional distribution, and the personnel with the appropriate expertise. This would be expected to raise the level of concentration in the industry, as well as raising the height of entry barriers based on capital requirements and personnel. The impact on the role of reputation and client contacts as an entry barrier may be mixed; reputation and contacts may be more important for Rule 415 issues that are negotiated, but less important as more Rule 415 issues are opened to some form of competitive bids. The impact of Rule 415 appears to be especially adverse to the regional underwriters, who are included less often, and for smaller amounts, in the smaller (or nonexistent) Rule 415 syndicates. If this adverse impact leads to a further reduction in the number of regional underwriters, the small and medium-sized corporations that have relied on these regional underwriters to manage the majority of their new issues and initial public offerings could also be adversely affected.

The rise in concentration should not automatically be equated with a decline in the vigor of competition in general, however, because the "ground rules" for competitive behavior have also been altered by the advent of Rule 415. Indeed, there is a general belief that the vigor of competition, at least for the business of larger corporations that have issues on the shelf, has been heightened by Rule 415. Investment banks solicit their business more aggressively, often without any prompting by the issuer, based on the investment bank's knowledge of what is on the shelf and thus potentially available for underwriting. The issuers themselves appear more willing to shop around, creating a greater degree of competitive bidding. These effects will be explored further in the discussion below of behavior and performance.

BEHAVIOR AND PERFORMANCE

The behavior and performance of firms in a market are analytically distinct. As was explained in the first section of this chapter, behavior characterizes what firms do in the market, and performance characterizes the outcomes. Nevertheless, the two categories are frequently linked closely. Pricing decisions (and pricing patterns) are usually considered to be behavior; but whether those prices approximate long-run marginal costs (and hence, whether excess, noncompetitive profits are being earned) is considered to be performance. Rather than trying to keep them apart, we will analyze them together. Our discussion will focus on prices, the quality of services rendered, and profits.

Prices

In a competitive market with easy entry, over any medium- to long-term period prices should reflect the cost of producing the relevant goods or services (including a normal profit return on invested capital). Substantial positive deviations of prices above costs (excess profits) are likely to induce output expansion by existing firms (who compete with each other for these extraordinarily profitable opportunities) and to attract entry by new firms (if these excess profits are expected to persist for any appreciable time); the added output causes prices to drop. This process should continue until prices return to levels that approximate long-run marginal costs. Similarly, substantial negative deviations of prices below costs are likely to lead to reduced output and to exit, until prices rise to levels that approximate long-run marginal costs.

Prices in a noncompetitive market structure are also likely to be sensitive to costs, but there is no automatic equilibrating mechanism, and prices may deviate from costs for long periods of time. Prices are likely to reflect noncost elements, such as the number or relative sizes of sellers and the bargaining power of buyers. The dynamics of pricing in an industry with a comparative handful of sellers may cause prices to be sticky and to fail to reflect cost changes over time, as the sellers fear that price changes may cause implicit understandings to unravel.

With this general background, we can now examine the prices for the services rendered by underwriters. As was described in the section entitled ''The Market and Its Characteristics,'' the underwriting of securities usually involves three functions (origination, underwriting proper, and distribution) that are usually provided to issuers as a package. In return for these services, the underwriters charge fees. These fees can either be expressed in terms of total revenues (e.g., $1 million in fees on a $10 million securities issue) or in percentage terms (e.g., 10%). The latter method is more convenient for our purposes, because it makes fees comparable across different size issues. It also conforms with industry usage, which frequently refers to the fees in terms of a percentage ''spread''—the difference between the price paid for a security by the buyer and the moneys received by the issuer, expressed as a percentage of the former. The spread, then, can be considered to be the price of underwriting services, expressed as a percentage of each dollar's worth of securities issued.

Patterns in Underwriting Fees.   A number of patterns are known to hold generally true for underwriting fees[42]:

Spreads tend to be smaller for debt issues than for equity issues.

Spreads tend to be smaller for well-known companies and for secondary issues than for the initial public offerings (IPOs) of relatively unknown companies.

Spreads tend to be smaller for large issuing companies than for small ones.

Spreads tend to be smaller for large issues (in dollar size) than for small issues.

Spreads (for public utilities) tend to be smaller for competitive underwritings than for negotiated underwritings.

This pattern, with the possible exception of the last comparison, appears to be roughly consistent with cost factors. The risk (on firm commitment underwritings) that the market price of an issue will decline between the time the underwriter makes a firm price commitment to the issuer and the time the entire issue is sold constitutes one major category of cost[43]; distribution efforts constitute another. Debt issues tend to be less volatile than equity issues; the issues of larger, more well-known issuers tend to be less volatile and easier to distribute than issues at the other end of the spectrum; and the fixed costs of the underwriting process appear to be substantial, so a larger issue that allows these fixed costs to be spread over a greater dollar value will have lower costs per dollar of securities issued. Even for the comparisons between competitive and negotiated underwritings, the latter may involve more services (e.g., advising, preparing documents) than the former, so that the latter are more costly to undertake. Thus, the specific pattern described above does appear to correlate with the likely cost difference of the varying kinds of issues and issuers.

This consistency with cost patterns does not, however, imply that the actual fee differentials among issues and issuers bear the close reflections of cost differences that we would expect to find in a competitive industry. We know that the underwriting costs of a debt issue are probably lower than those of an equity issue, and thus we would expect the spreads to be lower. But without a great deal more information, we cannot determine whether the spreads charged for high-quality, long-term, negotiated corporate debt issues (typically, around $7/8\%$) and the spreads charged for high-quality equity issues (typically, around 3%–4%) closely match the costs of underwriting each type of security. A companion paper by Giddy,[44] examining the volatility of newly offered equity issues, indicates that the likelihood of underwriters' experiencing a loss on equity issues is quite small. This evidence at least raises the question of whether the relative costs of underwriting equity issues are as great as the spread differential indicates.[45]

Further, the relative stability over time of at least some spreads—a spread of $7/8\%$ on high-quality, long-term corporate bonds has apparently persisted for a number of decades[46]—is not likely to be consistent with cost-based pricing. It is unlikely that underwriting costs, even expressed as a percentage spread, have remained this stable over long periods of time that have encompassed substantial cost changes and technology (electronics, telecommunications) changes.

Finally, two studies[47] of public utility securities flotations have found that issuer costs and spreads are significantly lower when an issuer can attract three or more underwriters to bid for the opportunity to underwrite its issue. Again, this evidence raises the suspicion that these spread differentials may be due to differences in competitive vigor rather than to cost differences.

An Empirical Examination of Spreads on Initial Public Offerings. As part of the research for this study, the authors undertook a fresh statistical examination of underwriting spreads in one relatively well-defined area: initial public offerings (IPOs) of equity by issuers whose securities were not previously traded publicly. Our purpose was to test hypotheses concerning the determinants of spreads on these issues; these determinants included both cost-based and noncost-based factors. To the extent that the latter provide significant explanations for the pattern of spreads, they may indicate that noncompetitive influences may be present in underwriting.

We chose equity IPOs as our area of investigation for two reasons. First, this narrowing of the broader underwriting area meant that we did not have to take into account (control for) the influences of differing degrees of seasoning and stock market track-record of experienced firms; it also meant that we could neglect the underwriting differences between equity and debt. Second, although they account for only a small fraction of the capital raised annually through securities flotations, IPOs represent an important means through which small and medium-size firms raise capital for new and expanding ventures. We hope that our study can provide some added insights into the functioning of this important sector of the nation's capital markets.[48]

Our study focused on IPOs coming to market in the first six months of 1981. The year 1981 was chosen so as to ensure that data from published sources would be available, while keeping the period close enough to the present to allow inferences for current conditions to be drawn. The first six months were chosen to limit the data-gathering burden, while maintaining a sample large enough to allow statistical reliability; this time period also happens to encompass the end of a "hot" period for new issues and the beginning of a somewhat "colder" period.[49]

Data availability caused the sample to be restricted to 216 IPOs during these six months. The spreads on these IPOs ranged from a high of 20% (on one issue; the next highest spread was 10% on a large number of issues) to a low of 5.9%; the average spread was 9.0%.

Our statistical study consisted of efforts to explain the pattern of (or variation in) the spreads of the various IPOs through the variation in other ("explanatory") variables. Our explanatory variables included both cost-oriented and noncost-oriented variables. The cost-oriented variables were the following:

The size of the issuers (expressed as the dollar value of assets)[50]; we would expect a greater size of issuer to have a negative effect on spreads, because greater size would imply less risk and less distribution effort.

The size of the issue (in dollars); we would expect a greater size of issue to have a negative effect on spreads, because of the economies of spreading fixed costs over a larger issue.

The broker loan rate at the time of issue; we would expect a higher rate to mean higher costs of financing the underwriter's inventory and hence to have a positive effect on spreads.

A measure of uncertainty in the capital markets during the days immediately preceding the offering (as expressed by the average of the squares of the day-to-day changes in the closing value of the NASDAQ Over-the-Counter Index); we would expect greater uncertainty to have a positive influence on spreads.

An indicator of whether the issue was more complicated than straight equity; we would expect complicated issues to involve greater distribution efforts and hence to imply higher spreads.

An indicator of whether the underwriting was "best efforts" (as opposed to "firm commitment"); a best efforts arrangement involves less risk to the underwriter, but it usually involves much smaller, less well known and riskier ventures that entail greater distribution effort; thus, the effect on spreads, in principle, could go in either direction[51], but our prior notion would be that best efforts arrangements would involve higher spreads.

We also included two variables that were not cost-oriented[52]:

The distance (in miles) of the issuer's location of business from a major underwriting financial center[53]; we would expect distance to have a positive effect, because distance might discourage the larger, nationally oriented underwriters from being interested in a particular issuer, leaving the latter with a more limited choice of a few local (regional) underwriters (dealer-brokers); that is, distance could limit competition.

An indicator of whether the lead manager of the underwriting was one of the large, nationally oriented underwriting firms[54]; an explanation of the influence of this variable will be provided below.

The statistical method we used was that of ordinary least squares multiple regression. This method allows the influence of each explanatory variable to be expressed separately, while controlling for (holding constant) the influences of the other variables. All variables[55] were converted into natural logarithms, and the ordinary least squares regression computations were then performed on these transformed variables.[56]

The results of this statisical investigation are presented in Table 5.6. (The figures in parentheses are the t-statistics of the estimated effects, providing an indication of

Table 5.6   Results of Ordinary Least Squares Regression to Explain IPO Underwriting Spreads[a]

The Percentage Change in IPO Spreads that Would Accompany a 10% Change in:	
Size of issuer	-0.4%
	$(\ 3.89)^b$
Size of issue	-0.5%
	$(\ 3.57)^b$
Broker loan rate	$+0.4\%$
	$(\ 0.57)$
Market uncertainty	-0.1%
	$(\ 1.15)$
Distance of issuer from major financial center	$+0.01\%$
	$(\ 0.57)$
The Percentage Change in IPO Spreads that Would Accompany:	
Complicated issue	$+4.1\%$
	$(\ 1.99)^b$
Best efforts underwriting	$+2.6\%$
	$(\ 1.40)$
Leading underwriter	-10.3%
	$(\ 3.99)^b$
Fraction of Variance in IPO Spreads Explained by Variables in the Model (R^2):	0.56
Number of Observations	216

[a]Figures in parenthesis are t-statistics.
[b]Statistically significant at a 95% (or better) level of confidence (one-tailed test).

their statistical reliability.) As can be seen, our model provides a reasonable fit to the data. Over half (56%) of the variance in IPO spreads can be explained statistically by the variables we have selected. All of the variables except the market uncertainty variable[57] have the predicted signs; the size of issuer, size of issue, complicated issue, and leading underwriter variables are statistically significant.[58]

Accordingly, it is clear that cost factors play an important role in explaining IPO spreads. This result will surely come as no surprise to those who are familiar with underwriting, but the strength and consistency of the results does (we believe) lend credence to our overall methods and model.

An equally interesting result is that at least one noncost variable—whether or not the lead underwriter was one of the large, nationally oriented firms—is also statistically and quantitatively significant. (Although the distance variable has the predicted sign, its effects are not statistically or quantitatively significant. Accordingly, it does not appear that IPO issuers who are located in the boondocks suffer a significant disadvantage in the price they pay for underwriting solely because of their location.) If the underwriter was one of the leading firms, the spread would tend to be 10% smaller; that is, the typical spread in the sample, 9.0% (or 9¢ per dollar of equity issued) would be reduced to 8.1% (or 8.1¢ per dollar of equity issued). For the average issue size in the sample, $7.6 million, the saving to the issuer would be $71,000. It is worth noting that this finding of a negative effect on spreads by the presence of a leading underwriter is consistent with the previous results reported by other researchers.[59]

We can offer two possible explanations for this tendency of the leading underwriter to be associated with lower IPO spreads.[60] The first involves increased competition. If an IPO issuer has been able to attract the attention of a leading underwriter, he has (in essence) probably been able to create a more competitive environment for the underwriting of his issue; he is not limited to the (usually small number of) local, smaller broker-dealers who would otherwise be interested in the underwriting. This added competition (implicit or explicit in the negotiations of the issuer with potential underwriters) causes the price (spread) of the underwriting services to be lower.[61] This explanation is consistent with the findings (mentioned earlier) that the presence of three or more bidders for the underwriting of a public utility securities flotation causes a decrease in spreads and issuer costs.

If this explanation is correct, then our estimate of the effect of attracting the attention of a leading underwriter is likely to be less than the true value, because we were not able to observe the instances in which an issuer was able to attract the attention of one or more leading underwriters, generate the competition that would cause spreads to be lower, and then nevertheless choose a smaller underwriter. In those instances, we would be falsely associating the lower fee with the smaller underwriter, whereas it would actually be caused by the unobserved competition that had been generated. Also, our explanation should not be interpreted as implying that the lower underwriting fee associated with a leading underwriter is necessarily at the level that a perfectly competitive market would generate; we only infer that more competition leads to a lower price.

An alternative explanation is that the leading underwriters are selecting (are attracted to) particular IPO issuers who are, in some way that is not measured by our other variables, less risky or have other lower-cost attributes than the remaining IPO issuers in our sample.[62] (Recall that this effect could not be occurring purely through the effects of the sizes of the issuers or the sizes of the issues selected by the leading underwriters, because these effects have already been taken into account in our ordinary least squares regression methods.) This alternative explanation would imply that spreads are lower in these IPOs because the underwriting costs of these IPOs are lower.

We are not able, at this stage, to offer any way of distinguishing between the two explanations. Indeed, they are not mutually contradictory, and they both may be part of the reason that spreads are lower when leading underwriters are present. To the extent that the former explanation is valid, however, these results indicate that more vigorous competition among underwriters could, at least for IPOs, yield lower prices for underwriting services, with benefits accruing to IPO issuers. The lower costs of raising capital that would accompany more competition in underwriting would encourage more rapid growth and development of small and medium-size companies in the U.S. economy.

The Effects of Rule 415.   As was noted in the section entitled "Market Structure," Rule 415 (the "shelf registration" rule), which was approved by the Securities and Exchange Commission and went into effect in March 1982, simplifies the issuing procedures for large issuers of new securities. Issuers can file a formal registration statement for certain types of new or secondary issues with the SEC and then place the issue "on the shelf" for up to two years, pulling some or all of the issue "off the shelf" at any time during those two years and selling it at comparatively short notice. This simplification may have reduced costs to some extent; but even more important, it appears to have simplified the underwriting process. Once the issue is "on the shelf," issuers appear to be more capable of shopping around or of "holding an auction" among potential underwriters. The mirror image of this process is that potential underwriters, knowing which companies have issues "on the shelf," apparently have been more vigorous in offering their services and soliciting business.[63]

The SEC has conducted a number of studies of the effects of Rule 415 on spreads.[64] These studies have found a consistent, significant effect: Costs to issuers have been lower on both equity and debt offerings that have been issued under Rule 415, as compared with those that were not covered by Rule 415 (holding other important influences constant). The effect on equity spreads is estimated to be a drop of 1.06¢ per dollar of equity issued. For debt, the effect is a drop of 30–40 basis points in issuing costs. Most of this cost decrease is due to lower offering yields, but industrial bond issuers also paid $1.78 less in underwriting spread per $1,000 bond.

It appears that the increased vigor of competition among underwriters is responsible for at least part of these reduced spreads.[65] The objections of a number of underwriters to the continuation of Rule 415 appear, at least in part, to be based on their unhappiness with the new level of competition they have faced.[66] Again, this evidence provides support for an argument that competition among underwriters has not been as vigorous as it might be. It is worth noting that in December 1983, when the SEC made Rule 415 permanent, the Commission permitted it to apply only to the issues of large, established corporations. Thus, smaller, newer companies are less likely to benefit from the added competition that Rule 415 has brought.

Service Quality

In return for the fees charged, underwriters provide the array of services that have already been described. Like all other goods and services, underwriting services can be provided at greater or lesser quality levels. Poor service (low quality) at a "standard" price can represent as much of a loss to issuers (and provide rewards to the exercise of market power) as an excessively high price for a "standard" quality of service.

In competitive markets, we expect to see an array of quality levels, with higher prices attached to higher quality goods and services and lower prices attached lower qualities. It is usually hard to judge the appropriateness of the quality levels and the prices that are attached to them. This difficulty applies equally well to underwriting services.

There is, however, one area in which underwriting services appear to be of glaringly poor quality: *the underpricing of new issues.* As was discussed above, one of the important services of an underwriter is the pricing of an issue (either setting the initial offer price for an equity issue or setting an offering yield for a debt issue). If the underwriter sets a price (for an equity issue) that the market thinks is too high (or an offering yield for a debt issue that is too low), the underwriter will be unable to sell the issue at that price (or yield), and the underwriter (in a firm commitment underwriting) will suffer a loss. If the underwriter sets a price that the market thinks is too low (or a yield that is too high), issuers are deprived of proceeds (or are saddled with higher interest costs) that more accurate pricing would have provided. In these latter circumstances, the initial buyers of the security enjoy windfall gains, because the price of the security quickly rises to the price that the market thinks is appropriate.

Since 1960 (and possibly as early as the 1930s[67]), the underwriting industry has consistently, on average, *underpriced* new equity issues by substantial margins: On average, initial buyers of new equity issues have been able to resell their holdings, within a few days, and achieve substantial price increases. Ritter[68] found that, for the period January 1960 through December 1982, the average underpricing for all new issues was 18.8%. During periods of "hot" new issue markets, the average underpricing was *42.1%* (during the "hot" period of January 1980 through March 1981 the average underpricing was *48.4%*!); during periods of "cold" markets, the average underpricing was "only" 9.2%. Again, these data imply that, on average, issuers of new equity received revenues (from their underwriters) that were 18.8% less than the market indicated was possible.

The explanation for underpricing remains a puzzle to academic researchers. Among the hypotheses that have been advanced are the following[69]: Underpricing occurs because of extreme risk-aversion among underwriters, who are very reluctant to be caught with unsold issues that they have priced too high[70]; it occurs as a means of compensating investors for informing themselves about the comparative merits of various new issues and also as a means of keeping uninformed investors in the market[71]; and it occurs as an expression of market power by underwriters vis-à-vis issuers, in which they do not keep the underprice margins for themselves directly but instead provide it to favored customers or to other brokerage houses, in return for other favors received (such as other underpriced issues) at other times.[72]

We are not in a position to assess the merits of the alternative hypotheses. To the extent that the last hypothesis is valid, however, more vigorous competition in underwriting would clearly increase the returns to issuers. To the extent that the first hypothesis is correct, the extreme risk aversion may nevertheless be a ''taste'' that underwriters have the luxury of indulging in because of the absence of sufficiently vigorous competition among themselves[73]; if competition were to become more vigorous (and/or if new firms that might have a less strong ''taste'' in this direction could enter, and/or if the institutional arrangements of underwriting were to change, so that underwriters could price more flexibly), underpricing would diminish, and issuers would clearly benefit.

Profits

Over a medium- to long-run period, profits (measured as a rate of return on equity) in a competitive industry should roughly equal profits in other competitive industries, allowing for differential degrees of risk. Profits (risk-adjusted) in an industry that are persistently above those of other industries are likely to be due to the exercise of market power—the maintenance of prices above long-run marginal costs—by firms in that industry, buttressed by barriers to the entry of new firms that would otherwise be attracted to the high profits and would otherwise drive the prices (and profits) down to competitive levels.

Unfortunately, the available data do not allow us to conclude anything definitively concerning the profitability of underwriting. Although it is frequently alleged that underwriting has been a highly profitable activity for the firms who engage in it,[74] there are no good data to allow us to verify this claim. All underwriters also engage in other aspects of the securities business, and only consolidated financial data for these firms are available. For the consolidated industry, underwriting revenues have typically accounted for 10% or less of overall revenues of these firms, so that it is impossible to extract much that is meaningful about underwriting profitability from the consolidated data.

Nevertheless, we believe it is worth noting that the securities industry's activities overall (of which underwriting has been a part) have been profitable. As Table 5.7 shows, for the nine years 1974–1982,[75] the firms in the securities industry earned a 15.0% average return on stockholders' equity[76]; during the same period, all manufacturing corporations earned an average return of 13.6%. For a shorter period, comparisons can also be made with the rates of return on equity earned by commercial banks; again, as Table 5.7 indicates, the profitability of the securities industry has been somewhat higher. It seems unlikely that underwriting has been a serious burden on the profitability of the securities industry.

Table 5.7   Rates of Return on Equity for the Securities Industry, for All
Manufacturing Corporations, and for Commercial Banks

	Securities Industry	All Manufacturing Corporations	All Insured Commerical Banks	Largest 25 Commercial Banks
1974	0.7%	14.9%	—	—
1975	16.6	11.6	—	—
1976	17.6	13.9	—	—
1977	6.9	14.2	11.8%	11.8%
1978	10.9	15.0	12.9	13.8
1979	15.6	16.4	13.9	—
1980	25.7	13.9	13.7	14.6
1981	18.9	13.6	13.2	13.9
1982	21.8	9.2	12.2	12.8
Average				
1974–82:	15.0	13.6	—	—
1977–82:	16.6	13.7	13.0	—
1977–78,				
80–82:	16.8	13.2	12.8	13.4

Sources: Securities Industry Association, *Securities Industry Yearbook,* various years (New York). U.S. Council of Economic Advisers, *Annual Report,* February 1984 (Washington, D.C.), p. 319. U.S. Department of Commerce, Bureau of Industrial Economics, *U.S. Industrial Outlook,* various issues (Washington, D.C.). Standard and Poors, Industry Surveys, *Banking and Other Financial Services, Basic Analysis,* various issues (New York).

THE LIKELY EFFECTS OF ENTRY BY COMMERCIAL BANK AFFILIATES

A Review of Structure-Behavior-Performance in Corporate Underwriting

A brief review of the structure, behavior, and performance in the underwriting of corporate securities can provide a basis for the following discussion of the likely effects of entry by commercial bank affiliates.

The market for underwriting the securities of large (e.g., Fortune 1000) companies is moderately concentrated, with the leading four underwriters together accounting for 40–50% of underwritings. The effective market may be yet more concentrated, because of the specialization among investment banking firms and the differing needs of differing issuers. Small and medium-size issuers may face a more restricted set of providers of services; if these issuers cannot attract the attention of one or more of the leading (usually, New York-based) underwriters, they may choose among only a handful of local (regional) broker-dealers. The effective concentration facing these issuers may be quite high.

Barriers to entry consist of the necessity to develop a network of contacts and distributional outlets, the establishment of reputation and prestige (customer loyalty), and the need to attract skilled personnel—plus the glaring barrier of Glass-Steagall's prohibition on commercial bank entry.

The service (or package of services) provided by underwriters is a complicated one; customers (issuers) may have a difficult time judging quality in making pricing comparisons among underwriters. But many of the customers are large corporations that have (or are acquiring) the financial expertise to make their own judgments and to shop around.

Fees appear to be related to cost factors in the industry. But some fees appear to have been unduly stable over long periods of time. And issuers who attract more competition to their issues appear to achieve lower underwriting fees (as indicated by the empirical evidence presented above and by the experience under Rule 415). These latter pieces of evidence indicate that competition in parts of the underwriting industry is not as vigorous as it might be. Further, the industry has a consistent tendency to underprice new issues—to the loss and detriment of issuers.

Finally, profits in the securities industry generally have been healthy, but specific information about the profitability of underwriting is not available.

The Effects of Entry on Competition

In general, the presence of more competitors in a market is not likely to harm the competitive process and may increase the vigor of competition, with better results for customers. The general case in favor of competition was outlined earlier—lower prices, greater efficiency, better service—and this argument should be equally valid for the entry of commercial banks into corporate underwriting.

The case of more competitors should not be overstated. If a market is already quite competitive, an increase in the number of sellers in the market may not make much difference. A few more producers of wheat are not likely to have a great effect on the wheat market.

Is corporate underwriting like the wheat market? The data on structure, behavior, and performance indicate otherwise. There do appear to be deficiencies in the competitive process for corporate underwriting. And, even for the wheat market, if one group of potential producers (who might have lower costs or superior technologies or innovative ideas) were systematically excluded from the market, we would have less confidence that the entry of those producers would have no effect on the market.

The entry of commercial bank affiliates would likely have a significant pro-competitive effect on corporate underwriting. Commercial banks have many of the characteristics that would allow them to become significant competitors. The large bank holding companies in financial centers would have the financial resources, reputation and prestige, network of contacts, and familiarity and experience in underwriting (from their experience in underwriting government general obligation bonds and, in some cases, Eurobonds) to compete with the current underwriters' offerings to large issuers. Commercial bank holding companies are the most likely candidates to offer competition in the market "niches" that were described in the section on "Market Structure." Smaller, regional commercial bank holding companies should also be capable of providing new competition to regional broker-dealers in offering underwriting services to small and medium-size companies. It should be noted that the beneficial effects on competition can arise even if most commercial banking organizations do not actually enter corporate underwriting. Just the knowledge that a firm may enter can serve to keep a market more competitive. With over 14,000 commercial banks in operation in the United States, the increase in the number of actual or potential competitors would be substantial.

Further, beyond the purely competitive aspects of commercial bank entry, there are two additional reasons why the presence of commercial bank affiliates should improve the prices received by equity issuers and decrease the issuing cost of debt issuers.[77] First, as we have noted above, the markets for securities, especially new securities, are ones of imperfect information; potential investors have imperfect information about securities issuers, and underwriters have imperfect information about who the potential investors for a new issue would be. With more search, more information can be gained, but search is costly. The addition of a new group of underwriters (commercial bank affiliates), with different contacts, customers, and information, should increase the potential market for any issue. Second, to the extent that commercial bank affiliates become additional market makers in particular securities issues, bid-ask spreads in those securities are likely to decline.[78] This decline in bid-ask spreads improves the liquidity of a security, which should improve investor interest in the security and thus increase the potential market for the issue.

Unfortunately, we cannot offer any quantitative estimate of the magnitudes of the beneficial effects of entry by commercial bank affiliates; there are no data that would support specific estimates. But we are quite confident of the direction of change: toward lower spreads and improved service and performance for issuers. Our confidence stems from two sources: (1) the evidence on concentration and behavior that have already been discussed; and (2) the evidence from a "natural experiment" that has occurred in a similar area: the underwriting of state and local government securities.

The Glass-Steagall Act allows commercial banks to underwrite the general obligation securities of state and local governments, but not the revenue bonds of these governments. Thus comparisons of underwriting fees and other issuer costs in these two areas (general obligation versus revenue), controlling for other influences, provides some strong inferences as to the likely effects of the presence of commercial banks in an underwriting market. Silber, surveying the available evidence, concluded that the evidence strongly supports the proposition that the presence of commercial banks in general obligation underwriting causes spreads to be significantly smaller and issuer costs to be significantly lower:

A rather pleasant surprise emerged from the empirical studies that were surveyed . . . Statistically significant impacts of bank eligibility on municipal borrowing costs emerged from virtually every research effort . . .

A rough idea of the magnitude of the savings to muncipalities that might follow bank underwriting of revenues was derived from various empirical studies . . . A . . . range of between $150 million and $300 million a year of savings to issuers is . . . the most likely impact. This range translates into a reduction of between 6.7 and 13.3 basis points, or in other words 1.1 to 2.2 percent of borrowing costs when municipal bond yields are at a 6 percent level.[79]

A survey of new studies published since Silber's review does not cause us to alter his general conclusions.[80] We see no reasons why similar results would not also occur in the underwriting of corporate securities.

Are There Potential Problems from Commercial Bank Entry?

It is sometimes claimed that entry by commercial bank affiliates into underwriting would harm performance in the market for underwriting rather than improve it or that entry would have a deleterious effect on bank behavior in other dimensions. We do not believe these objections have validity. We will deal with each in turn.

Predatory Behavior.   It is sometimes alleged that bank affiliates would engage in predatory behavior (e.g., charge excessively low prices or fees for their services), so as to drive out the competition, and then (when only one or a few banks remain) raise prices to reap high profits.

This scenario would make sense only if a commercial bank affiliate could be confident that little actual or potential competition would remain after the predatory actions. This outcome does not seem likely. The large underwriters are unlikely to be driven entirely from underwriting or to be reluctant to reenter if profitable opportunities arose. Further, predatory behavior clearly has not occurred in the areas (such as general obligation bond underwriting and private placements) where commercial banks currently compete with investment banks,[81] nor has it occurred in the areas where commercial banks compete among themselves. Further, the antitrust laws (notably, Section 2 of the Sherman Act) could be used by the injured parties or by the Justice Department to prevent such behavior. We thus consider such action most unlikely.

Tying.   It is sometimes feared that a commercial bank will tie its business loans to the requirement (or the strong suggestion) that the loan recipient also give its underwriting business to the bank's securities affiliate. This tying would allow commercial banks unfairly to monopolize underwriting.

Again, this scenario has little validity. To effect a tie, the tying party must have market power in the tying good (the commercial loan). But the structures of many loan markets (e.g., the national market for loans to large corporations; the markets in metropolitan areas for loans to medium-size companies) are reasonably competitive, and it is unlikely that a commercial bank would have the ability to tie underwriting to loans; the customer could easily go elsewhere for the loan. Further, even if a bank has market power in the loan market, it could usually extract the full monopoly profits through the interest charged on the loan.[82] There would be no increased "leverage" that it could use to extract extra profits in the underwriting market.[83]

By contrast, tying, in some instances, can serve a pro-competitive function in protecting goodwill or otherwise dealing with informational deficiencies or externalities in goods and services.[84] We are not sure whether tying might occur in underwriting for such reasons, but we believe that it is unlikely to occur for anticompetitive reasons. And, again, the antitrust laws (Section 3 of the Clayton Act) could be used to prevent anticompetitive tying.

Conflicts of Interest. It is sometimes alleged that corporate securities underwriting will create conflicts of interest for commercial banks. Either the bank will unwisely make loans to a shaky company whose securities its affiliate has underwritten, or it will shore up the shaky company by underwriting new securities (to protect or pay off the loans it has made to the company) and not provide the investing public with an accurate appraisal of the company's financial health.[85]

We do not believe that such potential conflicts of interest are appreciably different from those that are currently present in commercial banks and investment banks and that are not now considered to be serious problems. ''Chinese walls,'' plus the concern of institutions for their established reputations, appear to be adequate to handle the potential problems. We believe that the same would be true for corporate securities underwriting by commercial bank affiliates.[86]

Commercial Bank Safety and Soundness. It is sometimes alleged that the safety and soundness of commercial banks would be endangered by their entry into corporate underwriting.[87]

Again, we do not find this claim convincing. The safety and soundness of commercial banks do not seem to have been endangered by their participations in general obligation government bond underwriting. Further, corporate securities underwriting, as it is currently practiced, is certainly not very risky. Syndicates help share risk. Fees are healthy. And the current practice of underpricing offerings—both new issues (by an average of 18.8%!) and issues of seasoned issuers[88]—means that the risk is small that a bank affiliate will be caught with a sizable position in a security that has fallen significantly in price.[89] Even with the effects of the increased competition that we predict would accompany commercial bank affiliate entry (which would decrease spreads and reduce underpricing), the risks to bank affiliate underwriters still would not be great, and the sizes of the possible losses averaged over any reasonable period, relative to the sizes of banking organizations likely to engage in underwriting, would be unlikely to endanger any significant number of commercial banks.[90]

Fairness

It is sometimes claimed that, efficiency or competitive issues aside, it would simply be unfair or inequitable to allow commercial bank affiliates to enter corporate securities underwriting—that commercial banks have an unfair advantage of some sort.

Notions of fairness are frequently quite subjective, and we are not sure that we have much to contribute to this area. But we can put some arguments concerning fairness in perspective.

First, as we argued above, one possible source of unfairness—tying—is unlikely to arise for anticompetitive or monopolistic reasons.

Second, contrary to frequent allegations, commercial banks' access to low-cost funds through their deposit-taking functions does not give them an unfair advantage in competing with other financial institutions. A profit-seeking banking organization, in considering whether to undertake an activity and how to price it, will make its decisions on the basis of its *marginal cost* (or opportunity cost) of funds. And that marginal cost applies to funds attracted or lent at the margin—usually involving relatively high-cost funds obtained through the financial markets. Thus the *opportunity cost* of undertaking the activity in question would be the granting of a loan to a potential customer who is currently turned away, lending the funds in the financial markets, or obtaining fewer funds from the financial markets. In this important sense, the marginal costs of banking organizations are roughly comparable to those of other comparably-sized institutions,[91] and banking organizations do not possess a special or unfair advantage at the margin in undertaking other activities or competing with other financial institutions.[92]

This argument applies with equal validity to underwriting. Further, the cost of funds is a small component of underwriting costs (because underwriters normally finance an issue for only a short period of time), so any cost-of-funds advantage would not bulk large in a commercial bank affiliate's underwriting behavior.

Third, a commercial bank affiliate may have genuine efficiencies ("economies of scope"), such as the sharing of costs with their other bank activities, that would allow the bank to provide underwriting services at lower cost. We do not believe that such efficiencies should be considered an unfair advantage that commercial banks should not be allowed to exploit. To the contrary, they represent a genuine productivity and efficiency gain for the economy that should be encouraged.

Fourth, the past few years have seen the entry of investment banks (and other entities that are not commercial banks) into the area of commerical banking services, through the establishment of "nonbank banks" that make consumer loans, the expansion of consumer credit operations, the expansion of commercial credit operations, and the offering of checking-account-type services. For the same basic reasons that we favor commercial bank affiliate entry into corporate underwriting we also applaud this entry from the opposite direction. In this new era of expanded financial services and "one-stop financial shopping," we do not believe it unreasonable or unfair to allow commercial banks to enter corporate underwriting.

Finally, we are not sure how large the quantitative impact ("market share") of commercial bank affiliates in corporate underwriting would be. But that share is likely to be won through superior efficiency and innovative services. In a private enterprise economy, such competition, and the gains from such competition, should not be considered unfair.

CONCLUSION

The entry of commercial bank affiliates into the underwriting of corporate securities would provide valuable new competition in this area. Lower spreads and improved services, including better pricing of issues—in sum, lower costs of and superior opportunities for raising capital for issuers—would be the likely result, with benefits spreading throughout the U.S. economy. The possible drawbacks to such entry are minor and can be easily remedied.

The removal of unnecessary regulatory barriers and the consequent increased competitive vigor in markets are significant means of achieving the improvements in efficiency and productivity that are always important in an economy and are especially important for the American economy of the 1980s. Amending the Glass-Steagall Act to permit commercial bank affiliates to underwrite corporate securities would be a significant step toward this goal.

NOTES

[1] The historical reasons for this separation are complex and cannot be addressed in this chapter. More complete discussions of the history of Glass-Steagall are found in Flannery, ''An Economic Evaluation of Bank Securities Activities Before 1933,'' chapter 4 of this book; Golembe Associates, ''Commercial Banks and Investment Banks.'' Prepared for the Economics and Financial Research Division of the ABA, November 29, 1976; and Perkins, ''The Divorce of Commercial Banking: A History,'' *Banking Law Journal*, **88** (June 1971), pp. 483–528.

[2] Any standard microeconomics text provides the full theoretical structure that supports the case for competition. See, for example, Michael Bradley, *Microeconomics*. (Glenview, Ill.: Scott Foresman, 1980).

[3] For a more complex discussion, see Francis M. Bator, ''The Anatomy of Market Failure,'' *Quarterly Journal of Economics*, **72** (August 1958), pp. 351–379.

[4] See Steven Salop and Joseph Stiglitz, ''Bargains and Ripoffs,'' *Review of Economic Studies*, **44** (October 1977), pp. 493–510; Mark A. Satterthwaite, ''Consumer Information, Equilibrium Industry Price, and the Number of Sellers,'' *Bell Journal of Economics*, **10** (Autumn 1979), pp. 483–502; Alan Schwartz and Louis L. Wilde, ''Competitive Equilibria in Markets for Heterogeneous Goods Under Imperfect Information: A Theoretical Analysis with Policy Implications,'' *Bell Journal of Economics*, **13** (Spring 1982), pp. 181–183; and George A. Ackerlof, ''The Market of 'Lemons': Quality Uncertainty and the Market Mechanism,'' *Quarterly Journal of Economics*, **84** (August 1970), pp. 488–500.

[5] For a more complete discussion, see F. M. Scherer, *Industrial Market Structure and Economic Performance*, 2d ed. (Chicago: Rand McNally, 1980).

[6] For a summary of these differences, see Harvey J. Goldschmid et al. (eds.), *Industrial Concentration: The New Learning*. (Boston: Little, Brown, 1974).

[7] Samuel L. Hayes III et al., *Competition in the Investment Banking Industry*. (Cambridge, Mass.: Harvard University Press, 1983), also consider these to be the most important of the related services offered by investment banks.

[8] By 1982, over 4,000 commercial banks provided some form of brokerage services, in addition to their trust activities, and the number has grown since then.

[9] As reported in Ernest Bloch, ''Investment Banking,'' Graduate School of Business Administration, New York University, 1983.

[10] Matthew Clark and Anthony Saunders, ''Glass-Steagall Revisited: The Impact on Banks, Capital Markets, and the Smaller Investor,'' *Banking Law Journal*, 97 (October 1980), pp. 811–840.

[11] See Chapter 10.

[12] For example, Richard S. Bower, Dennis E. Logue, and Robert A. Jarrow, ''The Investment Banking Industry: A Preliminary Report on Its Structure and Competitiveness,'' Amos Tuck School of Business Administration, Dartmouth College, April 1979.

[13] For example, Clifford Smith, Jr., ''Alternative Methods for Raising Capital: Rights versus Underwritten Offerings,'' *Journal of Financial Economics*, **5** (December 1977), pp. 273–307.

[14]See Hayes et al., *Competition in Banking*.

[15]See Ervin Miller, "Background and Structure of the Industry," in Irwin Friend et al., *Investment Banking and the New Issues Market*. (Cleveland, World Publishing, 1967), pp. 80–175.

[16]The level of concentration at which this likelihood increases substantially is called the critical level of concentration. For a recent analysis of this issue, see Ralph M. Bradburd and A. Mead Over, Jr., "Organizational Costs, 'Sticky Equilibria' and Critical Levels of Concentration," *Review of Economics and Statistics*, **64** (February 1982), pp. 50–58.

[17]Ervin Miller, "Background and Structure of the Industry," in Irwin Friend et al., *Investment Banking and the New Issues Market*. (Cleveland: World Publishing, 1967), pp. 80–175, noted the trend toward declining concentration in the earlier period.

[18]Hayes et al., *Competition in Banking*, chap. 2.

[19]This is opposite to the relationship noted by Miller, "Background and Structure," who found that concentration in competitive bid underwriting was much higher than that found in negotiated underwriting, from the mid-1930s into the 1960s.

[20]In contrast, Miller, "Background and Structure," found that concentration was substantially higher in the underwriting of debt, from the mid-1930s into the 1960s.

[21]A bank can earn a share of these gross spread revenues by participating in the underwriting syndicate, without necessarily being a manager.

[22]For instance, firms smaller than the top 25 earned 48% of these revenues in 1971 and 33% in 1975, according the SEC *Staff Report on the Securities Industry in 1980*.

[23]Lack of data prevented separate consideration of negotiated and competitive bid underwritings.

[24]For a discussion, see Jonathan D. Ogur, "Competition and Market Share Instability," *Staff Report to the Federal Trade Commission*, Bureau of Economics, August 1976.

[25]Indeed, the latter two firms were in the top five in the mid-1930s.

[26]See Hayes, et al., *Competition in Banking*, Table 1.

[27]U.S. Securities and Exchange Commission and U.S. small Business Administration, *The Role of Regional Broker-Dealers in the Capital Formation Process: Underwriting, Market-Making and Securities Research Activities*. Phase II Report. (Washington, D.C.: August 1981), p. 13.

[28]For an empirical analysis of these propositions, see Howard H. Newman, "Strategic Groups and the Structure-Performance Relationship," *Review of Economics and Statistics*, 60 (August 1978), pp. 417–427.

[29]The national full-line firms were previously called national wire-houses.

[30]Samuel L. Hayes III, "Investment Banking: Power Structure in Flux," *Harvard Business Review*, **57** (January–February 1979), pp. 153–170.

[31]The discussion of entry barriers into distribution is based largely on the conclusions of Hayes, et al., *Competition in Banking*.

[32]See George J. Stigler, "A Theory of Oligopoly," *Journal of Political Economy*, **72** (February 1964), pp. 44–61.

[33]See Salop and Stiglitz, "Bargains and Ripoffs;" Satterthwaite, "Consumer Information;" and Schwartz and Wilde, "Competitive Equilibria."

[34]See Stigler, "A theory of Oligopoly."

[35]Letter from Mr. John C. Whitehead, Goldman Sachs, to the SEC, September 12, 1983 (SEC File No. S7-979).

[36]*Wall Street Journal*, "Salomon Brothers Led Competitors in '83 with $15.76 Billion in U.S. Underwritings," January 6, 1984.

[37]Letter from Mr. John C. Whitehead, Goldman Sachs, to the SEC, September 12, 1983 (SEC File No. S7-979), and *Wall Street Journal*, "Salomon Brothers."

[38]*Wall Street Journal*, "Salomon Brothers."

[39]Letter from Mr. John C. Whitehead, Goldman Sachs, to the SEC September 12, 1983 (SEC File No. S7-979).

[40]Letter from Mr. Robert E. Linton and Mr. Edward I. O'Brien, Securities Industry Association, to the SEC, September 12, 1983 (SEC File No. S7-979).

[41]Attachment to the letter from Mr. Jeffrey M. Schaefer, Securities Industry Association, to the SEC, September 16, 1983 (SEC File No. S7-979).

[42]See Hans R. Stoll, "The Pricing of Underwritten Offerings of Listed Common Stocks and the Compensation of Underwriters," *Journal of Economics and Business,* 28 (Winter 1976), pp. 96–103; Dennis E. Logue, "On the Pricing of Unseasoned Equity Issues: 1956–1969," *Journal of Financial and Quantitative Analysis,* 8 (January 1973), pp. 91–103; Frank J. Fabozzi and Richard R. West, "Negotiated versus Competitive Underwritings of Public Utility Bonds: Just One More Time," *Journal of Financial and Quantitative Analysis,* 16 (September 1981), pp. 323–339; Edward A. Dyl and Michael D. Joehnk, "Competitive versus Negotiated Underwriting of Public Utility Debt," *Bell Journal of Economics,* 7 (Autumn 1976), pp. 680–689; George G. C. Parker and Daniel Cooperman, "Competitive Bidding in the Underwriting of Public Utility Securities," *Journal of Financial and Quantitative Analysis,* 13 (December 1978), pp. 885–902; Gary D. Tallman et al., "Competitive versus Negotiated Underwriting Costs for Regulated Industries," *Financial Management,* 4 (Summer 1974), pp. 49–55; Dennis E. Logue and John R. Lindvall, "The Behavior of Investment Bankers: An Econometric Investigation," *Journal of Finance,* 29 (March 1974), pp. 203–215; Keith B. Johnson et al., "An Empirical Analysis of the Flotation Cost of Corporate Securities, 1971–1972," *Journal of Finance,* 30 (September 1975), pp. 1124–1133; M. Chapman Findley et al., "An Analysis of the Flotation Cost of Utility Bonds, 1971–1976," *Journal of Financial Research,* 2 (Fall 1979), pp. 133–142. Louis J. Ederington, "Uncertainty, Competition, and Costs in Corporate Bond Underwriting," *Journal of Financial Economics,* 2 (March 1975), pp. 71–94; Eric H. Sorenson, "The Impact of Underwriting Method and Bidder Competition Upon Corporate Bond Interest Cost," *Journal of Finance,* 34 (September 1979), pp. 863–869; Morris Mendelson, "Underwriting Compensation," in Irwin Friend et al., *Investment Banking and the New Issues Market.* (Cleveland: World Publishing, 1967), pp. 394–479; and Louis H. Ederington, "Negotiated versus Competitive Bidding for Corporate Bonds," *Journal of Finance,* 31 (March 1976), pp. 12–28.

[43]To the extent that individuals are risk averse, they will be willing to bear extra risk only if they are provided with extra compensation. It is in this sense that we categorize risk as a cost.

[44]See Ian H. Giddy, "Is Equity Underwriting Risky for Commercial Banks?" Chapter 6 of this book.

[45]Any price-cost differential comparisons always face, among other difficulties, the severe problem of allocating joint costs to different products or services.

[46]See Hayes, "Transformation of Banking Industry," and Mendelson, "Underwriting Compensation," p. 408.

[47]See Ederington, "Negotiated versus Competitive Bidding;" and Fabozzi and West, "Negotiated versus Competitive Underwritings."

[48]For other studies of IPOs, see Ibid.; Logue, "Pricing of Equity;" Logue and Lindvall, "Behavior of Bankers;" U.S. SEC-SBA, *The Role of Regional Broker-Dealers;* and U.S. Small Business Administration and U.S. Securities and Exchange Commission, *Initial Public Offerings of Common Stock: The Role of Regional Broker-Dealers in the Capital Formation Process.* Phase I Report. (Washington, D.C.: March 1980).

[49]See Jay R. Ritter, "The 'Hot Issue' Market of 1980," *Journal of Business,* 57 (April 1984), pp. 215–240.

[50]Data on sales revenues were not available for enough firms to allow sales to be the measure of size; all financial firms were dropped from the sample because the assets of a financial firm may stand in a different relationship to the firm's activities than is true of nonfinancial firms. In order to minimize the effects of reporting data on the reported size of assets (while also trying to keep the sample size as large as possible), we chose the first reported assets in the 12 months following the issue. This procedure means that the size of the issue itself affected reported asset size, but the procedure does not appear to have affected our results. (For a much smaller sample of 137 observations we were able to use pre-issue assets, and for a yet smaller sample of 123 observations we were able to use pre-issue sales. The results of those regressions were quite similar to those reported in the text below.) In four instances, the only reported assets data available were for a pre-issue date, whereas in three instances the only reported assets data were for a date in 1982 that was more than 12 months after the date of issue. A separate 0,1 dummy variable was used for each of these

special categories; the coefficients on these variables were not significant and are not reported in Table 5.6.

[51]See Mendelson, "Underwriting Compensation," pp. 443–444.

[52]Dummy variables (0,1) were also included originally if the issuer was involved in "hot" industries: electronics, energy, or medical services; also, a dummy variable was originally applied to issues in the first quarter of 1981, because this was supposed to be part of a "hot" market; see Ritter, "The 'Hot Issues' Market." None of these dummy variables showed any statistical significance, and all were dropped from subsequent analyses. The coefficients on the reported variables were not appreciably different in the equations containing these dummy variables.

[53]The financial centers were New York, Boston, Chicago, Atlanta, Houston, Los Angeles, and San Francisco. This list was taken from Hayes et al.; *Competition in Banking*, p. 129. Distance from New York only was also tried, with similar results.

[54]The list of the leading 25 underwriters in 1979, provided by Hayes et al., *Competition in Banking*, p. 130, was used.

[55]With the exception of the "presence or absence" variables, which took the form of 0,1 dummy variables.

[56]This method dampens the effects of extreme observations and allows the coefficients of the regression to be expressed in terms of the percentage effects of percentage changes in the variables (elasticities). It assumes that the unexplained portions of the dependent variable (spreads)—the "error terms"—are distributed log-normally. Alternative specifications involving only natural numbers or a mix of natural and logarithmic numbers were also tried, with the same basic results.

[57]It may be that the measure we chose to capture market uncertainty—the squared day-to-day percentage changes in the NASDAQ OTC index for the five days before the offering date—does not adequately capture the true uncertainty that underwriters face.

[58]Although the coefficient for the broker loan rate has the proper sign, it is statistically insignificant. Because underwriters typically have to finance the issue for only a few days, the lack of significance for this variable is not a serious failing of the model.

[59]See Mendelson, "Underwriting Compensation;" Logue and Lindvall, "Behavior of Bankers;" and Stoll, "Pricing of Offerings."

[60]If there were a "brand name" or high-quality effect from the presence of a leading underwriter, a positive effect on spreads would be expected. The negative effects that were found rule out this explanation.

[61]Mendelson, "Underwriting Compensation," and Stoll, "Pricing of Offerings," hypothesize that this effect occurs because the large underwriters have lower costs, due to economics of scale. We are unable to shed any light on this question. But the important point is that the issuer has been able to attract the attention of the large underwriter and thus benefits from the lower spread.

[62]For example, the leading underwriter might have taken a venture capital position in the issuer at an earlier date; in this case, the issuer would be better known to the underwriter and hence less risky. In a separate statistical investigation, we attempted to explain which underwriters (large versus small) would tend to underwrite an issue, using ordinary least squares, probit, and logit analysis. The only statistically significant explanatory variables were the size of the issue and the size of the issuer; other characteristics of the issuer (such as industry type) or issue (degree of complexity) were not significant. Approximately a third of the variance in the dependent variable could be explained.

It might be that a leading underwriter would offer a lower spred, thus gaining the issuer's business, but then underprice the issue by a greater extent than is the norm (see the text below), leaving the issuer on net no better (or perhaps even worse) off. We were able to test for this possibility with a smaller sample of 77 issues for which trading price data were available for the days following the date of issue. There was no significant correlation between the tendency of a leading underwriter to underwrite the issue and the extent of underpricing.

[63]See Beth McGoldrick, "Life with Rule 415," *Institutional Investor,* 17 (February 1982), pp. 129–133.

[64]See M. Wayne Marr and G. Rodney Thompson, "Shelf Registration and the Utility Industry," Department of Finance, Virginia Polytechnic Institute and State University, June 3, 1983; "The Rule 415 Experiment: Equity Markets" (SEC File No. S7-979, Sept. 8, 1983), and "Summary of 'Rule 415—The Ultimate Competitive Bid' " (SEC File No. S7-979, June 30, 1983).

[65]Some of the decrease in spreads may be due to the reduced level of services (and hence reduced costs) provided by the underwriter. It is worth noting that the reduced spreads have occurred despite the increase in concentration noted in the section on "Market Structure." This result provides a clear instance in which a change in institutional arrangements that allows buyers to shop among sellers more effectively has more than offset any effects that the concommitant increase in concentration might bring.

[66]See, for example, the letters by the Securities Industry Association (September 12, 1983) and by Merrill Lynch Capital Markets (September 12, 1983) to the SEC, commenting on Rule 415 (SEC File No. S7-979). The underwriting industry's objections to Rule 415 have much of the flavor of the industry's objections in the 1930s to competitive bidding. See Vincent P. Carosso, *Investment Banking in America: A History.* (Cambridge, Mass.: Harvard University Press, 1970), chap. 20.

[67]Ibid., p. 442.

[68]Jay R. Ritter, "The 'Hot Issue' Market of 1980," Wharton School, University of Pennsylvania, September 1982; "The 'Hot Issue' Market of 1980," *Journal of Business,* **57** (April 1984), pp. 215–240.

[69]It is also sometimes claimed that issuers like the fact that their equity price rises immediately, because this rise may make it easier for them to float equity in the future. This claim confuses the very short-term and any longer-term period. Issuers surely want to see their equity price rise over the long-term, because this rise reflects the market's confidence in the company's long-term prospects; such confidence does make the future issuance of equity easier. But the immediate price rise after an offering is simply a loss of potential revenues to the issuer.

[70]Barbara Goody Katz and Joel Owen. "Initial Public Offerings: An Equilibrium Model of Price Determination," Faculty of Business Administration, New York University, Working Paper #83–69, July 1983.

[71]See Harvey Leibenstein, "Allocative Efficiency vs. X-Efficiency," *American Economic Review,* 66 (June 1966), pp. 392–415, for an explanation of this "x-inefficiency" theory of behavior.

[72]Kevin R. Rock, "Why New Issues Are Underpriced," Ph.D. dissertation, University of Chicago, 1982.

[73]Richard R. West, "More On the Effects of Municipal Bond Monopsony," *Journal of Business,* **39** (April 1966), pp. 304–308.

[74]See Hayes, "Investment Banking"; "Transformation of Investment Banking"; and Neil Osborn, "What Happens After Glass-Steagall?" *Institutional Investor,* 16, (February 1928), pp. 67–78.

[75]Comparable data are not available for the manufacturing profit rates before 1974; it should be noted that the securities industry earned a negative profit in 1973, which would lower its 10-year average.

[76]Payments to partners (which include a component of true profits) are an important component of overall returns in the securities industry.

[77]These arguments are discussed by William L. Silber, *Municipal Revenue Bond Costs and Bank Underwriting: A Survey of the Evidence.* Salomon Brothers Center for the Study of Financial Institutions, Graduate School of Business Administration, New York University, Monograph Series in Finance and Economics, Monograph #1979–3, in the context of municipal bond underwriting; they are equally valid for corporate security underwriting.

[78]See George J. Benston and Robert L. Hagerman, "Determinants of Bid-Asked Spreads in the Over-the-Counter Market," *Journal of Financial Economics,* 1 (December 1974), pp. 353–364.

[79]Silber, *Municipal Revenue Bonds,* p. 45.

[80]See Robert J. Rogowski, "Underwriting Competition and Issuer Borrowing Costs in the Municipal Revenue Bond Market," *Journal of Bank Research,* **11** (Winter 1980), pp. 212–220; Benson et al., "Systematic Variation in Yield Spreads for Tax-Exempt General Obligation Bonds," *Journal of Financial and Quantitative Analysis,* **16** (December 1981), pp. 685–702; Robert M. Nauss and Bradford R. Keeler, "Optimizing Municipal Bond Bids," *Journal of Bank Research,* 12 (Autumn 1981), pp. 174–181; David S. Kidwell and Timothy V. Koch, "Why and When Do Revenue Bonds Yield More Than GOs?" *Journal of Portfolio Management,* **8** (Summer 1982), pp. 51–56; Kidwell and Koch, "The Behavior of the Interest Rate Differential Between Tax-Exempt Revenue and General Obligation Bonds: A Test of Risk Preferences and Market Segmentation," *Journal of Finance,* **37** (March 1982), pp. 63–73; Paul A. Leonard, "Some Factors Determining Municipal Bond Interest Costs," *Journal of Economics and Business,* **35** (1983), pp. 71–82; Ronald C. Braswell et al., "A Comparison of the True Interest Costs of Competitive and Negotiated

Underwritings in the Municipal Bond Market,'' *Journal of Money, Credit, and Banking,* **15** (February 1983), pp. 102–106; and George G. Kaufman, ''Municipal Bond Underwriting: Market Structure,'' *Journal of Bank Research,* **12** (Spring 1981), pp. 23–31.

[81]See Richard M. Levich, ''A View from the International Capital Markets,'' chapter 10 of this book.

[82]See Richard A. Posner, *Antitrust Law: An Economics Perspective.* Chicago: University of Chicago Press, 1976, pp. 161–184.

[83]Tying may be a means by which a firm with market power can practice price discrimination, through ''metering'' the demands of its customers. But ''metering'' would be operative in instances in which two close complements are tied, such as a tabulating machine company's tying punch cards to its machines. (See Meyer L. Burstein, ''A Theory of Full-Line Forcing,'' *Northwestern University Law Review,* **55** [1960–1961], pp. 62–95). Underwriting and commercial loans do not appear to be likely candidates for ''metering.''

[84]See Posner, *Antitrust Law,* pp. 161–184.

[85]See Anthony Saunders, ''Conflict of Interest: An Economic View,'' chapter 8 of this book.

[86]But, for a cautionary note on the dangers of separate subsidiaries, see Franklin R. Edwards, ''Banks and Securities: Legal and Economic Perspectives on the Glass-Steagall Act,'' in Lawrence G. Goldberg and Lawrence J. White (eds.), *The Deregulation of the Banking and Securities Industries.* (Lexington, Mass.: Lexington, 1979), pp. 273–291.

[87]See Anthony Saunders, ''Bank Safety and Soundness and the Risks of Corporate Securities Activities,'' chapter 7 of this book.

[88]See Stoll, ''Underwritten Offerings.''

[89]See Giddy, ''Is Equity Underwriting Risky?''

[90]One cannot, of course, guarantee that a small commercial bank affiliate would not engage in a series of imprudent underwritings, any more than one can guarantee that the bank would not make a series of imprudent loans. The purpose of public policy, however, should be not be to protect entrepreneurs (including bank owners and managers) from their own mistakes; the competitive market is the proper instrument for applying this discipline. If there are serious social problems from bank failure, they are best handled through FDIC insurance (especially if the premiums on that insurance are sensitive to risk).

[91]A possible exception to this statement is that the premiums a bank currently pays for FDIC insurance on deposits are not fully sensitive to risks at the margin.

[92]In essence, then, banks may enjoy windfalls from their access to low-cost deposits (although the eventual elimination of Regulation Q ceilings on interest rates on deposits should end even these windfalls and cause the marginal costs of deposits, including processing costs, to equal the marginal costs of other funds), but these windfalls do not give the bank any advantage at the margin.

REFERENCES

Ackerlof, George A. ''The Market for 'Lemons': Quality Uncertainty and the Market Mechanism,'' *Quarterly Journal of Economics,* **84** (August 1970), pp. 488–500.

Bator, Francis M. ''The Anatomy of Market Failure,'' *Quarterly Journal of Economics,* **72** (August 1958), pp. 351–379.

Benson, Earl D., David S. Kidwell, Timothy W. Koch, and Robert J. Rogowski. ''Systematic Variation in Yield Spreads for Tax-Exempt General Obligation Bonds,'' *Journal of Financial and Quantitative Analysis,* **16** (December 1981), pp. 685–702.

Benston, George J., and Robert L. Hagerman. ''Determinants of Bid-Asked Spreads in the Over-the-Counter Market,'' *Journal of Financial Economics,* **1** (December 1974), pp. 353–364.

Bloch, Ernest. ''Investment Banking,'' Graduate School of Business Administration, New York University, 1983.

Bower, Richard S., Dennis E. Logue, and Robert A. Jarrow. "The Investment Banking Industry: A Preliminary Report on Its Structure and Competitiveness," Amos Tuck School of Business Administration, Dartmouth College, April 1979.

Bradburd, Ralph M., and A. Mead Over, Jr. "Organizational Costs, 'Sticky Equilibria' and Critical Levels of Concentration," *Review of Economics and Statistics,* **64** (February 1982), pp. 50–58.

Bradley, Michael, *Microeconomics.* Glenview, Ill.: Scott Foresman, 1980.

Braswell, Ronald C., E. Joe Nosari, and DeWitt L. Sumners. "A Comparison of the True Interest Costs of Competitive and Negotiated Underwritings in the Municipal Bond Market," *Journal of Money, Credit, and Banking,* **15** (February 1983), pp. 102–106.

Burstein, Meyer L. "A Theory of Full-Line Forcing," *Northwestern University Law Review,* **55** (1960–1961), pp. 62–95.

Carosso, Vincent P. *Investment Banking in America: A History.* Cambridge, Mass.: Harvard University Press, 1970.

Clark, Matthew, and Anthony Saunders. "Glass-Steagall Revisited: The Impact on Banks, Capital Markets, and the Smaller Investors," *Banking Law Journal,* **97** (October 1980), pp. 811–840.

Dyl, Edward A., and Michael D. Joehnk, "Competitive versus Negotiated Underwriting of Public Utility Debt," *Bell Journal of Economics,* **7** (Autumn 1976), pp. 680–689.

Ederington, Louis H. "Uncertainty, Competition, and Costs in Corporate Bond Underwriting," *Journal of Financial Economics,* **2** (March 1975), pp. 71–94.

———. "Negotiated versus Competitive Bidding for Corporate Bonds," *Journal of Finance,* **31** (March 1976), pp. 17–28.

Edwards, Franklin R. "Banks and Securities: Legal and Economic Perspectives on the Glass-Steagall Act," in Lawrence G. Goldberg and Lawrence J. White (eds.), *The Deregulation of the Banking and Securities Industries.* Lexington, Mass.: D.C. Heath, 1979, pp. 273–291.

Fabozzi, Frank J., and Richard R. West. "Negotiated versus Competitive Underwritings of Public Utility Bonds: Just One More Time," *Journal of Financial and Quantitative Analysis,* **16** (September 1981), pp. 323–339.

Findley, M. Chapman, III, Keith B. Johnson, and T. Gregory Morton. "An Analysis of the Flotation Cost of Utility Bonds, 1971–76," *Journal of Financial Research,* **2** (Fall 1979), pp. 133–142.

Flannery, Mark J. "An Economic Evaluation of Bank Securities Activities Before 1933," chapter 4 of this book (1985).

Giddy, Ian H. "Is Equity Underwriting Risky for Commercial Banks?" chapter 6 of this book.

Goldschmid, Harvey J., H. Michael Mann, and J. Fred Weston (eds.), *Industrial Concentration: The New Learning.* Boston: Little, Brown, 1974.

Golembe Associates. "Commercial Banks and Investment Banks." Prepared for the Economics and Financial Research Division of the ABA, November 29, 1976.

Hayes, Samuel L., III. "Investment Banking: Power Structure in Flux," *Harvard Business Review,* **49** (March–April 1971), pp. 136–152.

Hayes, Samuel L., III. "The Transformation of Investment Banking," *Harvard Business Review,* **57** (January–February 1979), pp. 153–170.

Hayes, Samuel L., III. A. Michael Spence, and David Van Prang Marks. *Competition in the Investment Banking Industry.* Cambridge, Mass.: Harvard University Press, 1983.

Johnson, Keith B., T. Gregory Morton, and M. Chapman Findley, III. "An Empirical Analysis of the Flotation Cost of Corporate Securities, 1971–1972," *Journal of Finance,* **30** (September, 1975), pp. 1129–1133.

Katz, Barbara Goody, and Joel Owen. "Initial Public Offerings: An Equilibrium Model of Price Determination," Faculty of Business Administration, New York University, Working Paper #83-69, July 1983.

Kaufman, George G. "Municipal Bond Underwriting: Market Structure," *Journal of Bank Research,* **12** (Spring 1981), pp. 24–31.

Kidwell, David S., and Timothy W. Koch. "Why and When Do Revenue Bonds Yield More Than GOs?" *Journal of Portfolio Management*, **8** (Summer 1982a), pp. 51–56.

Kidwell, David S., and Timothy W. Koch. "The Behavior of the Interest Rate Differential Between Tax-Exempt Revenue and General Obligation Bonds: A Test of Risk Preferences and Market Segmentation," *Journal of Finance*, **37** (March 1982b), pp. 63–73.

Leibenstein, Harvey. "Allocative Efficiency vs. X-Efficiency," *American Economic Review*, **66** (June 1966), pp. 392–415.

Leonard, Paul A. "Some Factors Determining Municipal Revenue Bond Interest Costs," *Journal of Economics and Business*, **35** (1983), pp. 71–82.

Levich, Richard M. "A View from the International Capital Markets," chapter 10 of this book.

Logue, Dennis E, "On the Pricing of Unseasoned Equity Issues: 1956–1969," *Journal of Financial and Quantitative Analysis*, **8** (January 1973), pp. 91–103.

Logue, Dennis E., and John R. Lindvall, "The Behavior of Investment Bankers: An Econometric Investigation," *Journal of Finance*, **29** (March 1974), pp. 203–215.

McGoldrick, Beth. "Life with Rule 415," *Institutional Investor*, **17** (February 1983), pp. 129–133.

Marr, M. Wayne, and G. Rodney Thompson, "Shelf Registration and the Utility Industry," Department of Finance, Virginia Polytechnic Institute and State University, June 3, 1983.

Mendelson, Morris. "Underwriting Compensation," in Irwin Friend et al., *Investment Banking and the New Issues Market*. Cleveland: World Publishing, 1967, pp. 394–479.

Miller, Ervin. "Background and Structure of the Industry," in Irwin Friend et al., *Investment Banking and the New Issues Market*. Cleveland: World Publishing, 1967, pp. 80–175.

Nauss, Robert M., and Bradford R. Keeler. "Optimizing Municipal Bond Bids," *Journal of Bank Research*, **12** (Autumn 1981), pp. 174–181.

Newman, Howard H. "Strategic Groups and the Structure-Performance Relationship," *Review of Economics and Statistics*, **60** (August 1978), pp. 417–427.

Ogur, Jonathan D. "Competition and Market Share Instability," Staff Report to the Federal Trade Commission, Bureau of Economics, August 1976.

Osborn, Neil. "What Happens After Glass-Steagall?" *Institutional Investor*, **16** (February 1982), pp. 67–78.

Parker, George G. C., and Daniel Cooperman. "Competitive Bidding in the Underwriting of Public Utility Securities," *Journal of Financial and Quantitative Analysis*, **13** (December 1978), pp. 885–902.

Perkins, Edwin J. "The Divorce of Commercial and Investment Banking: A History," *Banking Law Journal*, **88** (June 1971), pp. 483–528.

Posner, Richard A. *Antitrust Law: An Economics Perspective*. Chicago: University of Chicago Press, 1976.

Ritter, Jay R. "The 'Hot Issue' Market of 1980," Wharton School, University of Pennsylvania, September 1982.

Ritter, Jay R. "The 'Hot Issue' Market of 1980," *Journal of Business*, **57** (April 1984), pp. 215–240.

Rock, Kevin R. "Why New Issues Are Underpriced," Ph.D. dissertation, University of Chicago, 1982.

Rogowski, Robert J. "Underwriting Competition and Issuer Borrowing Costs in the Municipal Revenue Bond Market," *Journal of Bank Research*, **11** (Winter 1980), pp. 212–220.

Salop, Steven, and Joseph Stiglitz. "Bargains and Ripoffs," *Review of Economic Studies*, **44** (October 1977), pp. 493–510.

Satterthwaite, Mark A. "Consumer Information, Equilibrium Industry Price, and the Number of Sellers," *Bell Journal of Economics*, **10** (Autumn 1979), pp. 483–502.

Saunders, Anthony. "Conflict of Interest: An Economic View," chapter 8 of this book.

Saunders, Anthony. "Bank Safety and Soundness and the Risks of Corporate Securities Activities," chapter 7 of this book.

Scherer, F. M. *Industrial Market Structure and Economic Performance*, 2d ed. Chicago: Rand McNally, 1980.

Schwartz, Alan, and Louis L. Wilde. "Competitive Equilibria in Markets for Heterogenous Goods Under Imperfect Information: A Theoretical Analysis with Policy Implications," *Bell Journal of Economics,* **13** (Spring 1982), pp. 181–193.

Silber, William L. *Municipal Revenue Bond Costs and Bank Underwriting: A Survey of the Evidence.* Salomon Brothers Center for the Study of Financial Institutions, Graduate School of Business Administration, New York University, Monograph Series in Finance and Economics, Monograph #1979-3.

Smith, Clifford W., Jr. "Alternative Methods for Raising Capital: Rights versus Underwritten Offerings," *Journal of Financial Economics,* **5** (December 1977), pp. 273–307.

Sorenson, Eric H. "The Impact of Underwriting Method and Bidder Competition Upon Corporate Bond Interest Cost," *Journal of Finance,* **34** (September 1979), pp. 863–869.

Stigler, George J. "A Theory of Oligopoly," *Journal of Political Economy,* **72** (February 1964), pp. 44–61.

Stoll, Hans R. "The Pricing of Underwritten Offerings of Listed Common Stocks and the Compensation of Underwriters," *Journal of Economics and Business,* **28** (Winter 1976), pp. 96–103.

Tallman, Gary D., David F. Rush, and Ronald W. Melicher. "Competitive versus Negotiated Underwriting Costs for Regulated Industries," *Financial Management,* 4 (September 1974), pp. 49–55.

U.S. Securities and Exchange Commission and U.S. Small Business Administration. *The Role of Regional Broker-Dealers in the Capital Formation Process: Underwriting, Market-Making and Securities Research Activities.* Phase II Report. Washington, D.C.: August 1981.

U.S. Small Business Administration and U.S. Securities and Exchange Commission. *Initial Public Offerings of Common Stock: The Role of Regional Broker-Dealers in the Capital Formation Process.* Phase I Report. Washington, D.C.: March 1980.

Wall Street Journal, "Salomon Brothers Led Competitors in '83 with $15.76 Billion in U.S. Underwritings," January 6, 1984.

West, Richard R. "New Issue Concessions on Municipal Bonds: A Case of Monopsony Pricing," *Journal of Business,* **38** (April 1965), pp. 135–148.

West, Richard R. "More On the Effects of Municipal Bond Monopsony," *Journal of Business,* **39** (April 1966), pp. 304–308.

Comment

THOMAS F. HUERTAS

Proponents of the continued separation of commercial and investment banking employ three myths in arguing against the repeal of Glass-Steagall. Briefly stated, these myths are:

That investment banking is inherently riskier than commercial banking and would therefore endanger the solvency of any commercial bank that engaged in investment banking.

That the union of commercial and investment banking presents such grave conflicts of interest that abuse is inevitable and harm to customers is unavoidable.

That the union of commercial and investment banking, were it permitted, would have insignificant impact on the cost of issuing new securities.

Chapter 5, by Pugel and White, convincingly debunks the third of these myths and shows that allowing the unification of commercial and investment banking will produce significant benefits. My comments therefore do not directly criticize the paper. Instead, I will review the same problem from a somewhat different perspective. This will further substantiate the results of Pugel and White.

The perspective is the theory of contestable markets. This states that limiting entry into an industry, particularly from firms most qualified and most likely to enter, inherently reduces economic efficiency. Limiting entry acts much like a quota on imports from a more efficient nation. It allows firms in the protected industry to fix prices, avoid risk-taking, and incur higher costs. Moreover, it provides a shield behind which firms in the protected industry can consolidate, so that the profitability of leading firms, even after higher costs are taken into account, is extraordinarily high. Thus Glass-Steagall could breed both inefficiency and monopoly, and repealing it could yield significant benefits.

Trends in the investment banking industry tend to bear this out. Prices for underwriting services, although not fixed by law, have been remarkably constant, both over time and as a proportion of the funds raised. For decades, the spread on underwriting new corporate debt issues held steady at 0.875%. As Pugel and White point out, it is highly unlikely that a market open to entry by commercial banks would have exhibited such behavior. Indeed, as Levich (see Chapter 10) has demonstrated, this has not been the case in the Eurobond market, where commercial banks have been free to enter.

Contrary to popular belief, investment banks have been loathe to assume risk, at least when underwriting new issues. When bidding on new issues, investment banks stack the deck in their favor. They consistently underprice new issues in order to guarantee the success of the offering. From the issuer's perspective, money is "left on the table." For example, in the case of initial public offerings of common stock, underwriters have underpriced issues by nearly 19% on the average.

Finally, there is significant concentration with the industry. In 1983 over 250 securities firms were engaged in underwriting corporate securities. Yet the top four firms managed 47% of the total dollar volume of corporate security underwritings, and the top eight firms managed 73%. This degree of concentration gives firms in the industry enough market power to generate supernormal profits. In fact, during the period 1980 to 1982, securities firms' rate of return on equity was 16.8%, 2.6% higher than that for all manufacturing corporations and 4% higher than that for all insured commercial banks.

The advent of Rule 415 may aggravate this situation. It puts underwriting on a bought deal basis, and considerably simplifies the registration process. It places a premium on capitalization, placing power and trading capability—precisely the strengths of the leading securities firms. It is therefore likely to lead to further consolidation within the securities industry rather than a significant reduction in underwriting costs. Initial results under Rule 415 bear this out. Origination has become more concentrated, and the size of the average underwriting syndicate has been significantly reduced from the 125–150 members employed in a normal offering to 20–40 members.

Finally, the securities industry itself is consolidating behind the shield provided by Glass-Steagall. During 1983–84, two mergers (Merrill Lynch—Becker and Shearson—Lehman) occurred among firms that were among the top 15 underwriters of corporate securities in 1983.

Who then would benefit from repeal of Glass-Steagall, and by now much? Corporations issuing securities would be a major beneficiary. Greater competition among underwriters would reduce underwriting fees and raise prices at which securities would be offered to the public. The entry of new firms would also increase the number of dealers in corporate securities. This would tend to improve the liquidity of the market, especially in corporate bonds. It would make securities more valuable to investors and enable firms to float securities at lower costs.

Smaller corporations, lower-rated corporations, and corporations entering the securities markets for the first time would particularly benefit. These firms have less bargaining power with underwriters but do generally have close relationships with commercial banks. Thus allowing commercial banks to underwrite securities would significantly increase the access of these firms to the securities markets and reduce the cost of borrowing for these firms.

Just how much costs would be reduced is difficult to say, but a calculation for corporate bonds, based on the approach developed by Giddy (Chapter 6), is revealing.

The risk of underwriting is equivalent to writing a covered call option on the bond with an exercise price equal to the offer price over expiration period of one week. The premium received for writing the option is the spread. In firm commitment underwriting, the investment banking syndicate offers the issuing firms a net price for the securities and adds a spread to arrive at an offering price to investors. Thus, the profits of a syndicate member are equal to the spread multiplied by its allotment, if the market price is equal to or exceeds the offering price — or to the difference of the market price and the net price, multiplied by the allotment, if the market price is below the offer price. The syndicate member realizes a loss only if the market price falls below the net price. How likely is this to be in the case of corporate bond underwriting?

The answer seems to be, not very likely. The risk involved in corporate bond underwriting is, strictly speaking, due only to the risk that the premium for default risk will change. Changes in the price of the bond due to changes in the general level of interest rates are a diversifiable risk and are not attributable to underwriting corporate securities (e.g., the underwriter can short the government bond of equivalent maturity or hedge itself in the futures market).

Changes in the premium for default risk have two causes: firm specific and class wide. Firm-specific changes in risk due to changes in leverage, etc. should be fully disclosed in the prospectus and are very unlikely to change during the underwriting period. Thus, the risk of underwriting corporate bonds amounts to losses that may arise due to changes in the premium for default risk on a given class of bonds. Loss will occur only if the decline price of the bond due to a change in the premium for default risk is greater than the spread, which usually amounts to 0.625% of par.

Based on an analysis of the week-to-week variance in corporate bond prices for 20 year straight bonds rated BAA and AAA, the underwriter of a corporate bond will incur a loss only 26% of the time. Nearly three-fourths of the time the underwriter will make a profit. In contrast, in the government securities market, which is open to entry by commercial banks and where spreads are consequently much narrower, the underwriter stands to lose money 47% of the time and to make money 53% of the time.

Entry by commercial banks into underwriting corporate securities would tend to bring the probability of profit from underwriting corporate bonds more into line with that involved in underwriting Treasury securities. Let's say the difference between the two were halved, so that the probability of profiting from underwriting corporate bonds fell from 74% to 63%. That would reduce the underwriting spread from $5/8$% to $3/8$%. Thus the price of underwriting services could fall by 40% as a result of commercial bank entry into corporate bond underwriting. This is a considerable saving in any corporate treasurer's book.

In sum, the approach taken here corroborates the results of Pugel and White. There are considerable benefits to allowing commercial banks to underwrite corporate securities. The costs of repealing Glass-Steagall are negligible. Both regulation and the self-interest of banks—whether commercial or investment—ensure safety and soundness and prevent abuses of conflict of interest. Thus benefits of repealing Glass-Steagall outweigh the costs. Glass-Steagall should therefore be repealed.

6 Is Equity Underwriting Risky for Commercial Bank Affiliates?

IAN H. GIDDY

This chapter examines the risks and returns in the U.S. corporate equity underwriting business. The issue of interest is whether underwriting risk is qualitatively or quantitatively different from the kinds of risks encountered in conventional commercial banking. The conceptual objective is to identify the character of the risk that arises when an investment banking syndicate agrees to purchase an issue of stock from a corporation and resell it to the public at a fixed price (the ''offer price''). The empirical objectives are to learn something about the riskiness of market price movements of equity shares during the days following an issue, and to measure the riskiness of the estimated net gains or losses incurred by underwriters. A companion study evaluates the riskiness of U.S. corporate bond underwriting.

Underwriting risk is only one of several major risks faced by investment banks, and by no means the dominant one. It is of considerable interest in itself, however, because it is imperfectly understood and because it has an asymmetrical character that requires special attention to the proper means of limiting the risk. Equity underwriters by convention and regulation set a fixed ''offering'' price to the public at the time the issue is underwritten. This produces potential one-sided risks as follows: If the aftermarket value of the issue is greater than the offer price, the investor who purchases the offering earns a profit because the underwriter must sell at the offer price. On the other hand, if the aftermarket price of the issue is less than the offer price, the underwriter will be unable to sell at the offer and will have to dispose of his or her shares at some lower price.

In the following section 2, the process of setting the offer price is described, and in the section following that it is argued that the level at which this price is set relative to the ''true'' market value produces a risk resembling that faced by the seller of a put option. The empirical section of the study employs data on offer prices, fees earned by the underwriters and distributors, and subsequent market prices to estimate the *net* gain or loss to the underwriting industry. Over 2500 issues were examined covering the period 1976 to 1983.

This method does not account for the internal costs faced by underwriters; nevertheless, the results are consistent with other studies[2] in that a net loss appears in a very small proportion of cases. The results show, moreover, that the key to limiting risk in underwriting is selling off the issue as soon as possible, even if that means selling at a loss. Thus equity underwriters can take as much, or as little, risk as they choose.

Is the underlying risk of equity underwriting necessarily greater than that of commercial or consumer lending? Both entail an asymmetric distribution of outcomes, and although loan values fluctuate less, equities are far more liquid, enabling underwriters to recognize and limit risks far earlier than lenders.

THE UNDERWRITING PROCESS

The investment banking function of "firm commitment" underwriting of corporate securities serves to guarantee to an issuer that a certain amount of shares will be sold at a certain price. The underwriter achieves this, typically, in the following manner.[3]

First, the managing or lead underwriter develops insights into a company over a period of time, simultaneously advising the company on the nature, volume, and timing of possible financings, and testing market sentiment or "appetite" for the company's equity.

When the demands of the market are perceived as matching the needs of the company, the investment house will "bring the firm to market" by assisting the issuer in preparing a "red herring" prospectus, a document that is filed with the Securities and Exchange Commission (SEC). The issue becomes publicly known, and the managing underwriter now seeks to form an underwriting syndicate. Although the issue is "in registration," the SEC may request amendments to the prospectus. Until there is a formula price, the final amendment is the "price amendment" (normally made on the morning of the day of issue) which sets the basis for the price to be paid to the issuer. At this stage the prospectus does not state an explicit offer price, but rather promises that the offer price will be set within some proximate range of the market price, for example, no higher than the last reported sale price (for a seasoned issue) plus $0.50 per share. Following this, the SEC permits the prospectus to become "effective" (in practice by accelerating the registration period). An agreement among the underwriters will then be signed. This provides for the several commitments of each to purchase their share of the issue at the net price. Shortly thereafter, a separate agreement between the underwriters and the issuer will be signed. The underwriters will seek expressions of interest on the part of institutional investors and broker-dealers, and a fixed offer price will be set at the end of that day—after the close of trading. A successful issue will be sold out within a very short period of time.

If the issue is not readily absorbed by the market at the public offering price, the underwriters will seek to sell the shares on the following days. If shares remain unsold, the syndicate "breaks" and underwriters are free to sell at the market price—presumably below the offer price.

Approximately one week after the hectic day during which the prospectus became effective and the various agreements are signed, the issue is "closed." The closing date is simply the date at which the issuer transfers ownership of the shares to the underwriters, who pay the issuer the agreed price per share; the underwriters then transfer ownership to those who bought shares from them at the offer price or below. The importance of this date is that no money changes hands until the closing—so that even if the underwriter is unable to sell the shares for several days, he or she incurs no carrying costs until the closing date. The same fact demonstrates the existence of a very strong incentive for underwriters to sell all shares before the closing date, even if doing so may mean suffering a loss.

The above description also should clarify the *period* over which the underwriter incurs a risk. This period (in the case of formula price offerings) is not from the time of price agreement with the issuer, but rather from the time at which the offer price is set. This is at the *end* of the business day of the effective date of the offer. Thus the closing price at the end of the first business day *following* the effective date is the relevant price to gauge one business day's risk to the underwriter, should part or all of the issue remain unsold.

The approval of Rule 415 by the SEC in 1982, permitting "shelf registration," has changed the underwriting process in important ways—in particular, it has enabled elimination of the relationship between the investment banker and his or her client during the pre- and post- "red herring" registration periods described above. Because companies can preregister a certain number of shares and later sell them ad hoc to the highest bidder in a matter of minutes, the firm itself is permitted to usurp much of the preparatory role played in regular underwriting by the investment banker. Once an underwriter has bid successfully for a 415 issue, however, he or she pays a net price and faces one-sided risk in exactly the same way as if the issue were conducted in the conventional fashion.

In both kinds of underwriting, the risk borne by the underwriters depends in large measure on their ability to gauge the market demand for the issue—how much would be bought at what prices?—and to buy at a price acceptable to the issuer but sufficiently below the offer price to accommodate the risk of not being able to sell at that price. Underwriters' skill lies also in their ability to line up buyers—that is, to "presell" the issue by obtaining indications of interest to purchase the shares at a price close to the current market price, if one exists, or otherwise at an indicative offer price. However, because no sales can legally be made until the offer price is actually set, these indications of interest can be rescinded. Where such uncertainties are greater, underwriters will seek to protect themselves by demanding a higher spread— a greater difference between the price paid to the issuer and the public offering price.[4]

REVENUES, COSTS, AND RISKS IN EQUITY UNDERWRITING

Investment banking firms that underwrite corporaate equity issues in the United States are ostensibly compensated for their services by a "gross spread." This is an amount that is agreed upon between the issuer and the underwriting syndicate, and expressed as a percentage of the "gross proceeds." For example, Hypo Ethical, Inc. issued 1.6

million shares of common stock at an offer price of $28.75 in 1983. The gross proceeds were thus $46 million. For their underwriting services (broadly defined to include advisory and distribution as well as risk-bearing services) the investment bankers received a gross spread of 4.38% of the gross proceeds, that is, $2,015,600. Of this amount, 16% was a management fee, paid to the syndicate managers, 16% was an underwriting compensation paid to each firm (including the managers) for that portion of the issue which it underwrote, and the remaining 68% was a selling concession, paid to the ''selling group'' of securities firms (including members of the underwriting syndicate) as an incentive for successful distribution of the issue at the offer price. The net proceeds received by Hypo were the gross proceeds less the spread, that is, $43,984,400.

In effect, the underwriting syndicate simply agrees to purchase the entire issue from the issuing company at a *net price* per share. The underwriters sell as many shares as the public will buy at an agreed-upon *offer price,* as long as the syndicate remains intact. If the offer price is set at or below the true market value (as perceived by the investing public), the entire issue will be sold almost immediately, usually within one day. The investment bankers will then pocket the entire spread, equal to the number of shares times the offer price received less than the net price paid the issuer. Out of this, of course, will come costs such as salaries and variable costs such as selling incentives.

If, on the other hand, the offer price is set above the true market value, the underwriters will be unable to sell all, or perhaps any, of the shares at the offer price. If, after a day, a week, or at most two weeks of attempting to sell the shares at the offer price, some or all shares remain unsold, the managers break the syndicate and the underwriters are free to sell their shares at whatever the market will pay—presumably, a price below the offer price, and perhaps even a price below the net price paid to the issuer.

The revenues and costs in each case can be described in the following stylized fashion[5]:

	If Offer Price < Market Price	If Offer Price ≥ Market Price
Revenues	No. of shares × offer price	No. of shares × market price
Cost of shares	No. of shares × net price	No. of shares × net price
Fixed costs	Salaries, etc.	Salaries, etc.
Contingent costs	Selling incentives to broker-dealers	Selling incentives to broker-dealers

The chief difference between the two circumstances is the lopsided nature of the underwriter's gain or loss, although the selling incentives paid to broker-dealers are greater when the latter succeed in distributing the issue at the public offering price, which may reduce the underwriter's risk somewhat. The set of outcomes facing the underwriter may be depicted as in Figure 6.1, which shows the net gain or loss from any given issue. If the market price after issue turns out to be above the offer price, the underwriting industry's gain is the whole spread and nothing but the spread, no

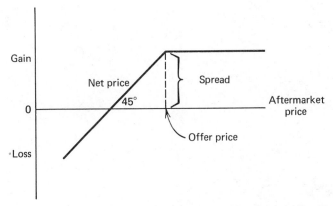

Figure 6.1 Net gain or loss from underwriting with a fixed public offering price

matter how high the issue's price goes. But to the extent that the market price falls below the offer price, the underwriter's net gain (or loss) is proportionately reduced.

Figure 6.1 is in fact a diagram familiar to finance theorists; it matches the profit profile from selling (or "writing") a put option. The writer of a put option sells someone (for a fee called the premium) the right to sell a security to the writer at a fixed ("strike") price within a given period. If the market price of the security falls below the strike price, the holder of the option can profit by purchasing at market and selling at the higher strike price. Because an option is a right that need not be exercised, the writer cannot gain, nor the buyer lose, more than the premium paid initially. In underwriting, the issuer sells to the underwriter at a fixed price, no matter what happens to the stock's market value; but if demand proves strong, the public, not the issuer, gains.

In sum, we can characterize U.S. equity underwriting risk as equivalent to that of writing a put option on the stock with an exercise price equal to the offer price and an expiration period ranging up to two weeks.[6]

Firm commitment underwriting, the dominant form,[7] was characterized in previous sections as being similar to writing a put option—with an upside gain no greater than the spread, and a downside loss theoretically limited only by the amount the stock can move while the issue remains in syndication. For any given issue, this may be illustrated as a truncated distribution, such as the diagram in Figure 6.2. Changes in equity prices may be roughly described by the log-normal distribution. But to the underwriter, the *entire right-hand side of that distribution is concentrated in one tall spike*. Precisely where that spike stands depends upon where the offer price has been set in relation to the expected value (mean) of the distribution of the stock's price changes.[8]

But now consider commercial banking, especially the normal business of matched-maturity deposit-taking and lending. For any given loan, ignoring expenses, the maximum the bank can earn is the spread between the lending rate and the deposit rate. The maximum that can be lost, however, is the entire amount of the loan, plus accrued

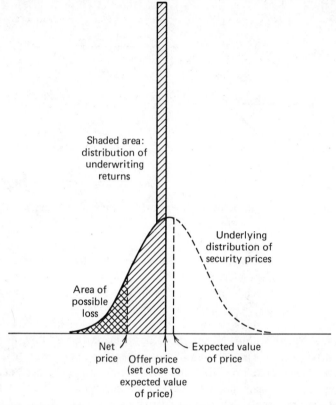

Figure 6.2   Underwriting versus commercial banking: distribution of possible returns

interest. Thus the distribution of returns that results is qualitatively identical to that of underwriting randomly-fluctuating securities: upside gain limited to (but concentrated in) the spread; and a range of potential downside losses distributed roughly lognormally and determined by the maximum potential fall in the value of the asset over the relevant holding period, as in writing a put option.

Thus the true difference between commercial lending risk and underwriting risk lies in the variability of asset prices and the length of the holding period—a quantitative rather than a qualitative difference. As one senior investment banker explained to the author:

> It is clear that the most fundamental difference between the commercial banker and the investment banker lies in their respective attitudes towards assets. The commercial banker seeks to acquire assets (make loans) which he can fund profitably (the interest rate earned on the loan exeeds the banker's cost of funds). The investment banker, on the other hand, traditionally treats an acquired asset as evidence of his having made a disastrous mistake. [His] primary concern is to resell his underwritten commitment, even at a loss, in order to free his capital for the next deal.

The distinction, then, lies in how each tries to limit the bottom half of the distribution: the commercial banker by holding low-risk assets and diversifying, and the underwriter by holding risky assets for an extremely limited period. In principle, neither financial service is inherently riskier than the other—the final risk depends on how successful each is in limiting the negative side of the distribution of returns. Although neither underwriting nor commercial lending risk can be measured directly with available data, we will now describe a method for approximating the distribution of underwriting returns. Later, a rough comparison with estimated commercial bank returns will be presented.

THE METHOD

This study employs data on U.S. equity issues during 1976–1983 to estimate the riskiness of equity underwriting. In principle we would have liked to have known *how much* of each issue was sold off at *what* prices, and when, and the *costs* faced by underwriters. Because these were unobtainable, we use publicly reported data and accordingly find it necessary to make some strong assumptions about the underwriting industry's revenues and costs. The riskiness of equity underwriting is measured in two stages.

First, we examine the behavior of equity prices in the secondary market on the days following stock issues, to discover the extent to which the market was able to absorb the issue without market price falling below the offer price, thus possibly forcing underwriters to sell the issue at a lower-than-anticipated price.

Second, we calculate the hypothetical gains or losses to the underwriters for each equity issue, by assuming that the underwriters buy the shares from the issuer at the net price (the offer price less the three sets of fees constituting the spread), and sell all shares at the offer price if the market equals or exceeds that level. If, after a certain number of days following issue, the market price has not reached the offer price, the underwriters are assumed to sell the entire issue at whatever the market price is on that day. In practice the underwriter is willing to bear market risk only for a very small number of days. In our tests we calculated results for three periods—one business day, five business days, and 10 business days.

The manner in which a particular issue's gain or loss for each of the three periods under market conditions was calculated is delineated in Table 6.1. Notice that, if a 5- or 10-day holding period is assumed, the stock's price may dip below the offer price on day 1, resulting in no sale, but recover by day 5 or 10, resulting in a sale at a higher price than that on day 1 but no higher than the offer price. On the other hand, if the market price is below the offer price on day 1 and even lower on the later date, the method assumes the syndicate then breaks and sells the whole issue at the latest price. Descriptive statistics and frequency distributions for the two sets of performance data were complied. The results are then summarized.

Before moving on to review the results, the reader should be aware of the limitations of this approach to measuring underwriting risk. First, the study does not pinpoint the risk to any single underwriter, but rather the gain or loss to the under-

Table 6.1   Calculation of Hypothetical Net Gains or Losses to Equity Underwriters

Assumed Period of Risk Taking	Market Conditions		Value of Net Gain or Loss
1 day	If Day 1 price ≥ offer price	then	No. of shares (Offer price-net price)
	Otherwise		No. of shares (Day 1 price-net price)
5 days	If Day 1 price ≥ offer price, or Day 5 price ≥ offer price	then	No. of shares (Offer price-net price)
	Otherwise		No. of shares (Day 5 price-net price)
10 days	If Day 1 price ≥ offer price, or Day 5 price ≥ offer price, or Day 10 price ≥ offer price	then	No. of shares (Offer price-net price)
	Otherwise		No. of shares (Day 10 price-net price)

Note: (1) Prices are closing prices for the stock on the first, fifth, and tenth business days
following the "effective date" of the issue.
(2) The net price is the price per share paid by the underwriters; that is, the offer price
less the per-share "spread."

writers as a group. In practice even the syndicate manager would not take more than,
say, 25% to 40% of most issues, and even major underwriters would each have underwriting commitments of less than 10% of a large issue. In addition, some of the
gain or loss is incurred by broker-dealers whose primary function is distribution rather
than underwriting in a strict sense. In the United States the two functions are impossible to separate, and are normally performed by the same firms. We also make no
distinction between those fees retained by the manager and those earned by the remainder of the underwriting syndicate. All the data allow us to do, in sum, is to take
a look at underwriting risk faced by the underwriters *as a group,* and not at the peculiar
risk faced by any given firm or segment.

Second, the "all-or-nothing" assumption is incorrect. Although a strong market
almost certainly means that an issue will be sold successfully, the fact that the secondary market price fell below the offer price almost certainly does *not* mean that
none of the shares could be sold at the offer price. In this respect our study overes-
timates the losses (or understates the gains) in cases where the offer price exceeds the
market price.

Offsetting this is the fact that in calculating net gains or losses we ignore both fixed
and variable costs faced by the underwriter, including those associated with promoting the deal. Although the author has been told that approximately one-sixth of
the gross spread is absorbed by out-of-pocket underwriting expenses, it has proved
impossible to verify this or any other assignation of the spread; so no attempt is made
to reduce the spread by some estimate of costs. In this respect the results overstate
the profits (or understate the net losses) from underwriting.

Finally, in cases where the underwriters found themselves forced to sell part or all of an issue at a price or prices below the offer price, one cannot be certain of what those prices were. The closing price on days 1, 5, and 10 following issue are simply estimates of the price underwriters may have received.

THE DATA

This study employs data on all public equity issues with a gross proceeds of at least $5 million registered with the Securities and Exchange Commission during the period 1976 through the third quarter of 1983, for which complete, usable figures were obtainable. The name, date of issue, number of shares, offer price, underwriting fee, management fee, and selling concession were matched with the stock's market price at the end of the first, fifth, and tenth business days after the issue date for 2540 issues. The study relied entirely on data that are publicly reported to the SEC and the closing market prices of each stock issued.

Some characteristics of the data can be seen in Table 6.2 and Figures 6.3 and 6.4. Of the total fees earned, almost precisely two-thirds were in the form of selling concession. The other third was divided equally between the underwriting and management fees. As expected, the higher risk associated with Initial Public Offerings (IPOs) results in a spread almost two percentage points higher, on average, than the mean spread of 5.42% for the entire sample. Very few equity issues are done on a comparative bidding basis, and all of these are utility issues. The spread is lower for competitive issues and, as may be seen in Figure 6.3, the average spread decreases from 5.69% for smaller issues to 3.33% for issues exceeding $75 million. Although this may reflect economies of scale, it may also be that bigger companies both make bigger issues and are perceived as having more stable stock prices. Figure 6.5 shows that no distinct trend in underwriting spread has appeared in the eight-year period; however, the annual averages are strongly influenced by the proportion of IPOs in each year, because IPOs carry a higher spread. For example, 1982 had a lower pro-

Table 6.2 Characteristics of Equity Underwriting Data (Issues above $5 million, January 1976–September 1983)

Features	All Issues	Of Which:		
		Negotiated	Competitive[a]	IPOs[b]
Number	2540	2468	72	604
Average gross spread[c]	5.46%	5.52%	3.22%	7.35%
Average underwriting fee[c]	1.10	1.12	0.45	1.60
Average management fee[c]	1.04	1.06	0.31	1.48
Average selling concession[c]	3.32	3.34	2.46	4.27

[a]All competitive issues were made by public utilities.

[b]Initial Public Offerings.

[c]Fees expressed as a percentage of the offer price.

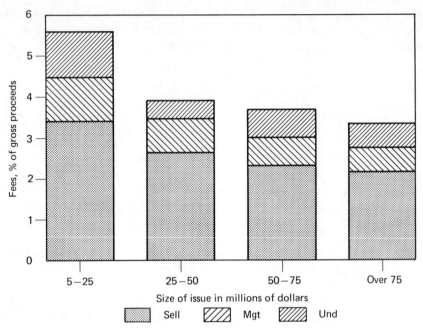

Figure 6.3 Average spread by size of issue: equity issues > $5M, 1976–1983

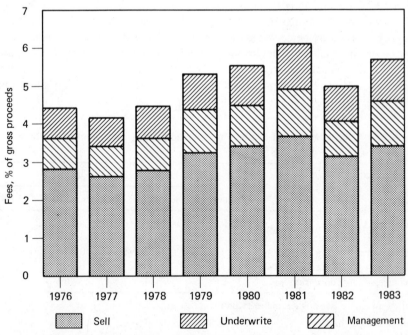

Figure 6.4 Underwriting compensation trends: equity sales > $5M

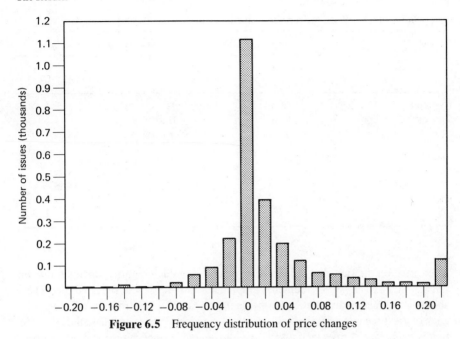

Figure 6.5 Frequency distribution of price changes

portion of IPOs than each of the surrounding years. Nevertheless, it is safe to say that no whittling-away of margins has occurred in equity underwriting during the period of 1976 to 1983 unlike certain other financial services.

THE RESULTS

In this section we present the results of our examination of the behavior of secondary market prices relative to the offer prices, followed by the evidence on estimated gains or losses to the underwriting industry produced by these price changes, taking into account the gross spread earned by the underwriters but ignoring their overhead costs.

Table 6.3 contains evidence on the size and variability of market prices relative to offer prices. As other studies have shown[9], we find that market prices exceed, on average, the offer price in the days following issue: by 2.6%, 3.0%, and 3.9% on the first, fifth, and tenth trading day after issue, respectively. In other words, equity issues are, on average, underpriced by U.S. investment bankers. The bottom half of the table shows that price rises outnumber price falls by about 17% and that a large number of issues (13%, on average) experience no price deviation from the offer price. In some cases this may reflect "stabilization" efforts on the part of the underwriters; in others it may reflect the stolid price behavior of seasoned stocks.

A more striking feature than the average price rise is the very substantial variation in percentage price changes. Even on the first day following offer, the standard deviation is over 10%. Considering that about 23% of all issues do not deviate from the

Table 6.3   Market Price Relative to Offer Price on Days Following Issue

	Percentage Deviation of Market From Offer Price by		
	First Day After Issue	Fifth Day After Issue	Tenth Day After Issue
Average	2.6	3.0	3.9
Standard deviation	10.8	13.0	15.58
Range	− 56 to + 181	− 59 to + 163	− 63 to + 150
Number of			
Rises	1064	1202	1295
Zero changes	582	267	155
Falls	894	1071	1090
Total	2540	2540	2540

offer price on the first day, this indicates a considerable volatility when the price is not stabilized. The point is depicted graphically in Figures 6.6, 6.7, and 6.8. These show the frequency distributions of percentage price changes from the offer price for each of the three intervals studied. As noted, a majority of issues fall on the plus side, that is, on balance prices tend to rise. Yet the degree of price movements experienced by a large number, indeed a majority, of issues is surely surprising. A 10% price change in a single trading day is a lot—and no less than 9.7% of the issues studied experienced price changes of this magnitude by day 1. On this basis, taken in isolation, anyone holding a position in such equities at the offering date is subject to a great deal of risk, unless there are offsetting factors.

Which, of course, there are. First, underwriters do not normally have a position in the issue, even for a single day: as noted earlier, they sell off most issues at the offer price almost immediately. Second, even when they do get stuck with an unsold issue, they have paid the net price, not the offer price—the offer less the spread. Finally, underwriters demand a higher spread for riskier issues; that is, they pay a lower net price to give themselves greater protection against the risk of having misjudged the price the market will pay. This phenomenon is verified in Figure 6.9, which shows the direct relationship between the size of the spread and the absolute magnitude of the price change by day 1. The spread rises from about 4% for nonstabilized issues whose price changed less than 1%, to about 7% for issues with price changes of over 10%.

The final and most important set of results shows the net gains and losses, calculated as described in the last section (Table 6.1). Do the *truncated* returns display the high riskiness that many have supposed must result from underwriting such volatile securities? First, looking at some summary statistics in Table 6.4, we find an *average net gain* of $1.28 million assuming the syndicate broke by the end of the first day following issue. On one occasion the underwriters, taken together, may have suffered a maximum loss of $10.35 million (or $13.84 million had they waited until the tenth day); but their maximum gain was more than twice as large. The standard

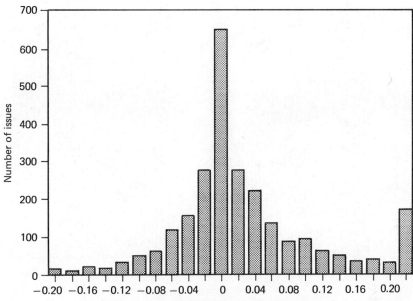

Figure 6.6 Frequency distribution of price changes

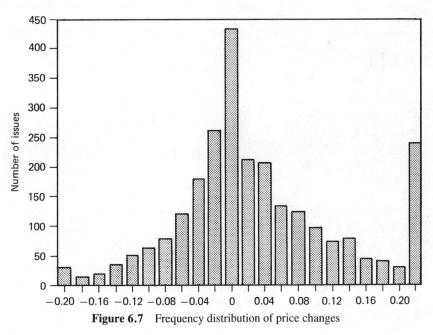

Figure 6.7 Frequency distribution of price changes

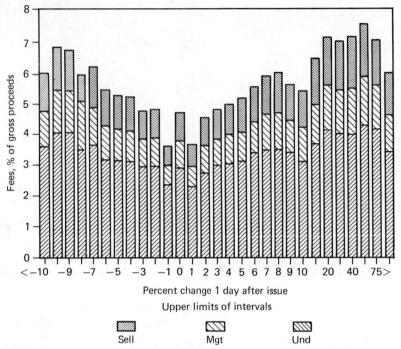

Figure 6.8 Fees are higher for riskier issues: all issues > $5M, 1976–1983

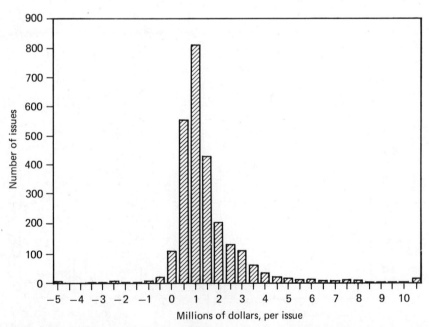

Figure 6.9 Frequency distribution of gains and losses: estimated gains/losses at day 1

Table 6.4 Hypothetical Net Gains or Losses to Underwriters (in millions of dollars)

	Gain/Loss Assuming Syndicate Broke on or Before		
	First Day After Issue	Fifth Day After Issue	Tenth Day After Issue
Average	1.28	1.14	1.12
Standard deviation	1.83	2.03	2.09
Range	− 10.35 to 25.58	− 18.72 to 25.58	− 13.84 to 25.58
Number of			
Net gains	2439	2254	2226
Net breakevens	5	3	3
Net losses	96	283	311
Total	2540	2540	2540

Note: This table shows the estimated *net* gain or loss to the underwriter as described in Table 6.1. "Net" means the price at which the underwriter was able to sell (lower of offer or market) minus the purchase price, but not taking into account the other costs.

deviation of returns was 1.83 (in millions of dollars) for a one-day holding period, rising to 2.09 for a 10-day holding period. What this number masks, however, is the fact that the average return lies considerably rightward of the zero point. As may be seen from the lower half of Table 6.4, even for a 10-day holding period only 311 issues or 12.2% of the total involved losses; this is reduced to 3.8% for a one-day holding period. The shape and location of the distribution of returns is evident in the histograms depicting the frequency distribution of returns (Figures 6.10 and 6.11). For day 1, in particular, the distribution is skewed with the great bulk of net returns concentrated in the zero to $2 million range; most of the remaining returns exceed $2 million, with several exceeding $10 million; a small proportion fall in the $0.5 to $0 million loss range; and a trivial proportion involve losses greater than $0.5 million. These histograms and Table 6.4 demonstrate that the quick sale of assets can largely eliminate the downside price risk of underwriting even volatile equity issues.

The last point is reinforced by a comparison of the numbers underlying the three frequency distributions of net returns. Table 6.5 lists the number of observations falling in each interval, ranging from losses exceeding $5 million to gains in excess of $10 million. The right-hand column measures the change in the number of returns in each interval arising from reducing the holding period from 10 days to one day. Although keeping a syndicate intact for 10 days provides a significantly higher probability of being able to sell at the offer price, this is offset by the much greater variability of stock prices over 10 days than over one day. The net effect is that the one-day holding period reduces the number of losses in *every* loss interval, although it reduces gains in only very few.

During the eight years covered by this study underwriters would undeniably have been better off if they had sold all securities by the end of day 1, even if some or all could not have been sold at the public offering price. Waiting 10 days raises the

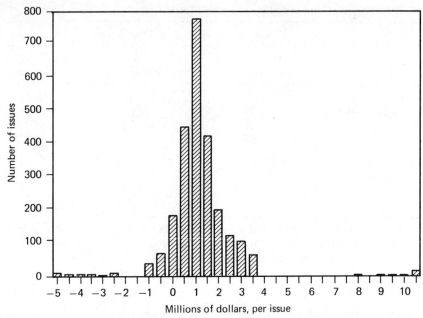

Figure 6.10   Frequency distribution of gains and losses: estimated gains/losses at day 5

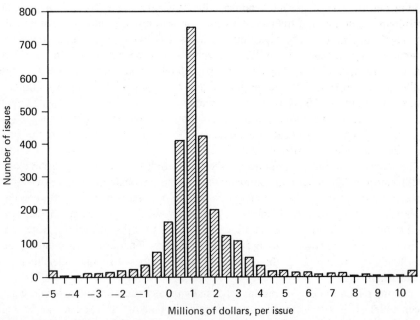

Figure 6.11   Frequency distribution of gains and losses: estimated gains/losses at day 10

Table 6.5 Frequency Distribution of Net Gains or Losses from Equity Underwriting, 1976–1983

Range in Millions	Number in Each Interval by Day 1	by Day 5	by Day 10	Difference Day 1–Day 10
≤ -5	4	9	17	-13
-5 to -4.5	0	4	2	-2
-4.5 to -4	0	4	1	-1
-4 to -3.5	1	4	8	-7
-3.5 to -3	1	3	7	-6
-3 to -2.5	4	7	12	-8
-2.5 to -2	2	14	17	-15
-2 to -1.5	3	12	21	-18
-1.5 to -1	6	32	34	-28
-1 to -0.5	19	63	71	-52
-0.5 to 0	106	178	168	-62
0 to 0.5	555	446	414	141
0.5 to 1	814	777	754	60
1 to 1.5	433	421	426	7
1.5 to 2	204	196	201	3
2 to 2.5	128	116	123	5
2.5 to 3	106	103	107	-1
3 to 3.5	58	58	59	-1
3.5 to 4	34	35	34	0
4 to 4.5	19	15	16	3
4.5 to 5	16	17	19	-3
5 to 5.5	13	11	11	2
5.5 to 6	11	10	11	0
6 to 6.5	9	6	6	3
6.5 to 7	4	8	8	-4
7 to 7.5	8	9	9	-2
7.5 to 8	4	3	3	1
8 to 8.5	3	4	5	-2
8.5 to 9	3	3	3	0
9 to 9.5	3	1	1	2
9.5 to 10	2	3	3	-1
$>$ 10	12	13	13	-1

Note: Net returns in this table are those calculated according to the procedure described in Table 6.1. Thus "net" for day 1, for example, means the lower of the offer price or the market price, less the underwriter's purchase price.

proportion of net losses from 4% to 12%, although it leaves the proportion of large gains (above $5 million) virtually unchanged at about 3%. This is hardly surprising, because the random walk theory of securities prices, reinforced by the evidence presented above, suggests that the longer the holding period the greater the volatility of prices. The 10-day syndicate faces a more widely dispersed probability distribution of price changes, but a fixed increase in the offer price that limits gains from upward movement. Thus it is hardly surprising that a greater proportion of losses result.

The final important aspect of equity underwriting results is the special nature of initial public offering (IPO) underwriting. Table 6.6 (top half) shows that when measured as before by the percentage deviation of aftermarket from offer price, IPOs are much more severely underpriced, on average, than other issues, and they are distinctly riskier. For example, on day 1 the average price change is +9.8% (compared to 2.6% for all issues) and the standard deviation is 23.4% (compared to 10.8%). Nevertheless, as the bottom half of Table 6.5 shows, the high spreads of IPOs produce net gains and losses that are not noticeably more risky than all issues: the range of gains/losses. The standard deviation of returns is higher for one-day returns but lower for 10-day returns.

Table 6.6   Initial Public Offerings

	First Day After Issue	Fifth Day After Issue	Tenth Day After Issue
	Percentage Deviation of Market from Offer Price		
Average	9.8	10.2	11.5
Standard deviation	23.4	27.2	31.7
Number of rises	349	349	350
Number of zero changes	118	69	41
Number of falls	136	185	212
	Net/Gain or Loss Once All Sold or Syndicate Breaks (in million of dollars)		
Average	1.34	1.17	1.11
Standard deviation	2.27	2.39	1.50
Number of gains	582	538	529
Number of breakdowns	1	0	0
Number of losses	20	65	74
Total number	603	603	603

Note: The top half of this table simply describes aftermarket price deviations (positive or negative) from the offer price. It is comparable to Table 3. The bottom half depicts, for IPOs, the distribution of the *truncated* returns. ''Net'' gain/loss means net price received (lower of offer or market) minus the purchase price, ignoring overhead and other costs.

COMPARISON WITH BOND UNDERWRITING

The previous section's findings on the reduced riskiness of shorter holding periods highlight what may be the most important conclusion of this study—that underwriting risk depends not so much on the riskiness of the underlying security, but rather on the pricing, the spread, and the length of time the securities are held.

This section pursues that point a little further. We compare our equity underwriting results with some crude estimates of the riskiness of corporate bond underwriting.

Bond underwriting is performed by commercial banks both in the United States (for general obligation municipal bonds) and in the Eurobond market (for corporate and other bonds) in a fashion similar to equity underwriting, with a fixed offer price and, in principle, a significant downside risk. We therefore sought to measure the riskiness of bond underwriting in a manner identical to that described above for equities.[11] Unfortunately, most bond trading is "over the counter," so few bonds have reliable aftermarket prices that can be compared with the offer price. Because bonds are much more uniform, commoditylike securities than equities, however, one can estimate any bond's price based on a "matrix" of market prices for traded bonds with similar attributes. This is called "matrix pricing." For our study, therefore, we used "matrix prices" supplied by Merrill Lynch bond traders wherever market prices were unavailable. These prices were available weekly, not daily, so we used the closing price on the Friday of the week of issue (same week), the following week, and the third week instead. Although it is not safe to assume that these represent true market values, we have been unable to identify any significant bias in the matrix pricing data that might distort our results. The study was limited to the period 1979–1983, because data for earlier years were grossly incomplete. Nevertheless, out of approximately 5000 issues examined, complete data were found for only 665 issues.

The overall results are summarized in Table 6.7. As in the previous table, the top half describes certain features of the distribution of price changes, whereas the lower half describes the estimated gains or losses.[12] It is widely assumed that bond underwriting is less risky than equity underwriting, because bond values are more stable than equity values. The latter is confirmed by the measures of riskiness of the bond price changes: Both the standard deviation and the range of bond price changes are far smaller than equity price changes (compare Table 6.3). On the other hand, the *average* price change is slightly negative for each of the three periods, indicating that the underpricing phenomenon observed for equities is absent for U.S. corporate bonds. All other things being equal, these taken together should produce higher, less risky returns from bond underwriting.

But this is not the case, as a comparison of the bottom half of Table 6.7 with Table 6.4 will confirm. Because bond underwriting *spreads* are much lower than equity spreads—typically about 0.6% to 0.8%, compared to 4%–7% for equities—the *net* return from bond underwriting appears to be lower, on average, than equity underwriting; indeed it is positive only if the syndicate breaks within the first week. Moreover, the standard deviation of gains and losses is about the same as for equity underwriting. This means that the coefficient of variation—the standard deviation

Table 6.7   Price Changes and Net Gains/Losses from Bond Underwriting

	Percentage Deviation of Market from Offer Price by:		
	Same Week	Second Week	Third Week
Average	−0.15	−0.32	−0.26
Standard deviation	2.03	2.68	3.15
Range	−11.19 to 11.20	−11.19 to 26.92	−12.39 to 26.92
Number of:			
Rises	246	259	268
Zero changes	72	32	29
Falls	347	374	368

	Net Gain/Loss Assuming Syndicate Broke on or Before: (in millions of dollars)		
	Same Week	Second Week	Third Week
Average	0.14	−0.01	−0.06
Standard deviation	.82	2.09	2.45
Range	−20.75 to 8.48	−20.75 to 5.73	−28.80 to 7.43
Number of:			
Net gains	473	470	474
Net breakevens	2	4	2
Net losses	190	191	189

Note: The top half of this table shows bond price changes from the offer price at the end of the week of the offering and of the two following weeks (daily data were unobtainable). The bottom half depicts the underwriters' truncated gains or losses, taking into account the price received (lower of offer or market) and the price paid but not overhead or other costs (the method described in Table 6.1). It is comparable to Table 6.4.

divided by the mean—is greater for bond underwriting than for equity underwriting. Finally, the proportion of net losses at each of the three dates is much higher for bonds than for equities.

Until evidence shows otherwise, therefore, we cannot conclude that equity underwriting is necessarily riskier than bond underwriting.

CAN UNDERWRITING RISK BE HEDGED?

Equity underwriting *can* be risky, simply because the underwriter of equity is dealing in a volatile security, and through mispricing, or insufficient spreads, or holding onto a falling stock for too long, the underwriter can in principle lose a great deal.

On the other hand, equity underwriting can be at least as safe as commercial lending, if the underlying risk is properly managed. Three approaches to limiting risk can be taken:

First, the size and proportion of losses evidently depends heavily on the holding period. By limiting the holding period to a few days or even a few hours, the U.S. underwriting industry can and does keep its risk to a minimal level. The crux here is having a sufficiently liquid market that the securities can be sold when desired.

Second, for any particular issue, the expected return to the underwriter depends on where the net and offer prices are set relative to the expected market price and the volatility of the stock. So the first step to protecting against underwriting losses is to set the net price low enough, and the offer price high enough, that the proportion of net losses can be kept to a minimum. Admittedly, in a competitive market the individual underwriter may not have much influence on the prices set. But the underwriter always has the choice of declining participation, just as commercial banks can decline to participate in risky, low-spread loans.

Third, this chapter has emphasized the lopsided character of underwriting risk, which is akin to that of writing a put option. But this suggests a third way to hedge. The proper way to hedge an asymmetric risk (underwriting) is with an asymmetric contract (an option). The underwriter can buy put options on the stock itself, if available, in an amount equal to the amount underwritten and with a strike price equal to the offer price. The gains from holding a put option will offset the losses from price falls, whereas the losses (if the stock rises) are limited to the purchase price of the option. The only disadvantage of this is that, if the market is pricing options and underwriting services correctly, the cost of the option premium will wipe out the portion of the spread that serves as a premium for risk-bearing. All that is left is the reward for distribution. This makes sense, however, because if the underwriter chooses to offer only distribution services and not to bear risk, the firm cannot expect to be rewarded for risk. The value of the options market is that it lets the underwriter make this choice. If no market for options in the particular stock exists, the underwriter can purchase options on an industry index or at worst on the overall market index. These will protect the firm from market risk, but not from the risk of having mispriced the issue nor from random events affecting the company that occur between the pricing and the sale of the shares.

In sum, the underwriting risk faced by any particular institution or the industry as a whole, and the impact of the underlying security's volatility can be (and normally is) reduced to a low level and it can be hedged. Whether any particular underwriter will choose to do so is a matter for the institution and its regulators to decide; but the same can be said of virtually every banking activity.

AN INTERPRETATION

We have sought to test the proposition that equity underwriting risk is qualitatively and quantitatively different from the normal risks of commercial banking. The arguments and evidence examined here demonstrate, we believe, that commercial lend-

Table 6.8 Components of Revenue of Securities Firms (Profits of NYSE member firms doing a public business)[a]

	1974 $	1974 %	1975 $	1975 %	1976 $	1976 %	1977 $	1977 %	1978 $	1978 %	1979 $	1979 %	1980 $	1980 %	1981 $	1981 %	1982 $	1982 %
Revenues																		
Securities Commissions	2303	48.9	2949	49.8	3163	45.8	2809	41.7	3779	42.8	4012	35.6	5671	35.5	5346	27.0	6021	25.9
Trading and Investments	623	13.2	916	15.5	1400	20.3	1296	19.3	1542	17.5	2671	23.7	3699	23.1	4813	24.3	5957	25.7
Interest on customer debt balances	604	12.8	455	7.7	565	8.2	754	11.2	1173	13.3	1651	14.7	2089	13.1	2890	14.6	2974	12.8
Underwriting	427	9.1	780	13.2	853	12.4	777	11.5	742	8.4	769	6.8	1307	8.2	1572	7.9	2319	10.0
Mutual fund sales	41	0.9	36	0.6	45	0.7	59	0.9	59	0.7	76	0.7	105	0.7	122	0.6	288	1.2
Commodity revenues	162	3.4	176	3.0	210	3.0	243	3.6	351	4.0	436	3.9	625	3.9	580	2.9	666	2.9
Other related to securities business	550	11.7	511	8.6	530	7.7	657	9.8	949	10.7	1296	11.5	1913	12.0	3254	16.4	3940	17.0
Other unrelated to securities business	NR[a]	NR[a]	105	1.8	136	2.0	135	2.0	237	2.7	353	3.1	577	3.6	1228	6.2	1047	4.5
Total Revenue	4710	100	5927	100	6902	100	6730	100	8832	100	11264	100	15986	100	19805	100	23212	100
Net Income	151		415		508		188		339		557		1158		1086		NA	

[a]Source: Standard & Poors Industry Survey, December 1983.

ing, like investment banking, involves a stictly limited upside gain (determined by the spread) and a downside risk associated with the variability of the assets price over a given holding period. Although the assets purchased in equity underwritings are much riskier than those purchased in commercial lending, investment bankers are able, in principle, to reduce the magnitude of any loss to a small percentage by reducing the holding period to a very short time interval. Observations of market practice suggest that this is indeed what happens—and the empirical evidence on the distribution of net gains and losses from equity underwriting confirms that doing so can reduce both the frequency and the magnitude of losses to a low level.

It was also shown that underwriting risk is in essence the risk of writing an uncovered put option on a stock with a very near expiration date. Consequently, underwriting risk can be hedged (albeit imperfectly) by buying put options, enabling the underwriters to lay off much of the risk of underwriting should they so choose.

We conclude by trying to place this study in proper perspective. As an examination of Table 6.8 will verify, underwriting per se averages only about 10% of securities firms' revenues. Far larger earnings come from trading and from brokerage commissions. The major influence on brokerage profitability is the volume of business. Because this applies to discount brokerage earnings as much as any other segment, perhaps commercial banks have *already* entered one of the more risky aspects of the securities industry. Dealing, on the other hand, is inherently risky *if* the firm chooses to take a large exposed position. But this applies to government bond and foreign exchange dealing, already done by banks, at least as much as to equity dealing. The risk borne by an individual bank depends on the size of the position taken and the length of time it is held in relation to the volatility of the underlying security.

Finally, both underwriting and dealing, as practiced by U.S. securities firms, are safer than commercial lending in one major respect. The assets held are liquid, can be disposed of easily, and their marketability allows frequent marking-to-the-market of the value of the firm's portfolio.[13] If, as can be argued, the key source of depositors' risk lies in the time lag associated with measuring the value of banks' assets, the exposure of the regulator/insurer can be ameliorated by turning Glass-Steagall on its head: that is, by insisting that depository institutions deal only in assets with transparent market values—as is done in the underwriting of public equity issues.

ACKNOWLEDGMENTS

The author has benefited from conversations with Ingo Walter, Anthony Saunders, and others, and from the computing assistance of Larry Bjorkman and Douglas MacKenzie.

NOTES

[1]See Ian H. Giddy, "Risk and Returns for Bond Underwriting," Working Paper, New York University, 1984.

[2]See Frank K. Reilly and K. Hatfield, "Investor Experience with New Stock Issues," *Financial Analysts Journal,* 25 (1969), pp. 73–80; J. G. McDonald and A. K. Fisher, "New Issue Stock Price Behavior," *Journal of Finance,* 27 (1972), pp. 97–102; Dennis E. Logue, "On the Pricing of Unseasoned Equity Offerings: 1965–1969," *Journal of Financial and Quantitative Analysis,* 8 (1973), pp. 91–103; Roger Ibbotson, "Price Performance of Common Stock New Issues," *Journal of Financial Economics,* 30, No. 4 (1975), pp. 235–272; Ibbotson, "Common Stock New Issues Revisited," Working Paper No. 84, Center for Research in Security Prices, University of Chicago, 1982; Roger G. Ibbotson and Jeffrey J. Jaffe, "Hot Issue Markets," *Journal of Finance,* 30, No. 4 (September 1975), pp. 1027–1042.

[3]For details, see Hayes et al., *Competition in the Investment Banking Industry.* (Cambridge, Mass.: Harvard University Press, 1983); or Vincent P. Carosso, *Investment Banking in America: A History.* (Cambridge, Mass.: Harvard University Press, 1970).

[4]L. H. Ederington, "Uncertainty, Competition and Costs in Corporate Bond Underwriting," *Journal of Financial Economics,* 2 (1975), pp. 71–94; and Dennis E. Logue and J. R. Lindvall, "The Behavior of Investment Bankers: An Econometric Investigation," *Journal of Finance,* 24 (1974), pp. 203–215, have analyzed underwriters' compensation as a function of various characteristics of the underwriter and the new issue offered.

[5]As will be seen later, the absence of data will force us to ignore, for empirical testing, the fixed and contingent costs noted in the table.

[6]A word of classification as to the nature of the optionlike character of underwriting risk. What happens is that the underwriter takes two steps: (1) The firm buys the shares at a below-market price, (2) then gives the public an option to buy the shares at the offer price. The latter is a call option with an exercise price = the offer price. The underwriter is in effect writing a covered call option. From the theory of option reversals and conversions, we know that a long position in a security combined with a short call is equivalent to a short put option. That is why underwriting risk resembles the risk of selling a put.

[7]Academic writers such as Gershon Mandelker and Arthur Raviv ("Investment Banking: An Economic Analysis of Optimal Underwriting Contracts," *Journal of Finance,* 32 [June 1977], pp. 683–694), have characterized three kinds of underwriting and the risks associated with each. These are: a "best efforts" contract (in which the underwriter is employed only for distribution and faces no market risk at all); a "stand-by" contract (in which the banker binds himself to purchasing all the securities that the issuing corporation may be unable to sell at a prespecified price); and "firm commitment" underwriting as described in the previous section. Only the latter is of interest, because the first is not underwriting and the second is now very rare.

[8]Mathematically, if $f(x)$ is the distribution of equity price changes in the relevant period after offer, and $F(x)$ the cumulative distribution, then the expected value of the truncated underwriting distribution is

Expected value $= [F(\alpha) - F(\text{offer price})] \times (\text{offer price} - \text{net price})$

$$+ \int_{\text{net price}}^{\text{offer price}} f(x)[x - \text{net price}] - \int_{0}^{\text{net price}} f(x)\,[\text{net price} - x]$$

[9]Ibbotson, "Price Performance,"; and Ritters, " 'Hot issue' Market."

[10]For the risk-limiting techniques of Eurobond underwriting by commercial bank affiliates, see Chapter 10 of this book.

[11]The method and results are described more fully in Ian H. Giddy, "Risk and Returns from Bond Underwriting," Working Paper, New York University, 1984.

[12]The estimated net gains or losses are calculated in the same manner as for equities (see Table 6.1), that is, taking into account the assumed sale price less the purchase price, but not taking into account overhead or other costs.

[13]As a banker familiar with both areas pointed out, knowing the market value of your portfolio provides a strong incentive to cut your losses short by disposing of assets quickly before their deterioration progresses too far. Therefore one could argue that commercial banks which held only marketable assets would be less risky than those who suffer the sudden trauma of writing down the book value of loans.

REFERENCES

Black, Fischer, and Myron Scholes. "The Pricing of Options and Corporate Liabilities," *Journal of Political Economy* 81 (August, 1973), pp. 637–654.

Carosso, Vincent P. *Investment Banking in America: A History.* Cambridge, Mass: Harvard University Press, 1970.

Ederington, L. H. "Uncertainty, Competition and Costs in Corporate Bond Underwriting," *Journal of Financial Economics* 2 (March 1975), pp. 71–94.

Giddy, Ian H. "Risk and Returns from Bond Underwriting," *Working Paper,* New York University, 1984.

Hayes, Samuel L., Michael A. Spence, and David V.P. Marks. *Competition in the Investment Banking Industry.* Cambridge, Mass: Harvard University Press, 1983.

Hayes, Samuel L. "Investment Banking: "Power Structure in Flux," *Harvard Business Review* (March–April, 1971), pp. 136–152.

Ibbotson, Roger G. "Common Stock New Issues Revisited," Working Paper No. 84, Center for Research in Security Prices, University of Chicago, 1982.

Ibbotson, Roger G. "Price Performance of Common Stock New Issues," *Journal of Financial Economics,* (September, 1975), pp. 235–272.

Ibbotson, Roger G., and Jeffrey J. Jaffe. "Hot Issue Markets," *Journal of Finance,* **30,** No. 4 (September, 1975), pp. 1027–1042.

Logue, Dennis E. "On the Pricing of Unseasoned Equity Offerings: 1965–1969," *Journal of Financial and Quantitative Analysis,* **8** (September, 1973), pp. 91–103.

Logue, Dennis E., and J. R. Lindvall. "The Behavior of Investment Bankers: An Econometric Investigation," *Journal of Finance,* **24** (March, 1974), pp. 203–215.

McDonald, J. G., and A. K. Fisher. "New Issue Stock Price Behavior," *Journal of Finance,* **27** (March, 1972), pp. 97–102.

Mandelker, Gershon, and Artur Raviv. "Investment Banking: An Economic Analysis of Optimal Underwriting Contracts," *Journal of Finance,* **32** (June, 1977), pp. 683–694.

Reilly, Frank K., and K. Hatfield. "Investor Experience with New Stock Issues," *Financial Analysts Journal,* **25** (1969), pp. 73–80.

Ritter, Jay R. "The 'Hot Issue' Market of 1980," Working Paper, University of Pennsylvania (September, 1982).

Rock, Kevin R. "Why Are New Issues Underpriced?" Unpublished Ph.D. Dissertation, University of Chicago, 1982.

7 Bank Safety and Soundness and the Risks of Corporate Securities Activities

ANTHONY SAUNDERS

One of the most important concerns of the Fed, in examining the case for bank holding company expansion into nonbank activities, is the unfavorable effects these activities might have on bank safety and soundness.[1] This chapter examines the implications of potential problems that could affect nonbank affiliate within a holding company structure.

In the following section the riskiness of two major underwriting or trading activities currently permissible for banks is analyzed. These activities are municipal general obligation bond underwriting and foreign exchange trading and dealing. It is argued that although these activities share many of the risks attributed to corporate securities underwriting and trading (see Chapter 6 for a full discussion of these risks) they have not yet caused any systematic losses or solvency problems for the banks concerned. Moreover, in the section on ''Possible Risk Reducing Factors,'' it is argued that there are likely to be activity and geographic diversification benefits which will result from banks expanding into security-type activities. These diversification benefits could work to reduce the overall risk of failure of the bank holding company and therefore the bank. In the section on ''Possible Risk Increasing Factors,'' some factors are identified and discussed that might impact adversely on bank safety and soundness, if bank holding companies were to undertake corporate securities activities. These adverse factors include the use of bank dividends to support an ailing affiliate, loans to the affiliate that turn bad, adverse confidence problems, and potential legal liabilities. In the section on ''Evidence from the Capital Market,'' studies of the investors' perceptions of the riskiness of nonbank activities of holding companies are discussed. Finally, the last section summarizes and discusses certain policy implications and recommendations.

BANK MUNICIPAL BOND UNDERWRITING AND FOREIGN EXCHANGE TRADING

In assessing the case for commercial bank affiliates engaging in corporate securities activities it is useful to begin by comparing some of the risk characteristics of corporate bond underwriting with those of municipal bond underwriting, an activity in which banks have been heavily engaged (with the notable exception of revenue bonds) for a number of years without apparent problems. Indeed, no contemporary failure of a bank or bank holding company as been attributed to losses on municipal bond underwritings.[2]

For individual issues, the corporate bond market tends to be deeper than the municipal bond market. Lamb and Rappaport[3] showed that over the period 1970–1978 an average of 7884 municipal issues (general obligation and revenue bonds) came to market each year, compared with only 426 publicly offered corporate debt issues. In 1982 the number of corporate debt issues was even lower, at 374.[4] However, the aggregate dollar value of all new municipal bond issues was never more than twice the aggregate dollar value of corporate bond issues. The relative market sizes for the three most recent years are shown in Table 7.1. These data imply that the *average* size of a corporate bond issue is larger than that of municipal issue.

Further insights into the relative depth of the corporate and municipal bond markets can be gained by examining the total volume of corporate and municipal bonds outstanding each year, as well as the distribution of investor holdings of those bonds. Some relevant data are shown in Tables 7.2 and 7.3.

Note that the actual value of corporate bonds *outstanding* in Table 7.2 is larger than municipal obligations (although this is partly because the available flow-of-funds figures do not distinguish between public and private placements, and because corporate bonds tend to be of longer maturity than municipal general obligation bonds). The ownership patterns reflected in Table 7.3 are particularly interesting. Specifically, the corporate bond market is dominated to a greater extent by institutional investors (such as insurance companies and pension funds) than is the municipal bond market. Block trades in the corporate bond market dominate trades on the official exchanges as discussed in Bloch.[5] Such block trading activity is far less common in the municipal bond market.

If large *average* new issue size is combined with a more active secondary market

Table 7.1   New Issues of State and Local Obligation and Public Offerings of Corporate Debt ($ millions)

	1980	1981	1982
General obligation	14,100	12,394	21,088
Revenue	34,267	35,338	57,862
Total	48,367	47,732	78,950
Public offering of corporate bonds	41,587	37,653	43,428

Source: Federal Reserve Bulletin.

Table 7.2   Corporate and State and Local Bonds
Outstanding ($ billions)

	1980	1981	1982
Corporate bonds	373.9	397.8	420.2
State and local	320.2	342.5	389.7

Source: Federal Reserve Board of Governors Flow of
Funds Tables (February 22, 1983).

(e.g., between large institutions), this would tend to dampen the relative price risk on corporate bonds (as compared with the market for municipals) caused by thinness in market demand. Specifically, the deeper a financial market, the less a price should change following any given buy or sell transaction. This is clearly shown in previous research by Fisher.[6] Thus $25 million of unsold municipal bonds left in an underwriter's inventory after the closing of the offer period will tend to command on average a greater (percent) price discount than an equivalent amount of corporate bonds if sold at one time (or over a short time interval).

To get a general idea of the relative volatility of rates on corporates and general obligation municipal bonds, the means and standard deviations of Moody's Aaa series on corporate bonds[7] and state and local general obligation bonds were computed from the monthly series reported in the *Federal Reserve Bulletin* over the period from January 1978 to March 1983. The results are shown in Table 7.4.

As can be seen from the table, the standard deviation of the yields on general obligation bonds (a measure of risk) is slightly larger than on obligation bonds, although this difference is not statistically significant at any meaningful confidence

Table 7.3   Holders of Corporate and State and Local Bonds in 1982 (%)[a,b]

	Corporate Bonds	State and Local Bonds
Households	12.8	35.9
Commercial banks	1.6	34.1
Insurance companies	39.7	21.0
Mutual funds	2.0	4.7
State and local government retirement funds	18.7	1.0
Other (includes private pension plans)	25.2	3.3

Source: Federal Reserve Board of Governors Flow of Funds Tables (February 22, 1983).
[a]Includes industrial revenue bonds for state and local government obligations, and foreign bonds for corporate bonds.
[b]No separation is made in the flow of funds between public offerings and private placements.

Table 7.4　Means and Standard Deviation of Yields (%) on Corporate and Municipal Obligation Bonds, January 1978–March 1983

	Mean	Standard Deviation
Corporate bonds	11.6608	2.28004
Municipal general obligation	8.14508	2.31579

Source: Federal Reserve Bulletin, various issues.

level. The coefficient of variation (standard deviation divided by the mean), however, was greater for municipal bonds (0.2843) than for corporate bonds (0.1955). This implies that municipal bond yields (and price equivalents) were more volatile than those on corporate bonds over the period of study. To any extent, the potential for interest rate risk appears to be no *greater* for corporate bonds than it is for municipal general obligation bonds—an underwriting activity in which banks themselves are already engaged. Indeed, despite this relative volatility result only one major bank holding company (Chemical) suffered a number of sizable losses on its securities trading account over the period 1976–1982. The profit and loss figures for the 15 largest bank holding companies are presented in Table 7.5. Although these figures include profits and commissions on government securities and foreign bond trading as well as municipals, they are indicative of the generally profitable nature of these activities. Moreover, even in the case of the largest loss—$17.2 million by Chemical in 1979—this amounted to only 1.58% of its common equity capital.

Similar results emerge when the profits (losses) from the foreign exchange trading activities of major bank players are analyzed. At least 119 banks in the United States had foreign exchange trading operations, as of April 1983, up from 90 in March 1980, and the total volume of foreign exchange trading was $702 billion in April 1983 compared with $491 billion in March 1980. These banks operate in the foreign exchange markets either on their own account (as market makers) or on behalf of multinational corporations and other customers. The major risk facing the foreign exchange trader in a bank is one of timing, that is, of selecting the optimum moment to buy and sell funds. This in turn will largely depend on the traders' expectations regarding future movements in exchange rates. The highly volatile nature of spot exchange rates in the post-Smithsonian era have been well documented as have the problems of hedging foreign currency risk in such an environment. Hence, an important question is whether banks that stand at the center of the foreign exchange market—both in making the market and buying and selling on behalf of customers—have suffered major losses on their foreign exchange operations.

The foreign exchange profits for bank holding companies who were the major players in the foreign exchange market are shown in Appendix I for the period 1976–1985.[8] As can be seen, the only loss was $934,000 by Security Pacific Corporation in 1979—equal to 0.1% of the value of its common equity. Further, for some holding companies—Bank America, Chase Manhattan, Citicorp, and J. P. Morgan—income from foreign exchange transactions has generally supplied over 10% of *all* noninterest

Table 7.5   Trading Account Profit and Commissions 15 Largest Bank Holding Companies, 1976–1982 ($ millions)

BHC	1976	1977	1978	1979	1980	1981	1982
Bank America	10.3	8.5	13.5	11.9	30.7	40.0	86.9
Citicorp	49.0	37.1	20.6	54.8	71.0	88.0	125.0
Chase	13.9	5.0	1.5	5.8	14.1	28.0	31.3
Manufacturers Hanover	6.1	4.9	6.1	6.8	10.4	16.4	18.9
Morgan	29.4	(3.5)	6.1	14.2	28.5	12.8	50.0
Chemical	11.3	(2.6)	(2.9)	(17.2)	(7.7)	19.3	33.6
Continental Illinois	17.3	11.0	11.3	15.7	6.1	27.9	39.9
First Interstate	—	4.0	2.1	4.9	2.9	15.1	15.7
Bankers Trust	—	4.0	11.0	27.1	50.0	39.5	81.1
Security Pacific	6.2	3.0	2.5	6.4	17.5	12.9	19.7
First Chicago	13.9	10.4	5.8	6.0	8.2	10.8	8.4
Crocker	—	(0.3)	(0.9)	1.8	7.0	0.5	16.4
Wells Fargo	5.2	4.2	3.7	5.3	12.2	16.2	21.0
Inter First	—	1.3	0.8	1.5	1.3	1.5	2.6
Mellon	2.9	(0.2)	0.7	0.7	1.6	3.9	9.9

Source: Moody's Bank and Finance Manual and Various Annual Reports.

income earned by the holding company. Thus even in this high-risk environment of flexible and volatile exchange rates, no *systematic* record of losses and therefore threats to safety and soundness are evident for the banks involved.

POSSIBLE RISK-REDUCING FACTORS

The expansion of a bank holding company into new activities such as securities underwriting (and dealing) may also serve to reduce the risk to the bank by increasing the level and reducing the underlying variance (risk) of holding company profits. Conceptually, the potential diversification gains of a bank holding company take two forms: (1) gains through activity (or product) diversification, and (2) gains through geographic diversification.

Activity Diversification

By engaging in activity or scope diversification,[9] the holding company may assume less risk if the net cash flows or profits of the bank (the holding company's primary asset) are imperfectly correlated with those of activities undertaken by nonbanking affiliates. In general, the lower the correlation between bank profits and profits from other activities (e.g., consumer finance, leasing, corporate securities underwriting, etc.) the lower will be the variance of holding company profits for any *given* level of expected profit or return.[10] Thus a crucial question in evaluating the gains from holding company expansion is the degree to which profits or returns on bank activities are correlated with other (nonbanking) activities. Not surprisingly, there have been a number of empirical studies evaluating this question, three of which are reviewed here.

Heggestad[11] using the IRS's *Corporate Source Book of Income,* derived profitability data for different activity (industry) groups that were at that time—or might in the future—be parts of a bank holding company. Apart from banks, 13 other industry groups were investigated. Heggestad found that, over the period 1953–1967, six of the 13 activities had returns (profits) that were negatively correlated with returns from commercial banking. Interestingly, one of these was between commercial banks and holding/investment companies[12] with a correlation coefficient of -0.12.

Eisemann[13] considered the gains from risk diversification where the bank holding company is assumed to be (1) limited to diversifying into currently allowable activities only, (2) allowed to diversify into activities that have been neither permitted nor ruled nonallowable (so-called possible activities), and (3) allowed to diversify into activities that have been ruled nonallowable, such as investment banking. Nine activities were viewed as permissible, seven as possible, and five as nonallowable. As a proxy for the profitability of these activities, average rates of return on the stocks of firms principally engaged in these various activities were calculated on a monthly basis over the December 1961 to December 1968 period. Three "efficient activity frontiers" were calculated according to the set of activities viewed as being available to the bank. The efficient frontier shows the combination of activities that minimize a holding company's risk (standard deviation of returns) for each level of expected return.

The major results were that: (1) by allowing both possible and nonallowable activities such as securities underwriting to be undertaken, the holding company could earn a significantly higher return per unit of risk than when constrained to permissible activities only, and (2) investment banking could display a (potentially) significant risk-reducing role in the overall portfolio of holding company activities. Specifically, with respect to (2) above, investment banking was found to be a particularly important activity in all of the low-risk (low standard deviation) holding company activity portfolios—with an optimal component, as part of the holding company, of between 11% and 19%.[14] Eisemann's findings thus suggest that investment banking activities might significantly improve the overall risk-return characteristics of a bank holding company.

Meinster and Johnson[15] use profit data from an existing bank holding company and its subsidiaries to compute an *efficient* set of company activities.[16] This efficient holding company structure can be compared with the actual profitability and risk of the *existing* holding company and the bank subsidiary, when viewed in isolation. The bank holding company analyzed owned one bank, two leasing subsidiaries, five consumer finance subsidiaries, a mortgage bank subsidiary, a bank management consulting firm, and one financial service and two foreign banking subsidiaries. The cash flow, or profit data for each subsidiary were derived from balance-sheet and income statements over the 1973–I to 1977–II period. The mean quarterly return and standard deviation of returns for the bank subsidiary, viewed in isolation from the rest of the holding company, were 0.00527 and 0.00151, respectively, with an average return per unit of risk ratio of 3.490. When other activities were considered and the efficient set of activities for the holding company calculated, it was found that *all* existing subsidiaries were included in the efficient set. This even encompassed those activities with higher profit variances and lower average profits than the bank itself, because these subsidiaries generated profits that were low or even negatively correlated with those of the bank. This efficient holding company was found to provide significant risk reduction gains when compared to the weighting of activities in the existing holding company.[17] Further, even the inefficiently diversified (existing) holding company was found to outperform the bank itself, with a return per unit of risk ratio of 3.758 compared to 3.490 for the bank viewed in isolation.[18]

Finally, a study by Wall and Eisenbeis[19] analyzing the correlations between bank (or bank holding company) earnings and the earnings from selected nonbank activities of banks found that over the period 1970–1980 the correlation between bank and security broker/dealer earnings was -0.17821, and that between bank holding companies and security broker/dealers was -0.16985.

Overall, then, these studies suggest that important risk-diversification gains may be available to a bank holding company through *efficient* activity diversification, with these gains working to insulate the bank from the failure of, or losses on, any single acitivity.

Finally, for another perspective on the underlying relationship between the core activities of commercial and investment banks, in Figure 7.1 the quarterly *changes* in C and I loans were plotted against the quarterly changes in (new) publicly offered

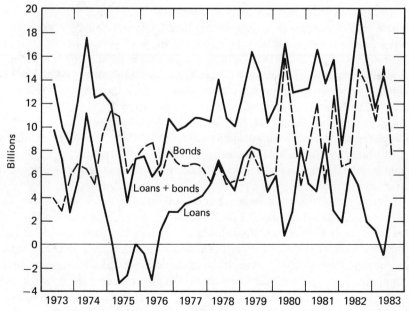

Figure 7.1   Change in C&I loans versus publicly offered nonconvertible debt (Largely corporate debt issues. Excludes syndicated agencies, federal, state, and local issues, as well as tax-exempt pollution control financings and swaps.)

nonconvertible debt issues for the 1973–1983 period. Visual inspection suggests that these time series offers move in opposite directions; this especially appears to be true in the post-1980 period. Indeed, the partial correlation coefficient between the two series is -0.5, which again suggests that significant diversification opportunities may be present.

Geographic Diversification

Under the 1927 McFadden Act and the 1956 Bank Holding Company Act, banks face severe restrictions on their ability either to branch or buy other banks across state lines. Although there has been some elasticity introduced by emergency purchase and assumptions of out-of-state banks, the passage of reciprocal interstate banking laws (e.g., by the New England states, the growth of interstate ATM and ACH networks, the expansion of Edge Act corporations and loan production offices, and the purchase of S&Ls by out-of-state banks, the degree of interstate banking is (arguably) still quite small. This limits the ability of banks to diversify their earnings regionally. For example, the fast-growing states in the Sunbelt have been a particularly profitable area for banks and bank holding companies located there, compared with those confined to states in the industrialized Midwest and Northeast. This seems to be reflected in relative rates of growth in bank assets.[20] These differential profits reflect both regional business cycles and the degree of competition in those areas. Thus interstate banking restrictions often lead to unequal rates of return on bank capital across regions, with many banks earning excess returns because of regulatory restrictions and localized monopoly power rather than institutional efficiency.

These opportunity losses are further amplified for banks in states where there are also restrictions on intrastate branching. Indeed, of the 50 states plus the District of Columbia, less than half (24) can be designated as full branching states, whereas 16 have limited branching powers and 11 are basically unit-banking states. The bank holding company structure provides a substitute vehicle through which banks can enjoy indirectly some of the benefits of regional diversification. For example, Eisenbeis[21] presents evidence which shows that by far the largest number of *one* bank holding companies exist in unit-banking states, followed by limited-branching and then full-branching states. More recently, Eisenbeis[22] showed that, in the past, the economic gains from geographic diversification have dominated those from pure activity diversification.

Currently a bank holding company can acquire affiliates across state lines in over 20 different activities designated by the Fed as being closely related to banking.[23] So, for example, both Citicorp and BankAmerica Corp have consumer finance affiliates in over 40 different states. By acquiring affiliates in other states, the bank holding company can arbitrage away some of the discrepancies in regional rates of return, resulting in a more efficient interregional allocation of scarce capital resources. This benefits society and results in a more regionally diversified earnings stream for the holding company. These is also evidence[24] to show that there are some rather substantial regional differences in corporate securities flotation costs, partly due to the concentration of underwriters in the Northeast. Thus significant profit opportunities might be available to (one) bank holding companies which establish securities affiliates in ''less traditional'' investment banking states and service small and regional firms that have previously been excluded from the primary capital market.

POSSIBLE RISK-INCREASING FACTORS

There are at least four direct and indirect routes through which a bank might be adversely affected by holding company expansion into securities activities using a separately capitalized affiliate.

Upstreaming Dividend Payments to the Holding Company

This possibility arises if the capital positions of either the affiliate or the holding company were significantly weakened by major underwriting losses. Under such circumstances, the holding company has the option of (1) closing the affiliate, for example, by declaring bankruptcy; (2) selling it off to outside buyers, if any are available; or (3) seeking to increase its capital base. The latter option is perhaps the most desirable. Suppose the banking affiliate of the holding company is healthy and has substantial earnings. The holding company might use these earnings by inducing bank managers to pay abnormally high dividends to the holding company parent, thereby generating funds for additional capital investment in the securities affiliate in difficulty. This is tantamount to milking the bank (the cash cow) to the benefit of the affiliate (the dog), although it appears to make little business sense and is constrained by statutory limits on bank dividends.

There are a number of factors that would tend to limit such a diversion of funds. First, the Fed ostensibly monitors dividend payments by banks, and is therefore in a position to flag exceptionally large increases in bank dividend pay-out ratios.[25] Second, such behavior rarely is wise from a profit- or value-maximizing perspective of holding-company shareholders. Assuming holding company management wishes to maximize the profits (or market value) of the overall corporation, by redistributing capital from the bank to the securities affiliate it is likely to forgo a number of profitable (positive net present value) future growth or investment opportunities that might arise with respect to the bank. Instead, these funds would be used as an incremental investment in a currently low-profit venture—the securities affiliate. Such a redirection of capital can only be rationalized on economic grounds[26] if the holding company's management perceives ex ante that the *future* growth opportunities for the currently unprofitable affiliate are somehow greater than those available to the bank.[27]

Loans to the Securities Affiliate or Holding Company

An alternative way in which the bank can be used by its holding company to aid a failing or distressed securities affiliate is through intercompany loans.[28] The Bank Holding Company Act, as amended, and the Federal Reserve Act, Section 23A, however, place strict limits on the amount of loans a bank can make to any single nonbank holding company affiliate to 10% of capital (with a 20% limit on loans to all nonbank affiliates combined), with all such loans having to be collateralized between 100% and 130% of the size of the loan. In essence, this collateral requirement converts these loans into risk-free instruments from the bank's perspective. Nevertheless, to the extent that the bank has alternative investment or lending opportunities that can generate expected risk-adjusted returns greater than the risk-free rate charged to the securities affiliate, such loans involve an opportunity cost to the bank's shareholders, and reduce profits below the attainable maximum. It should be noted, however, that in a (perfectly) competitive loan market the expected risk-adjusted returns on loans will, in equilibrium, just equal the return on risk-free loans, so that this opportunity cost would tend toward zero.

The Confidence Problem

A more serious and indirect route through which the bank might be affected by the financial difficulties of an affiliate is the so-called confidence problem. Publicized financial difficulties of a securities affiliate may lead to a loss of confidence on the part of depositors or other liability holders in the safety and soundness (or reputation) of the bank or in the quality of the bank's management, resulting either in a run-off of liabilities or an increase in the required risk premium demanded by liability holders. The classic confidence problem results in a run on a bank by depositors following the announcement of some adverse information or rumor (well founded or not). This forces the bank to liquidate its assets at current market rates (often at a loss), to meet the demand for funds, forcing it even further toward insolvency. Banks are particularly susceptible to this type of run because outside depositors and investors often have imperfect and inadequate information about the true value of bank assets, and this encourages ''me-first'' behavior in withdrawing funds. This information problem is partly due to accounting valuation rules, absence of secondary markets for loans, as well as limited disclosure rules.

A recent example of a run on a bank fueled by concern as to the true value of bank assets (especially energy-related loans) was Continental Illinois, in May 1984. Note that ''confidence problems'' as described for banks are less likely to arise for a securities affiliate (in a bank holding company) because their will be less uncertainty about the value of its assets in the eyes of outside creditors and bondholders. The main reason for this is that the assets of securities firms, by their very nature, are market-to-market, whereas such market valuation is usually absent for bank assets such as loans.

The likelihood of such a confidence problem affecting a bank generally will depend on (1) the ratio of uninsured to insured depositors,[29] (2) depositors' expectations regarding the behavior or reaction of the regulatory authorities in the event a bank encounters difficulties, (3) the size of the bank and its holding company's capital-assets ratio (or the level of its capital-adequacy), and (4) the degree of depositor consensus regarding the true solvency position or quality of assets of the bank.

Because only the largest bank holding companies are likely to have corporate securities affiliates, and their bank subsidiaries will tend to have the greatest ratio of uninsured to insured deposits,[30] such banks would appear to be more susceptible to deposit withdrawals by large, sophisticated, uninsured depositors than smaller banks following adverse information regarding a nonbank affiliate. Acting against this susceptibility to deposit runs (or liability drains), however, is the fact that the social costs of large bank failures are such that large depositors would expect the Fed (via the discount window) or the FDIC to take action to prevent outright failure. After short-term loans from the discount window have been exhausted or the Fed has decided to limit its exposure, the usual method by which outright failure is prevented is through purchase and assumption—whereby the FDIC seeks a merging partner to assume the failing bank's (good) assets and liabilities.

A case that generally ran along these lines was the assumption of Franklin National Bank of New York in 1974 by a consortium of six European banks, becoming the European American Bank. More recently, the FDIC has extended direct loans to a failing bank (the First National Bank of Midland, Texas, in 1983 and Continental Illinois in 1984), as it did in the case of the First Pennsylvania Bank in 1980.[31] Moreover, a bank in trouble may be taken over by a competing institution without active participation of the FDIC, although perhaps with its encouragement. An example here might be the Seafirst-Bank of America case in 1983.

To the extent that depositors view regulators as standing ready to provide direct or indirect support to a failing bank, their deposits are implicitly insured, and any adverse confidence effects resulting from difficulties of a securities affiliate should be rather limited. On the other hand, if regulators send signals that they intend to impose greater market discipline in the future by allowing more banks to fail outright (liquidating bank assets and "paying off" creditors and depositors), then the confidence problem becomes more acute.[32]

Perhaps the most *likely* result of a confidence problem caused by difficulties at the securities affiliate would be to increase the risk premiums demanded on deposits issued by the bank such as large CDs (so-called tiering). Under these circumstances the bank would still have an ability to fund itself, albeit at a higher cost. Of course, this would tend to squeeze a bank's net interest income and earnings and might adversely impact its ability to maintain an adequate capital-asset ratio. In extreme cases, however, such as the Continental Illinois case, banks can be effectively rationed out of the money market for a period until either a rescue package is arranged by regulators (as in the case of Continental Illinois) or the bank is closed or sold off.

It is important to note there that the reasons given for most bank failures are either bad loans and/or bank mismanagement.[33] In a recent study[34], the causes of failure of every commercial bank between 1971 and 1982 were traced. Of the 120 banks[35] that failed, the main reasons were given as:

Loans	90
Other business reasons	36
Illegal activities	20
Nonbanking activities of holding company subsidiaries	1

The only failure directly attributable to the involvement of a bank with a holding company affiliate was that of Hamilton National Bank of Chattanooga, Tennessee, which closed in 1976 with deposits of $336.3 million (or 4.9% of the total deposits of all closed banks over the 1971–1982 period). The main reason for the demise of this bank was the behavior of the holding company, Hamilton Bankshares, which transferred poor quality real estate loans from its troubled mortgage subsidiary (Hamilton Mortgage Corp.) to its banking subsidiaries—principally the Hamilton National Bank. Within one week of the bank's closure, the holding company and three of its nonbanking affiliates (including the Hamilton Mortgage Corp.) filed voluntary bankruptcy petitions.

Finally, banks and bank holding companies can ameliorate confidence problems, in part, by improving their capital-asset ratios (i.e., by self-insurance).[36] Capital-asset ratios measure the degree of protection, or cushion, that depositors have in the event of loan losses or other contingencies, which adversely affect the probability of deposit repayment. Banks and bank holding companies, by increasing their capital adequacy, can send favorable signals to the money markets regarding their intention to maintain safety and soundness.

Contingent Liabilities

A further risk to the bank arises if it is held legally responsible for the losses of the affiliate and/or the holding company. As has been discussed by Black et al.,[37] the major question is the extent or ability of the unsatisfied creditors of the affiliate or the holding company itself to lay claim to the capital or assets of the bank. Following Henn,[38] the general rule appears to be that creditors of the affiliate have no claim on the bank's assets. Nevertheless, there may be exceptions, under the principle of estoppel, through which creditors may be able to make a justifiable claim if they can show that the affiliate or bank holding company misled them into believing that they were dealing with the bank instead. Elsewhere, this has been called "piercing the corporate veil."[39]

Black et al.[40] suggest that if the following four circumstances are present, creditors of the affiliate may be able to make an estoppel argument: (1) the name of the affiliate providing the securities underwriting is similar to the bank, or the same services (i.e., securities underwriting) are also undertaken by the bank; (2) the complaining creditor is a member of the general public rather than being a "sophisticated" businessperson or investor; (3) the creditor is a contract creditor, such as a customer; and (4) the nonbanking activity is either a traditional banking service or is so closely related as to suggest to the customer that he or she is dealing with the bank rather than the holding company and its affiliate.

Most of these circumstances can be avoided, or are unlikely to arise in securities underwriting. Given that underwriting of corporate securities would almost certainly take place through a separately capitalized affiliate of the holding company, the name linkage can be remedied by ensuring that the affiliate has a title which is clearly distinguishable from that of the bank.[41] This might prove costly to the bank, however, because it amounts to changing a positive marketing asset into a liability. The second circumstance is unlikely to arise because the customers of the affiliate are likely to be either sophisticated middle- or large-sized corporate securities issuers and/or large institutions, such as pension funds. Although most underwritings take the form of a contractual arrangement (case 3), it is debatable as to whether securities underwriting has been a traditional banking service, or that underwriting is so closely related to banking as to induce the customer to believe that he or she is dealing with the bank, as in case 4.

Thus although the principle of estoppel may impose a contingent, off-balance sheet liability on the bank, the expected value of this liability is likely to be small. Moreover, to the extent that it is nonzero, banks can always increase their capital to protect depositors accordingly. Indeed, there has been an increasing trend, shown by both regulators and bank analysts,[42] toward judging a bank's capital by the protection it gives depositors against both on- and off-balance sheet contingencies. Of course, increasing a bank's capital for this purpose is not cost free to the bank, the holding company, or its shareholders.

EVIDENCE FROM THE CAPITAL MARKET

In the previous sections the possible risk-increasing and reducing factors that might impact a bank subsidiary when a holding company expands into new activities (specifically corporate securities underwriting) were discussed. We evaluate next the evidence from capital market studies. The motivation for using capital market data is that, in an efficient capital market, stock prices and in particular stock market returns will quickly reflect changes in information regarding the underlying riskiness and profitability of banks and bank holding companies.[43]

The 1982 Aharony and Swary study sought to determine whether the 1970 amendments to the Bank Holding Company Act, whereby the permissible set of activities of bank holding companies was significantly reduced, adversely affected holding company profits, while at the same time decreasing their risk.

Prior to 1970, bank holding companies were engaged in a wide array of nonbanking activities, including agricultural production, food store ownership, and railroad transportation companies (see Appendix II). Moreover, they held 42 affiliates defined as security brokers, dealers, and flotation companies. The 1970 amendments restricted activities to only those "closely related to banking," and required divestiture of nonpermissible activities. Initially the Federal Reserve designated only 10 activities as closely related to banking (increased to over 20 at the time of writing).

Aharony and Swary[44] analyzed the risk and return performance of 33 (previously unregulated) one-bank holding companies relative to a control group of 15 independent banks in the period before and after the amendments to the Act were introduced. The methodology used to test for risk-return differences over time, and between bank groups, was the capital asset pricing model (or market model). This is summarized in Appendix III.

The only statistically significant effect on stockholder returns (*negative* abnormal returns) found for the group of one-bank holding companies occurred in the so-called post-adjustment phase (September 1972 to November 1973) by which time the amendment had already been in operation for over 21 months. The banks in the independent control group also suffered abnormal declines in their returns over the same period, however, so that it is not clear whether this effect was the result of a delayed impact of the 1970 legislation, or generally adverse factors affecting all banks in this period. Because it was also observed that the returns on bank holding company and independent bank stocks followed similar patterns over the entire time-period studied (November 1968 to November 1973), it might be inferred that the decline in returns was largely due to general economic factors affecting *all* bank profits. The authors then looked for changes in risk, measured here by the variance of returns on bank stocks (see Appendix III). Contrary to prior expectations, it was found that the variance of one-bank holding company returns in the post-adjustment phase (September 1972 to November 1973) was actually *greater* than the variance of returns in the preenactment period (November 1968 to January 1970).[45] Similar patterns were observed in the variance of returns for the control group of independent banks. Thus as in the case of mean returns, it appears to have been mainly changes in general market factors—rather than the 1970 amendments—which were the prime cause of increases in return variance over the period of study.[46]

Overall, it appears that capital market investors heavily discounted the effects of the 1970 legislation on bank holding company risks and returns. That is, capital market investors appeared to view holding companies relative to independent banks as no more risky in the pre-1970 period as in the post-1970 period. This result gains further support from a more recent study[47] in which the authors found that, over the 1968–1980 period, the dominant factor changing the riskiness (variance of returns) of bank holding company stocks was shifts in general market risk factors (i.e., economic conditions), rather than changes in investors' risk perceptions regarding the underlying riskiness of activities undertaken by (one) bank holding companies.[48]

Elsewhere Swary[49] has examined the effects of individual Federal Reserve approval or denial decisions[50] on the riskiness (variance of stock returns) of the acquiring bank holding companies. Seventy-four applications were reviewed over the period 1971–1976 of which 21 were denied and 53 approved. It was found that the Fed's approval/denial decision had a significant effect on risk during the post-decision period of the acquiring holding company. Specifically it was found that in denying an application for expansion, the variance of returns (riskiness) of the holding company *increased* in the post-decision period, whereas no statistically significant changes in risk occurred for those companies whose applications were approved. Because a major risk-increasing factor in the denial cases was due to greater idiosyncratic (or firm-specific) risk, this suggests that loss of important diversification opportunities may well have been a significant cause of the increase in the variance of returns. Thus restrictions on, or denials of, applications for holding company expansion may increase the risk of specific bank holding companies and therefore, indirectly, weaken the safety and soundness of the banking subsidiary itself. However, an alternative interpretation of this result is that the Fed has better information regarding the financial situation (capital adequacy, etc.) of the holding company than outside investors. In this case, Fed denials send adverse signals to investors regarding the safety and soundness of the holding company, resulting in an increase in investors' required rates of return to hold their stocks.

SUMMARY AND CONCLUSIONS

This chapter addressed the question of bank insulation from the activities of securities affiliates in the same holding company structure. It was argued that existing bank activities in municipal bonds and foreign exchange appear to have caused no systematic safety and soundness problems. Moreover, new activities may have well-defined geographic and activity diversification benefits which reduce the variance of holding company profits (risk). However, four possible risks (to the bank) resulting from securities activities were identified. These were: (1) upstreaming bank dividends (or fees or tax payments) to the holding company; (2) loans to (or purchase of assets from) the affiliate or holding company; (3) a run on the bank/or increase in the bank's cost of funds because of a crisis of confidence in the bank following the announcement of adverse information regarding the affiliate; and (4) piercing the corporate veil (*via* the principle of estoppel), under which affiliate's creditors may lay claim to the assets of the bank. Nevertheless, in each of these cases, the risk exposure to the bank appeared to be relatively moderate and controllable, whereas capital market studies suggested that the restrictive provisions of the 1970 Bank Holding Company Act amendments had no (negative) impact on holding company risk, with general economic factors appearing to be the major determinants of changes in both holding company and independent bank risk over recent time periods.

Finally, it is perhaps appropriate to note that in 1982 Congress permitted and indeed encouraged bank entry into the real-goods sector in passing the Export Trading Company Act. This legislation has many of the same consequences as would involvement by bank holding companies in domestic corporate securities activities. In particular, it adds to the effective diversification of bank holding companies while limiting possible spillovers of problems to the affiliated commercial bank. The ETC legislation may thus contribute to bank safety and soundness in much the same way as has been argued here.

In summary, given the economic and empirical evidence discussed in this chapter, there appears to be no firm grounds—based on bank safety and soundness—for continuing to prohibit bank holding company acquisition of securities underwriting affiliates. Even if regulators perceived that some (nontrivial) risk to bank safety and soundness exists, this could be accommodated by requiring all banks and holding companies affiliated with underwriters to build up their capital. Alternatively, the FDIC could levy risk-related, rather than size-related insurance premiums. These premiums might reflect the quality of bank's portfolio as well as the off-balance sheet or contingent risks and claims that could arise through bank affiliation with securities and other nonbanking affiliates. Such a risk-related insurance scheme has been extensively suggested in the academic and professional literature.[51] Although such a scheme is easy to suggest, there are a number of problems in making it operational. Nevertheless, in November 1983 the FDIC notified Congress of its intention to introduce a risk-related scheme in the near future.

NOTES

[1]See E. G. Corrigan, "Are Banks Special?," Federal Reserve Bank of Minneapolis *Annual Report, 1982.* P.A. Volcker, Statement Before the Committee on Banking, Housing and Urban Affairs, U.S. Senate, September 13, 1983.

[2]This despite the fact that the potential exposure to municipal bond underwriting losses is increased by the underwriting taking place within a department of the bank itself or a subsidiary of the bank, rather than through a separately capitalized affiliate of a bank holding company.

[3]R. Lamb and S. P. Rappaport, *Municipal Bonds: The Comprehensive Review of Tax-Exempt Securities and Public Finance.* New York: Mc-Graw Hill, 1980.

[4]A recent estimate suggested that there were over 1.5 million different municipal issues outstanding.

[5]E. Bloch, *Investment Banking,* unpublished manuscript, Graduate Business School, New York University, 1983.

[6]L. Fisher, "Determinats of Risk Premiums on Corporate Bonds," *Journal of Political Economy,* 1959, pp. 217–237.

[7]Seasoned issues only.

[8]These figures are not strictly comparable among banks because not all compute their profits and losses in the same way. Some bank figures do not reflect such factors as currency translation losses and gains and brokerage commissions. But they all reflect such factors as operating costs, salaries, benefits, telex, and other communications costs.

[9]E. J. Kane, "Accelerating Inflation, Technological Innovation, and the Decreasing Effectiveness of Bank Regulation," *Journal of Finance* (1981), pp. 355–367.

[10]The average return or profit for bank holding company will be $\sum_{i=1}^{n} x_i r_i$, where x_i is the proportion of holding company assets invested in that activity and r_i is the rate of return (or profit) on capital invested in that activity. The standard deviation (a measure of variability) of holding company profit will be equal to $[i = \sum_{i-1}^{n} X_i^2 \sigma_i^2 + 2[\sum_i \frac{n}{i} x^2 \sigma^2 + 2\sum_{i-j} \frac{n}{} x_i x_j \pi_{ij} \sigma_i \sigma_j]_1/_2$, where σ_i, σ_j are the standard deviations of returns from individual activities and π_{ij} is the correlation between returns from different activities. As can be seen, as π_{ij} falls from $+1$ to -1, the standard deviation of holding company profits falls toward zero.

[11]A. Heggestad, "Riskiness of Investments in Nonbank Activities by Bank Holding Companies," *Journal of Economics and Business* (1975), pp. 219–223.

[12]IRS Code 6048.

[13]P. C. Eisemann, "Diversification and the Cogeneric Banking Holding Company," *Journal of Bank Research* (1976), pp. 68–77.

[14]It should be noted that returns on investment banking were based on a very small sample of publicly traded firms. Thus the return figures used may have been unrepresentative of returns in the whole investment banking industry.

[15]D. R. Meinster and R. D. Johnson, "Banking Holding Company Diversification and the Risk of Capital Impairment," *Bell Journal of Economics* (1979), pp. 683–694.

[16]Again, those that minimize risk for any given return.

[17]That is, although the same activities were included in both the efficient and actual holding company, the relative proportions with which each activity should be undertaken (i.e., capital invested) differed.

[18]However, Meinster and Johnson ("Bank Holding Companies," 1979) showed that this result is reversed if allowance was made for "double-leveraging" by the holding company.

[19]L. Wall and R. A. Eisenbeis, "Bank Holding Company Non-Banking Activities and Risk." Paper presented to the Conference on Bank Structure and Compilation, Federal Reserve Bank of Chicago.

[20]The American Bankers Association (*Statistical Information on the Financial Service Industry,* 1981, p. 134) reports that the growth in bank assets over the period 1970–1980 was 257% for Texas, 254% for New Mexico, and 228% for Arizona, compared with 138% for Pennsylvania, 133% for New York, and 116% for Ohio.

[21]R. A. Eisenbeis, "Financial Innovation and the Growth of Bank Holding Companies." Proceedings from a Conference on *Bank Structure and Competition,* Federal Reserve Bank of Chicago, April 27–28, 1978.

[22]J. Guttentag and R. Herring, "Credit Rationing and Financial Disorder," *Working Paper,* University of Pennsylvania, Wharton School, 1982.

[23]Two recent additions are discount brokerage and export trading companies.

[24]For example see H. Stoll, "Small Firms' Access to Public Equity Financing," forthcoming in P. M. Horvitz and R. R. Pettit (eds.), *Financing Small Business.* Greenwich, Conn.: JAI Press.

[25]Moreover, national banks and state-chartered banks that are members of the Federal Reserve System must receive the Fed's approval to pay dividends greater than net profits for a given year and those retained in the two previous years. Further, the recently imposed capital and loan loss reserve requirements under the 1983 International Lending Supervision Act will severely constrain the abilities of large banks to pay excessive dividends in the near future.

[26]We ignore for the moment the economic value of upholding the name or reputation of the affiliate and/ or its holding company. In particular, a good reputation (and associated goodwill) has very positive economic value (see A. Saunders, "Conflicts of Interest," *Working Paper,* New York University, Graduate School of Business Administration, January 1984.)

[27]More subtle forms of upstreaming might also take place: (1) banks might upstream deferred taxes to the holding company and/or pay its tax contribution to the holding company "as if" its liability were being assessed independently from the holding company, so that any tax savings from filing a conslidated return accrue to the holding company; (2) fees paid by the bank for services provided by the holding company may be boosted or inflated, achieving the same effect as higher dividend payouts to the holding company. Moreover, these may be harder for the Fed and other regulators to monitor.

[28]It might also be argued that the bank itself could purchase some of the unsold bonds in the securities affiliate's inventory. This is analogous to banks buying up poor real estate loans made by REITs in the mid-1970, as alleged in Investment Company's Institute *Misadventures in Banking: Bank Promotion of Pooled Investment Funds,* Washington, D.C., 1979. However, the holdings of corporate bonds by banks appear to be limited by a quantity (10% of capital) and a quality rule (investment grade Baa or better). Moreover, the tax disadvantages of a bank (and any other corporation with taxable status) buying such bonds would tend to limit the attractiveness of such an operation. This is quite apart from any legal and regulatory consequences relating to conflict of interest. Also possible is that bonds could be dumped with clients of the bank's trust department, although such an action would be in breach of the bank's fudiciary responsibilities and is therefore illegal (see Saunders, "Conflicts of Interest," 1984).

[29]In 1980 the aggregate of all deposits held by individuals with values of $100,000 or less, for all insured commercial banks, was 71.6% (*FDIC Annual Report,* 1980).

[30]A. Saunders, "Conflicts of Interest," *WP,* New York University, Graduate School of Business Adminsitration, January 1984.

[31]Note that 27 other private banks also shared in the bail-out scheme by buying warrants as well.

[32]The ICI (*Misadventures in Banking,* 1979) reports the case of the Beverly Hills Bancorp in 1974, when the announcement of a large default on a loan made by the bank holding company resulted in a run-off in deposits of 15% at the affiliated bank. Ultimately this bank was sold to Wells Fargo. J. F. Sinkey, Jr. "Adverse Publicity and Bank Deposit Flows," *Journal of Bank Reserach* (1975a, pp. 109–112; "The Failure of United States National Bank of San Diego: A Portfolio and Performance Analysis," *Journal of*

Bank Reserach (1975b), pp. 8–24, discusses evidence from a large number of individual bank failures. Specifically he found that adverse publicity scarcely affected small banks, whereas depositors in Franklin National were very sensitive to "bad" information or publicity. Moreover, adverse information led to large withdrawals from small insured-demand and time and savings accounts.

[33]See Sinkey, "Adverse Publicity," 1975a; "Failure of U.S. Bank," 1975b; and Sinkey and D. A. Walker, "Problem Banks: Identification and Characteristics," *Journal of Bank Research* (1975), pp. 208–217.

[34]See Morgan Guaranty, "An Investigation of Commercial Bank Failures," Internal Memorandum, September 1, 1983.

[35]The total exceeds 120, because some banks closures fell into more than one category.

[36]For all one-bank holding companies with deposits of over $150 million, capital adequacy is determined by the Fed-OCC on a consolidated as well as individual bank basis (see Fed-OCC release [1981]). Capital adequacy is measured by both the ratio of total bank capital to assets and primary capital to assets, where primary capital excludes subordinated debt.

[37]See F. Black, M. H. Miller, and R. A. Posner, "An Approach to the Regulation of Bank Holding Companies," *Journal of Businss* (1978), pp. 379–411.

[38]H. G. Henn, *Handbook of the Law of Corporations and Other Business Enterprises,* 2d ed. St. Paul, Minn.; West Publishing, 1970.

[39]See Eisenbeis "Financial Innovation," p. 1978 and P. M. Horvitz, "Bank Holding Company Regulation: Discussion," proceedings from a Conference on Bank Structure and Competition, Federal Reserve Bank of Chicago, April 27–28, 1978.

[40]"Approach to Regulation," 1978.

[41]Incidentially, it might be noted that many of Chase's problems with Chase REIT were caused by the common linkage of names (see Investment Company's Institute, "Misadventures in Banking," 1979.)

[42]See Salomon Brothers Inc., "Primary Capital Ratios: The Potential Implications of Standby Letters of Credit," *Bank Weekly,* October 7, 1983.

[43]Three major studies in this area are by Aharony and Swary "Effects of the 1970 Act," 1981; and I. Swary, "Bank Acquisition of Non-bank Firms: An Empirical Analysis of Administrative Decision," *Journal of Banking and Finance* (1983), pp. 213–230.

[44]"Effects of the 1970 Act," 1981.

[45]However, in the so-called adjustment period, just after the legislation was passed, the variance of returns did fall below the preenactment level.

[46]The β's, or systematic risk coefficients of one-bank holding companies and independent banks, showed no significant changes between the pre-enactment and post-enactment phases, whereas the variance of market returns Var $(\bar{R}_{mt})$ increased significantly compared to Var$(\bar{\epsilon}_{jt})$ the banking group (or firm) specific risk.

[47]See Aharony and Swary, "Bank Performance," 1982.

[48]These would cause changes in either the systematic or idiosyncratic risk measures.

[49]"Bank Acquisition," 1983.

[50]Under Section 4(c)8 of the 1970 Amendments to the Banking Holding Company Act.

[51]See S. D. Buser, A. H. Chen and E. J. Kane, "Federal Deposit Insurance, Regulatory Policy and Optimal Bank Capital," *Journal of Finance,* 1981, pp. 51–60; and S. Lee, "Why Some Banks May Pay More for Deposit Insurance," *Business Week* (January 1984), for example. Securities firms have also expressed concerns about the organization of FDIC insurance (see *New York Times* report, January 1, 1984 [Section D].)

Appendix 1: Analysis of Foreign Exchange Profits

	PD-End Assets ($MIL)	PD-End Common Equity ($MIL)	Foreign Exchange Trading Income	FX Prof. as % Avg. Assets	FX Prof. % Nonint Inc.	FX Prof. % Nonint Inc. Less Nonrecur. Items	FX Prof. as % PTX Inc. (FTE)	FX Inc. as % NII + Oth Inc.
Bank of Boston Corporation								
1982	18267.4	884.1	14,039	0.08	5.88	5.88	5.33	1.63
1981	16809.1	820.5	18,030	0.11	9.06	9.06	7.36	2.27
1980	15948.5	730.0	9,420	0.06	5.55	5.55	4.44	1.38
1979	13759.8	649.1	6,285	0.05	5.10	5.10	3.64	1.14
1978	11557.1	590.6	5,932	0.05	5.83	5.83	4.43	1.34
1977	10301.6	549.7	4,208	0.04	4.37	4.37	4.32	1.18
Bankamerica Corporation								
1982	122220.8	4277.0	141,500	0.12	13.81	13.81	20.75	3.37
1981	121158.3	4090.6	119,200	0.11	13.86	13.86	14.60	3.13
1980	111617.3	3908.4	101,100	0.10	12.11	12.46	8.42	2.69
1979	108389.3	3462.0	90,200	0.10	15.27	15.27	7.97	2.69
1978	94902.5	3038.7	63,700	0.08	12.32	12.32	6.14	2.13
1977	81988.6	2691.2	54,064	0.08	12.12	12.12	6.62	2.20
1976	73912.9	2421.6	51,640	0.08	12.90	12.90	7.61	2.44
Bankers Trust New York Corporation								
1982	40427.1	1405.8	46,257	0.12	11.01	12.09	9.65	3.52
1981	34213.0	1180.6	30,780	0.09	9.70	10.00	8.08	2.85
1980	34201.6	1009.6	22,815	0.07	6.91	8.64	5.43	2.09
1979	30952.9	778.6	16,604	0.06	7.87	7.87	6.47	2.03
1978	25863.3	705.8	23,058	0.09	12.80	13.17	13.64	3.28
1977	23057.3	666.8	12,839	0.06	8.43	8.43	11.40	2.09
1976	21812.5	647.8	16,499	0.08	10.92	10.92	12.52	2.66

	PD-End Assets ($MIL)	PD-End Common Equity ($MIL)	Foreign Exchange Trading Income	FX Prof. as % Avg. Assets	FX Prof. % Nonint Inc.	FX Prof. % Nonint Inc. Less Nonrecur. Items	FX Prof. as % PTX Inc. (FTE)	FX Inc. as % NII + Oth Inc.
Chase Manhattan Corporation, The								
1982	80862.9	2761.4	130,513	0.17	17.20	12.63	21.73	4.35
1981	77839.3	2592.7	123,440	0.16	17.99	17.99	14.10	4.59
1980	76189.6	2282.7	96,518	0.14	16.55	17.00	13.47	4.18
1979	64708.0	2026.5	77,027	0.13	17.57	17.57	11.74	3.82
1978	61171.5	1821.1	74,696	0.14	19.75	19.75	16.58	4.35
1977	53180.3	1718.3	48,540	0.10	14.17	14.17	16.10	3.27
1976	45637.7	1667.1	47,425	0.11	16.09	16.09	17.51	3.34
Chemical New York Corporation								
1982	48274.8	1586.0	55,513	0.12	14.25	14.25	9.58	3.04
1981	44916.9	1420.2	39,490	0.09	11.86	12.89	8.82	2.66
1980	41066.1	1207.2	34,824	0.09	15.11	15.11	8.78	2.80
1979	39375.3	1090.2	9,895	0.03	5.69	6.02	3.25	0.96
1978	32769.7	1009.9	19,205	0.06	12.77	12.77	7.28	2.05
1977	30705.9	941.8	6,619	0.02	5.24	5.24	2.77	0.79
1976	26613.8	885.9	5,384	0.02	3.91	3.91	2.46	0.67
Citicorp								
1982	129997.0	4815.0	241,000	0.20	14.69	14.99	16.50	4.57
1981	119232.0	4281.0	265,000	0.23	16.39	17.49	27.60	6.32
1980	114920.0	3891.0	175,000	0.16	14.94	14.94	18.62	4.61
1979	106370.6	3598.0	113,600	0.12	14.09	14.09	11.31	3.35
1978	88194.7	3186.0	172,400	0.22	23.34	23.34	18.22	5.58
1977	77112.4	2862.6	68,000	0.10	15.46	15.46	9.67	2.75
1976	64155.9	2660.7	62,300	0.11	13.64	13.64	8.40	2.65

Continental Illinois Corporation								
1982	42899.4	1709.9	19,500	0.04	6.08	6.31	12.88	1.48
1981	46971.8	1710.7	34,300	0.08	10.64	10.64	7.01	2.78
1980	42089.4	1524.9	31,013	0.08	12.73	12.73	7.26	2.87
1979	35790.1	1362.9	11,293	0.03	5.44	5.44	3.22	1.28
1978	31058.7	1225.7	20,011	0.07	12.00	12.00	6.30	2.62
1977	25800.3	1012.1	15,330	0.07	10.99	10.99	5.42	2.33
1976	21984.9	912.4	8,873	0.04	7.10	7.10	3.48	1.42
First Chicago Corporation								
1982	35876.4	1366.3	27,155	0.08	8.72	8.72	10.18	2.74
1981	33562.4	1271.9	27,975	0.09	9.85	9.85	12.97	3.32
1980	28699.4	1201.8	21,808	0.08	9.05	9.05	18.54	3.22
1979	30181.8	1184.3	11,195	0.04	5.91	5.91	5.54	1.71
1978	24066.1	1120.0	13,079	0.06	7.13	7.13	5.50	1.93
1977	22614.0	1030.9	8,438	0.04	5.92	5.92	3.90	1.42
Irving Bank Corporation								
1982	19514.3	686.8	16,056	0.08	12.20	12.27	10.07	2.52
1981	18227.2	638.1	11,570	0.06	9.67	9.69	5.74	1.82
1980	18089.8	567.2	14,478	0.09	13.36	13.62	7.87	2.48
1979	16702.4	504.7	10,307	0.07	11.37	11.45	7.06	2.11
1978	13975.4	457.2	4,300	0.03	5.86	5.89	3.56	1.08
1977	12586.0	420.4	3,600	0.03	5.66	5.72	3.53	1.04
Manufacturers Hanover Corporation								
1982	64040.6	2073.5	29,956	0.05	5.99	5.74	5.06	1.45
1981	59108.5	1900.3	28,600	0.05	6.12	7.81	5.28	1.64
1980	55522.2	1708.6	15,000	0.03	5.26	5.75	2.95	1.03
1979	47675.4	1555.0	15,200	0.04	6.95	7.39	3.25	1.18
1978	40605.8	1400.3	12,400	0.04	6.55	6.55	2.95	1.11
1977	35787.6	1281.6	8,482	0.03	5.03	5.03	2.29	0.87
1976	31482.8	1085.9	8,620	0.03	5.89	5.89	2.67	0.96

	PD-End Assets ($MIL)	PD-End Common Equity ($MIL)	Foreign Exchange Trading Income	FX Prof. as % Avg. Assets	FX Prof. % Nonint Inc.	FX Prof. % Nonint Inc. Less Nonrecur. Items	FX Prof. as % PTX Inc. (FTE)	FX Inc. as % NII + Oth Inc.
Marine Midland Banks, Inc.								
1982	20238.8	881.0	26,988	0.14	18.53	18.53	15.95	3.71
1981	18682.5	819.3	32,367	0.18	22.95	22.95	18.64	4.89
1980	17479.6	759.4	20,655	0.12	20.69	20.69	16.86	3.83
1979	15728.2	477.9	11,011	0.07	15.54	15.54	13.42	2.53
1978	14289.4	448.2	6,663	0.05	11.63	11.63	11.42	1.73
1977	12137.2	429.9	4,100	0.04	7.01	7.20	9.25	1.16
Mellon National Corporation								
1982	20294.4	1067.6	5,555	0.03	3.34	3.34	2.12	0.78
1981	18447.9	976.6	6,057	0.04	5.19	5.36	2.62	1.06
1980	16156.5	901.2	5,848	0.04	5.66	5.77	2.81	1.18
1979	13507.7	825.5	4,227	0.03	5.22	5.22	2.26	0.95
1978	11684.8	765.1	7,277	0.07	10.13	10.13	4.32	1.84
1977	9921.1	713.3	3,891	0.04	6.44	6.44	2.85	1.11
1976	9352.7	670.2	2,266	0.02	3.87	3.90	1.82	0.72
Morgan, J. P. & Co. Incorporated								
1982	58597.0	2710.0	57,000	0.10	11.50	11.50	5.88	3.19
1981	53522.0	2420.0	106,000	0.20	21.85	23.01	12.79	7.11
1980	51990.6	2180.4	62,826	0.13	14.56	15.16	7.74	4.40
1979	43487.7	1949.3	35,894	0.09	11.90	11.90	5.54	3.13
1978	38536.2	1759.7	56,385	0.17	18.85	20.15	9.35	5.40
1977	31663.8	1591.6	40,322	0.14	17.46	17.46	7.87	4.45
1976	28765.5	1455.5	33,844	0.13	13.42	13.42	6.97	3.85

NBD Bancorp Inc.							
1982	12406.9	750.0	2,036	0.02	2.49	2.49	1.38	0.44
1981	12144.9	698.2	2,898	0.03	3.88	3.88	2.27	0.73
1980	10869.0	661.4	2,777	0.03	4.55	4.55	1.94	0.73
1979	9506.4	608.0	2,499	0.03	4.78	4.78	1.67	0.68
Security Pacific Corporation							
1982	36991.0	1469.4	3,300	0.01	0.73	0.83	0.80	0.20
1981	32999.1	1323.2	20,340	0.07	6.00	6.00	5.20	1.45
1980	27794.2	1170.3	11,858	0.04	4.40	4.40	3.42	0.98
1979	24923.4	1042.4	−934	0.00	−0.46	−0.46	−0.29	−0.09
1978	21632.6	920.0	3,983	0.02	2.59	2.59	1.40	0.44
1977	18717.2	779.1	1,945	0.01	1.40	1.40	0.90	0.26
1976	16385.0	711.0	1,536	0.01	1.19	1.14	0.92	0.24

Coefficient of Variation—Foreign Exchange Profits for Companies with 7 or More Years of Data in Ascending Order of Coefficient of Variation

Name	Number Year	Avg. FX Prof. as % Avg. Assets	Std. Dev. FX Prof. as % Avg. Assets	Coeff. of Variation	Rank
Bankamerica Corporation	8	0.10	0.015	0.156	1
Chase Manhattan Corporation, The	8	0.13	0.025	0.188	2
Manufacturers Hanover Corporation	8	0.04	0.008	0.215	3
Bankers Trust New York Corporation	8	0.08	0.021	0.247	4
Morgan, J. P. & Co. Incorporated	8	0.14	0.035	0.260	5
Citicorp	8	0.16	0.054	0.334	6
Bank of Boston Corporation	8	0.07	0.026	0.398	7
Continental Illinois Corporation	8	0.06	0.022	0.401	8
Mellon National Corporation	9	0.04	0.016	0.408	9
Chemical New York Corporation	8	0.06	0.038	0.669	10
Security Pacific Corporation	8	0.02	0.023	1.001	11

Appendix II: December 1972 One-Bank Holding Companies[a]
Date of entry by one-bank holding companies into nonbank activities, by two-digit SIC classification.

Primarily in SIC No.	Description of activity	Before 1930	1930–39	1940–49	1950–59	1960–64	1965–70
01	Agricultural production		2	1	1	10	15
07	Agricultural services and hunting				2	7	12
08	Forestry	1					1
10	Metal mining						4
12	Bituminous coal and lignite mining	3					3
13	Crude petroleum and natural gas				1	2	19
14	Mining and quarrying nonmetallic minerals, ex. fuel				2	1	5
15	Building construction—general contractors				1	1	14
16	Construction other than building	1				3	7
17	Construction—special trade contractors				1	1	11
19	Ordnance and accessories		1				
20	Food and kindred products	1			4	4	21
22	Textile mill products	1				2	16
24	Lumber and wood products, ex. furniture	1				1	7
25	Furniture and fixtures						6
26	Paper and allied products	1			1	2	11
27	Printing and publishing	1		2	4	6	13
28	Chemicals and allied products		1		3	4	8
29	Petroleum refining and related industries				3		1
30	Rubber and misc. plastic products		2			1	3
31	Leather and leather products						3
32	Stone, clay, glass, and concrete products				3	2	10
33	Primary metals				6	1	16
					1		
34	Fabricated metal products		1		4	20	
35	Machinery, ex. electrical			1	2	2	24

Appendix II: *(Continued)*

Primarily in SIC No.	Description of activity	Before 1930	1930–39	1940–49	1950–59	1960–64	1965–70
36	Electrical machinery				3	7	23
37	Transportation equipment				2	1	6
38	Instruments				2	1	2
39	Misc. manufacturing industries					2	3
40	Railroad transportation	1					3
41	Local suburban and interurban passenger transportation				2	1	
42	Motor freight transportation and warehousing				6	4	11
44	Water transportation		1	1		1	33
45	Transportation by air				1	2	5
46	Pipeline transportation					1	2
47	Transportation services			2	3	1	27
48	Communication					8	27
49	Electric gas and sanitary services	3			5	7	12
50	Wholesale trade	1	1	3	13	14	51
52	Building materials, hardware, farm equipment dealers	1		1		3	6
53	Retail trade—general merchandise	1	1			4	8
54	Food stores				1	10	2
55	Auto dealers and gasoline service stations					4	9
56	Apparel and accessory stores				1		
57	Furniture, home furnishings, and equipment stores					1	4
58	Eating and drinking places					2	4
59	Misc. retail stores					2	16
60	Banking	1	1	5	3	5	99
61	Credit agencies other than banks	10	9	1	60	115	359
62	Security and commodity brokers, dealers, exchanges				4	8	61

Code	Industry						Total
63	Insurance carriers	1		2	24	32	147
64	Insurance agents, brokers, and service	1		3	12	27	140
65	Real estate	7	4	22	57	105	478
66	Combinations of real estate, insurance, loans, law offices						1
67	Holding and other investment companies	5	3	7	33	46	481
70	Hotels, rooming houses, and other lodging			2		1	7
72	Personal services			2		1	1
73	Misc. business services	2	3	4	10	22	168
75	Auto repair, auto services, and garages	1				2	19
76	Misc. repair services				1		1
78	Motion pictures				1		2
79	Amusement and recreation services				3		6
80	Medical and other health services					2	7
82	Educational services						3
86	Nonprofit membership organizations				3		3
89	Misc. services				1	2	77
99	Nonclassifiable establishments	1		2		2	7
	Total	43	34	58	290	503	2,571

Source: Federal Reserve Bulletin December 1972, Vol. 58, No. 12.

ᵃTabulation is based on the "principal" SIC activities reported for non-bank subsidiaries. It includes each nonbank subsidiary of a holding company regardless of how many subsidiaries are reported in the same principal two-digit group. Inactive subsidiaries are excluded. There are 18 nonbank subsidiaries for which either the principal SIC activities or the date of acquisition or formation was not provided. These data should be interpreted with caution because the number of entries into the various activities for each time period reflect only those nonbank subsidiaries that were still owned by one-bank holding companies as of December 31, 1970. If, for example, a one-bank holding company acquired or formed a nonbank subsidiary between 1930 and 1939 and disposed of that subsidiary prior to December 31, 1970, it would not be reflected here. Consequently, the number of formations and acquisitions reported is understated in earlier time periods.

Note.—Periods showing date of entry indicate when OBHC's formed or acquired nonbank subsidiaries.

One-Bank Holding Companies December 1972

Diversification patterns of one-bank holding companies, December 31, 1970

SIC No.	Description of activity	Number[a]	SIC No.	Description of activity	Number[a]
011	Field crops	11	225	Knitting mills	4
012	Fruits, tree nuts, and vegetables	7	226	Dyeing and finishing textiles	1
013	Livestock	59	227	Floor covering mills	4
014	General farms	28	229	Misc. textile goods	5
019	Misc. agriculture	1	242	Sawmills and planing mills	4
071	Agricultural services, ex. animal husbandry and horticulture	6	243	Millwork, veneer, plywood	6
			244	Wooden containers	1
072	Animal husbandry	11	249	Misc. wood products	4
081	Timber tracts	4	251	Household furniture	5
086	Gathering forest products	1	252	Office furniture	2
			253	Public building furniture	1
101	Iron ores	1	254	Partitions, shelving	1
102	Copper ores	1	262	Paper mills, ex. building paper mills	3
103	Lead and zinc	1	263	Paperboard mills	1
105	Bauxite	1	264	Converted paper and paperboard products	5
108	Metal mining services	1	265	Paperboard containers and boxes	5
109	Misc. metal ores	2	266	Building paper and board mills	1
121	Bituminous coal and lignite mining	2	271	Newspapers: Publishing and printing	4
131	Crude petroleum and natural gas	10	272	Periodicals: Publishing and printing	4
132	Natural gas liquids	1	273	Books	2
138	Oil and gas field services	9	274	Miscellaneous publishing	8
141	Dimension stone	2	275	Commercial printing	9
142	Crushed stone	1	276	Manifold business forms	1
144	Sand and gravel	3	277	Greeting card publishing	2
145	Clay, ceramic, and refractory minerals	3	278	Blankbooks and loose leaf binders	3
148	Nonmetallic minerals, ex. fuels	2	279	Service for printing	1

Code	Description	
149	Misc. nonmetallic minerals, ex. fuels	1
151	General building contractor	19
161	Highway and steel construction	1
162	Heavy construction, ex. highway and street	8
171	Plumbing, heating (ex. electrical), and air conditioning	3
172	Painting, paper hanging, and decorating	3
173	Electrical work	4
175	Carpeting and flooring	1
176	Roofing and sheet metal work	1
177	Concrete work	1
179	Misc. special trade contractors	7
192	Ammunition, ex. small arms	2
195	Small arms	1
196	Small arms ammunition	1
199	Ordnance and accessories n.e.c.	1
201	Meat products	1
202	Dairy products	2
203	Canned and preserved fruits, vegetables, and seafood	6
204	Grain mill products	3
205	Bakery products	2
206	Sugar	2
207	Confectionary and related products	2
208	Beverages	5
209	Misc. food preparation	4
222	Broad woven fabric mills, manmade fibers, and silk	3
223	Broad woven fabric mills, wool	1
224	Narrow fabrics	1
281	Industrial inorganic and organic chemicals	7
282	Plastic materials and synthetic rubber resin	4
283	Drugs	3
284	Soap, detergents, perfumes, and cosmetics	7
285	Paints, varnishes, and lacquers	4
286	Gum and wood chemicals	1
287	Agricultural chemicals	4
289	Misc. chemical products	3
291	Petroleum refining	4
295	Paving and roofing materials	3
299	Misc. products of petroleum and coal	1
301	Tires and inner tubes	2
302	Rubber footwear	1
303	Reclaimed rubber	1
306	Fabricated rubber products n.e.c.	4
307	Misc. plastics products	8
311	Leather tanning and finishing	1
312	Industrial leather belting	1
314	Footwear, ex. rubber	1
321	Flat glass	2
323	Glass products	1
325	Structural clay products	1
326	Pottery and related products	1
327	Concrete, gypsum, and plaster products	6
329	Abrasives, asbestos, and misc. nonmetallic mineral products	5
331	Blast furnaces, steel works, and rolling and finishing mills	6
333	Primary smelting and refining of nonferrous metals	1

Table (Continued)

SIC No.	Description of activity	Number[a]	SIC No.	Description of activity	Number[a]
334	Secondary smelting of nonferrous metals	2	444	Transportation on rivers and canals	1
335	Rolling, drawing, and extruding of nonferrous metals	3	445	Local water transportation	3
336	Nonferrous foundries	2	446	Services for water transportation	4
339	Misc. primary metal products	1	451	Air transportation, certified carriers	5
341	Metal cans	2	452	Air transportation, noncertified carriers	1
342	Cutlery, hand tools, and general hardware	3	458	Fixed facilities for air transportation	4
343	Heating apparatus, ex. electrical, and plumbing fixtures	3	461	Pipelines, ex. natural gas	3
344	Fabricated structural metal products	16	471	Freight forwarding	3
345	Screw machine products	4	472	Arrangement of transportation	36
346	Metal stampings	3	473	Stockyards	3
347	Coating and engraving	2	474	Rental of railroad cars	1
349	Misc. fabricated metal products	5	478	Misc. services for transportation	1
351	Engines and turbines	2	481	Telephone communication	1
352	Farm machinery and equipment	4	483	Radio and TV broadcasts	11
353	Construction and mining equipment	6	489	Communication services n.e.c.	7
354	Metalworking machinery	9	491	Electric companies and systems	2
355	Special industrial machinery	4	492	Gas companies and systems	2
356	General industrial machinery	4	494	Water supply	7
357	Office computing and accounting machines	3	495	Sanitary services	7
358	Service industry machines	6	497	Irrigation systems	3
359	Misc. machinery, ex. electrical	3	501	Wholesale motor vehicles and auto equipment	9
361	Electrical transmission and distribution equipment	3	502	Wholesale drugs, chemicals, and allied products	5
362	Electrical industrial apparatus	3	503	Piece goods, notions, apparel	4

Code	Industry	Count
363	Household appliances	2
364	Electric lighting and wiring equipment	4
365	Radio and TV receiving sets	6
366	Communication equipment	9
367	Electronic components and accessories	12
369	Misc. electrical machinery	5
371	Motor vehicles and equipment	7
372	Aircraft and parts	1
374	Railroad equipment	1
379	Misc. transportation equipment	3
381	Engineering, laboratory, and scientific equipment	1
382	Instruments for measuring and weighing physical characteristics	5
383	Optical instruments	3
384	Surgical and medical supplies	2
386	Photographic equipment	3
387	Watches and clocks	1
393	Musical instruments	3
394	Toys and athletic goods	2
395	Pens and pencils	1
399	Misc. manufacturing industries	2
401	Railroads	3
411	Local and suburban passenger transportation	1
421	Trucking	8
422	Public warehousing	18
423	Terminal facilities for motor freight transportation	1
441	Deep sea foreign transportation	2
442	Deep sea domestic transportation	1
504	Groceries and related products	11
505	Farm products, raw materials	7
506	Electrical goods	10
507	Hardware, and plumbing and heating supplies	2
508	Machinery, equipment, and supplies	11
509	Misc. wholesalers	34
521	Lumber and building materials dealers	16
523	Paint, glass, and wallpaper stores	1
524	Electrical supply stores	2
525	Hardware and farm equipment	11
531	Department stores	8
532	Mail order houses	6
533	Variety stores	1
535	Direct selling establishments	1
539	Misc. general merchandise stores	7
541	Grocery stores	10
542	Meat and fish markets	1
545	Dairy products stores	3
551	Motor vehicle dealers	9
553	Tire, battery, and accessory dealers	2
554	Gasoline service stations	7
559	Misc. aircraft, marine, and auto dealers	6
561	Men's and boy's clothing stores	1
562	Women's ready-to-wear stores	2
563	Women's specialty stores	1
564	Child's and infant wear	1
565	Family clothing stores	2
571	Furniture and home furnishings, ex. appliance stores	6
572	Household appliance stores	1

Table (Continued)

SIC No.	Description of activity	Number[a]	SIC No.	Description of activity	Number[a]
573	Radio, TV, and music stores	2	673	Trusts	22
581	Eating and drinking places	14	679	Misc. investing institutions	57
591	Drug and proprietary stores	6			
595	Sporting goods and bike stores	1	701	Hotels and motels	20
596	Farm and garden supply stores	7	703	Trailer parks and camps	5
598	Fuel and ice dealers	4	704	Membership hotels	2
599	Retail stores n.e.c.	7	721	Laundries and cleaning plants	4
			726	Funeral services and crematories	3
602	Commercial and stock savings banks	36	729	Misc. personal services	1
603	Mutual savings banks	1	731	Advertising	18
604	Trust companies not engaged in deposit banking	5	732	Consumer credit reporting agencies	9
			733	Duplicating, mailing, and stenographic services	2
605	Establishments performing functions closely related to banking	78	734	Services to dwellings and other buildings	11
611	Rediscount and financing institutions for credit agencies other than banks	5	739	Business services n.e.c.	214
			751	Auto rentals w/o drivers	28
612	Savings and loan associations	27	752	Auto parking	3
613	Agricultural credit institutions	18	762	Electrical repair shops	2
614	Personal credit institutions	114	769	Misc. repair shops	3
615	Business credit institutions	173	781	Motion picture production and distribution	4
616	Loan correspondents and brokers	61	783	Motion picture theaters	1

Code	Activity	Number
621	Security brokers, dealers, and flotation companies	42
622	Commodity contracts brokers and dealers	6
628	Services allied with the exchange of securities or commodities	32
631	Life insurance	73
632	Accident and health insurance	38
633	Fire, marine, and casualty insurance	40
635	Surety insurance	32
636	Title insurance	12
639	Insurance carriers n.e.c.	7
641	Insurance agents, brokers, and service	604
651	Real estate operators (ex. developers) and lessors	439
653	Agents, brokers, and managers	127
654	Title abstract companies	10
655	Subdividers and developers	91
656	Operative builders	28
661	Combinations of real estate, insurance, loans, law offices	7
672	Investment companies	35
793	Bowling alleys and pool establishments	2
794	Sports promoters and commercial operators	10
806	Hospitals	2
809	Health and allied services n.e.c.	5
811	Legal services	1
821	Elementary and secondary schools	1
822	Colleges and universities	3
824	Correspondence and vocational schools	3
829	Schools n.e.c.	1
862	Professional membership organizations	1
863	Labor unions	1
867	Charitable organizations	6
869	Nonprofit membership organizations n.e.c.	2
891	Engineering and architectural services	4
893	Accounting, auditing, and bookkeeping services	136
899	Services n.e.c.	4
990	Nonclassifiable establishments	9

[a]Number of one-bank holding companies that are engaged in the activity either directly or through a subsidiary. Subsidiaries classified as inactive are not included in this tabulation.

APPENDIX III: A NOTE ON THE CAPITAL ASSET PRICING MODEL

In the capital asset pricing model the equilibrium return on any security j over the time period t, will be equal to:

$$\tilde{R}_{jt} = \alpha_j + \beta_j \tilde{R}_{mt} + \tilde{\epsilon}_{jt}$$

where $\tilde{R}_{jt}$ is the uncertain return on security j over week t, $\tilde{R}_{mt}$ is the uncertain return of the "market portolio" (here, the value weighted index of all common stocks on the NYSE and AMEX), β_j is the systematic risk of the security and equal to $\text{Cov}(\tilde{R}_{jt}, \tilde{R}_{mt})/\text{Var}(R_{mt})$, $\tilde{\epsilon}_{jt}$ is the idiosyncratic or firm specific risk of the security, and $\epsilon_{jt} \sim N(0, \sigma^2)$. Finally, α_j is the abnormal or excess return on the stock such that $\alpha_j = E(\tilde{R}_{jt}) - B_j E(\tilde{R}_{mt})$. Note that the variance (or the riskiness) of the jth stock is:

$$\text{Var}(\tilde{R}_{jt}) = \beta^2_j \text{Var}(\tilde{R}_{mt}) + \text{Var}(\tilde{\epsilon}_{jt})$$

Thus the variance of returns is dependent on the size of the stocks β or systematic risk, the variance of market returns $(\tilde{R}_{mt})$, and the variance of firm specific risk $(\tilde{\epsilon}_{jt})$.

REFERENCES

Aharony, J., and I. Swary. "Effects of the 1970 Bank Holding Company Act: Evidence from Capital Markets," *Journal of Finance* (1981), pp. 841–853.

Aharony, J., and I. Swary. "Bank Performance and Risk 1968–1980," New York University, Graduate School of Business Administration *Working Paper*, 1982.

American Bankers Association, *Statistical Information on the Financial Service Industry,* Washington, D.C., 1981.

Baltensperger, E. "Alternative Approaches to the Theory of the Banking Firm," *Journal of Monetary Economics* (1980), pp. 1–37.

Black, F., M. H. Miller, and R. A. Posner. "An Approach to the Regulation of Bank Holding Companies," *Journal of Business* (1978), pp. 379–411.

Bloch, E. *Investment Banking,* unpublished manuscript, Graduate School of Business Administration, New York University, 1983.

Buser, S. D., A. H. Chen, and E. H. Kane. "Federal Deposit Insurance, Regulatory Policy and Optimal Bank Capital," *Journal of Finance* (1981), pp. 51–60.

Cagan, P. "The Monetary Dynamics of Hyperinflation," in M. Friedman (ed.), *Studies in the Quantity Theory of Money.* Chicago: University of Chicago Press, 1956.

Corrigan, E. G. "Are Banks Special?," Federal Reserve Bank of Minneapolis *Annual Report,* 1982.

Carosso, V. P. *Investment Banking in America.* Cambridge, Mass.: Harvard University Press, 1970.

Eisemann, P. C. "Diversification and the Cogeneric Banking Holding Company," *Journal of Bank Research* (1976), pp. 68–77.

Eisenbeis, R. A. "Financial Innovation and the Growth of Bank Holding Companies." Proceedings from a Conference on *Bank Structure and Competition,* Federal Reserve Bank of Chicago, April 27–28, 1978.

Eisenbeis, R. A., R. S. Harris, and J. Lakonishok. "Benefits of Bank Diversification: The Evidence from Shareholder Returns," forthcoming *Journal of Finance.*

Fama, E. F. "Banking in the Theory of Finance," *Journal of Monetary Economics* (1980), pp. 39–57.

Federal Reserve Board of Governors—Office of the Comptroller of the Currency, "Capital Adequacy Guidelines," released December 17, 1981.

Fisher, L. "Determinants of Risk Premiums on Corporate Bonds," *Journal of Political Economy* (1959), pp. 217–237.

Galai, D., and R. Masulis. "The Option Pricing Model and the Risk-Factor of Stocks," *Journal of Financial Economics* (1976), pp. 53–81.

Giddy, I. H. "Risk and Returns from Bond Underwriting," *Working Paper,* Columbia University, Graduate Business School, December 1983.

Goodman, L. S. "New Options Markets," *Federal Reserve Bank of New York Quarterly Review* (Autumn 1983), pp. 35–47.

Guttentag, J., and R. Herring. "Credit Rationing and Financial Disorder," *Working Paper,* University of Pennsylvania, Wharton School, 1982.

Hayes, S. L. "Investment Banking: Power Structure in Flux," *Harvard Business Review* (1971), pp. 136–152.

Heggestad, A. "Riskiness of Investments in Nonbank Activities by Bank Holding Companies," *Journal of Economics and Business* (1975), pp. 219–223.

Henn, H. G. *Handbook of the Law of Corporations and Other Business Enterprises,* 2d ed. St. Paul, Minn.: West Publishing, 1970.

Horvitz, P. M. "Bank Holding Company Regulation: Discussion." Proceedings from a Conference on Bank Structure and Competition, Federal Reserve Bank of Chicago, April 27–28, 1978.

Ibbotson, R. G. "Price Performance of Common Stock New Issues," *Journal of Financial Economics* (1975), pp. 235–272.

Investment Company Institute, *Misadventures in Banking: Bank Promotion of Pooled Investment Funds,* Washington, D. C., 1979.

Kane, E. J. "Accelerating Inflation, Technological Innovation, and the Decreasing Effectiveness of Bank Regulation," *Journal of Finance* (1981), pp. 355–367.

Lamb, R., and S. P. Rappaport. *Municipal Bonds: The Comprehensive Review of Tax-Exempt Securities and Public Finance.* New York: Mc-Graw Hill, 1980.

Lee, S. "Why Some Banks May Pay More for Deposit Insurance," *Business Week* (January 1984).

Meinster, D. R. and R. D. Johnson. "Bank Holding Company Diversification and the Risk of Capital Impairment," *Bell Journal of Economics* (1979), pp. 683–694.

Morgan Guaranty. "An Investigation of Commercial Bank Failures," Internal Memorandum, September 1, 1983.

Patinkin, D. "Financial Intermediaries and the Logical Structure of Monetary Theory," *American Economic Review* (1961), pp. 95–116.

Public Securities Association. *A Staff Analysis of Certain Aspects of the Underwriting of General Obligation and Reserve Bonds,* New York, 1978.

Ritter, L. S., and W. L. Silber. *Principles of Money, Banking and Financial Markets,* 3d ed. New York: Basic Books, 1980.

Salomon Brothers Inc. "Primary Capital Ratios: The Potential Implications of Standby Letters of Credit," *Bank Weekly* (October 7, 1983).

Saunders, A., and T.S.Y. Ho. "A Micro Model of the Federal Funds Market," *Working Paper,* New York University, Graduate School of Business Administration, 1983.

A. Saunders. "Conflicts of Interest," *Working Paper,* New York University, Graduate School of Business Administration, January 1984.

Schwartz, R. A., and D. K. Whitcomb. "Implicit Transfers in the Extension of Trade Credit," in K. Boulding and T. Wilson (eds.) *Channels of Redistribution Through the Financial System: The Grants Economics of Money and Credit.* New York: Praeger, 1978.

Sinkey, J. F., Jr. "Adverse Publicity and Bank Deposit Flows," *Journal of Bank Research* (1975a), pp. 109–112.

Sinkey, J. F., Jr. "The Failure of United States National Bank of San Diego: A Portfolio and Performance Analysis," *Journal of Bank Research* (1975b), pp. 8–24.

Sinkey, J. F., Jr., and D. A. Walker. "Problem Banks: Identification and Characteristics," *Journal of Bank Research* (1975), pp. 208–217.

R. Startz. "Implicit Interest and Demand Deposits," *Journal of Monetary Economics* (1979), pp. 515–534.

Stoll, H. "Small Firms' Access to Public Equity Financing," forthcoming in P. M. Horvitz and R. R. Pettit (eds.), *Financing Small Business*. Greenwich, Conn.: JAI Press.

I. Swary. "Bank Acquisition of Non-Bank Firms: An Empirical Analysis of Administrative Decision," *Journal of Banking and Finance* (1983), pp. 213–230.

Volcker, P. A. Statement Before the Committee on Banking, Housing and Urban Affairs, United States Senate, September 13, 1983.

Wall, L., and R. A. Eisenbeis. "Bank Holding Company Non-Banking Activities and Risk." Paper presented to the Conference on Bank Structure and Competition, Federal Reserve Bank of Chicago.

Wilson, R. "The Theory of Syndicates," *Econometrica* (1968), pp. 119–132.

8 Conflicts of Interest: An Economic View

ANTHONY SAUNDERS

Potential conflicts of interest arise in most seller-buyer relationships. That this is so can be seen from definitions of conflicts of interest found in the literature. Schotland, for example, argues that potential conflicts exist in "a situation in which two or more interests are legitimately present and competing or conflicting. The individual (or firm) making a decision that will affect these interests may have a larger stake in one of them than in other(s).[1]" Edwards defines a potential conflict as arising "whenever one is serving two or more interests and can put one person in a better position at the expense of another."[2]

These quotes imply that potential conflicts are likely to exist in most business situations and are likely to be increasing functions of the size of the customer base and the number of activities engaged in by that business. Thus, a single product firm with a narrow customer base may face fewer potential conflicts than a multiproduct (activity) bank holding company with a great diversity of customers. This perhaps explains why potential conflicts of interest have been viewed with concern by regulators of bank holding companies. Nevertheless, although restricting bank holding company activities may reduce the private and social costs of conflicts of interest— which include any pecuniary penalties suffered by an injured party and the misallocation of society's resources that may result—such restrictions also have harmful effects. In particular, restricting bank holding company activities limits their ability to diversify business risk, and may limit their enjoyment of potential economies of scope and scale as well as limiting the degree of competition in various financial markets. These limitations may have negative effects on society.

Thus in the case of bank holding companies expanding into corporate securities activities, the public policy issue at stake is how troublesome are potential conflicts of interest (including questions of bank safety and soundness) relative to the benefits of activity expansion, greater competition with existing security firms, economies of scope and scale, and so on. If the economic incentives to exploit conflicts appear to be large, this may be an important reason for restricting the expansion of bank holding companies into this area. On the other hand, if the incentives to exploit conflicts are relatively small, restrictive legislation may be harmful on a net cost-benefit basis.

In the following section the potential conflicts that may arise if holding companies expand into corporate securities activities are reviewed. The potential conflicts described are those repeatedly identified in the existing literature by the securities industry and other analysts. The section entitled "Incentives to Exploit Conflicts" considers the economic conditions (or incentive structures) under which these potential conflicts are likely to be exploited. This is followed, in the section entitled "Factors Mitigating Conflict Exploitation," by a parallel discussion of economic incentives that tend to mitigate "conflict exploitation." Finally, the last section provides a summary and a set of conclusions related to this issue.[3]

TYPES OF CONFLICTS

In order to understand the types of conflict that may arise, it is useful to consider the organizational form, or structure, through which corporate securities activities of bank holding companies are likely to take place. Specifically, corporate securities underwriting and dealing might occur (1) within the bank itself (e.g., in a department separated from commercial banking operations, as is the case with most municipal bond underwriting activities today[4], (2) in a subsidiary of the bank—as may be the case for Eurobond underwritings, or (3) in a separately capitalized affiliate of the holding company, similar in manner to the leasing, data processing, and consumer finance subsidiaries that are common in the current bank holding company structure. Because the latter organizational form is the most likely of these alternatives, potential conflicts are examined below "as if" underwriting takes place within an affiliate of the bank holding company.

The potential conflicts to be discussed have either been raised at Congressional hearings leading up to the Glass-Steagall Act in the early 1930s,[5] or have been suggested more recently by industry observers or by the securities industry in opposing bank involvement in private bebt placements, open and closed-end mutual funds, REITs, and other securities-related activities.[6]

The potential conflicts most often mentioned are:

The conflict between the promotional role of the investment banker and the commercial banker's obligation to provide disinterested advice to depositors

Using the bank's securities affiliate to issue new securities to repay unprofitable loans

Economic tie-ins of different holding company products

Placing unsold securities in the bank's trust accounts

Conflicts resulting from director interlocks

Bank loans to support buying of a security issue

Imprudent loans to issuers of securities underwritten by the affiliate

Bank loans to its affiliate to keep it in business

Informational advantages regarding current and future customers

Although it is difficult to develop a well-defined taxonomy for these conflicts, it might be noted that they either involve conflicts among different customers (selling conflicts), conflicts that directly threaten the safety and soundness of the bank (conflicts with depositors interests), and conflicts that involve informational advantages (insider information). Generally, the first five conflicts are of the customer or selling type, the next three involve safety and soundness issues, whereas the last involves questions of insider information.

Each of these potential conflicts is discussed in more detail below.

The Conflict Between the Promotional Role of the Investment Banker and the Commercial Banker's Obligation to Provide Disinterested Advice to Depositors

Concern regarding conflict in the advisory role of banks with respect to depositors played a significant role in the debate leading up to the passage of the Glass-Steagall Act.[7] The prevailing view at the time appeared to be that the underwriting of securities through bank affiliates, given the need of those affiliates to be viewed as having been underwritten successfully, created pressure on banks to help place the securities underwritten by those affiliates. At the same time, banks were viewed as agents dispensing disinterested investment advice to their deposit customers (including correspondent banks), either free of charge or for an explicit or implicit fee (e.g., compensating balances). It was argued that once bankers had a direct or indirect stake in the securities activities of an affiliate, investment advice to customers would no longer be impartial. Indeed, banks might promote the securities underwritten by their own affiliates as good portfolio investments, even when superior investments are available elsewhere.

At the time, Senator Glass and others evidently believed that such promotional activity (pressure) was pervasive in the relationships that major banks had formed with their correspondents. Many of the bonds sold by the securities operations of money center banks to correspondents in various parts of the United States appear to have been relatively low-quality issues of South American countries, the proceeds of which were used to finance railroads and other development projects. The price decline of many of these securities, and the associated losses incurred by many small banks, has been viewed as an important factor in the surge of bank failures that occurred during the 1929–1933 period.[8]

Today, by diversifying into other activities, banks have developed a promotional interest in selling a number of nonbanking products to their customers. For example, Citibank has circulated letters to its New York retail depositors promoting the sale of life insurance offered by its banking subsidiary in South Dakota, whereas similar promotional activities at the retail level have occurred with bank-operated REITs, mutual funds, and discount brokerage services.[9]

The promotional role of banks has also been identified in connection with the international debt problems of the 1980s. Selldowns of syndicated loans by managers and co-managers focusing on fee income, to participating banks around the world, bear some similarity to the sale of foreign bonds to correspondents some 50 years earlier.[10] An even more intense promotional role developed in the early 1980s, when many of these syndicated loans matured and the debt of the foreign borrowers had to be restructured, with considerable pressure brought to bear on smaller banks to roll over loans and even increase them.[11]

The point at issue here is that the modern bank holding company has an inherent promotional role, both with respect to depositors and borrowers as well as co-lenders and purchasers of fee-based and other services. Promotion is a core element in most financial firms, and banking is no exception. This was true at the time the Glass-Steagall Act was passed, and it is still true today. The crucial question is under what conditions will the promotional activities of banks, when they gain access to corporate securities activities, harm, or conflict with, the best interests of bank customers. If, for example, customers are fully informed and banks face competition, no obvious financial harm should result. These points are examined further in the section on "Incentives to Exploit Conflicts" and "Factors Mitigating Conflict Exploitation."

Using the Bank's Securities Affiliate to Issue New Securities to Repay "Unprofitable" Loans

A number of scenarios have been suggested in the literature as underlying this "debt restructuring" potential conflict. In each case the bank, by using the underwriting ability of its securities affiliate, may be able to transfer risk from itself to the issuing firm's equity holders, or to new or existing bondholders of the issuing firm.

Consider the case where a firm has loans outstanding to a bank, and also has some bonds outstanding in addition to shareholder equity. Suppose bank management is risk averse and fears that, before the loan is repaid, there is an increased probability that the firm will default. Moreover, assume that these loans are only partly collateralized. The bank has an incentive to avoid any expected losses on its loans. It might avoid such losses by pressuring the firm into issuing new bonds through its securities affiliate and directing the cash proceeds of the new issue toward paying off the bank loan early. In so doing, the bank will eliminate its portfolio exposure to default risk, and its affiliate would earn a fee on the new issue underwriting. It should be noted, however, that the bank has more direct options other than debt restructuring in such cases. For example, it could renegotiate loan terms (interest rates) and/or ask the firm to pledge more collateral, thereby "repricing" the loan so as to extract a risk-premium comensurate with the new risk. Hence, debt-restructuring might be viewed as a potential alternative that arises only if these options are unavailable to the bank (i.e., it is a term loan with no provisions in the covenants for such actions). Certainly, the transaction costs to the bank of a renegotiation of loan terms should be less (except for resetting residual risk) than that involved in a debt restructuring exercise.

A question arises as to who bears the risk following a debt restructuring operation. This will depend directly on the *quality* of financial information revealed to prospective new bondholders regarding the financial situation of the issuing firm, and the *relative* seniority of the new bond issue compared with bond issues outstanding. Suppose full information disclosure has taken place, so that there are no information asymmetry problems. Investors will impound unbiased risk premiums into the prices or discounts required to purchase the new issue, whereas old bond prices will fully reflect all relevant and *known* financial information relating to the firm.

If, in the absence of differential collateral, bonded debt (new and old) and bank loans have equal seniority, so that new bondholders' claims will be equivalent to the bank's claims they replace, the bank will emerge from restructuring whole, bondholders, both new and existing, will receive an appropriate return adjusted for risk, whereas shareholders' interests will be affected by the increased cost of debt attributable to the sale of new bonds at a sizable discount.

A different scenario emerges if bank debt was *junior* to the old bonds, but the new bonds that are issued, as replacement financing are of equivalent seniority to the old bonds. The *unexpected* announcement of the new bond issue will now cause a drop in the price of existing (old) bonds. This assumes that the old bonds were traded on the assumption that no additional bonds would be issued. It occurs because the increase in the supply of bonds of equivalent seniority serves to dilute the effective asset protection of the existing bondholders' claims, so that, in the event of bankruptcy, the value of their per-dollar protection against the firm's assets has been reduced. Only if the new debt issue is subordinated to existing bonds will this dilution in value, or wealth transfer, be avoided. This, in turn, will depend on the nature of the protective covenants regarding the relative seniority of any new debt issue written into existing (old) bond indentures. Existing bondholders may thus suffer a capital loss through risk being transferred from the bank *via* the new issue mechanism. The *dilution effect* in general has been well-documented in the finance literature.[12] It should be noted that the issuing firm's shareholders also stand to lose if the new issue of debt commands a relatively high discount compared to the interest cost of the bank loan, because this reduces the firm's current and expected future net earnings and thus the market value of equity. To avoid or minimize such losses, stockholders have an incentive to issue new bonds with the *maximum* seniority possible—because these will command smaller discounts than relatively junior claims—whereas, as noted above, old bondholders prefer that any new debt issues be as junior as possible. As a result, the interests of the stockholders and existing bondholders of the firm directly conflict.

Two scenarios have been sketched above which assume a full information world. In both cases the shareholders are likely to lose (at least in the short term) from a debt restructuring that pays off bank loans. Existing bondholders lose only if the bank debt was junior to bonded debt, as in the second scenario. New bondholders do not lose. The basic "debt restructuring" conflict in these cases is therefore between the bank and the firm's shareholders, and it seems unlikely that the latter would *voluntarily* suffer a wealth loss whether or not the bank had a securities underwriting affiliate. Moreover, because the bank is relinquishing the loan customer, it is not clear what "pressure" it could bring to bear on that firm's stockholders to initiate a debt-restructuring exercise. Clearly, it no longer has any market power over the customer.

Of more concern is the case where the issuing firm and/or the bank's securities affiliate fail to make full disclosure of information regarding the increased default risk of the issuer. This is a world of asymmetry of information between issuers and investors. In this case the firm's stockholders might have an incentive *not* to disclose information, because the new bond issue might then be "overpriced" in relation to its true (or underlying) market value, thereby reducing the effective cost of the new issue to the firm.[13] In this case, the bank affiliate and the issuing firm's shareholders shift risk to *both* the new and existing bondholders. Conceivably they might be able to transfer all of the increased default risk to the bondholders. Of course, when the true financial problems of the issuing firm are subsequently revealed (perhaps on bankruptcy), both the issuer and the underwriter are potentially exposed to a class action suit on behalf of the bondholders. Even then, debt restructuring might conceivably benefit the bank and its holding company if the gains from salvaging the loan exceed the expected costs of litigation and damage to its reputation. This latter cost may be quite significant, however, if incurred repeatedly over many such restructurings.

Finally, it can be argued that the potential for debt restructuring involving new bond issues exists today, especially because banks act as financial advisers to many large firms. For example, a commercial bank might advise a firm to use an existing investment banking firm to underwrite a new issue and pay off its bank loans with the proceeds. The difference between this case and one in which there is a securities affiliate of the same bank's holding company is essentially one of degree. That is, does the combination of loan repayments and underwriting fees, as in the bank-affiliate case, increase the probability of debt restructuring compared to that when underwriting is undertaken by nonaffiliated firms?

Economic Tie-ins

As noted in the first section, it is common to view the bank holding company as a multiproduct firm offering a full range of services to customers. This range of services, when it includes corporate securities underwriting, may lead to *economic* tie-ins, with bank customers being pressured into "buying" the underwriting services of the securities affiliate even if they could float new issues on more favorable terms elsewhere.

The major leverage a bank has over customers is through its lending function and as a guarantor (e.g., letters of credit). Threats of credit rationing, curtailing, or nonrenewal of credit lines or increasing the cost of funds could all impose future costs on a firm. Thus the total costs, explicit and implicit, of using outside underwriters may outweigh interest or flotation cost savings, if any. A bank is unlikely to tie in large firms in this manner, because these firms tend to diversify their lines of credit. Smaller firms, however, may be more susceptible, because they usually have a closer relationship with local banks. Moreover, there is considerable empirical evidence that banks do credit ration smaller customers.[14] By making the availability of loans and other bank services *contingent* on the use of the services of the securities affiliate, the affiliate may be able to attract customers from traditional investment bankers.

This effect would be mitigated, however, if, as is likely, investment banks are also given full commercial banking powers (through affiliates) in any future deregulation.

Placing Unsold Securities in the Bank's Trust Accounts

This potential conflict might arise if, at the end of the offer period, the securities affiliate of a bank holding company has securities remaining in its inventory that can only be sold off at a loss to outside investors—that is, at a price below the firm commitment price. To avoid such losses, the affiliate may seek to place the securities at favorable prices in other parts of the holding company, such as with the trust accounts of the affiliated bank. Schotland has documented an extensive list of potential conflicts that arise in trust activities of banks, one of which is disposing of unwanted securities in fiduciary accounts.[15] Although disposing of unwanted securities in large institutional trust or pension fund accounts is unlikely—because owners of these accounts closely monitor performance—this pressure is absent in the management of smaller personal trusts over which banks, as trustees, have considerable discretionary control. Even in these cases, however, a number of legal and regulatory constraints exist to limit abuse of fiduciary responsibilities.

The "dumping" of securities directly in the bank's own portfolio, a concern expressed in the proceedings leading up to the Glass-Steagall Act, seems even less likely. First, the bank holding company itself would not obviously gain, because the underwriting loss is simply transferred to the bank. Second, national banks are subject to strict quantitative limits on the amount of corporate bonds they can buy (less than 10% of capital) as well as qualitative restrictions on those bonds (Baa or better).[16] Third, there are often considerable tax disadvantages for a bank that buys corporate bonds rather than municipal bonds.

Director Interlocks Between Bank Holding Companies and Nonfinancial Firms

With the ability of bank securities affiliates to underwrite debt and equity issues, the potential conflicts arising from director interlocks between banks and other firms may become more important. For example, a 1979 Senate Staff Study[17] found 182 separate director interlocks between the five largest U.S. banks and the five largest U.S. nonfinancial corporations. Moreover the ICI[18] estimated that, at the end of 1977, federally chartered banks (through their trust departments) controlled 19.5% of the stock of General Motors, 20.6% of Exxon, and over 30% of Ford, Caterpillar Tractor, K Mart, and Kellogg.

The combination of director interlocks and large holdings of corporate stock in bank trust departments, together with the ability of a bank holding company affiliate to offer underwriting services, may increase the potential for conflicts of interest. For example, financing decisions made at the boardroom level such as loans versus bond issues, bonds versus equity, and the choice of underwriter may well be influenced, either directly or indirectly, by the presence and voting powers of bank directors.

Nevertheless, it seems unlikely that a single bank director on boards of nonbank corporations would have sufficient voting or persuasive powers to cause the board consistently to act against the best interests of the vast majority of its shareholders. Indeed, as discussed in the following section, directors (and senior managers) are becoming increasingly exposed to liability regarding decisions made in the board-room.

Bank Loans to Support the Price of a Security

In acting as an underwriter (especially as a lead underwriter or syndicate manager), the securities affiliate may want its underwriting effort to be as successful as possible. This may be especially true for new entrants into the underwriting business. For bank-affiliated new entrants, bank loans may be made (at relatively favorable rates) to third-party investors on the understanding that part or all of these funds would be used to purchase certain new issues underwritten by the affiliate and its syndicates. In such a case, bank loans could be used to support (or subsidize) the prices of those securities, sending false signals to other capital market investors and potential new issuers re-garding the true market performance of the underwriter, as well as possibly affecting the safety and soundness of the bank and its depositors. As discussed in the section entitled, "Factors Mitigating Conflict Exploitation," it would be surprising if such activities ultimately failed to attract the attention of bank examiners and regulators. Moreover, this operation clearly depends on the existence of a high degree of infor-mation imperfection (or asymmetries) in the capital market.

Imprudent Loans to Issuers of Securities Underwritten by the Affiliates

This is essentially the reverse of the debt-restructuring conflict discussed earlier. Sup-pose a new issue of bonds is undertaken, and the investment projects financed by the proceeds fail, or there is some other negative impact on the issuing firm's cash flows that serve to increase its default risk. To prevent the firm from failing, and/or to avoid possible litigation costs arising from bondholders' claims against the securities affil-iate (relating to informational disclosure and lack of due diligence), the bank may make new loans to keep the firm afloat in the hope that its financial situation will improve in the future.

If the new loans of the bank are subordinated to the claims of existing bondholders, the market values of outstanding bonds will tend to rise—as the assets of the firms have expanded, while the stock of bonds remains unchanged. Bank management may thus be implicitly subsidizing the risky claims of the issuing firm's bondholders in conflict with the best interests of its depositors (i.e., by threatening the bank's safety and soundness through imprudent loans).[19]

The Bank May Make Direct Loans to its Securities Affiliate

If the securities affiliate is separately capitalized, it might seek to increase leverage through loans from the banking arm of the holding company. Although direct loans from a bank to its affiliate are subject to a ceiling of 10% of bank capital, must be backed by more than 100% collateral, and must be on market terms, it is still possible that such loans could be made at less than the appropriately determined risk-free interest rate. In such a case, the protection of bank depositors (via earnings) will be weakened. Further, because money is fungible, loans could also be made to third-party banks and on-lent to the securities affiliate—perhaps for a direct fee or an increase in compensating balances held with third-party banks—in order to circumvent the 10%-of-capital loan ceiling. (Note that this technique could be used currently to finance any large external customer of the bank.) As in cases (6) and (7) such actions involve potential conflicts between the bank and its depositors and may threaten its safety and soundness.[20]

Informational Advantages Regarding Competitors

As bank holding companies and other financial and nonfinancial firms cross traditional market and product boundaries, they will encounter increasing competition. Because bank-affiliate underwriters may become privy to any inside or as yet unannounced information regarding firms whose securities they underwrite, this information (regarding other firms) may be disseminated to other affiliates of the holding company to generate a competitive advantage in lending, leasing, and so on.[21] However, this potential "insider information" conflict is present in virtually all existing corporate security underwriting situations and is currently subject to the close scrutiny and penalties of the SEC. This would also likely be the case if bank holding companies were allowed to underwrite corporate securities.

INCENTIVES TO EXPLOIT CONFLICTS

The preceding section has catalogued the major potential conflicts of interest identified in the *existing literature*. Most of these have been put forward by the securities industry to make a case against allowing banks to take part in securities-related activities. The key conceptual issue, given the definition of conflicts of interest in the section on "Types of Conflicts," is whether or not it is in the self-interest of those directly involved in decision making, in particular the directors or managers of the bank holding company and its affiliates, to exploit a conflict *opportunity* in each case in which it arises. What environment or incentives exist that would lead to such exploitation, and what are the corresponding disincentives? In this section the major economic incentives to exploit such conflicts are analyzed. The following section gives an analysis of the disincentives.

It is argued below that the major incentives to exploit conflicts emanate either from: (1) agency problems within the holding company, (2) incentives resulting from the current structuring of deposit insurance, and/or (3) from different size of capital investment by the holding company in the bank and its affiliates. On the other hand, substantial disincentives exist in the form of: (1) the value of preserving the bank's and its affiliate's reputation, (2) the market for corporate control (or managerial services), (3) the market for bank and securities affiliate products and services, (4) the monitoring of managerial behavior by bond rating agencies, and (5) the monitoring of managerial behavior by regulatory agencies.

Perhaps the most interesting conclusion is that conflict-of-interest situations can only profitably be exploited if either (1) there are information imperfections (or asymmetries) that exist between contracting parties (i.e., buyers and sellers), and/or (2) the markets for labor services and commercial and investment bank final products (services) are imperfectly competitive. Thus the necessary conditions for "profitable" exploitation of conflicts of interest are imperfect information and imperfect competition. Hence, to the extent that financial information is speedily and widely disseminated to buyers and the markets for financial services are competitive, the economic incentives to exploit conflicts will be relatively small.

Agency Problems

Most of the potential conflicts described in the section on "Types of Conflicts" involved to varying degrees the bank subsidiary, its securities underwriting affiliate, and the issuing firm. Analysis of these conflicts is made difficult by noting that the bank holding company is not a monolithic whole, but rather a complex amalgam of contracts, relationships, and financial arrangements that link together bondholders, depositors (in the case of the bank), shareholders, and managers—each with a more or less well-defined set of objectives.

Specifically, the bank and its securities affiliate will have the same controlling group of shareholders (those of the holding company) represented by a single board of directors. Moreover, following traditional corporate finance theory[22] for example, it can be assumed that the best interests of the shareholders are served by seeking to maximize the present value of current and future profits of the holding company. This will be directly reflected in the value of the holding company's stocks in the equity market.

The basic issues at stake are (1) whether the shareholders of an organization that seeks to maximize long-run profits can impose their objectives on the managers who run that organization, and (2) whether maximization of long-run profits is conducive (or not conducive) to conflict exploitation. It is argued below that the objective of long-run profit maximization is generally conducive to conflict control, and that managerial compensation structures, when used appropriately, can tie managerial interests to those of the stockholders.

The major agency problem which arises is that although shareholders are the ultimate controlling and risk-bearing principals in a holding company, direct decision making for both the bank and the securities affiliate will usually be in the hands of managers (or agents). This includes day-to-day decisions about whether or not to exploit potential conflicts. Generally, one might expect managers of the bank and the underwriting affiliate not only to have different objectives, but more important, to have objectives that differ from those of the shareholders of the holding company (and the board of directors who are the shareholders representatives).

There is a growing literature on the problems that arise when there is separation of ownership from control in large organizations, such as bank holding companies.[23] This literature also examines the reasons why the objectives of managers and stockholders in such organizations tend to differ.[24] The major distinction between managerial and shareholder objectives is believed to involve the decision horizon.[25] A manager's tenure with an organization tends to be relatively short compared to the lifetime of a firm—which is theoretically indefinite. As a result, it is argued that managers may place much greater value on short-run profits—even at the cost of market reputation and long-run profits. Thus managers may be *less* concerned about the future profits (and reputation) of the firm than shareholders and their representatives on the board of directors, whose claims are valued according to the entire stream of both current and expected future profits. Under such conditions, managers may have greater incentives to exploit conflicts for short-run profit opportunities than if the manager's and shareholder's interests were identical. Even in managerially controlled firms, however, by optimally manipulating managerial compensation schemes, boards of directors can partly resolve horizon differences and therefore lessen the probability that conflicts will be in fact be exploited.[26]

In both banking and securities underwriting activities, bonuses and profit-sharing schemes appear to be extremely important components of managerial salaries. Three types of bonus or compensation scheme can be identified,[27] and their potential for conflict control analyzed, assuming that it is in the shareholders' best interest (e.g., through long-run reputation effects) to avoid such conflicts.[28] These are: (1) bonuses or profit-sharing of both bank and securities affiliate managers tied to the (consolidated) current profits of the holding company; (2) bonuses or profit-sharing of securities affiliate managers tied to the current profits of the affiliate only, whereas those of bank managers are tied to bank profits; and (3) bank and securities affiliate management bonuses tied to the market value of the shares of the holding company.

Bonuses tied to the consolidated *current* profits of the holding company would seem to be the least desirable form of compensation if the objective is to avoid managerial incentives for conflict exploitation. Among the reasons for this are first, because this type of bonus simply accentuates the horizon differences between managers and holding company shareholders (i.e., the incentives for managerial short-run profit maximizing are increased). Second, the managers of the underwriting affiliate and the bank have clear incentives to form coalitions in order to ensure that current consolidated profits of the holding company increase—even at the expense of the current profitability of one or other of the bank and its affiliate. For example, under this type of bonus scheme a bank may be willing to make subsidized loans to its affiliate, or to a third party, to support the prices of stock underwritten by that affiliate, even if the expected profits (or returns) on these loans are low. As long as the net profit generated by the underwriter *via* these loans *more than compensates* for bank losses, the consolidated profits of the holding company will increase and so will managerial bonuses. This type of bonus plan also creates incentives for managers to exploit tie-ins designed to promote the sale of securities to depositors, and to restructure debt through new issues, because any collective bank-securities affiliate activity that produces a *net* increase in total short-run profits benefits both managerial teams.

A superior, common compensation scheme is one that links management bonuses directly to the current profits of the particular affiliate or department of the holding company in which they are employed. This essentially involves separate profit centers within an organization. Although profit centers do not resolve the fundamental manager-shareholder horizon problem, they go a long way toward controlling the coalition of interests problem. For example, it is less likely that "unsound loans" would be made to an affiliate, because any losses on interest or principal would serve only to reduce bank managers' bonuses, whereas those of affiliate managers may well increase if the loans serve to increase underwriting profits. Unless bank managers are unduly altruistic, it is unlikely that they would voluntarily accept this type of income transfer.[29] Thus with bonus separation, a number of the conflicts described earlier, such as tie-ins, information dissemination, third-party or direct loans, and promotional sales of stock or bonds seem less likely to occur.

An ideal bonus scheme in terms of internal conflict control is one that ties management compensation to the *separately* valued stock of the bank and its securities affiliate. Such a scheme would solve the managerial *horizon* problem—because managers of both the bank and the securities affiliate would now be concerned with the long-run profits and reputation of their respective organizations—as well as the *coalition* problem, because the stock of each part of the holding company would be valued separately. Unfortunately, market values are usually available only for the shares of the overall holding company, so that stock bonus plans are usually linked to the overall market values of the latter, thus failing to resolve the coalition of interests problem.[30] Nevertheless, tying managers to shareholders and board decision horizons does reduce the *present value* of forming coalitions in order to exploit conflicts.

Managerial stock bonus plans can be implemented through (1) stock options; (2) stock appreciation rights, which are like stock options but the holder receives cash, not shares, at maturity; (3) restricted stock (i.e., common stock with restrictions on transferability); and (4) phantom stock, which is like restricted stock except that when the restrictions expire the manager receives the cash value of the stock rather than the stock itself.[31] If managerial bonuses or profit-sharing represent significant components of the overall compensation package, then stockholders through their representatives on the board of directors can impose a reasonable degree of *internal* control over incentives for conflict exploitation.

Even in the absence of, or weakness in, *internal* controls (or "carrots") regarding managerial incentives to exploit conflicts, there are at least four *external* forces (or "sticks") that limit managers from diverging too far from long-run holding company profit maximization through conflict exploitation for short-run gains. Two are "market control" mechanisms and two are regulatory or "outside agent" control mechanisms:

1. The market for corporate control
2. The market for the bank and securities affiliate products and services
3. The monitoring of managerial behavior by bond rating agencies
4. The monitoring of managerial behavior by regulatory agencies

Discussion of the conflict controlling roles of (3) and (4) is deferred to the next section.

The idea underlying the market for corporate control, as developed by Jensen and Meckling, and Jensen and Ruback[32] is that the current managers of the banking and securities affiliates are just two of many potential teams offering their managerial services to a holding company's shareholders in the professional labor market. Should existing managers overtly pursue short-run profit maximization by exploiting conflicts and adversely affecting or damaging the reputation of the enterprise, then shareholders, through the board and senior holding company management, will have an incentive to go to the labor market and replace them with managers whose objectives are more closely aligned with their own (i.e., long-run profit maximization).[33]

A good example of the managerial control in action was the Chase-Drysdale affair. In May 1982, following the failure of Drysdale Government Securities, Chase Manhattan (as agents for Drysdale in securities repurchase transactions) paid $160 million in interest due on $4 billion worth of government securities that had been borrowed by Drysdale Securities. Although it was not clear whether Chase Manhattan was legally liable, it paid to preserve its market reputation and to prevent the failure of a number of small security dealers.[34] Nine Chase officials were forced to leave, including two senior executives. Further, Chase established a litigation committee in the summer of 1982 to research the possibility of taking legal action against these same officers.

> The Committee was formed to determine whether the corporation or the bank has any legal claims against any of their present or former directors or officers in connection with the Drysdale Government Securities, Inc. and Penn State Bank, N.A. situations and, if so, is authorized to cause such legal claims to be initiated or pursued if the Committee determines that it would be in the best interest of the Corporation or the Bank to do so.[35]

Further, it is not only the act of firing but also the threat of firing (and potential future liability) that acts as a deterrent to managerial behavior contrary to the best interests of the shareholders.

The ability of managers to exploit conflicts is further limited by the degree of market power held by the bank and/or its affiliate managers over customers (e.g., depositors, borrowers, and issuing firms). For example, tie-ins can only be exploited if the bank has a substantial degree of market power over the issuing firm in the provision of loans or other services. If a firm has a number of lenders and credit lines available, it is less likely to accede to bank pressure in that direction. Smaller firms or large firms in financial distress are likely to be the most susceptible to this type of pressure.[36] Similar arguments can be made regarding the pressures to restructure debt. The deregulation of the financial system, together with the technological and information revolutions currently under way in financial services, means that even smaller firms will eventually be able to escape or at least mitigate tie-ins and similar pressures. Indeed, in a world of full and perfect competition between buyers and sellers of financial services, and in which each of the market participants is fully informed (see below), it would be impossible for any seller to exploit a potential conflict of interest, because the buyer would be immediately aware of the situation and would switch his or her demand to another market competitor or impound any potential loss in the price he or she is willing to pay.

Moral Hazard and FDIC Insurance

Even though the objective of shareholders and boards of directors can be assumed to focus on maximization of the value of the firm, it has been argued,[37] that the current system of fixed-premium deposit insurance levied by the FDIC creates incentives for banks to increase the level of risk taken above the *optimally priced insurance* level.[38] Under the current deposit insurance scheme, two banks of equal deposit size and insured/uninsured deposit mixes, but with radically different asset and off-balance sheet risks, would be subject to the same FDIC insurance premiums.

Merton[39] has argued that this type of fixed-fee or premium insurance is isomorphic to selling a put option to the bank's shareholders (i.e., the holding company). Using standard Black and Scholes[40] option pricing theory, Merton[41] demonstrates that the value of this option increases as the underlying riskiness of the bank's assets is increased. Thus by increasing the variance of asset returns, the bank can transfer risk to the FDIC and outside depositors. One way in which bank shareholders could allow risk to increase is by placing a lower value on maintaining the bank's reputation in controlling and monitoring conflict exploitation by its managers.

The incentives for banks to take additional risks are also increased by the implicit insurance provided to large debt holders (depositors) when the FDIC uses purchase and assumption, rather than payoff methods to prevent bank failures. For depositors in surviving banks, this method of bank reorganization signals that the FDIC has no taste for imposing market discipline on large depositors of failing banks, which in turn lowers the cost of bank funds (deposits) below that which would otherwise exist if market discipline prevailed.

One direct method for resolving this ''moral hazard'' problem is for the insurance agency to levy premiums that are a function of the on- *and* off-balance sheet risks of the bank. Although such a method is difficult to implement, its benefits may well outweigh the costs of implementation. At the very least, the FDIC would be better able to control the incentives for risk-taking and conflict exploitation implicit in the existing fixed-premium insurance scheme. At the time of writing, there is a strong possibility that a system of risk-related deposit insurance will be presented to Congress at some point.[42]

Different Capital Investments by the Holding Company in its Bank and Affiliate

Incentives to exploit potential conflicts might exist when the holding company (1) has either very different levels of capital invested in two subsidiaries (e.g., the bank and the securities affiliate), and/or (2) one or all of the subsidiaries are not 100% owned, (i.e., there are some external shareholders).

To illustrate the incentives, consider a holding company with two wholly owned subsidiaries. In one the holding company has invested relatively large amounts of capital, whereas in the other its capital investment is small (perhaps it is highly levered). Assume that the high-equity investment subsidiary is having financial difficulties and faces some risk of bankruptcy. To protect their capital investment in that subsidiary, the shareholders of the holding company have an incentive either to shift inferior assets to the low capital investment subsidiary and/or use the funds of the low capital subsidiary (such as in the form of loans) to protect their investment in the highly capitalized subsidiary. The greater the disparity in capital investments among subsidiaries the greater will be this type of incentive. In effect, the shareholders of the holding company generally have an incentive to transfer risk to that part of the holding company where their capital investment is the smallest. These parts may also be highly levered and/or only partly owned (with other outside shareholders in existence).

If we view these subsidiaries as a bank and its securities affiliate, it seems likely that most bank holding companies will have more capital invested in the bank than in the securities affiliate. Thus any bankruptcy risk shifting is more likely to be from the bank to the securities affiliate rather than vice versa, thereby ruling out the potential safety and soundness conflicts discussed previously under "Types of Conflicts."[43]

FACTORS MITIGATING CONFLICT EXPLOITATION

Just as there are factors that would tend to create incentives to exploit conflicts of interest (with respect to the corporate securities business of bank holding company affiliates), other factors exist that would tend to limit this problem. These involve the value of the holding company as a going concern, the role of securities rating services, as well as the supervisory and regulatory process.

The Value of Reputation and the Quality of Information

As discussed in the previous section most of the corporate finance literature concerns the (normative) paradigm that shareholders seek to maximize long-run profits. Given that shareholders, through boards of directors, do indeed seek to maximize long-term profits, they will be vitally concerned with building and maintaining a long-term relationship with their customers (by not exploiting conflicts) as long as the market for bank products (services) is competitive and information is disseminated widely and quickly among customers.[44] As Bull has noted:

> . . authors have suggested that concern by the firm for its reputation or brand name
> . . . may lead the employer [principal] to fulfill his part of the contract. In other words,
> an appeal is made to a third party, here the market rather than the court for enforcement.[45]

Thus reputation, or the stock of "goodwill," can be viewed as an asset of the firm which has real value to existing shareholders and is reflected in binding commitments or "implicit" contracts with its customers. In this view, banking and securities underwriting activities undertaken by a holding company with its customers are economic "games" that take place in a repeated, or dynamic market setting. Although the net profit from exploiting a conflict with a given customer, such as promoting the sale of tainted securities or tie-ins, may be positive in the short-run (i.e., at one point in time), in the long run the exploitation of conflicts (breach of the implicit contract) may eventually damage the reputation of the holding company and its various affiliates, and therefore hamper its future growth and profit prospects.

Specifically, customers who feel they have been exploited will seek to move their businesses to another institution, whereas adverse publicity will tend to deter potential customers from forming permanent relationships with the bank and/or its securities affiliate. In particular, the greater the flow of information among (potential) customers, the higher will be the costs to the bank of exploiting any conflict.[46] Indeed, in a world of perfectly competitive financial markets and no information asymmetries (or complete information), conflicts of interest cannot be profitably exploited because all parties (buyers and sellers) are fully aware of any potential conflicts that will be fully reflected in prices and/or other contractual terms.

Hence, the more value that is placed on customer goodwill (which in turn is a function of the degree of competition and information imperfection in the markets in which it operates), the greater are the incentives of stockholders and their boards to monitor and control the behavior of managers in order to reserve the value of that assset. Indeed, throughout the commercial banking and investment banking literature, the importance of building and maintaining customer relationships and reputations is repeatedly emphasized.[47]

Rating Agencies

In the previous section the external *market* mechanisms involved in monitoring and controlling managerial incentives to exploit conflicts were discussed. Here we examine the role of the bond rating agencies as external "nonmarket" monitoring agents.

The role of bond rating agencies (e.g., Moody's, Standard & Poor's) is to monitor, externally and independently, the financial performance and safety of bond issuing firms, and to provide investors with information regarding the default risk attached to those bonds. For example, if carried out successfully, this monitoring function would make it difficult for a bank-affiliated underwriter to unload a new issue of debt above its "true" market value (as discussed in the second conflict in the section on "The Types of Conflicts").

Thus the critical question is how successful the bond rating agencies are in detecting changes in the default risk of securities issuing firms *prior* to the offering date. Because there have been relatively few bond defaults in the postwar period, studies of the default prediction abilities of bond rating agencies have been unable to provide conclusive results.[48] When the sample period is extended back to include the pre-World War II period, however, there appears to have been an inverse relationship between changes in bond ratings and default rates.[49] Other studies have sought to examine the extent to which bond ratings explain the systematic risks or "betas" of corporate bonds.[50] Urwitz,[51] using a large sample of bonds, found that the rank correlation between bond default risk ratings and bond beta's (systematic risk) was in the order of 0.8. From this evidence, it seems that rating agencies are fairly successful predicting the systematic risk of bonds.[52]

Although this evidence is supportive of the view that rating agencies have done a relatively good job, on average, in signaling to investors information regarding the risk of new issues, some commentators argue that there have been serious failures as well. Perhaps the most recently publicized case has been the bonds issued by the Washington Public Power Supply System (WPPSS) to finance the construction of five nuclear plants in Washington State. Despite cost overruns and delays, which had been apparent since the middle of 1980, S&P continued to rate the bonds (issued to build the first three plants) as AAA until January 1983, whereas the bonds on the final two riskier plants were only downgraded from A to BBB+ in January 1982. Moody's had the first three plants A1 until May 1983 with the last two at A1 until June 1981. The long time delays between identifying the increased risk of default and the ratings changes on bonds issued by WPPSS has led to considerable criticism of the rating agencies, including the accusation that they have become so heavily institutionalized that they can only respond *after* the fact and not before.[53] Currently, a class-action suit is outstanding against the primary underwriters, Merrill Lynch and Salomon Brothers, alleging failure to exercise due diligence in disclosing information regarding WPPSS.

However, because bond rating agencies, like banks, have to maintain a reputation in order that their evaluations remain credible and have informational value to the purchaser, they have to be on average correct. (Note that in a world of perfect information, bond rating agencies are of no value to investors.) Thus in an environment of information asymmetries or imperfections, rating agencies provide the crucial function of improving the quality and increasing the availability of information disseminated to the investors. This, as noted above, makes it more costly for banks or their affiliates to exploit conflicts. Indeed perfect bond ratings would eliminate all potentially profitable conflict opportunities in debt restructuring.

Examinations by Regulatory Authorities, and Margin and Collateral Requirements

Margin requirements on broker/dealer loans and collateral requirements on loans to affiliates, combined with direct monitoring of these requirements by regulatory authorities, impose further *external* nonmarket constraints on conflict exploitation.

Currently, margin requirements limit the maximum leverage multiplier on broker/dealer loans to two. This ratio, if maintained, limits the ability of banks to make third-party loans to support the price of securities underwritten by their affiliates. As noted earlier, direct bank loans to affiliates are subject to a 10% of capital ceiling and must be backed by at least 100% collateral. Violation of these restrictions would lead to costly penalties being imposed on managers and/or shareholders if discovered by the Fed, FDIC, or other regulatory agencies with examination authority. Regulatory examination thus provides an additional disincentive to exploit conflicts. The more efficient are examiners, the more costly, in expected value terms, will be the exploitation of a potential conflict—with costs or penalties ranging from fines and criminal prosecution of bank officers to bank charter revocation.[54]

For efficiency in examinations there has to be coordination between those examining the bank, its trust department, and the securities affiliate. This suggests that optimal surveillance might be achieved when each part of the holding company is examined by a single regulatory authority such as the Fed, which is currently the major regulator of bank holding companies.

As an external mechanism of conflict control, surveillance would probably be least efficient if different regulatory agencies had examination powers and took an adversarial (rather than cooperative) stance over interagency information exchange. This might be the outcome if the Fed remained the primary regulator of the bank and its trust department, whereas the SEC emerged as the primary regulator of the securities affiliate.[55] Specifically, as noted by Sametz et al.[56], the SEC and the Federal Reserve have had different rules and regulations pertaining to disclosure, annual statements, insider information, enforcement and prosecution, and record keeping, as well as competition and market structure.

SUMMARY AND CONCLUSIONS

This chapter has examined the potential conflicts of interest that might arise if bank holding companies are allowed to acquire or establish separately capitalized securities affiliates. Nine potential conflicts previously identified in the literature were outlined and discussed. Each involved a complex interaction of forces between the bank, the securities affiliate, and/or the issuer. Even within each of these organizations the objectives of managers, bondholders, depositors, shareholders, and their boards of directors tend to differ. It was argued that in seeking to maximize long-run profits, shareholders and directors need to preserve the reputation of the holding company and its affiliates with their customers, and are therefore likely to avoid exploitation of conflicts. This is particularly true if information is easily and quickly disseminated to existing and potential customers and markets for financial products are competitive.

This objective may not be the same for managers of the bank or its securities affiliate, however, who may be more concerned with maximizing short-run profits, which could lead to exploiting conflict opportunities. This difference in decision horizons creates incentives for directors, acting in the interest of shareholders, to closely monitor the performance of managers and to structure managerial compensation packages in a manner that ties managerial objectives more closely to those of the ultimate owners of the enterprise. Different methods of bonding managerial objectives to those of shareholders were discussed, and it was argued that managerial bonuses, based on the market value of the holding company stock, are a useful *internal* mechanism of conflict control.

Even when internal control mechanisms are absent, there are at least four *external* control mechanisms that define or limit the probability of conflict exploitation. These are: (1) the market for corporate control and managerial services, (2) the competitive nature of the market for commercial and investment banking products and services, (3) the default risk assessments of bond rating agencies, and (4) the examination and penalty powers of regulatory agencies. Specifically, the greater the degree of competition between financial institutions and the better the quality (and quantity) of information available to their customers the more costly (less profitable) it is to exploit any potential conflict. The financial services industry is becoming increasingly competitive and the quality of information being made available by firms and their outside monitoring agencies is continuously being refined and improved with the help of technology.[57] Thus it is not clear that the benefits of regulating the activities of holding companies, measured in terms of conflict prevention, outweigh the costs such as loss of activity and geographic diversification and/or loss of economics of scope and scale.

NOTES

[1]R. A. Schotland, in *Abuse on Wall Street: Conflicts of Interest in the Securities Markets.* (Westport, Conn.: Quorum Books, 1980).

[2]F. R. Edwards, "Banks and Securities Activities: Legal and Economic Perspectives on the Glass Steagall Act" in L. Goldberg and L. J. White (eds.), *The Deregulation of the Banking and Securities Industries,* (Lexington, Mass.: D.C. Heath, 1979).

[3]In papers by A. Saunders "An Economic Perspective on Bank Uniqueness and Corporate Securities Activities," *Working Paper,* New York University, 1983, and I. H. Giddy "Risk and Returns From Bond Underwriting," *Working Paper,* Columbia University, December 1983.

[4]It might be noted that, under the proposed Financial Institutions Deregulation Act, all municipal bond underwriting would take place in separately capitalized affiliates of bank holding companies (see R. C. Clark, "Deregulation Hearings Raise Conflict of Interest Issue," *Trust and Estates* (April 1982), pp. 15–16.

[5]See, for example, Congressional Record, 75th U.S. Congress, *Statement* by Senator Glass on May 10, 1932, for example.

[6]Investment Company Institute, *Misadventures in Banking: Bank Promotion of Pooled Investment Funds,* Washington, D.C., 1979, Securities Industry Association, *Private Placement Activities of Commercial Banks,* Memorandum to the Federal Reserve Board of Governors, May 1977, L. Perkins, "The Divorce of Commercial and Investment Banking: A History," *Banking Law Journal* (1971).

[7]See Perkins, "Divorce of Investment Banking," 1971, p. 87.

[8]See Congressional Record, 75th U.S. Congress, *Statement* by Senator Glass on May 10, 1932.

[9]See Investment Company Institute, *Misadvantages in Banking: Bank Promotion of Pooled Investment Funds,* Washington, D.C., 1979.

[10]For a perceptive analysis of the similarities between foreign loans and bonds (see J. Sachs in P. Wachtel (ed.), *Crises in the Economic and Financial Structure.* (Lexington, Mass.: D.C. Heath, 1982).

[11]One example of the potential conflict surfaced when the Michigan National Bank (a $1.75 billion bank in Detroit) decided to sue Citicorp, demanding the return of $5 million loaned to Pemex. Michigan National purchased a $5 million participation in a loan totaling $45 million in May 1982, which was expected to be outstanding for a short period of time. However, Citicorp asked for three subsequent 90-day extensions until July 26, 1983. At that time Michigan National told Citicorp it did not wish to extend the loan beyond July. Moreover, it claimed that Citicorp extended the Pemex loan in violation of its intention and the participation agreement, which called for prior consent of the smaller bank.

[12]See P. Asquith, and D. Mullins Jr., "Equity Issues and Stock Price Dilution," *Working Paper,* Harvard Business School, 1983. L. Dann and W. H. Mikkelson, "Debt Issuance and Capital Structure Change:

Impact on Stockholder Wealth," *Working Paper*, University of Oregon, 1982. M. C. Jensen, and C. W. Smith, Jr., "Stockholders, Manager and Creditor Interests: Applications of Agency Theory," *Working Paper*, University of Rochester, 1983.

[13]However, the affiliate may assure a broader market for the issue, that is, minimize the risk of being left with these bonds in its trading inventory at the end of the offer period.

[14]See W. J. Garvin, "The Small Business Capital Gap: The Special Case of Minority Enterprise," *Journal of Finance* (1971), pp. 445–457; D. G. Harris, "Credit Rationing of Commercial Banks: Some Empirical Evidence," *Journal of Money, Credit and Banking* (1974), pp. 227–240, for example.

[15]See Schotland, *Abuse on Wall Street*, 1980, p. 134.

[16]See D. V. Austin and M. Tincher, "Corporate Securities in Commercial Bank Investment Portfolios," *Bankers Magazine* (May–June 1979), pp. 62–69.

[17]See Senate Staff Study, 95th Congress, 2d Session, *Interlocking Directorates Among the Major U.S. Corporations*, 1978.

[18]See Investment Company Institute, 1979.

[19]In the case where deposits are insured the conflict is then between the best interests of the insurance agency and the bank.

[20]As noted by H. E. Buschgen ("The Universal Banking System in the Federal Republic of Germany," *Journal of Corporate Law and Securities Regulation* [1979], pp. 1–27), this type of abuse is not unknown in banking systems such as Germany, where the case of Schroder, Munchmeyer, Hengst and Co. (SMH) and the industrial conglomerate IBH Holding A.G. received considerable attention in 1983. Loans by German banks are subject to a strict ceiling of 75% of bank capital. To avoid these ceilings the parent of SMH channeled additional loans to IBH and its affiliates, through extra-national (or "offshore") banking subsidiaries in Luxembourg and Finzag, a Swiss factoring company. By the time IBH's financial difficulties became public, it was estimated that SMH's total exposure to IBH amounted to more than 400% of its capital and reserves, and triggered SMH's demise.

[21]See T. Campbell, "Optimal Investment Decisions and the Value of Confidentiality," *Journal of Financial and Quantitative Analysis* (1979), pp. 913–924 for a discussion on the value of information confidentiality.

[22]See *Inside the Administration*, 2, No. 25 (December 16, 1983). G. Hawkins, "Risk and Private Placement Debt Covenants," *Working Paper*, University of California, Berkeley, 1983.

[22]See Hawkins, "Risk and Placement Debt," 1983; and J. F. Weston and E. F. Brigham, *Essentials of Managerial Finance*, 3d ed. (Hinsdale, Ill.: Dryden Press, 1974), for example.

[23]See O. E. Williamson, "A Model of Rational Managerial Behavior," in R. M. Cyert and J. G. March (eds.) *A Behavioral Theory of the Firm*. (Englewood Cliffs, N.J.: Prentice-Hall, 1963) for example.

[24]See M. C. Jensen and W. H. Meckling, "Theory of the Firm: Managerial Behavior, Agency Costs and Ownership Structure," *Journal of Financial Economics* (1976), pp. 305–360.

[25]Other differences usually cited are: (1) effort expended by managers is often viewed as bad (negative utility), whereas for stockholders increased managerial effort increases the value of the firm, and (2) the risk preferences of managers and stockholders may differ according to whether the latter are less or more risk-averse than the former.

[26]See M. Blumstein, "Its Wall Street Bonus Time," *New York Times* (December 15, 1983), p. D7.

[27]One type of bonus (not analyzed here) because it merely serves to accentuate management-shareholder conflicts and control problems) is related to loan or transactions *volume* generated by different departments or areas. It might be noted that such a bonus system was operational at Chase Manhattan until very recently.

[28]See the section entitled "Factors Mitigating Conflict Exploitation" for a discussion of the value of a reputation.

[29]This assumes, of course, that side payments between securities affiliate managers and bank managers are absent. Moreover, managers in the securities affiliate are likely to have, on average, a much high base-level of compensation than those in commercial banking. This will serve only to increase the reluctance of commercial bank managers to undertake further income transfers voluntarily.

[30]Directors could impute separate "shadow" market values for the stock of the bank and its affiliate, and compute some annual exchange price linking these values with the overall holding company. Such a contrived scheme might be preferable to that of linking bonuses to the value of the stock in the overall holding company.

[31]M. C. Jensen and R. S. Ruback, "The Market for Corporate Control: The Scientific Evidence," *Journal of Financial Economics* (1983), pp. 5–50.

[32]See Jensen and Meckling, "Theory of the Firm," 1976, pp. 305–360; and Jensen and Ruback, "Market for Corporate Control," (1983), pp. 5–50.

[33]However, managerial change will only occur when the perceived benefits of managerial reorganization outweigh the expected costs involved. Often only a major crisis will cause managerial reorganization, although less dramatic personnel shifts can have the same effect.

[34]See Federal Reserve Bank of New York, *A Report on Drysdale and Other Recent Problems of Firms Involved in the Government Securities Market,* September 15, 1982.

[35]Chase Manhattan Corporation, *Notice of Annual Meeting and Proxy Statement,* 1982. As the comment implies a somewhat similar result occurred in the case of Chase managers responsible in the 1983 Penn Square loan participation losses, where their actions were similarly held to be adverse to the interests of the organization as a whole.

[36]See Garvin, "Small Business Capital Gap," 1971; and D. G. Harris, "Credit Rationing of Commercial Banks: Some Empirical Evidence," *Journal of Money, Credit and Banking* (1974), pp. 227–240.

[37]See Buser et al., "Federal Deposit Insurance," 1981; and R. C. Merton, "An Analytic Derivation of the Cost of Deposit Insurance and Loan Guarantees: An Application of Modern Option Pricing Theory," *Journal of Banking and Finance* (1977), pp. 3–11. R. C. Merton, "On the Cost of Deposit Insurance When There Are Surveillance Costs," *Journal of Business,*)1978), pp. 439–452.

[38]This implies that the value of stockholders' claims may increase even if the value of the firm (the sum of the values of stockholder, bondholder, and government agency claims—in the case of deposit insurance) falls.

[39]Merton, "An Analytic Derivation"; and Merton, "Cost of Deposit Insurance," 1978.

[40]See Black and Scholes, "Pricing of Options," 1973.

[41]See Merton, "An Analytic Derivation," 1977.

[42]See S. Lee, "Why Some Banks May Pay More for Deposit Insurance," *Business Week* (January 1984).

[43]If securities firms were to buy up banks, however, the incentives to shift risk might work in the other direction and pose problems concerning bank safety and soundness.

[44]This view is developed in B. Klein and K. Leffler, "The Role of Market Forces in Assuring Contractual Performance," *Journal of Political Economy* (1981), pp. 615–641, and in L. Telser "A Theory of Self-Enforcing Agreements," *Journal of Business* (1980), pp. 27–44.

[45]Bull, "Implicit Contracts," 1983, pp. 658–671.

[46]See Klein and Leffler, "Role of Market Forces," 1981, pp. 615–641, for a similar argument.

[47]See, for example, Bloch, *Investment Banking,* 1983; and Carosso, *Investment Banking in America,* 1970.

[48]However, there has been a widely observed negative relationship between ratings and bond yields.

[49]See R. West, "Bond Ratings, Bond Yields, and Financial Regulation: Some Findings," *Journal of Law and Economics* (1973), pp. 159–168, for a review of these studies.

[50]Where the "beta" measures the covariance of the return on a bond with the return on the market, divided by the variance of market returns. It should be noted that investors might be vitally concerned with the idiosyncratic or unsystematic risk of a bond, especially if they hold relatively undiversified portfolios.

[51]R. West, "Bond Ratings, Bond Yields, and Financial Regulation: Some Findings," *Journal of Law and Economics* (1973), pp. 159–168.

[52]Elsewhere, R. Kaplan and G. Urwitz, "Statistical Methods of Bond Ratings: A Methodological Inquiry," *Journal of Business* (1979), pp. 231–261 have developed a model to *predict* bond ratings. After

testing a number of models, the authors found that a relatively small number of accounting and financial-market variables were sufficient to "explain" bond ratings. The variables found to be important were: (1) the ratio of cash flow before interest and tax to total interest payments, (2) the ratio of long-term debt to total assets, (3) the ratio of net income to total assets, (4) total assets, (5) subordination, (6) the beta of the firm's equity, and (7) the variance of the firm's equity. Although these may not be the exact variables used by rating agencies (which are, of course, confidential) Kaplan and Urwitz correctly rated 62% of the bonds in their sample, and no bond was placed more than one category away from its "true" agency rating. Thus even outside investors, using a small subset of variables, might come close to replicating the default-risk evaluation systems of the bond rating agencies.

[53]See Brimelow, "Shock Waves," 1983, pp. 46–48. A potential conflict of interest also existed between the WPPSS and the rating agencies, because WPPSS has paid these agencies more than $400,000 over 10 years to rate their bonds.

[54]H. K. Wu, "New Evidence on the Accuracy of Bank Examiner Loan Criticisms: An Intertemporal Cross-Section Analysis," *Working Paper,* University of Alabama, 1983 presents extensive evidence from the files of the OCC which shows that in 1975 only 14.5% of loans charged off had failed to be classified previously as either OLEM, Substandard, Doubtful, Loss, or some combination of these criticisms.

[55]It might be noted that this is the form which has been suggested by the Bush Task Force on a New Federal Banking Agency. In a November 1983 draft, it is proposed that all securities regulation of Bank Holding Companies be transferred to the SEC, (see *Inside the Administration,* 2, No. 25, December 16, 1983).

[56]A. Sametz, M. Keenan, E. Bloch, and L. Goldberg, "Securities Activities of Commercial Banks: An Evaluation of Current Developments and Regulatory Issues," *Journal of Comparative Law and Securities Regulation* (1979), pp. 155–194.

[57]The quality and quantity of corporate financial information available to outside investors is likely to be increased considerably in 1985 when the SEC puts its EDGAR System (Electronic Data Gathering and Retrieval System) into effect. Under this system companies will electronically file quarterly and annual reports with the SEC, whereas investors, brokers, and dealers will gain direct access to those files through their own office (or home) computer terminals. Thus information should be disseminated in a far more timely fashion and be available to a much wider audience.

REFERENCES

Asquith, P., and D. Mullins Jr. "Equity Issues and Stock Price Dilution," *Working Paper,* Harvard Business, School, 1983.

Austin, D. V., and M. Tincher. "Corporate Securities in Commercial Bank Investment Portfolios," *Bankers Magazine* (May–June 1979), pp. 62–69.

Black, F., and M. Scholes. "The Pricing of Options and Corporate Liabilities," *Journal of Political Economy* (1973), pp. 637–659.

Bloch, E. *Investment Banking,* manuscript, Graduate School of Business Administration, New York University, 1983.

Blumstein, M., "It's Wall Street Bonus Time," *New York Times* (December 15, 1983), p. D7.

Brimelow, P., "Shock Waves from Whoops Roll East," *Fortune Magazine* (July 25, 1983), pp. 46–48.

C. Bull, "Implicit Contracts in the Absence of Enforcement and Risk Aversion," *American Economic Review* (1983), pp. 658–671.

Buser, S. D., A. H. Chen, and E. J. Kane. "Federal Deposit Insurance, Regulatory Pricing and Optimal Bank Capital," *Journal of Finance* (1981), pp. 56–60.

Bushgen, H. E. "The Universal Banking System in the Federal Republic of Germany," *Journal of Corporate Law and Securities Regulation* (1979), pp. 1–27.

Campbell, T., "Optimal Investment Decisions and the Value of Confidentiality," *Journal of Financial and Quantitative Analysis* (1979), pp. 913–924.

Carosso, V. P. *Investment Banking in America: A History*, Cambridge, Mass.: Harvard University Press, 1970.

Chase Manhattan Corporation, *Notice of Annual Meeting and Proxy Statement*, 1982.

Clark, R. C. "Deregulation Hearings Raise Conflict of Interest Issue," *Trust and Estates* (April 1982), pp. 15–16.

Congressional Record, 75th U.S. Congress, *Statement* by Senator Glass on May 10, 1932.

Dann, L., and W. H. Mikkelson. "Debt Issuance and Capital Structure Change: Impact on Stockholder Wealth," *Working Paper*, University of Oregon, 1982.

Edwards, F. R. "Banks and Securities Activities: Legal and Economic Pespectives on the Glass Steagall Act," in L. Goldberg and L. J. White (eds.), *The Deregulation of the Banking and Securities Industries*. Lexington, Mass.: D.C. Heath, 1979.

Federal Reserve Bank of New York, *A Report on Drysdale and Other Recent Problems of Firms Involved in the Government Securities Market*, September 15, 1982.

Garvin, W. J. "The Small Business Capital Gap: The Special Case of Minority Enterprise," *Journal of Finance* (1971), pp. 445–457.

Giddy, I. H. "Risk and Returns From Bond Underwriting," *Working Paper*, Columbia University, December 1983.

Golembe Associates. *Commercial Banks and Investment Banks*. Paper prepared for the Economic and Financial Research Division of the American Bankers Association, November 29, 1976.

Harris, D. G. "Credit Rationing of Commercial Banks: Some Empirical Evidence," *Journal of Money, Credit and Banking* (1974), pp. 227–240.

Hawkins, D. G. "Risk and Private Placement Debt Covenants," *Working Paper*, University of California, Berkeley, 1983.

Inside the Administration, 2, No. 25 (December 16, 1983).

Investment Company Institute. *Misadventures in Banking: Bank Promotion of Pooled Investment Funds*. Washington, D.C., 1979.

Jensen, M. C., and W. H. Meckling. "Theory of the Firm: Managerial Behavior, Agency Costs and Ownership Structure," *Journal of Financial Economics* (1976), pp. 305–360.

Jensen, M. C., and R. S. Ruback. "The Market for Corporate Control: The Scientific Evidence," *Journal of Financial Economics* (1983), pp. 5–50.

Jensen, M. C., and C. W. Smith, Jr. "Stockholders, Manager and Creditor Interests: Applications of Agency Theory," *Working Paper*, University of Rochester, 1983.

Kaplan, R., and G. Urwitz. "Statistical Methods of Bond Ratings: A Methodological Inquiry," *Journal of Business* (1979), pp. 231–261.

Klein, B., and K. Leffler. "The Role of Market Forces in Assuring Contractual Performance," *Journal of Political Economy* (1981), pp. 615–641.

Lee, S. "Why Some Banks May Pay More for Deposit Insurance," *Business Week* (January 1984).

Merton, R. C. "An Analytic Derivation of the Cost of Deposit Insurance and Loan Guarantees: An Application of Modern Option Pricing Theory," *Journal of Banking and Finance* (1977), pp. 3–11.

Merton, R. C. "On the Cost of Deposit Insurance When There Are Surveillance Costs," *Journal of Business* (1978), pp. 439–452.

New York Clearing House Association. *Commercial Bank Private Placement Advisory Services*, April 1977.

Perkins, L. "The Divorce of Commercial and Investment Banking: A History," *Banking Law Journal* (1971).

Sachs, J., in P. Wachtel (ed.), *Crises in the Economic and Financial Structure*. Lexington, Mass.: D.C. Heath, 1982.

Sametz, A., M. Keenan, E. Bloch, and L. Goldberg. "Securities Activities of Commercial Banks: An Evaluation of Current Developments and Regulatory Issues," *Journal of Comparative Law and Securities Regulation* (1979), pp. 155–194.

Saunders, A. "An Economic Perspective on Bank Uniqueness and Corporate Securities Activities," *Working Paper,* New York University, 1983.

Schotland, R. A., *Abuse on Wall Street: Conflicts of Interest in the Securities Markets,* Westport, Conn.: Quorum Books, 1980.

Securities Industry Association. *Private Placement Activities of Commercial Banks,* Memorandum to the Federal Reserve Board of Governors, May 1977.

Senate Staff Study, 95th Congress, 2d Session, *Interlocking Directorates Among the Major U.S. Corporations,* 1978.

Smith, C., and J. Warner. "On Financial Contracting: An Analysis of Board Covenants," *Journal of Financial Economics* (1979), pp. 117–162.

Telser, L. "A Theory of Self-Enforcing Agreements," *Journal of Business* (1980), pp. 27–44.

Urwitz, G. "On the Pricing of Corporate Bonds: The Mean-Variance Model and Market Determined Risk Measures," *Working Paper,* Carnegie-Mellon University, 1975.

Van Horne, J. C. *Financial Management and Policy,* 4th ed. Englewood Cliffs, N.J.: Prentice-Hall, 1977.

West, R. "Bond Ratings, Bond Yields, and Financial Regulation: Some Findings," *Journal of Law and Economics* (1973), pp. 159–168.

Weston, J. F., and E. F. Brigham. *Essentials of Managerial Finance,* 3d ed., Hinsdale, Ill.: Dryden Press, 1974.

Williams, H. M. Chairman of the SEC Statement before the Subcommittee on Financial Institutions, Regulation and Insurance of the House Committee on Banking, Finance and Urban Affairs, October 17, 1979.

Williamson, O. E. "A Model of Rational Managerial Behavior," in R. M. Cyert and J. G. March (eds.), *A Behavioral Theory of the Firm.* Englewood Cliffs, N.J.: Prentice-Hall, 1963.

Wu, H. K. "New Evidence on the Accuracy of Bank Examiner Loan Criticisms: An Intertemporal Cross-Section Analysis," *Working Paper,* University of Alabama, 1983.

9 Conflicts of Interest: A Legal View

EDWARD J. KELLY III

Congress' principal objective in enacting the Glass-Steagall Act was to restore public confidence in the banking system. Congress viewed the Act's separation of commercial and investment banking as an integral part of this effort for two reasons. First, Congress believed that severing the ties between commercial and investment banking would eliminate a significant threat to the safety and soundness of the commercial banking system. Second, Congress believed that separating commercial and investment banking would prevent the recurrence and future exploitation of the conflicts of interest it believed were associated with commercial banks' participation in the securities markets.[1] As the Supreme Court stated in *Investment Co. Institute v. Camp:*

> Congress acted to keep commercial banks out of the investment banking business largely because it believed that the promotional incentives of investment banking and the investment banker's pecuniary stake in the success of particular investment opportunities was destructive of prudent and disinterested commercial banking and of public confidence in the commerical banking system.[2]

Although opponents of relaxing Glass-Steagall's prohibitions rely heavily on the alleged threat such a relaxation would pose to the stability of the commercial banking system, they also invariably invoke the specter of abuses associated with the exploitation of conflicts of interest.[3]

In 1971, for example, the President's Commission on Financial Structure and Regulation stated that Congress' decision to separate commercial and investment banking "was prompted by the conflicts of interest that developed when the same organization handled the two functions."[4] The Commission went on to assert: "The possibility of conflict of interest would still exist if banks were again permitted to underwrite new issues of corporate securities. The Commission, therefore, strongly recommends the continued prohibition against bank underwriting of private securities issues."[5] More recently, one commentator has suggested that "the conflicts of interest arising from commercial bank investment banking activity provide the most compelling basis for Glass-Steagall's continued support in Congress and the courts."[6]

It is clear that the conflicts of interest issue must be addressed as part of any discussion of the wisdom of permitting expanded securities activities on the part of commercial banks or their affiliates. This chapter briefly discusses the nature of "conflicts of interest" in this context. It then identifies the conflicts commonly alleged to be associated with commercial banks' involvement in the securities markets and examines existing and potential responses to these conflicts. Finally, there is a discussion on the merits of prohibiting rather than regulating certain commercial bank securities activities.

BACKGROUND

It is difficult to formulate a precise definition of conflict of interest. One commentator has suggested that a conflict of interest

> . . . denotes a situation in which two or more interests are legitimately present and competing or conflicting. The individual (or firm) making a decision that will affect those interests may have a larger stake in one of them than in the other(s), but he is expected—in fact, obligated—to serve each as if it were his own, regardless of his actual stake.[7]

Another commentator has stated simply that a "conflict of interest arises whenever one is serving two or more interests and can put one person in a better position at the expense of another."[8] As will become apparent, the notion of conflicts of interest as applied to banks is very broad. This is due, at least in part, to the special role banks play in our society. In testimony before Congress, Paul Volcker, Chairman of the Board of Governors of the Federal Reserve System, stated:

> Public policy has long recognized the importance of protecting the safety and soundness of banks and depository institutions generally: they perform a unique and critical role in the financial system as operators of the payments system, as custodians of the bulk of liquid savings, as unbiased suppliers of short-term credit, and as the critical link between monetary policy and the economy.[9]

As Chairman Volcker's statement implies, a special role carries with it special duties. During the Senate debate on one version of the Glass-Steagall Act in 1932, Senator Bulkley stated that "acceptance of deposits from the public is in itself a public trust . . ."[10] Banks are viewed as owing a duty to depositors to keep their money safe and to pursue practices and policies consistent with assuring the solvency of the bank. This perceived duty to depositors (and to the public in view of banks' role in the payments and monetary system) leaves little room for bank activities that are seen as involving any substantial risk. Although the pursuit of such activities might lead to increased profits, it would also pose a threat to bank safety and soundness and put a bank in conflict with its perceived duties to depositors and the public. In addition, banks' importance to the economy has given rise to the commonly accepted view that they have an obligation to borrowers and to the public to serve as impartial suppliers of credit. When these broad duties to depositors, borrowers, and the public are considered in combination with banks' more narrow duties as fiduciaries for their trust accounts, for example, it becomes apparent that banks might be confronted with a number of potential conflicts of interest. Although one may question the precise legal basis for holding banks to such expansive duties, it is important to recognize that a deeply ingrained sense of these obligations appears to have considerable influence on discussions of "conflicts of interest" in this area.

CONFLICTS COMMONLY ALLEGED TO BE ASSOCIATED WITH COMMERCIAL BANKS' SECURITIES ACTIVITIES[11]

The starting point for a discussion of the conflicts of interest commonly alleged to be associated with commercial banks' securities activities is the Appendix to the hearings on the Glass-Steagall Act held by a subcommittee of the Senate Committee on Banking and Currency in 1931.[12] At least three of the commonly alleged conflicts are drawn from that Appendix.

First, the subcommittee expressed concern that an affiliation between a commercial bank and a securities company might lead to loan and securities transactions between the bank and its affiliate that would be damaging to the bank. The subcommittee stated that "[t]he most direct manner in which the affiliate may impair the liquidity of the bank is through . . . borrowing."[13] The subcommittee noted that "[t]he loan relationship as it exists between the bank and its affiliate differs from that prevailing with the general run of the bank's customers in an essential respect," and went on to explain that "[w]hen dealing with its affiliate, the bank is really dealing with itself, in view of the identity of ownership and management that is established."[14] As a result, "there tends to be a breaking down of those limitations on the extension of credit which the bank sets up in other cases to guard against the making of excessive or poorly-secured loans."[15] With respect to securities transactions, the subcommittee pointed out that the bank, in an effort to insure the survival of the affiliate or to protect it from losses, might purchase securities from the affiliate to relieve it of excess holdings.[16]

The second conflict drawn from the Appendix relates to a bank's fiduciary obligations to its trust accounts. In this regard, the subcommittee suggested that "[i]n the case of a trust company or a bank with a trust department, the possession of a security affiliate may adversely affect the independence with which fiduciary activities are exercised."[17] In less delicate terms, the concern is that a bank might use its trust accounts as a dumping ground for securities underwritten or distributed by its affiliate.[18]

The third alleged conflict relates to a bank's credit policies and is based on the subcommittee's assertion that a bank "may lend much more freely to customers on issues sponsored by the security affiliate, in order to facilitate their distribution, than it would otherwise do.''[19] The subcommittee also suggested that it might prove more difficult for the bank ''to insist upon the maintenance of adequate margins on these security loans than on other such advances, in view of the fact that customers are encouraged to make the loans by the bank's own affiliate.''[20]

The fourth and fifth commonly alleged conflicts are drawn from Senator Bulkley's remarks during the debate on an early version of the Glass-Steagall Act in 1932. During those remarks Bulkley noted that banks might convert bad loans ''into bond issues to be sold to savings depositors of the same banks . . .''[21] In addition, Bulkley discussed what he viewed as a fundamental conflict between the role of commercial banker and investment banking activities. He stated:

> The banker ought to be regarded as the financial confidant and mentor of his depositors. This underlying relationship is a natural and desirable one with respect to all depositors, although the aspects of it and the kind of advice called for will necessarily vary a great deal from the poor widow whose life savings are evidenced by a savings passbook to the great corporation requiring financial aid in the development of intricate business problems.

> Obviously, the banker who has nothing to sell to his depositors is much better qualified to advise disinterestedly and to regard diligently the safety of depositors than the banker who uses the list of depositors in his savings department to distribute circulars concerning the advantages of this, that, or the other investment on which the bank is to receive an originating profit or an underwriting profit or a distribution profit or a trading profit or any combination of such profits.[22]

The sixth alleged conflict is drawn from the Supreme Court's opinion in *Investment Co. Institute v. Camp*. In *Camp*, the Court reviewed the legislative history of the Glass-Steagall Act and discussed in detail the ''more subtle hazards'' that had influenced Congress' decision to separate commercial and investment banking.[23] During that discussion the Court discussed one conflict that does not appear to have been mentioned explicitly in the legislative history. The Court stated:

> [T]he pressure to sell a particular investment and to make the affiliate successful might create a risk that the bank would make its credit facilities more freely available to those companies in whose stocks or securities the affiliate has invested or become otherwise involved. Congress feared that banks might even go so far as to make unsound loans to these companies.[24]

The final two conflicts commonly alleged to be associated with commercial banks' involvement in securities activities are drawn from the literature in the area. One relates to a commercial bank's lending policies and is based on the possibility that a bank might ''tie'' the extension of credit to the extension of other services provided by the bank or its affiliates.[25] In order to obtain credit, a customer would have to agree to purchase the other service as well. The other potential conflict relates to the possibility that a commercial bank and its securities affiliates might enjoy, and exploit, informational advantages obtained through exchange of information about their respective clients.[26]

The eight potential conflicts identified above are the ones most commonly cited in connection with proposals to permit expanded bank securities activities. The next section examines the extent to which the law could control each of these potential conflicts.

LEGAL RESPONSES[27]

Loan and Securities Transactions Between a Bank and Its Securities Affiliate

It is probably reasonable to assume that a bank would try to assist any affiliate that was experiencing financial difficulties or was in danger of failing. The special problem posed by a bank's relationship with an affiliate engaged in the securities business, at least in Congress' view, is that securities activities are especially risky. This increases the likelihood that a bank would be forced to come to the aid of such an affiliate. Moreover, given the nature of "public confidence," the existence of an unprofitable affiliate, even if the affiliate were not assisted substantially by the bank, might shake public confidence in the bank, thereby threatening the interests of depositors and the public.

Assuming for purposes of argument that this conflict presented a severe problem at the time of the passage of the Glass-Steagall Act, it should not be an insurmountable problem today. Section 13 of the Banking Act of 1933 added a new Section 23A to the Federal Reserve Act, which imposed limitations on a member bank's transactions with its affiliates.[28] In 1982, this section was amended and strengthened.[29] The provision now limits the aggregate amount of "covered transactions" between a member bank and an affiliate to 10% of the capital stock and surplus of the bank.[30] "Covered transactions" include loans or extensions of credit to an affiliate; purchases of, or investments in, securities issued by an affiliate; purchases of assets, including assets subject to an agreement to repurchase; the acceptance of securities issued by an affiliate as collateral security for a loan or extension of credit to any person or company; and the issuance of a guarantee, acceptance, or letter of credit, including an endorsement or standby letter of credit, on behalf of an affiliate.[31] Moreover, the section imposes stringent collateral requirements on "[e]ach loan or extension of credit to, or guarantee, acceptance, or letter of credit issued on behalf of, an affiliate . . ."[32] In addition, the section prohibits a bank from purchasing "a low-quality asset from an affiliate unless the bank . . ., pursuant to an independent credit evaluation, committed itself to purchase such asset prior to the time such asset was acquired by the affiliate."[33] Finally, the section requires all transactions between banks and their affiliates to be "on terms and conditions that are consistent with safe and sound banking practices."[34] This particular provision is designed to assure that no transactions between banks and their affiliates will affect adversely the financial condition of the bank. Two commentators have described this provision as "a second line of defense to protect banks—the first line being the quantitative limitations and the collateral requirements."[35]

It is also noteworthy that a recent proposal to permit bank affiliates to engage in expanded securities activities includes a provision adding a new Section 23B to the Federal Reserve Act.[36] This new section would permit member banks to engage in certain transactions with any affiliate ''only if the terms and conditions of the transaction, including credit standards, [were] substantially the same as, or at least as favorable to the bank as, those prevailing at the time for comparable transactions with nonaffiliated companies.''[37] In addition to the transactions covered by Section 23A, this new section would apply to ''any transaction in which an affiliate act[ed] as an agent or broker or receive[d] a fee for its services to the bank or to any other person,'' among others.[38]

The new section would also prohibit a bank and its affiliates from ''advertising, or entering into an agreement suggesting, that the bank [was] in any way responsible for its affiliates' obligations.''[39] Finally, the new section would prohibit a bank, ''whether acting as principal or fiduciary, from knowingly either purchasing or acquiring, during the existence of any underwriting or selling syndicate, any obligation for which an affiliate . . . [was] a principal underwriter.''[40]

Section 23A addresses effectively the problem of damaging securities and loan transactions between a bank and its securities affiliate. By strictly limiting such transactions, this section would insulate the resources of the bank and assure depositors that an unprofitable affiliate would not threaten the solvency of the bank.

Trust Accounts

Although there was some evidence that banks used their trust accounts as a ''dumping ground'' for securities underwritten or distributed by their securities affiliates during the 1920s and early 1930s,[41] it is as clear now as it was then that such activities are illegal. During the Senate debate on an early version of the Glass-Steagall Act in 1932, Senator Bulkley stated that ''[i]t is a long-established rule of English and American law that a trustee may not profit by dealing with his trust estate.''[42] In its report following the Stock Exchange Practices Hearings, the Senate Committee on Banking and Currency noted that these practices violated a ''fundamental fiduciary duty to the *cestui* trust. . . .''[43]

The same common law rules prohibiting self-dealing by a trustee would apply to these transactions today. These rules are very strict; they clearly apply to transactions between a trustee and its affiliates.[44] They also apply to purchases by a corporate trustee from a syndicate of which it is a member and in whose profits it shares.[45] Even if the transaction is fair to the beneficiaries and any losses on the investment are not caused by self-dealing on the part of the trustee, the trustee is liable.[46] As the court stated in *Albright v. Jefferson Country National Bank:*

> The law . . . does not inquire whether the transaction was fair or unfair. The value of the rule depends in part upon its rigorous and inflexible enforcement. If a corporate fiduciary has placed itself in a position where its interest or the interests of its stockholders *may* conflict with the interests of the *cestui,* the law ''stops the inquiry when the relation is disclosed, and sets aside the transaction or refuses to enforce it, at the instance of the party whom the fiduciary undertook to represent, without undertaking to deal with the question of abstract justice in the particular case.''[47]

The common law prohibition against self-dealing has been reinforced by statute and regulation. Some states have codified the prohibition against self-dealing by state-charted bank trustees.[48] The Employee Retirement Income Security Act of 1974 treats self-dealing as a ''prohibited transaction,''[49] and substantial penalties are imposed for any violation by fiduciaries of employee benefit plans.[50] In addition, the Comptroller of the Currency has promulgated regulations prohibiting self-dealing by national banks.[51] Moreover, regulations proposed by the Federal Deposit Insurance Corporation to govern the securities activities of state nonmember insured banks include a provision that would prohibit such a bank from purchasing ''as fiduciary or co-fiduciary any security currently distributed, currently underwritten, or issued by such . . . affiliate . . . unless the purchase is expressly authorized by the trust instrument, court order, or local law, or specific authority for the purchase is obtained from all interested parties after full disclosure.''[52]

It is noteworthy that the potential conflict presented by an affiliation between a bank, a fiduciary, and a securities company is no different than the one that already exists for securities firms that provide investment advisory services and engage in underwriting and dealing, or for banks that underwrite and deal in U.S. government or municipal securities.[53] It appears that existing legal rules have been effective in preventing exploitation of these potential conflicts. In 1975, the Department of the Treasury stated that ''while the potential for conflict exists, there is no record of actual conflicts arising from commercial bank underwriting of general obligation municipals during the past 40 years that they have engaged in such activity.''[54] The Department went on to note that ''[t]his issue was probed extensively in 1967 hearings before the Subcommittee on Financial Institutions of the Senate Committee on Banking and Currency'' and opponents of commercial bank underwriting of revenue bonds ''were unable to present a single instance where a bank had been guilty of a conflict of interest in underwriting and dealing in general obligation issues.''[55] Similarly, in a 1977 study of commercial bank private placement activities the Federal Reserve Board Staff stated:

> There has been no evidence . . . of any conflict of interest arising from the placement of securities with bank managed funds. . . . Any substantial conflicts of interest that arose probably would be detected by trust department examination procedures, in effect for many years, which have been directed to ensuring the appropriate discharge of fiduciary responsibilities. And, as indicated above, examiners have been instructed to devote increased attention to possible conflicts that could result from bank assisted private placements.[56]

This statement also highlights the important role played by bank examiners in the detection of abuses. The examination process could and undoubtedly would be used to police bank trustees' purchases of securities from their securities affiliates.[57]

Bank Loans to Facilitate Distribution of Securities

This alleged conflict reflects both a concern that a bank might make imprudent loans to facilitate the distribution of a security underwritten or distributed by its affiliate, and that a bank's credit policies might be distorted by its desire to assist its affiliate. Even disregarding the question of the economic rationality of these potential loans,[58] the severity of the problems posed by them is mitigated by provisions of the Securities Exchange Act of 1934. Section 7 of the Exchange Act authorized the Federal Reserve Board to promulgate regulations governing loans to finance the purchase of equity securities.[59] These regulations apply both to bank and nonbank lenders that finance the purchase or carrying of margin stock when these lenders are secured directly or indirectly by margin stock.[60] They restrict the amount a bank could loan to a customer on securities distributed by the bank's securities affiliate. Moreover, Section 11(d)(1) of the Exchange Act prohibits a securities firm from directly or indirectly arranging for "the extension or maintenance of credit to or for a customer on any security . . which was part of a new issue in the distribution of which [the firm] participated as a member of a selling syndicate or a group within 30 days prior to such transaction. . . ."[61] Finally, the regulations proposed by the Federal Deposit Insurance Corporation to govern the securities activities of state nonmember insured banks include a provision that prohibits such a bank from "[e]xtend[ing] credit or mak[ing] any loan where the purpose of the extension of credit or loan is to acquire . . . any stock, bond, debenture, note or other security currently underwritten or distributed by [its] . . . affiliate. . . ."[62] These proposed regulations suggest that it would not be difficult or impractical to limit further the possibility that this potential abuse might occur.

Conversion of Bad Bank Loans into Bond Issues

The conversion of bad bank loans into bond issues appears to present a "conflict" not with a bank's perceived duty to its depositors or to the public to assure the solvency of the bank, but with the bank's, or more particularly its affiliate's, duty to the investing public. In this respect, it is somewhat different from the conflicts previously discussed. In his remarks during the Senate debate, however, Senator Bulkley raised the possibility that this practice might create a conflict between the bank and its depositors, because the unsound bonds would be sold to "savings depositors of the same bank. . . ."[63] Despite this twist, the alleged "conflict" basically presents a securities law problem. The advent of detailed securities laws, which impose extensive regulation on securities offerings and provide investors with effective remedies, has reduced substantially the severity of the problem presented by this "conflict."

The Securities Act of 1933 dealt broadly with the issuance and distribution of securities to the public.[64] The Act includes detailed disclosure requirements[65] and prohibits fraud in the offer or sale of securities.[66] As applied to this particular alleged "conflict," the Act would require disclosures concerning not only the financial condition of the issuer,[67] but also the intended use of the proceeds from the offering.[68] Failure to comply with these requirements could result in civil[69] and criminal liability.[70] In short, the securities laws make it highly unlikely that a bank would be able to convert its bad loans into bond issues distributed by its securities affiliate to an unwitting public.

In a 1978 report on the private placement activities of commercial banks, the Comptroller of the Currency, the Federal Reserve Board, and the Federal Deposit Insurance Corporation stated that no cases were found of "funds raised through bank-advised private placements being used to repay bank loans to the issuer that were delinquent or classified as substandard or worse.''[71]

Commercial Banker versus Investment Banker

Senator Bulkley's suggestion that the role of the commercial banker is fundamentally inconsistent with investment banking activities appears to be based on his notion that ''[t]he banker ought to be regarded as the financial confidant and mentor of his depositors'' with an attendant obligation to provide them with disinterested investment advice.[72] In Bulkley's view, the promotional pressures inherent in investment banking activities prevent a commercial banker from discharging his obligations to depositors. Although one may reasonably question whether a commercial banker has any express or implied duty to provide his depositors with disinterested investment advice, the most striking thing about Bulkley's ideas is how inconsistent they are with current market realities. In today's dynamic financial services market, commercial bankers have a variety of services and products to sell to their depositors in which they have a ''salesman's stake.''[73] These bankers are also involved in intense competition with other financial institutions for depositors' funds and the opportunity to offer them services.[74]

Moreover, commercial banks are engaged in investment banking activities such as underwriting and dealing in U.S. government and general obligation securities. In addition, commercial bank affiliates offer a range of services from which they hope to make a profit. Even assuming that there is some validity to Bulkley's notions about the proper role of commercial bankers, and that permitting commercial bank affiliates to engage in expanded securities activities would pose a qualitatively different threat to bankers' fulfillment of this role than the services and products currently offered by banks and their affiliates, it would be possible to regulate the ''conflicts'' that might arise.[75]

It would be simple, for example, to address Bulkley's specific objection to a banker's using ''the list of depositors in his savings department to distribute circulars concerning the advantage of this, that, or the other investment on which the bank is to receive an originating profit or an underwriting profit or a distribution profit or a trading profit or any combination of such profits.''[76] This practice could be prohibited. In its regulations authorizing bank holding companies and their nonbanking subsidiaries to provide investment advisory services to certain investment companies, the Federal Reserve Board prohibits bank holding companies from distributing sales literature or prospectuses or from making any such literature available to the public at any office of the holding company.[77] Moreover, the regulations state that ''officers and employees of bank subsidiaries should be instructed not to express any opinion with respect to advisability of purchase of securities of any investment company for which the bank holding company acts as an investment adviser.''[78] Finally, the regulations prohibit bank holding companies from furnishing the names of bank customers to the fund or its distributor.[79] Regulations similar to these could be used to insulate depositors from pressure to invest in securities underwritten or distributed by a bank's securities affiliate.

It is important to recognize that securities firms, which may combine the functions of underwriter, broker, dealer, and investment adviser, frequently confront a severe conflict between their duty to provide their clients with impartial investment advice and the promotional pressures associated with their activities.[80] As the Securities and Exchange Commission has stated:

> [T]he over-the-counter house which conducts a brokerage business and which also takes underwriting positions . . . is under temptation to induce its brokerage customers to purchase securities which it is anxious to sell. . . . Whenever the broker and dealer functions are thus combined the profit motive inherent in the latter may be sufficient to color investment advice or otherwise affect the brokerage service rendered to customers.[81]

In recognition of this potential conflict, the securities laws include disclosure requirements,[82] antifraud provisions,[83] and other rules and regulations designed to insure that the conflict is not exploited.[84] Similarly, when a securities firm acts as an investment adviser, it may be tempted to advise clients to purchase securities in which it has an interest. The Investment Advisers Act, however, was designed "to eliminate, or at least expose, all conflicts of interest which might tempt an investment adviser—consciously or unconsciously to render advice which was not disinterested."[85] Moreover, the courts have treated an investment adviser as a fiduciary with an "affirmative duty of 'utmost good faith, and full and fair disclosure of all material facts,' as well as an affirmative obligation 'to employ reasonable care to avoid misleading' his clients."[86]

The SEC has stated that "the duty of an investment adviser to refrain from fraudulent conduct includes an obligation to disclose material facts to his clients whenever the failure to do so would defraud or operate as a fraud or deceit upon any client or prospective client."[87] In this regard, "the adviser's duty to disclose material facts is particularly pertinent whenever the adviser is in a situation involving a conflict, or potential conflict, of interest with a client."[88] These rules and regulations reflect the fact that it is possible, and practical, to control the effect of promotional pressures on an organization's duties to its clients.

Bank Loans to Clients of Its Securities Affilate

The suggestion that a bank might make unsound loans to its affiliate's investment banking clients appears to reflect a dual concern over the bank's duty to depositors and the public to preserve the solvency of the bank and over the potential distortion of the bank's credit decisions.

At the outset, it is noteworthy that this conflict is similar to potential conflicts which already exist. It is possible, for example, that a bank might make unsound loans to trust department customers,[89] or that a bank's trust department might invest in securities of borrowers.[90] These potential conflicts are controlled through the bank examination process.[91] There appears to be no reason that the potential conflict at issue here could not be controlled in the same way. Banks' lending practices are a primary focus of bank regulatory authorities, and a pattern of unsound loans to clients of a bank's securities affiliate would be likely to be uncovered.[92]

It would also be possible to prohibit banks from lending to clients of the securities affiliate during the time the securities affiliate was underwriting or distributing the securities of that client. In this regard, the Federal Deposit Insurance Corporation's proposed regulations governing the securities activities of state nonmember insured banks prohibit such banks from extending credit or making any loans "directly or indirectly to any company the stocks, bonds, debentures, notes or other securities which are currently underwritten or distributed by an affiliate of the bank unless the company's [securities] that are underwritten or distributed (i) qualify as investment quality debt securities, or (ii) qualify as investment quality equity securities" under standards established by the Federal Deposit Insurance Corporation.[93]

The concern that a bank might make an unsound loan to an investment banking client of its affiliate in order to enhance the marketability of a planned securities issue assumes both that the securities affiliate would make the economically questionable decision to underwrite the securities of a presumably weak company, and that the bank would place its funds at risk in an amount greatly exceeding the potential earnings of the securities affiliate.[94] Even accepting the validity of these assumptions (and the validity of the latter assumption is surely exceedingly questionable), the concern over the threat to the bank's solvency could be addressed through use of the examination process to police such loans. Moreover, any related concern over the distribution of unsound securities to unwitting investors is addressed by the securities laws.

Tying

The suggestion that a bank might "tie" the extension of credit to the extension of other services provided by the bank or its affiliates appears to reflect a concern over the potential distortion of credit decisions and a more traditional concern over the concentration of economic resources, which is especially pronounced with respect to banks.[95]

It should be noted that banks and their affiliates already offer a range of services other than lending which might be tied to the extension of credit. Moreover, the threat of tying arrangements is not confined to the banking industry. As a theoretical matter, such arrangements can be made in any context in which a firm offers more than one service or sells more than one product.

Certain tying arrangements are *per se* illegal under the antitrust laws.[96] In *Fortner Enterprises v. United States,* a case involving credit, the Supreme Court stated that tying arrangements are illegal whenever the defendant has sufficient market power over the tying product and a substantial volume of commerce in the tied product is foreclosed by the tying arrangement.[97] The "sufficient market power" standard "does not . . . require that the defendant have a monopoly or even a dominant position throughout the market for the tying product."[98] The Court stated that "the economic power over the tying product can be sufficient even though the power falls short of dominance and even though the power exists only with respect to some of the buyers in the market."[99] The Court asserted that "the presence of any appreciable restraint on competition provides a sufficient reason for invalidating the tie."[100] In the Court's view, "[s]uch appreciable restraint results whenever the seller can exert some power over some of the buyers in the market, even if his power is not complete over them and over all other buyers in the market.''[101] The Court's rather expansive definition of ''sufficient market power'' was based on its view that ''tying arrangements generally serve no legitimate business purpose that cannot be achieved in some less restrictive way. . . .''[102] With respect to the second requirement, the Court stated that ''the controlling consideration is simply whether a total amount of business, substantial enough in terms of dollar-volume so as not to be merely *de minimis,* is foreclosed to competitors by the tie. . . .''[103]

In addition to the stringent protection the antitrust laws afford against tying arrangements, Section 106(b) of the Bank Holding Company Act Amendments of 1970 specifically prohibits tying arrangements.[104] In *Parsons Steel v. First Alabama Bank of Montgomery,* the Court stated that ''the purpose and effect of [Section 106(b)] is to apply the general principles of the Sherman Antitrust Act prohibiting anticompetitive tying arrangements specifically to the field of commercial banking, without requiring plaintiffs to establish the economic power of a bank and specific anticompetitive effects of tying arrangements. . . .''[105] Section 106(b) also has been described as making it ''illegal *per se* for banks to enter into tying arrangements.''[106]

Although the antitrust and banking laws address effectively the possibility that banks might illegally tie the extension of credit to the provision of other services, it should be noted that in view of the competitive nature of the credit market it is unlikely that tying arrangements will ever be a problem. One commentator has noted that ''[e]ven in times of tight money, banks are unlikely to possess leverage over many bank loan customers who have other bank or nonbank financing options.''[107] Similarly, the President's Council of Economic Advisers has stated:

> Another argument is that financial intermediaries would be able to compete unfairly by tying loans to the purchase of other services. It is not likely, however, that many financial intermediaries would find tying arrangements advantageous. Tying arrangements are a way in which a firm with market power can circumvent laws against price discrimination and increase its profits by selling different customers different quantities of tied-in products. It is unlikely that many banks have such market power, but even if some do, they could directly price discriminate by charging different interest rates to different customers.[108]

Finally, any concern over voluntary tying arrangements or ''tying effect''[109] appears to be largely unjustified in view of the competitive nature of the credit markets. In this regard, the Federal Reserve Board ''believes that the potential for 'voluntary tying' is structural, based upon the nature of competition in the relevant market areas, and that voluntary tying is not a problem in competitive markets.''[110]

Informational Advantages

The suggestion that a bank and its securities affiliate might secure, and exploit, informational advantages obtained through exchanges of information about their respective clients reflects a concern over possible breaches of the bank's and its affiliate's duties to their clients. It is important to recognize, however, that banks already face a similar problem stemming from the combination of commercial lending and trust functions.[111] Moreover, securities firms have confronted this problem for decades.[112] As a result, both banks and securities firms are experienced in the construction of "Chinese walls."[113] These walls are used to prevent the flow of material, nonpublic information between the underwriting and brokerage departments of a securities firm or the commercial lending and trust departments of a bank. Chinese walls could easily be adapted to prevent the flow of material, nonpublic information between a bank and its securities affiliate, especially because the bank and its affiliate would be separate corporate entities.

In addition, bank examinations are now used to police the effectiveness of walls and to detect the use of material, nonpublic information in trust department trading activities.[114] Such examinations could serve a similar function if banks were permitted to be affiliated with securities companies. Finally, the securities laws prohibit the use of material, nonpublic information in securities trading and provide effective remedies for violations of this prohibition.[115]

PROHIBITION VERSUS REGULATION

The potential conflicts that would be faced by banks if they were permitted to be affiliated with a company engaged in a full range of investment banking activities do not appear to be any more severe than those already faced by banks or securities firms individually.[116] Moreover, it is clear that existing law, adaptations of existing rules and regulations, or, in some cases, additional regulation would be sufficient to control any potential conflicts that might arise.[117] In this light, one is forced to question why banks have not been permitted to become affiliated with companies engaged in the securities business.

It is possible that the continued separation of commercial and investment banking might be justified on the ground that it is a necessary prophylactic. This theory would suggest that in view of the range of potential conflicts presented by a bank's affiliation with a securities firm and the difficulties associated with detecting the exploitation of these conflicts, it is good policy simply to prohibit such affiliations.[118] This potential justification fails, however, for it proves too much. Rigid adherence to the underlying theory would require similar rules prohibiting combinations of trust and commercial lending functions in a bank or underwriting, brokerage, dealing, and investment advisory functions in a securities firm. Given that the conflicts faced by banks affiliated with securities companies would not be qualitatively different from those faced by each firm individually, and that it would be possible to control such conflicts legally, it is impossible to explain why the "prophylaxis" theory should be any more persuasive in the case of banks with securities affiliates than it is in the case of banks with trust departments or securities firms with underwriting and brokerage departments.

A second plausible justification for prohibiting banks from affiliating with securities firms rests on the notion (referred to earlier in this chapter) that banks are somehow "special."[119] According to this theory, it would be unwise to risk the shock to public confidence that might result if banks were found to be exploiting conflict situations. As one commentator has stated:

> Congress generally has sought to prevent banks from engaging in activities which give rise to conflicts of interest before they arise because public trust is so important to the banking system's soundness. Moreover, although bank exposure to possible conflicts of interest can weaken public trust, disclosure of or punishment for conflicts would not restore public trust but only confirm the bank's misbehavior to the public. Thus, it is sound policy to prevent banks from engaging in activities unnecessary to effective banking which create possible conflicts of interest.[120]

There are two responses to this argument. First, banks are not the only institutions that are dependent on public confidence. In this regard, one commentator has noted that the "securities business rests on public confidence, confidence that the brokers and dealers with whom the public transacts business are properly qualified and held to standards of fair dealing, and confidence that customers' funds or securities are safe and will be handed over at the proper time."[121] Moreover, it is impossible to dispute the important role that securities firms play in our economy, crucial as they are to fulfilling the capital requirements of business. But despite the potential conflicts that pervade the securities industry, Congress has chosen to control these conflicts through regulation rather than through an enforced separation of functions. Second, it is arguable that detailed regulation of potential conflicts and careful monitoring of abuses in fact increases rather than erodes public confidence in an industry.

One commentator has noted that

> . . . [p]ublic confidence [in securities firms] is clearly enhanced by rules ensuring that brokers are financially responsible, that securities will not be lost or stolen, that a firm's books and records are accurate, that brokers are required to "know" their customers and to make only those recommendations that are suitable for those customers, and so forth.[122]

Admittedly, it is difficult to predict how the public, and in particular depositors, might react if a bank, or its affiliate, were discovered to be engaged in abusive practices. It seems likely, however, that so long as such abuses were isolated, which they would be likely to be,[123] the shock to public confidence would not be too severe, especially if depositors and the public were confident that a system of careful regulation had been developed to control any abuses.

The real question surrounding a decision to permit commercial banks to affiliate with securities companies is not whether the potential conflicts that would be created could be controlled legally. They could be. Instead, the real question (which is beyond the scope of this chapter) is whether the benefits of permitting bank affiliates to engage in expanded securities activities would exceed the costs of such a decision, including the risk that public confidence in a bank might be shaken by possible disclosures of illegal activity on the part of the bank or its securities affiliate. Suggestions that the potential conflicts which would be created by permitting bank affiliates to engage in expanded securities activities would be impossible or too difficult to control legally are not only inaccurate, but also tend to obscure the need to address this central question.

CONCLUSION

The Glass-Steagall Act was enacted in the midst of "a regulatory void."[124] Since the time the Act was passed, a regulatory structure governing banks and securities companies has developed that could be adapted to control the potential conflicts of interest which played a crucial role in Congress' decision to separate commercial and investment banking. The difficulty, or alleged impossibility, of regulating these conflicts is no longer a persuasive argument for prohibiting commercial banks from being affiliated with firms engaged in the securities business.

NOTES

[1]See generally Chapter 3 supra. See also, e.g., Karmel, Glass-Steagall: Some Critical Reflections, 97 BANKING L.J. 631, 640 (1980). ("The prohibition of conflicts of interest perceived by Congress as improper is basic to the Glass-Steagall Act. Functional segregation of commercial and investment banking is a respectable regulatory mechanism for preventing conflicts of interest. Although in other areas Federal law has resolved conflicts of interest by disclosure, the elimination of possible conflict situations is obviously more effective.")

[2]401 U.S. 617, 634 (1971).

[3]See, e.g., Statement of Richard H. Jenrette, Chairman, Securities Industry Association, on S. 2181 and S. 2134 before the Senate Committee on Banking, Housing and Urban Affairs, App. B (March 7, 1984).

[4]THE REPORT OF THE PRESIDENT'S COMMISSION ON FINANCIAL STRUCTURE AND REGULATION 52 (1971).

[5]Id.

[6]Note, A Conduct-Oriented Approach to the Glass-Steagall Act, 91 YALE L.J. 102, 106 (1981).

[7]Schotland, Introduction, in ABUSE ON WALL STREET: CONFLICTS OF INTEREST IN THE SECURITIES MARKETS 4 (1980).

[8]Edwards, Banks and Securities Activities: Legal and Economic Perspectives on the Glass-Steagall Act, in THE DEREGULATION OF THE BANKING AND SECURITIES INDUSTRIES 282 (L. Goldberg & L. White eds. 1979).

[9]Statement of Paul A. Volcker, Chairman, Board of Governors of the Federal Reserve System, before the House Committee on Banking, Finance and Urban Affairs 3 (June 12, 1984). See also Wall & Eisenbeis, Risk Considerations in Deregulating Bank Activities, in FEDERAL RESERVE BANK OF ATLANTA, ECONOMIC REVIEW 7–8 (May 1984).

[10]75 CONG. REC. 9913 (daily ed. May 10, 1932) (statement of Sen. Bulkley). During the same speech Senator Bulkley suggested that a "banker ought to be regarded as the financial confidant and mentor of his depositors." Id., at 9912. He later stressed that the separation of commercial and investment banking would provide depositors with significant protection "by prohibiting a banker from having an interest contrary to his depositors, by prohibiting him from being interested in securities which he recommends to his depositor to buy, by keeping him in such position that he may be free and independent to pass on credits without the embarrassment of having brought back to him the very securities that he sold to his depositors and being asked to loan upon them. We feel that by removing the bankers from the temptation of using credit in such a way as to make a good background and foundation for the flotation of more security issues we are protecting the depositors." Id., at 9914.

[11]For general discussions of one or more of the conflicts discussed in this sectionn, see ECONOMIC REPORT OF THE PRESIDENT 161 (1984); U.S. DEPARTMENT OF TREASURY, PUBLIC POLICY ASPECTS OF BANK SECURITIES ACTIVITIES 13, 22, 28–29 (1975) [hereinafter TREASURY PAPER]; V. Carosso, INVESTMENT BANKING IN AMERICA 332–33 (1970); Note, *Restrictions on Bank Underwriting of Corporate Securities: A Proposal for More Permissive Regulation*, 97 HARV. L. REV. 720, 722 (1984); Note, *National Banks and the Brokerage Business: The Comptroller's New Reading of the Glass-Steagall Act*, 69 VA. L. REV. 1303, 1308–09 (1983); Pitt & Williams, *Glass-Steagall Act: Key Issues for the Financial Services Industry*, 11 SEC. REG. L.J. 234, 236–37 (1983); Note, *Glass-Steagall: A Proposal for Regulation Rather than Prohibition*, 47 ALBANY L. REV. 1378, 1381–82 (1983); Note, *A Conduct-Oriented Approach to the Glass-Steagall Act*, 91 YALE L.J. 102, 104–05, 108–09 (1981); Note, *Commercial Bank Private Placement Activity: Cracking Glass-Steagall*, 27 CATH. U. L. REV. 743, 749–50 (1978); Peach, *The Security Affiliates of National Banks*, in WALL STREET AND THE SECURITY MARKETS 113–14 (V. Carosso ed. 1975); Perkins, *The Divorce of Commercial and Investment Banking: A History*, 88 BANKING L.J. 483, 503 (1971).

[12]*Operation of the National and Federal Reserve Banking Systems: Hearings Pursuant to S. Res. 71 Before a Subcomm. of the Senate Comm. on Banking and Currency*, 71st Cong., 3d Sess. (1931) [hereinafter *S. Res. 71 Hearings*].

[13]*Id.* at 1064. The subcommittees stated that debtor-creditor relationships between banks and their affiliates were "very prevalent." Id. at 1063. In the subcommittee's view this was at least partially attributable to the close connection "in the public mind" between a bank and its affiliates. If the affiliates suffered losses, "it [was] practically unthinkable that they would be allowed to fail." Instead, "the bank ould normally support [an affiliate] by additional loans or other aid, thus becoming more deeply involved itself." *Id.*

[14]*Id.*, at 1066.

[15]*Id.*

[16]*Id.*, at 1064.

[17]*Id.*

[18]Some evidence of this practice was uncovered during the Stock Exchange Practices Hearings. In the report issued following those hearings, the Senate Committee on Banking and Currency stated:

> A most vicious practice faciliated and encouraged by the group banking system was the device whereby individual trusts were exploited by the unit trust companies for the benefit of the group. In the administration of individual trusts by the unit trust companies, either as executor, administrator, guardian or trustee, it was a common practice to sell to the trusts securities which were sponsored by the security unit of the Group company, or which the security affiliate had a substantial interest in disposing. The trust company, as trustee, was violating a fundamental fiduciary duty to the cestui trust in purchasing, as trustee, securities in which the trustee or the affiliated units of the Group company had a pecuniary interest. The activities of the Detroit Trust Co., the unit trust company of the Detroit Bankers Co., was a glaring example of this reprehensible conduct.

S. REP. NO. 1455, 73d Cong., 2d Sess. 281 (1934). *See also Stock Exchange Practices: Hearings Before the Senate Comm. on Banking and Currency on S. Res. 84 and S. Res. 56*, 73d Cong., 2d Sess. 7986, 8063-68 (1834); V. Corosso, note 11 *supra*, at 332–33; Jenrette, note 3 *supra*, at App. B-6.

In discussing the abuses uncovered during the Stock Exchange Practices Hearings, one commentator has noted: "Congress' investigation was not a systematic industry-wide examination. It is therefore difficult to ascertain the pervasiveness of these abuses and whether commercial banks' investment security activity inevitably leads to such abuses." Note, *Glass-Steagall: A Proposal for Regulation Rather than Prohibition*, 47 ALBANY L. REV. 1382–83 (1983). Similarly, two other commentators have stated: "[W]e actually have very little idea of how great a role the majority of affiliates played in the abuses. The stock market crash merely presaged the spectacular economic collapse which brought down the good with the bad, and the investigation of investment affiliates is somewhat less thorough than is popularly imagined." Whitesell & Kelly, *Is the Glass-Steagall Act Obsolete?*, 87 BANKING L.J. 387, 395–96 (1970).

[19]*S. Res. 71 Hearings*, note 12 *supra*, at 1064.

[20]*Id.*

²¹75 CONG. REC. 9912 (daily ed. May 10, 1932) (statement of Sen. Bulkley). *See also* Perkins, note 11 *supra,* at 503.

²²75 CONG. REC. 9912 (daily ed. May 10, 1932) (statement of Sen. Bulkley).

²³401 U.S., at 630–34.

²⁴*Id.* at 631. The Court appears to have based its identification of this congressional concern on statements made by the Senate subcommittee in the appendix to the S. Res. 71 Hearings and on similar statements made by Senator Bulkley. *See id.,* at 631 n. 22.

²⁵*See, e.g.,* ECONOMIC REPORT OF THE PRESIDENT 162 (1984); TREASURY PAPER, note 11 *supra,* at 22; Solomon, *Bank Product Deregulation: Some Antitrust Tradeoffs,* in FEDERAL RESERVE BANK OF ATLANTA, ECONOMIC REVIEW 20, 25 (May 1984); Note, *A Conduct-Oriented Approach to the Glass-Steagall Act,* 91 YALE L.J. 102, 108–09 (1981). As described by one commentator, "a 'tie' means that a customer's purchase of one product is conditioned on the purchase of another product." Solomon, *supra,* at 25.

²⁶*See, e.g.,* Note, *Restrictions on Bank Underwriting of Corporate Securities: A Proposal for More Permissive Regulation,* 97 HARV. L. REV. 720, 722, 729–30 (1984); Note, *National Banks and the Brokerage Business: The Comptroller's New Reading of the Glass-Steagall Act,* 69 VA. L. REV. 1303, 1345–46 (1983).

²⁷The discussion in this section is based on the assumption that affiliates of commercial banks, rather than the banks themselves, would conduct any new securities activities that might be authorized as a result of legislation relaxing the prohibitions of the Glass-Steagall Act. The rationale for granting any new authority to bank affiliates, rather than to banks, rests on safety and soundness considerations. A securities affiliate, operated as a subsidiary of a bank holding company, would be only indirectly related to the bank. This structure would appear to present a less significant threat to bank safety and soundness than a structure that would permit banks to engage directly in expanded securities activities. *See, e.g.,* Statement of Donald T. Regan, Secretary of the Treasury, Before the House Committee on Banking, Finance and Urban Affairs 5 (June 19, 1984). ("Depositories and the Federal deposit insurance system [would be] insulated from the risks of nonbanking activities by a requirement that these activities be conducted upstream of the depository institution or through commonly controlled affiliates so that the bank's earnings and capital are not involved and cannot be impaired.") Moreover, the discussion is based on the assumption that a bank's securities affiliate, irrespective of the exemptions enjoyed by banks from various securities law statutes, would be subject to the full range of securities laws applicable to their activities. This makes sense from the standpoints of both competitive equity and regulatory efficiency. *See, e.g.,* Regan, *supra,* at 5; Note, *Restrictions on Bank Underwriting of Corporate Securities: A Proposal for More Permissive Regulation,* 97 HARV. L. REV. 720, 731 n. 78 (1984); Note, *Glass-Steagall: A Proposal for Regulation Rather than Prohibition,* 47 ALBANY L. REV. 1378, 1386 n. 39 (1983); Evans, *Regulation of Bank Securities Activities,* 91 BANKING L.J. 611 (1974). It should be noted, however, that at least one commentator believes that potential conflict of interest problems stemming from a decision to permit banks to engage in expanded securities activities would be less severe if banks were permitted to engage in these activities directly. *See* Edwards, note 8 *supra,* at 285–87.

²⁸12 U.S.C. sec. 371c.

²⁹Pub. L. No. 97-320, sec. 410(b), 96 Stat. 1515 (1982). *See generally* Rose & Talley, *Bank Transactions with Affiliates: The New Section 23A,* 100 BANKING L.J. 423 (1983).

³⁰12 U.S.C. sec. 371c(a)(1)(A). The aggregate amount of "covered transactions" between a member bank and all its affiliates is limited to 20% of the capital stock and surplus of the member bank. *Id.,* at sec. 371c(a)(1)(B).

³¹*Id.,* at sec. 371c(b)(7).

³²*Id.,* at sec. 371c(c).

³³*Id.,* at sec. 371c(a)(3).

³⁴*Id.,* at sec. 371c(a)(4).

³⁵Rose & Talley, note 29 *supra,* at 437–38.

³⁶*See* S. 1609, 98th Cong., 1st Sess. sec. 15, 129 CONG. REC. 9718 (daily ed. July 12, 1983).

[37]129 CONG. REC. 9727 (daily ed. July 12, 1983) (section-by-section analysis of S. 1609).

[38]*Id.*

[39]*Id.*, at 9728.

[40]*Id.*

[41]*See* note 18 *supra* and accompanying text.

[42]75 CONG. REC. 9912 (daily ed. May 10, 1932) (statement of Sen. Bulkley).

[43]S. REP. No. 1455, 73d Cong., 2d Sess. 281 (1934).

[44]*See, e.g.,* 2A. SCOTT, THE LAW OF TRUSTS sec. 170 (3d ed. 1967).

[45]*See id.,* at sec. 170.13.

[46]*See id.,* at sec. 170. *See also Magruder V. Drury,* 235 U.S. 106, 119–20 (1914).

[47]292 N.Y. 31, 40 (1944) (emphasis in original). *See also In re Ryan,* 291 N.Y. 376, 405–06 (1943).

[48]*See, e.g.,* N.Y. BANKING LAW sec. 100-b, subd. 1 (McKinney 1971) (''[N]o corporate fiduciary shall purchase securities from itself'').

[49]29 U.S.C. sec. 1106; 26 U.S.C. sec. 4975(c).

[50]29 U.S.C. sec. 1106; 26 U.S.C. sec. 4975(a), (b). Moreover, a fiduciary is permitted to purchase securities from another member of a syndicate of which the fiduciary or an affiliate is a member only if neither is a manager of the syndicate and if certain other restrictive conditions are met. *See* 40 Fed. Reg. 50,845, 50,848–49 (U.S. Dept. of Labor Prohibited Transaction Class Exemption 75–1 (Oct. 31, 1975)).

[51]12 C.F.R. sec. 9.12(a) states:

> Unless lawfully authorized by the instrument creating the relationship, or by court order or by local law, funds held by a national bank as fiduciary shall not be invested in stock or obligations of, or property acquired from, the bank or its directors, officers, or employees, or individuals with whom there exists such a connection, or organizations in which there exists such an interest, as might affect the best judgment of the bank in acquiring the property, or in stock or obligations of, or property acquired from, affiliates of the bank or their directors, officers, or employees.

In addition, the prohibition against self-dealing extends to purchases of securities from another member of a syndicate of which a trustee or an affiliate is a member, while the syndicate is open, if all members are responsible for a share of any unsold securities. *See* Comptroller of the Currency, TBC-19 (Sept. 25, 1981). *See also* THE NEW YORK CLEARING HOUSE ASSOCIATION, COMMERCIAL BANK PRIVATE PLACEMENT ADVISORY SERVICES 23 (1977).

[52]49 Fed. Reg. 18,497, 18,507 (May 1, 1984) (section 337.4(e)(1) of proposed regulations).

[53]*See, e.g.,* THE NEW YORK CLEARING HOUSE ASSOCIATION, note 51 *supra,* at 23. *See also* 17 C.F.R. sec. 241.10181; 38 Fed. Reg. 17,201 (June 29, 1973) (An underwriter of any offering has a self-interest in the success of that offering and in disposing of his commitment. The placement of a portion of that offering in discretionary accounts thus raises . . . a potential conflict of interest. It is a violation of the antifraud provisions of the federal securities laws if such an underwriter fails to make full and effective disclosure of this conflict to the customers involved. Full and effective disclosure, where the underwriter acts as principal, generally will require disclosure to and the consent of its clients not only that [the underwriter] proposes to deal with them for [its] own account but also of all other facts which may be material to the formulation of an independent opinion by the client as to the advisability of entering into the transaction.

[54]TREASURY PAPER, note 11 *supra,* at 35. Similarly, in a 1974 report, the Senate Committee on Banking, Housing and Urban Affairs stated: ''Banks have been underwriting general obligation bonds for the last 34 years without apparent abuses. . . . [N]one of the opponents of the bill could provide the Committee with documented evidence that banks have, in fact, abused their authority to underwrite general obligation bonds.'' S. REP. NO. 1120, 93d Cong., 2d Sess. 14 (1974).

[55]TREASURY PAPER, note 11 *supra,* at 35 n. 41.

[56]FEDERAL RESERVE BOARD STAFF STUDY, COMMERCIAL BANK PRIVATE PLACEMENT ACTIVITIES 65 (1977). *See also* COMPTROLLER OF CURRENCY, FEDERAL DEPOSIT INSURANCE CORPORATION & FEDERAL RESERVE BOARD, COMMERCIAL BANK PRIVATE PLACEMENT ACTIVITIES 2 (1978).

[57]*See, e.g., id.,* at 14; FEDERAL RESERVE BOARD STAFF STUDY, note 56 *supra,* at 79–80; Note, *Restrictions on Bank Underwriting of Corporate Securities: A Proposal for More Permissive Regulation,* 97 HARV. L. REV. 720, 730 & n. 72, 737 (1984). Federal bank regulatory agencies have the authority to examine bank affiliates. *See* 12 U.S.C. secs. 325, 481, 1820(b), 1844(c); Note, *Commercial Bank Private Placement Activity: Cracking Glass-Steagall,* 27 CATH. U. L. REV. 743, 760 (1978).

[58]It would appear to make little sense for a bank to expose itself to the losses associated with unsound loans so that its affiliate could earn a fraction of those potential losses on the sale of securities. Moreover, as a threshold matter, it would appear to make little sense for a bank's securities affiliate to agree to underwrite or distribute the securities of a financially troubled company.

In approving a bank holding company's acquisition of a discount brokerage firm, the Federal Reserve Board stated:

> The possibility that Bank might make unsound loans to Schwab customers to maximize Schwab's profits is not substantial and is neither based on evidence nor reasonable. Moreover, it would not be rational for Bank to place its own funds at risk in an unsound loan merely to increase brokerage commissions earned by Schwab.

BankAmerica Corporation, 69 FED. RES. BULL. 105, 113 (1983).

[59]15 U.S.C. sec. 78g.

[60]12 C.F.R. secs. 207, 220, 221. Under the regulations, "margin stock" includes equity securities registered or having unlisted trading privileges on a national securities exchange, OTC stocks appearing on the Federal Reserve's periodically published list, warrants to buy margin stock and debt securities convertible into margin stock. *See* 12 C.F.R. sec. 221.2.

[61]15 U.S.C. sec. 78k(d)(1).

[62]49 Fed. Reg. 18,497, 18,508 (May 1, 1984) (section 337.4(e)(5) of the proposed regulations).

[63]75 CONG. REC. 9912 (daily ed. May 10, 1932) (statement of Sen. Bulkley). *See* note 21 *supra* and accompanying text.

[64]15 U.S.C. sec. 77a, *et seq.*

[65]*See, e.g., id.,* at secs, 77g, 77j, 77aa.

[66]*Id.,* at sec. 77q.

[67]*Id.,* at sec. 77aa.

[68]*Id.,* at sec. 77aa(13) (Schedule A). Disclosure is required of "the principal purposes for which the net proceeds to the [issuer] from the securities to be offered are intended to be used and the approximate amount intended to be used for each such purpose." 17 C.F.R. sec. 229.504. In cases in which the issuer "has no current specific plan for the proceeds, or a significant portion thereof, the [issuer] shall so state and discuss the principal reasons for the offering." *Id.*

[69]*See, e.g.,* 15 U.S.C. secs. 77k, 77l.

[70]*See, e.g., id.,* at sec. 77x. *See also* THE NEW YORK CLEARING HOUSE ASSOCIATION, note 51 *supra,* at 24.

[71]COMPTROLLER OF CURRENCY, FEDERAL DEPOSIT INSURANCE CORPORATION & FEDERAL RESERVE BOARD, note 56 *supra,* at 2. As this statement suggests, any abuses that might arise also could be controlled through the bank examination process. *See generally* Siebert, *Commentary,* in SECURITIES ACTIVITIES OF COMMERCIAL BANKS 147–49 (A. Sametz ed. 1981).

[72]75 CONG. REC. 9912 (daily ed. May 10, 1932) (statement of Sen. Bulkley).

[73]*See generally* 12 C.F.R. sec. 225.4.

[74]*See, e.g.,* King & Whitehead, *Introduction,* in FEDERAL RESERVE BANK OF ATLANTA, ECONOMIC REVIEW 5 (May 1984); Note, *Glass-Steagall: A Proprosal for Regulation Rather than Prohibition,* 47 ALBANY L. REV. 1378, 1386 (1983). *See also Investment Co. Institute v. Camp,* 401 U.S. 617, 644 (1971) (Blackmun, J., dissenting) ("A bank offers its fiduciary services in an atmosphere of vigorous competition. One need only observe the current and continuous advertising of claimed fiduciary skills to know that this is so and that the business is one for profit. In the fiduciary area a bank is engaged in direct competition with other investment concepts and with nonbanking fiduciaries").

[75]One commentator has stated:

> Clearly, the potential conflicts-of-interest abuses that arise out of banks' doing a securities business
> are quite similar to those that exist already as a result of banks' engaging in multiple traditional
> banking activities. About the only thing that can be said is that by allowing banks to engage in even
> more activities, we may increase the potential for abuse. Even so, it is by no means obvious that
> these potential abuses cannot be adequately controlled by regulatory sanction.

Edwards, note 8 *supra,* at 284.
It should be noted that there is a certain irony associated with the notion that the commercial banker's role
as a purveyor of disinterested investment advice should be preserved. In view of the fact that banks or their
affiliates are not permitted to engage in a full-fledged securities business, one may reasonably question
the value of whatever advice they have to offer.

[76]75 CONG. REC. 9912 (daily ed. May 10, 1932) (statement of Sen. Bulkley). Apparently, there were
instances during the 1920s and early 1930s in which banks referred their depositors to their securities
affiliates. *See, e.g.,* S. REP. NO. 1455, 73d Cong., 2d Sess. 163 (1934) ("Commercial banks found a
fertile field among its depositors for purchasers of security issues which their investment affiliates were
sponsoring. These banks, violating their fiduciary duty to depositors seeking disinterested investment
counsel from their bankers, referred these depositors to the affiliates for advice. These depositors were
then sold securities in which the affiliates had a pecuniary interest"); *S. Res. 71 Hearings,* note 12 *supra,*
at 1064 (noting "tendency of the selling organization of the affiliate to consider the bank's depositors as
its preferred list of sales prospects"); V. CAROSSO, note 11 *supra,* at 332; Jenrette, note 3 *supra,* at App.
B-3.

[77]12 C.F.R. sec. 225.125(h). These regulations were upheld by the Supreme Court in *Bd. of Govs., FRS
v. Investment Company Inst.,* 450 U.S. 46 (1981).

[78]12 C.F.R. sec. 225.125(h).

[79]*Id.* In its proposed regulations to govern the securities activities of insured state nonmember banks, the
FDIC included a provision that prohibits "any employee of the affiliate who is also an employee of the
bank" from conducting "any securities activities on behalf of the affiliate on the premises of the bank that
involve customer contact. . . ." 49 Fed. Reg. 18,497, 18,507 (May 1, 1984) (section 337.4(c)(4) of the
proposed regulations).

[80]*See generally* ECONOMIC REPORT OF THE PRESIDENT 161 (1984); N. Wolfson, CONFLICTS OF INTEREST:
INVESTMENT BANKING (1976); V. CAROSSO, note 11 *supra,* at 378; Note, *National Banks and the Brokerage Business: The Comptroller's New Reading of the Glass-Steagall Act,* 69 VA. L. REV. 1303, 1345
(1983).

[81]N. Wolfson, note 80 *supra,* at 61, *quoting* SECURITIES AND EXCHANGE COMMISSION, REPORT ON THE
FEASIBILITY AND ADVISABILITY OF THE COMPLETE SEGREGATION OF THE FUNCTIONS OF DEALER AND
BROKER (1936).

[82]*See, e.g.,* 15 U.S.C. secs. 77g, 77j, 77aa, 781, 78m, 78bb(a)(2).

[83]*See, e.g., id.,* at secs. 77q, 78i, 78j, 78o(c)(1). *See also* 17 C.F.R. secs. 240.10b-5, 240.15c1-6,
240.15c1-7.

[84]*See, e.g., id.,* at 240.15b10-2 ("Every nonmember broker or dealer and associated person shall observe
high standards of commercial honor and just and equitable principles of trade in the conduct of his business"); *id.,* at 240.15b10-3:

> Every nonmember broker or dealer and every associated person who recommends to a customer
> the purchase, sale or exchange of any security shall have reasonable grounds to believe that the
> recommendation is not unsuitable for such customer on the basis of information furnished by such
> customer after reasonable inquiry concerning the customer's investment objectives, financial sit-
> uation and needs, and any other information known by such broker or dealer or associated person.

See also, New York Exchange Rule 405. *See generally* Note, *National Banks and the Brokerage Business:
The Comptroller's New Reading of the Glass-Steagall Act,* 69 VA. L. REV. 1303, 1345 n.233 (1983);
Note, *Commercial Bank Private Placement Activity: Cracking Glass-Steagall,* 27 CATH. U. L. REV. 743,
760–61 (1978).

[85]*SEC v. Capital Gains Bureau,* 375 U.S. 180, 191–92 (1963). The Investment Advisers Act is codified at 15 U.S.C. sec. 80b-1, *et seq.*

[86]*SEC. v. Capital Gains B:ireau,* 375 U.S. 180, 194 (1963) (footnotes omitted).

[87]46 Fed. Reg. 41,771, 41,774 (Aug. 18, 1981) (SEC Release No. IA-770).

[88]*Id.*

[89]*See, e.g.,* Note, *Restrictions on Bank Underwriting of Corporate Securities: A Proposal for More Permissive Regulation,* 97 HARV. L. REV. 720, 737 (1984).

[90]*See, e.g.,* TREASURY PAPER, note 11 *supra,* at 17; E. Herman, CONFLICTS OF INTEREST: COMMERCIAL BANK TRUST DEPARTMENTS 27–29, 45, 53–54 (1975); Note, *Restrictions on Bank Underwriting of Corporate Securities: A Proposal for More Permissive Regulation,* 97 HARV. L. REV. 720, 730 (1984); Edwards, note 8 *supra,* at 284; Siebert, note 71 *supra,* at 147–49.

[91]*See, e.g.,* Note, *Restrictions on Bank Underwriting of Corporate Securities: A Proposal for More Permissive Regulation,* 97 HARV. L. REV.720, 730 & n.72, 737 (1984); Siebert, note 71 *supra,* at 147–49.

[92]*See, e.g.,* THE NEW YORK CLEARING HOUSE ASSOCIATION, note 51 *supra,* at 24; Note, *Glass-Steagall: A Proposal for Regulation Rather than Prohibition,* 47 ALBANY L. REV. 1378, 1385, 1386 n.39 (1983); Note, *Commercial Bank Private Placement Activity: Cracking Glass-Steagall,* 27 CATH. U. L. REV. 743, 760 (1978).

[93]49 Fed. Reg. 18,497, 18,507 (May 1, 1984) (section 337.4(e)(3) of the proposed regulations). The regulations do not prohibit a bank from ''honoring a loan commitment or revolving loan agreement or funding a line of credit where the loan commitment, revolving loan agreement, or line of credit was entered into prior in time to the underwriting or distribution.'' *Id.,* at 18,507–508 n.6.

[94]The concern that a bank might make an unsound loan to ''shore up'' a company with which its securities affiliate had previously had an investment banking relationship appears to be equally unjustified. As the New York Clearing House Association has noted in a similar context:

> This theoretical conflict of interest does not result in any realistic danger of abuse. This conflict can only be meaningful if bank management would risk the bank's own assets to protect private placement revenues which are far less than the amount of the assets placed at risk by any such loan. In other words, the conflict can only result in abuse if bank management consciously exposes its own assets to unjustified risk.

THE NEW YORK CLEARING HOUSE ASSOCIATION, Note 51 *supra,* at 24.

[95]*See, e.g.,* TREASURY PAPER, note 11 *supra,* at 22; Note, *A Conduct-Oriented Approach to the Glass-Steagall Act,* 91 YALE L. J. 102, 108–09 (1981).

[96]*See Fortner Enterprises v. U.S. Steel,* 394 U.S. 495, 498 (1969).

[97]*Id.,* at 497–98.

[98]*Id.,* at 502.

[99]*Id.,* at 502–03

[100]*Id.,* at 503.

[101]*Id.*

[102]*Id.*

[103]*Id.,* at 501.

[104]12 U.S.C. sec. 1972.

[105]679 F.2d 242, 245 (CA11 1982).

[106]TREASURY PAPER, Note 11 *supra,* at 22. *See also* Note, *National Banks and the Brokerage Business: The Comptroller's New Reading of the Glass-Steagall Act,* 69 VA. L. REV. 1303, 1346 n.238 (1983) (''A bank which pressured investors seeking credit to use the bank's brokerage services or the services of the bank's brokerage affiliate would be subject to a civil suit for use of an illegal tying arrangement''). The Federal Deposit Insurance Corporation's proposed regulations to govern the activities of state non-member insured banks also include a provision prohibiting such a bank from ''directly or indirectly condition[ing] any loan or extension of credit to any company on the requirement that the company con-

tract with, or agree to contract with, the bank's . . . affiliate to underwrite or distribute the company's securities. . . ." 49 Fed. Reg. 18,497, 18,508 (May 1, 1984) (section 337.4(e)(8) of the proposed regulations).

[107]Solomon, Note 25 *supra,* at 25.

[108]ECONOMIC REPORT OF THE PRESIDENT 162 (1984).

[109]*See, e.g.,* TREASURY PAPER, Note 11 *supra,* at 22–23; Note, *A Conduct-Oriented Approach to the Glass-Steagall Act,* 91 YALE L.J. 102, 108–09 (1981).

[110]*In re Citicorp,* [1981–82 Transfer Binder] FED. BANKING L. REP. (CCH) par. 98,708 at 85,303 (1981).

[111]*See, e.g.,* E. HERMAN, Note 90 *supra,* at 73; Herzel & Colling, *The Chinese Wall Revisited,* 6 CORP. L. REV. 116 (1983); Note, *Commercial Bank Private Placement Activity: Cracking Glass-Steagall,* 27 CATH. U. L. REV. 743, 764 (1978).

[112]*See, e.g.,* N. WOLFSON, Note 80 *supra;* Lipton & Mazur, *The Chinese Wall Solution to the Conflicts Problems of Securities Firms,* 50 N.Y.U. L. REV. 459 (1975).

[113]*See generally* Herzel & Colling, Note 111 *supra;* Lipton & Mazur, note 112 *supra;* Lybecker, *Regulation of Bank Trust Department Investment Activities: Seven Gaps, Eight Remedies,* 90 BANKING L.J. 912, 924 (1973); Note, *National Banks and the Brokerage Business: The Comptroller's New Reading of the Glass-Steagall Act,* 69 VA. L. REV. 1303, 1346 n.234 (1983).

[114]*See, e.g.,* FEDERAL RESERVE BOARD STAFF STUDY, Note 56 *supra,* at 79–80; Siebert, note 71 *supra,* at 147–49.

[115]*See* 15 U.S.C. sec. 78j; 17 C.F.R. sec. 240.10b-5. *See also SEC v. Texas Gulf Sulphur Co.,* 401 F.2d 833 (CA2 1968), *cert. denied,* 394 U.S. 976 (1969).

[116]*See, e.g.,* Edwards, Note 8 *supra,* at 284 ("[T]he kinds of conflicts of interest that arise from commercial banking-securities business ties are quite similar to those that already exist, and therefore would be amenable to the same types of regulatory control"); Note, *Restrictions on Bank Underwriting of Corporate Securities: A Proposal for More Permissive Regulation,* 97 HARV. L. REV. 720, 731 (1984) ("[T]he potential conflicts of interest posed to depository institutions by investment banking do not differ from those that already face commercial and investment banks").

[117]*See* Notes 28–115 *supra* and accompanying text.

[118]This justification appears to have had a significant influence on the Supreme Court's opinion in *Investment Co. Institute v. Camp,* 401 U.S. 617 (1971).

[119]*See* Notes 9–10 *supra* and accompanying text. *But see* White, *Commentary,* in SECURITIES ACTIVITIES OF COMMERCIAL BANKS 51, 53 (A. Sametz. [ed.] 1981) ("I would argue that we must start thinking of banks as closer to [other businesses] rather than as very special institutions that have these very special problems of conflict of interest").

[120]Note, *National Banks and the Brokerage Business: The Comptroller's New Reading of the Glass-Steagall Act,* 69 VA. L. REV. 1303, 1346–47 (1983). *See also* Evans, Note 27 *supra,* at 618 ("Bank requirements and standards are enforced in a 'discreet' way out of concern that public knowledge of improper bank activities would cause a loss of confidence by depositors and thus jeopardize the stability so necessary to our banking system").

[121]E. O'Brien, *In the Middle of the Regulation-Deregulation Road,* in THE DEREGULATION OF THE BANKING AND SECURITIES INDUSTRIES 134 (L. Goldberg & L. White [eds.] 1979).

[122]*Id.*

[123]In this regard, one commentator has stated:

> [I]t is imperative to recognize that the self-serving opportunities present in conflict-of-interest situations are usually not exploited. If such were not the case, fiduciary relationships would seldom have survived, reputations would rarely be intact, and the law would have had to intervene for more frequently than it has.

Schotland, *Preface,* in E. HERMAN, note 90 *supra,* at xv.

[124]Whitesell & Kelly, note 18 *supra,* at 395.

REFERENCES

V. Carosso, INVESTMENT BANKING IN AMERICA (1970).

COMPTROLLER OF CURRENCY, FEDERAL DEPOSIT INSURANCE CORPORATION & FEDERAL RESERVE BOARD, COMMERCIAL BANK PRIVATE PLACEMENT ACTIVITIES (1978).

ECONOMIC REPORT OF THE PRESIDENT (1984).

Franklin Edwards, *Banks and Securities Activities: Legal and Economic Perspectives on the Glass-Steagall Act,* in THE DEREGULATION OF THE BANKING AND SECURITIES INDUSTRIES (L. Goldberg & L. White eds., 1979).

Evans, *Regulation of Bank Securities Activities,* 91 BANKING L. J. 611 (1974).

FEDERAL RESERVE BOARD STAFF STUDY, COMMERCIAL BANK PRIVATE PLACEMENT ACTIVITIES (1971).

E. Herman, CONFLICTS OF INTEREST: COMMERCIAL BANK TRUST DEPARTMENTS (1975).

Herzel and Colling, *The Chinese Wall Revisited,* 6 CORP. L. REV. 116 (1983).

Karmel, *Glass-Steagall: Some Critical Reflections,* 97 BANKING L. J. 631 (1980).

King and Whitehead, *Introduction,* in Federal Reserve Bank of Atlanta, ECONOMIC REVIEW 5 (May 1984).

Lipton and Mazur, *The Chinese Wall Solution to the Conflicts Problems of Securities Firms,* 50 N.Y.U. L. REV. 459 (1975).

Lybecker, *Regulation of Bank Trust Department Investment Activities: Seven Gaps, Eight Remedies,* 90 BANKING L. J. 912 (1973).

THE NEW YORK CLEARING HOUSE ASSOCIATION, COMMERCIAL BANK PRIVATE PLACEMENT ADVISORY SERVICES (1977).

Note, *Restrictions on Bank Underwriting of Corporate Securities: A Proposal for More Permissive Regulation,* 97 HARV. L. REV. 720 (1984).

Note, *National Banks and Brokerage Business: The Comptroller's New Reading of the Glass-Steagall Act,* 69 VA. L. REV. 1303 (1983).

Note, *Glass-Steagall: A Proposal for Regulation Rather than Prohibition,* 47 ALBANY L. REV. 1378 (1983).

Note, *A Conduct-Oriented Approach to the Glass-Steagall Act,* 91 YALE L. J. 102 (1981).

Note, *Commercial Bank Private Placement Activity: Cracking Glass-Steagall,* 27 CATH. U. L. REV. 743 (1978).

O'Brien, *In the Middle of the Regulation-Deregulation Road,* in THE DEREGULATION OF THE BANKING AND SECURITIES INDUSTRIES (L. Goldberg & L. White eds. 1979).

Operation of the National and Federal Reserve Banking Systems: Hearings Pursuant to S. Res. 71 Before a Subcomm. of the Senate Comm. on Banking and Currency, 71st Cong., 3d Sess. (1931).

Peach, *The Security Affiliates of National Banks,* in WALL STREET AND THE SECURITY MARKETS (V. Carosso ed., 1975).

Perkins, *The Divorce of Commercial and Investment Banking: A History,* 88 BANKING L. J. 483 (1971).

Pitt and Williams, *the Glass-Steagall Act: Key Issues for the Financial Services Industry,* 11 SEC. REG. L. J. 234 (1983).

Rose and Talley, *Bank Transactions with Affiliates: The New Section 23A,* 100 BANKING L. J. 423 (1983).

S. REP. No. 1455, 73d Cong., 2d Sess. (1934).

Schotland, *Introduction,* in ABUSE ON WALL STREET; CONFLICTS OF INTEREST IN THE SECURITIES MARKETS (1980).

A. Scott, THE LAW OF TRUSTS (3d ed. 1967).

Siebert, *Commentary,* in SECURITIES ACTIVITIES OF COMMERCIAL BANKS (A. Sametz ed., 1981).

Solomon, *Bank Product Deregulation: Some Antitrust Tradeoffs,* in Federal Reserve Bank of Atlanta, ECONOMIC REVIEW 20 (May 1984).

Stock Exchange Practices: Hearings Before the Senate Comm. on Banking and Currency on S. Res. 84 and S. Res. 56, 73d Cong., 2d Sess. (1934).

THE REPORT OF THE PRESIDENT'S COMMISSION ON FINANCIAL STRUCTURE AND REGULATION (1971).

U.S. DEPARTMENT OF TREASURY, PUBLIC POLICY ASPECTS OF BANK SECURITIES ACTIVITIES (1975).

Wall and Eisenbeis, *Risk Considerations in Deregulating Bank Activities,* in Federal Reserve Bank of Atlanta, ECONOMIC REVIEW (May 1984).

White, *Commentary,* in SECURITIES ACTIVITIES OF COMMERCIAL BANKS (A. Sametz ed. 1981).

Whitesell & Kelly, *Is the Glass-Steagall Act Obsolete?,* 87 BANKING L. J. 387 (1970).

N. WOLFSON, CONFLICTS OF INTEREST: INVESTMENT BANKING (1976).

10 A View from the International Capital Markets

RICHARD M. LEVICH

A major question facing U.S. policymakers today is whether existing restrictions on securities activities of U.S. commercial banks should be abolished as part of a broader program of banking and financial market deregulation, or whether policymakers should preserve the status quo. In the discussion of this issue, two points are often overlooked:

1. An essentially unregulated securities market, the Eurobond market, has existed for over 20 years.
2. U.S. commercial bank affiliates have been important participants in the Euro-bond market and—where they are permitted to do so—in foreign securities markets as well.[1]

This historical experience suggests that it may be appropriate to examine the behavior of international capital markets, and to ascertain what lessons, if any, they hold for financial deregulation in the United States.

The purpose of this chapter is to offer a contribution to the debate on deregulation of investment banking activities by drawing on the experience in international capital markets. The evidence presented addresses two broad sets of issues:

1. Is it possible for private agents to organize the underwriting of securities, issuing and dealing functions in an efficient manner without restricting competitive forces?
2. Does the presence of agents (i.e., commercial banks) who engage in related financial transactions (e.g., accepting deposits, lending, managing trust funds, etc.) have any adverse effects on the underwriting and issuing markets, on related financial transactions (e.g., unbiased credit evaluations), or on the basic safety and soundness of the banking system?

One major segment of the international capital market, the Eurobond market, is our laboratory for exploring the first question. The Eurobond market, although not entirely free of regulation, operates under substantially fewer restrictions than those placed on domestic and foreign bond issues. In particular, there are no regulatory restrictions on firms wishing to engage in underwriting or dealing activities. Only economic factors—adequate financial capital, human capital, and appropriate technology—make it costly for firms to enter (or leave) the Eurobond market.

The Eurobond market may thus be studied as an example of how well the underwriting and issuing functions of a primary market are performed in an environment that is largely unregulated and open to competitive forces. Certain characteristics of the market—the concentration of underwriters, the allegiance of issuers to underwriters, the cost of underwriting services, and the cost of funds to issuers—might be taken as a standard of comparison against other markets.

In addressing the second question, the Eurobond market again offers a potentially useful source of evidence. Major foreign banks and offshore subsidiaries of U.S. bank holding companies compete head-to-head with more specialized investment banking or issuing houses. It will generally be the case that the major foreign and U.S. commercial banks will offer related financial services to corporate issuers and fiduciary services to other bank customers. Consequently, these banks may be thought to be more exposed to problems of conflict of interest and abuse of fiduciary trust than may be the case with more specialized issuing houses. The record of the Eurobond market is open to examination in this regard.

The second question might also be approached in another manner, by analyzing the primary issue markets in countries other than the United States. In many industrial countries commercial banking and investment banking are not formally separated, and commercial banks are not prohibited from underwriting corporate securities, including equities.[2] These foreign market settings offer another opportunity to analyze whether the combination of commercial and investment banking within one financial institution allows for a smoothly functioning primary issue market in which potential conflict of interest problems are manageable and public confidence in the safety and soundness of banks is maintained.[3]

Because of the great differences in macroeconomic policies, fiscal incentives and the institutional environment, however, we will argue that the experience with combined commercial and investment banking outside the United States is less relevant for our study. Indeed it will be argued that the thrust of regulation itself is fundamentally different in other industrial countries than in the United States.[4]

Consequently, we propose to focus on the Eurobond market as an arena in which both of our above research questions can be addressed. The Eurobond market is, first, an example of a largely unregulated market and second, a market in which institutions take on underwriting and investment banking duties in addition to their commercial banking functions. We propose that the analysis of the Eurobond market, in general, and the role played by banking institutions, in particular, is directly relevant for assessing the implications of expanding competition in the United States by allowing separately capitalized securities affiliates of commercial banks to engage in investment banking activities.

Our methodology is not that of formal hypothesis testing. Rather, we claim that the Eurobond market and the U.S. corporate securities markets are comparable in the sense that our findings concerning the degree of competition or advantages to borrowers and lenders might apply equally to U.S. securities markets were the Glass-Steagall act to be abolished.[5] Our approach, therefore, is to appraise the overall development and success of the Eurobond market with its attendant problems and risks. We then attempt to infer what lessons there are in this experience for deregulation of U.S. financial markets.

The evidence presented in this chapter suggests that the Eurobond market has indeed "succeeded" in the sense that the market can survive without articifial support and continues to fulfill the very real demands of both borrowers and lenders. In the early years, the market enjoyed "protection" because of U.S. policies that pushed borrowers offshore. Still, fixed income securities underwriting could hardly be labeled risk-free in the post-Bretton Woods decade. Demand for Eurobond issues fluctuated with both exchange rate and interest rate expectations. To protect their interests while developing the market, underwriters adopted a variety of protective measures—for example, dealing with AAA clients to minimize credit risks; establishing large syndicates to spread underwriting risks; setting transaction costs high enough to provide an adequate cushion; and establishing "gray markets" to minimize the price risk of unsold securities.[6]

In addition, our analysis suggests that if the United States allows commercial banking and investment banking activities to take place within the context of a single bank holding company, the result will not be a system of "universal banks" that resembles those existing in Europe. This is because the concentration in the banking industry is, and is likely to remain, far less in the United States than in Europe; the linkages between corporations and banks are weaker in the United States than in Europe; and the thrust of regulation is vastly dissimilar. Furthermore, if the U.S. commercial banks were permitted to engage in investment banking activities, they would do so within the framework of regulations to establish minimum capital requirements for the new banking activities, and to insure adequate separation of personnel and organization between commercial and investment banking activities.[7] As a result, only a minority of the nation's 14,000 commercial banks would qualify to establish investment banking operations.

Evidence from the Eurobond market strongly suggests that, within its essentially unregulated environment with no artificial barriers to entry, underwriters have indeed behaved prudently. They organized a market, allowing substantial benefits to both borrowers and lenders, without incurring substantial risks. The evidence offers good reason to believe that U.S. commercial bank holding companies could similarly behave prudently in competition with U.S. investment banking houses without undermining the basic safety and soundness of the system. Regulation and supervision of commercial bank-related corporate securities underwriting and dealing activities would establish minimum capital requirements, adequate disclosure of information, and sufficient separation from commercial banking operations. The increased competition would in all likelihood result in significant net benefits to the economy at a minimal increase in risk.

The plan for the chapter is as follows. In the following section we present background information on the Eurobond market. The evidence clearly shows that the

Eurobond market is a major financial market offering a variety of advantages over domestic markets for both borrowers and lenders. An appraisal of the underwriting strategies and competitive characteristics in the Eurobond market is offered in the section entitled "Appraising the Performance of the Eurobond Market." The evidence presented here on industry concentration and switching among lead managers suggests greater competition in the Eurobond market than in U.S. corporate underwriting. In the section entitled "Problems and Risks in the Eurobond Market," we identify some of the problems and risks that have been associated with Eurobond market operations and review some of the corrective steps and innovations that have been introduced to deal with them. The scope for transplanting the spirit of Eurobond market competition is explored in the section entitled "Scope for Increasing Competition in U.S. Investment Banking." A summary and conclusions follow in the final section.

BACKGROUND INFORMATION ON THE EUROBOND MARKET

The purpose of this section is to describe the important operating characteristics of the Eurobond market, and to present a variety of statistical data indicating the size and scope of the market. We intend to show that the Eurobond market is indeed a major financial market, and that our later findings concerning the behavior of underwriters and investment bankers in this market may be indicative of behavior in other major markets such as the United States, were it to allow securities affiliates of commercial banks to compete in the financial services industry.

Citing World Bank records, Mendelsohn[8] reports that the first Eurobond was issued in 1957 for Petrofina S.A., the Belgian petroleum company. The issue was denominated in U.S. dollars in the amount of $5 million.[9] In 1982, the total of new Eurobond issues surpassed $50 billion.[10] Individual issues have sometimes exceeded $500 million.[11] By comparison, total bond issues in the United States by private institutions totaled $53.4 billion in 1982. Public government issues raised another $324.9 billion.[12]

The Petrofina issue illustrates the two key features of a Eurobond. A Eurobond is (1) underwritten by an international syndicate, and (2) offered for sale simultaneously in a number of countries. As a consequence of (2), the issue is usually denominated in a currency (or unit of account) that is foreign to a large number of the buyers. Mendelsohn[13] points out that with the introduction of the "bought deal," in which a single underwriter commits to an entire issue in advance, the first of these dimensions of a Eurobond may be lost as a distinctive feature of Eurobond issues.

In contrast, a *foreign bond* is an obligation of a foreign company that is underwritten by a syndicate of domestic investment banks, denominated in domestic currency and offered for sale in the domestic market. Examples of foreign bonds are *Yankee bonds,* dollar obligations of non-U.S. firms underwritten and issued in the United States, and *Samurai bonds,* yen obligations of non-Japanese firms underwritten and issued in Japan.

Table 10.1 presents data on the yearly flow of international bond issues. On av-

Table 10.1 Internal Bond Issues, 1970–1981

Dates	Eurobonds	Foreign (Outside U.S.)	Foreign (Inside U.S.)	Total	Eurobonds	Foreign (Outside U.S.)	Foreign (Inside U.S.)	Total
	(in millions)				(percentage)			
1970	US$2,966	US$378	US$1,216	US$4,560	65.0%	8.3%	26.6%	100.0%
1971	3,642	1,538	1,104	6,284	58.0	24.5	17.6	100.0
1972	6,335	2,060	1,353	9,748	65.0	21.1	13.9	100.0
1973	4,193	2,626	1,019	7,838	53.5	33.5	13.0	100.0
1974	2,134	1,432	3,291	6,857	31.1	20.9	48.0	100.0
1975	8,567	4,884	6,460	19,911	43.0	24.5	32.4	100.0
1976	14,328	7,586	10,602	32,516	44.1	23.3	32.6	100.0
1977	17,735	7,185	7,286	32,206	55.1	22.3	22.6	100.0
1978	14,125	14,359	5,795	34,279	41.2	41.9	16.3	100.0
1979	18,726	17,749	4,515	40,990	45.7	43.3	11.0	100.0
1980	23,970	14,521	3,429	41,920	57.2	34.6	8.2	100.0
1981	31,616	13,817	7,552	52,985	59.7	26.1	14.3	100.0
Average	12,361	7,344	4,468	24,174	51.1	30.4	18.5	100.0

Source: Morgan Guaranty Trust Company, *World Financial Markets*, various issues.

erage, the share of Eurobonds and foreign bonds in the market is roughly equal. The average annual growth rate of Eurobond issues over the period 1970–1981 was 22%. Many of the important characteristics of the various bond issues are displayed for comparison in Table 10.2.

We wish to focus our attention next on differences in regulatory treatment and issuing costs, factors that should influence the propensity of borrowers and lenders to converge on a particular market. We have been careful not to suggest that the Eurobond market operates in a climate free from all regulation. Although there is no official regulation of the Eurobond market per se, every Eurobond issue "must conform with the laws and regulations of the country in which it is offered for sale."[14] However, this does *not* mean meeting local requirements for public offerings. For example, bonds may be offered for sale initially in the United States if they are registered with the SEC under the 1933 Act. Eurobonds are not registered under the 1933 Act, although they can still be sold in the United States *after* distribution abroad has been completed and they have been seasoned in the *secondary market*.[15] In practice, many foreign countries apply less restrictive regulations than exist in the United States, or apply fewer restrictions on Eurobonds than on domestic bonds. In most cases, the method of offering Eurobonds allows them not to be classified as "public offerings," and they are, therefore, not national securities subject to regulation.[16]

Because Eurobonds are issued under minimal formal regulatory control, the issuer avoids the kind of detailed and standardized disclosure requirements that are part of U.S. bond issues. Document preparation can be costly for U.S. issuers in the domestic capital market, but it may be prohibitive for non-U.S. firms in cases where accounting statements are not in accordance with American principles or where there is great reluctance to release certain types of information to the public. Eurobonds are frequently exchange-listed (in Luxembourg, London, or Singapore) and therefore disclosure requirements must conform to exchange practices in those financial centers. Exchange listing is a device to increase the marketability of bonds among institutions and is not a necessary (but highly desirable) feature of Eurobonds. In practice, very few secondary market transactions take place on the exchanges.[17] Regulation, therefore, is largely absent.

Unlike bond issues in the United States, the timing of domestic and foreign issues abroad is generally controlled by the local regulatory body.[18] Queuing of new issues is an important tool of macroeconomic policy outside the United States. In this manner, governments seek to avoid "congestion" in the capital market, achieve interest rate targets, allocate places in the queue according to national economic or sectional priorities, and allow the government a clear run at local capital markets.

Although it is claimed that queuing regulations do not operate in the Eurobond market, in fact this is only true in the U.S. and Canadian dollar segments of the market.[19] In other markets, notably Germany, the authorities do in fact regulate the issuance of Eurobonds denominated in domestic currency.[20] Again, these rules reflect the operation of macroeconomic policy within a small, open economy in which policymakers attempt to manage their exchange rate as well as interest rates. For domestic authorities, control over the volume of offshore issues denominated in domestic currency is important for achieving exchange rate and interest rate targets. Presumably,

Table 10.2 Comparative Characteristics of Bond Issues in International Bond Markets

	Domestic Bonds (U.S. Market)	Foreign Bonds (non-U.S. Market)	Eurobond Market
1. Regulatory bodies	Securities and Exchange Commission	Official agency approval	Minimum regulatory control
2. Disclosure requirements	More detailed higher initial expense higher ongoing expense may be onerous to non-U.S. firms	Variable	Determined by markets practice
3. Issuing costs	0.75–1.0%	Variable to 4.0%	2.0–2.5%
4. Rating required	Yes	Usually not	No
5. Listing	Listing separate	Listing usual	Listing usual
6. Queuing	No formal queue	Usually queue	No queue
7. Currency of denomination	U.S. does not restrict use of $	Many foreign countries (Germany, Switzerland) restrict use, part of queuing	No restrictions on U.S. and Canadian $
8. Speed	Relatively slow Rule 415 may speed up process.	Variable	Usually fast "Bought deal"
9. Borrower/Issuer incentives	Largest market, greater depth Disclosure may be costly to foreigners	Local visibility, Diversification of sources	Lower annual interest expense Speed of placement to capture advantageous windows Cannot sell issue in U.S. until 90-day seasoning
10. Lender/Investor incentives	Greater depth and liquidity More standarized information disclosed	Currency diversification gain	Currency gains Bearer bonds No withholding tax on interest

Source: Adapted from Antione W. Van Agtmael, "Issuance of Eurobonds: Syndication and Underwriting Techniques and Costs," Section 5.2 in A. George I. Giddy (eds.), International Finance Handbook. (New York: Wiley, 1983), p. 5.

authorities could prohibit domestic sales of any unauthorized issue, which would effectively destroy the market for it. Only the United States and Canada do not place restrictions on the use of their currencies for Eurobonds. Mendelsohn [21] argues, therefore, that only the U.S. and Canadian dollar segments of the market are "true" Eurobonds, reflecting pure market forces.

Because of these regulatory differences, a Eurodollar bond issue can usually be organized and placed more quickly than a comparable U.S. domestic market issue. SEC Rule 415, permitting shelf registration, has reduced the time necessary to launch a U.S. domestic issue, but the Eurobond market may still have certain advantages, especially in the case of a "bought deal." [22] Speed allows the issuer the benefit of seizing favorable "windows" when interest rates are viewed as being unusually low.

Gross spreads in Eurobond issues appear to be relatively high when compared to the U.S. domestic market, but moderate to low in comparison with other European markets (see Table 10.6). It is generally agreed that the selling concession built into Eurobonds is relatively high, and that this plays an important role in primary market pricing (as we will discuss in the next two sections). [23] Offsetting the high spreads, annual interest expense is generally lower in the Eurobond market than in domestic markets. The average size of this interest differential is difficult to measure, but in May 1982, the yield advantage of the Eurobond market to U.S. borrowers was roughly 75 basis points for a five-year issue. [24] Investors have been willing to pay a higher price for Eurobonds than, for example, comparable domestic bonds of the same U.S. firm because Eurobonds are generally issued in bearer form, and there are no taxes withheld on interest payments. Recent U.S. legislation has removed the 30% withholding tax on new issues of government and corporate bonds sold to foreigners. This new development may pose a considerable challenge to the Eurobond market. Historically, however, the actual cost of funds has been lower in either the Eurobond market or domestic capital markets, depending on prevailing conditions.

The overall growth in Eurobond issues was pointed out in Table 10.1. It is important to highlight other key dimensions of the market. Table 10.3 shows the breakdown of Eurobond issuers. Almost half of all issues were by governments, state enterprises, or international organizations. U.S. companies were responsible for 13.5% of all issues. The distribution of Eurobond issues by currency of denomination is reported in Table 10.4. Overall, the Eurodollar segment accounts for two-thirds of

Table 10.3   Eurobond Issues, 1972–1981

	Value (in millions)	Percentage
U.S companies	US$19,088	13.5
Non-U.S. companies	52,855	37.3
State enterprises	35,777	25.2
Governments	20,743	14.6
International organizations	13,266	9.4

Source: Morgan Guaranty Trust Company, *World Financial Markets,* various issues.

Table 10.4 Eurobond Issues by Currency of Denomination, 1972–1981 (in millions of U.S. dollars)

Currency	1972	1973	1974	1975	1976	1977	1978	1979	1980	1981	1972–1981 (percentage)
U.S. dollar	$3,908	$2,447	$996	$3,738	$9,125	$11,628	$7,290	$12,565	$16,427	$26,830	67.0%
Deutsche mark	1,129	1,025	344	2,278	2,713	4,109	5,251	3,626	3,607	1,277	17.9
Dutch guilder	393	194	381	719	502	361	394	531	1,043	529	2.9
Canadian dollar	15	0	60	558	1,407	674	0	425	279	634	2.9
French franc	491	166	0	293	39	0	0	NA	NA	NA	0.7
European Composite Units	0	99	174	371	99	28	165	253	65	309	1.1
Other	398	262	179	610	443	935	1,025	1,326	2,549	2,037	6.9

Source. Morgan Guaranty Trust Company. *World Financial Markets*, various issues.

Note. NA—figures not available.

**Table 10.5   Secondary Market
Turnover: Trading Volume, 1972–1982
($ billion equivalent)**

	Euro-clear	Cedel	Total
1972	11.0	6.0	17.0
1973	11.1	10.2	21.3
1974	8.2	8.1	16.3
1975	14.3	14.2	28.5
1976	37.0	29.7	66.7
1977	65.2	38.6	103.8
1978	77.1	39.7	116.8
1979	102.8	54.7	157.5
1980	160.5	80.3	240.8
1981	242.0	155.0	397.0
1982	510.0	332.0	842.0

Sources: Years 1972–1980 are from Frederick G. Fisher, *International Bonds.*
(London: Euromoney Publications, 1981),
p. 177. Years 1981–1982 are from Peter,
Koenig, "The Great Liquidity Debate,"
Institutional Investor, (May 1983a), pp.
153–66.

Note: Total excludes the majority of
deutsche mark denominated bonds, which
are handled through the German Kassen-
vereine system.

the market, but there is considerable variation from year to year. In 1978, when the
dollar was declining sharply on foreign exchange markets, the Eurodollar segment
was 51.6% of the market. In 1982, with foreign exchange conditions reversed, the
Eurodollar share reached 85%. The average size for new Eurodollar issues exceeds
$100 million (see Figure 10.1), a good deal larger than for nondollar denominated
issues. Secondary market trading in Eurobonds has grown simultaneously with new
issue volume, as illustrated in Table 10.5. The average maturities for new Eurobond
issues is plotted in Figure 10.3. The general trend for maturities is clearly downward,
reflecting the increase in risks associated with interest rate and exchange rate
volatility.

APPRAISING THE PERFORMANCE OF THE EUROBOND MARKET

In this section we offer an analysis of the performance of the Eurobond market as an
institution. We begin by describing the initial conditions when the first Eurobond
issues were launched. A discussion of strategic steps taken by Eurobond underwriters
in order to develop the market follows, and we then assess the competitive conditions
that have resulted in Eurobond underwriting.

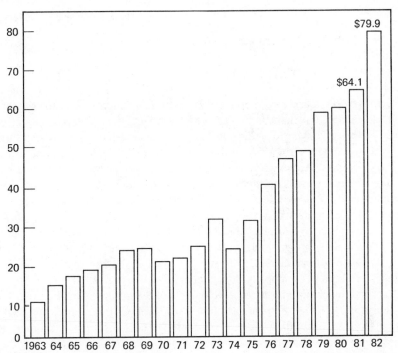

Figure 10.1a Growth in Eurobond issue size, 1963–1980 (average issue amount $ million equivalent)

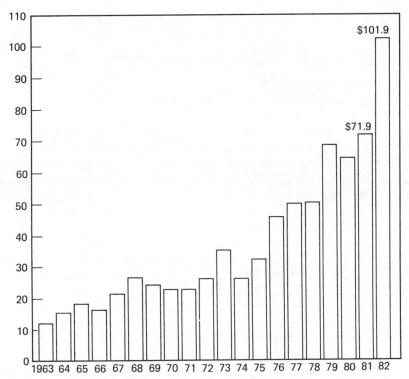

Figure 10.1b Growth of Eurodollar bond issue size, 1963–1980 (average issue amount $ million)

Economic Policies and Euromarkets in 1963

As noted earlier, the first Eurobond issue occurred in 1957. Over $500 million was raised through 22 Eurobond issues over the period 1957–1962.[25] At about this time the Euro*currency* market—the offshore market for short-term loans and deposits— was taking shape. Given the large share of international transactions denominated in dollars, it was reasonable to predict that Europeans and other offshore residents would soon demand longer-term offshore assets denominated in dollars, as well as Euro- currency deposits. Although natural forces were in place, the development of the Eurobond market was enhanced by the enactment of the Interest Equalization Tax in the United States, taking effect on July 18, 1963.[26] The IET was proposed as a tem- porary measure to reduce U.S. capital outflows and take pressure off the U.S. balance of payments deficit. The IET operated like an excise tax on American purchases of new or outstanding foreign stocks and bonds. To no one's surprise, the IET effectively closed the Yankee bond market; to the surprise of some, the foreign borrowers simply migrated offshore to London and Luxembourg.[27]

A second major stimulus to the development of the Eurobond market was the im- position of the Office of Foreign Direction Investment (OFDI) controls on U.S. mul- tinationals financing of their overseas ventures. The controls began in February 1965 on a voluntary basis and were made mandatory in January 1968 to reduce U.S. capital outflows and improve the balance of payments. By 1968, the OFDI controls effec- tively forced U.S. multinationals offshore to meet their financing needs for foreign projects.

Both the IET and OFDI controls were extended several times until January 1974, when both were scrapped. In 1974, with both foreign borrowers and U.S. multina- tionals free to use U.S. capital markets, the volume of Eurobond issues fell to $2.1 billion, its low for the decade. However, volume has been rising sharply and more or less steadily ever since.

The Eurobond market has survived and prospered because it satisfies economic demands that are not fulfilled by other markets. Earlier, it was suggested that some demand for Eurobonds is natural, because many non-Americans desire to issue or hold dollar-denominated securities. Demand was increased further because securities sold by U.S. companies domestically are generally in registered form, and, until July 1984, the United States applied a 30% withholding tax on interest payments to for- eigners. One could also argue that for some groups of borrowers (e.g., large, well- known firms) and investors (e.g., large, well-informed), domestic security market regulations represent a disincentive that can be reduced with little risk by taking trans- actions offshore.[28]

Fisher[29] notes with appropriate irony that the U.S. IET controls, "intentionally prejudicial" to non-American borrowers, ultimately led to the "largest international capital market the world has known." The 1963–1974 period of relative protection was essential for Euromarket participants to develop professional relationships among themselves, client relationships with issuers, as well as the issuing techniques ap- propriate to the new market.[30] It would be a mistake, however, to assume that the Eurobond market developed in a risk-free environment. As in any securities market, interest-rate and credit uncertainties led to investment and underwriting risks. In addition, the currency of denomination for most Eurobonds was foreign to most investors, and so underwriters faced the risk that demand for bonds would shift because of unexpected exchange rate movements. As we have seen (Table 10.4) investors were more willing to accumulate an issue if the currency of denomination was expected to appreciate. Existing Eurobond underwriters always faced the risk that the IET would be scrapped, and in 1974, when the IET was finally eliminated and OFDI controls were phased out, Eurobond market volume collapsed to one-third the 1972 level (Table 10.1). Finally, because there were no regulatory barriers to entry, existing underwriters have faced the risk of entry by new competitors. And as we have seen, this competition may also come from the U.S. domestic market now that withholding taxes on interest payments to foreigners have been abolished.

Strategies of Eurobond Underwriters

To operate in this new market, Eurobond underwriters developed a variety of strategies and techniques to expand the market while controlling risks. The standard syndicate structure in the Eurobond market is described by the three-tier framework illustrated in Figure 10.2. Members of the underwriting syndicate agree to buy the issue from the issuer. In the U.S. domestic market, all underwriters are signatories to the underwriting agreement, and therefore have a "direct (several) obligation to the issuer.[31] In the Eurobond market, *underwriters* (as the term appears in Figure 10.2) in Englishstyle (but not Americanstyle) deals bear *no* obligation to the issuer.[32]

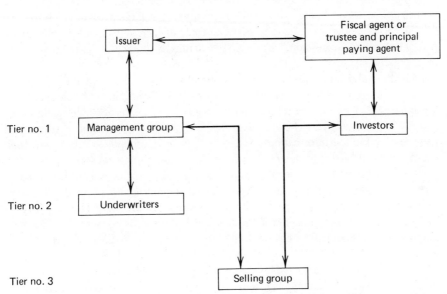

Figure 10.2   Three-Tier Framework for Eurobond syndication. (*Source:* Frederick G. Fisher, *International Bonds,* Euromoney Publications, London, 1981, p. 75.)

There is also a selling group with no underwriting responsibility. Once an allocation of securities is made, all parties are free to sell the issue as they see fit.[33] The lead management group attempts to instill discipline through economic incentives and disincentives, such as refusing to invite a seller into future syndicates. Large syndicates are used in efforts to maximize market demand and insure a successful issue. In the late 1970s, underwriting groups grew to 175 firms, with an additional 150 members in the selling group.[34] Naturally in groups this large, some members would be unable to place their full allocation, resulting in price-stabilization and discipline problems for the lead managers. Because Eurobonds are chiefly in bearer form, members of the selling group could unload unwanted bonds in a discreet way with little probability of being traced.[35]

The *gray market* or *premarket* involves a set of activities that formalize trading in Eurobonds prior to the official offering date. Professional dealers display their transaction prices over the Reuters Monitor and a market price is established.[36] Other sources publish gray market prices more widely.[37] The gray market reduces risks for members of the selling group by allowing them to participate in an organized market if conditions (demand for bonds, interest rate, or exchange rate developments, etc.) do not evolve as expected. The gray market also alleviates risks for lead managers because it provides additional information on the market's response to the issue (i.e., the extent of dumping) and whether the terms of the issue ought to be altered. The gray market can, in addition, provide information on the extent of ''overpricing'' to investors who pay full price on the day of issue. This concern arises because, as we noted in the previous section, there is reason to believe that spreads (in particular the selling concession) are relatively high on the Eurobond market. A large selling concession may have been appropriate in terms of sales to individuals or as a sweetener to attract sellers in a newly developing market. But large institutional buyers in the Eurobond market have had the power to force distributing groups to share all or part of the selling concession.[38] The market can thus exhibit a two-tier pricing system on any given issue.[39]

Managers and underwriters in the Eurobond market have adopted a number of straightforward procedures to increase the demand for bonds and to be compensated for additional risks. The Eurobond market began as a market for high-quality borrowers, and it continues to be dominated by recognized names. Higher quality compensates for limited information disclosure.[40] Most Eurobonds are listed on stock exchanges, as a marketing device to make the securities eligible for some institutional portfolios, to comply with legal requirements for sales in many countries, and to promote investor confidence. Both Moody's and Standard & Poor provide Eurobond ratings services. Spreads increase with the maturity of Eurobonds (see Table 10.6) to compensate for the greater risks involved.[41] We have also observed the average maturity of Eurobonds has declined (see Figure 10.3) as interest-rate risk has increased.

Eurobond underwriters have invented or adapted other innovative syndication approaches and issuing techniques. Prior to 1979, the standard Eurobond invitation telex included the expected coupon rate based on current market conditions. In contrast, U.S. domestic issues were priced on a yield basis after intensive discussions between

Table 10.6   Comparative Gross Spreads in International Bond Markets

	Total	Underwriting Commission	Management Fee	Selling Concession
U.S. domestic market				
estimate 1[a]	0.875–1.0%	0.175	0.200	0.500
estimate 2[b]	0.75 –1.0	NA	NA	NA
estimate 3[c]	0.60 –1.5	NA	NA	NA
Foreign Equity and Bond Markets				
United Kingdom[d]				
Domestic bond market	2.5%	NA	NA	NA
Germany[e]				
Stocks	4.0%	NA	NA	NA
Bonds				
Public	1.625–2.0	0.375–0.5	0–0.25	1.125–1.25
Industrial	2.5	1.00	0.25	1.25
International	1.75 –2.0	0.50 –0.75	0.25	1.00
France[f]				
Bonds				
First category	1.75%	0.50	0.10	1.15
Second category	3.00	0.75	0.25	2.00
Switzerland[g]				
Bonds				
Government	1.50%	NA	NA	NA
Foreign	3.00	NA	NA	NA
Eurobond market[h]				
Under 5 years	2.00%	0.375	0.375	1.25
5–8 years	2.25	0.375	0.375	1.25
more than 8 years	2.50	0.500	0.500	1.50

Notes: [a]M. S. Mendelsohn, *Money on the Move.* (New York: McGraw-Hill, 1980), p. 183; and Mendelsohn "Eurobond Markets," 1983, p. 18.

[b]Antoine W., Van Agtmael, "Issuance of Eurobonds: Syndication and Underwriting Techniques and Costs," Section 5.2 in A. George I. Giddy (eds.), *International Finance Handbook,* (New York: Wiley, 1983), p. 5.

[c]Frederick G. Fisher, "Imagination Wins Again," *Euromoney* (February 1981), p. 81.

[d]James E. Maycock, "United Kingdom: Banking, Money and Bond Markets," Section 4.3 in A. George and I. Giddy (eds.), *International Finance Handbook.* (New York: Wiley, 1983), p. 5.

[e]Gunter Dufey, and Krishnan, E., "West Germany: Banking, Money and Bond Markets," Section 4.4 in A. George and I. Giddy (eds.), *International Finance Handbook.* (New York: Wiley, 1983), p. 22.

[f]Florin Aftalion, and Bompaire, Frederick, "France: Banking, Money and Bond Markets," Section 4.5 in A. George and I. Giddy (eds.), *International Finance Handbook,* (New York: Wiley), 1983, p. 7.

[g]Mario A. Corti, "Switzerland: Banking, Money and Bond Markets," Section 4.6 in A. George and I. Giddy (eds.), *International Finance Handbook.* (New York: Wiley, 1983), pp. 40, 45.

[h]M. S. Mendelsohn, *Money on the Move.* (New York: McGraw-Hill, 1980), p. 184

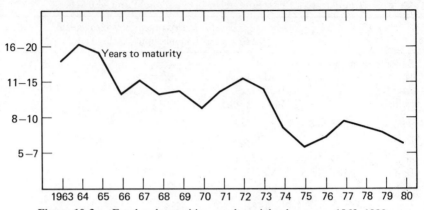

Figure 10.3a   Eurobond maturities: yearly weighted average, 1963–1980

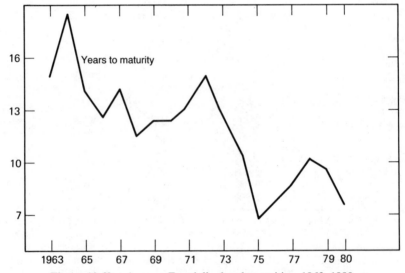

Figure 10.3b   Average Eurodollar bond maturities, 1963–1980

the lead manager and other syndicate members. Consequently a U.S. syndicate could better fix a yield consistent with secondary market conditions and investor demand. Coupon, issue price, and total commissions were set after the selling period without being indicated in the invitation telex.[42] The Eurobond market adapted this U.S. market practice, known as *yield pricing,* enabling the lead manager to work with a smaller syndicate, improve pricing control, better estimate demand, and reduce the need for discipline.

The *bought deal* or pre-underwritten issue was introduced in early 1979. The underwriter telexes that funds are available on specific terms for a short period. If the deal is accepted and successful, the issue should close quickly, the lead manager alone placing most or all of the issue. Under volatile market conditions, the speed of a bought deal is valuable to issuers, but the manager is exposed to greater underwriting risks.[43]

Other examples of issuing techniques are the *auction issue, conversion issue, multiple-tranche issue, deferred purchase issue, convertible issue,* issues *indexed to commodities* or *currencies,* and issues *with warrants attached.*[44] To some extent, these techniques may be viewed as fads or sweeteners to address uncertainties that momentarily concern the market. Some issuing innovations, such as *floating rate notes,* however, have captured substantial market shares and seem to be a permanent and growing feature of the market.[45]

Finally, we should mention the role of Euro-clear and Cedel, the two computerized depositary, clearing and information networks for the Eurobond market. Both systems were founded by private parties—Euro-clear in 1968 by Morgan Guaranty Trust Company and Cedel in 1971 by a group of shareholder institutions. In 1972, Morgan Guaranty sold 97% of its interest in Euro-clear to a group of 120 user shareholders,[46] but it continues to manage the system. In 1980, a bridge linking the two systems came into operation.[47] Fisher[48] argues that competition has forced the two systems to become increasingly similar, but Euro-clear maintains a two-thirds market share (see Table 10.5). Both systems, in conjunction with the Reuters Monitor, have improved the technological efficiency of trading in the Eurobond market and promoted new-issue volume.

Asssessing Competitive Conditions in the Eurobond Market

In an important sense, a free market that grows from nonexistence to $50 billion annual new issues in 20 years is a success, by definition. Clearly, the Eurobond market brings together a large number of willing borrowers and lenders with substantial benefits to both groups. Beyond gains to the direct participants, the market fills a gap in international capital markets, speeding the traditional recycling of funds in the 1970s and allowing time for adjustment between deficit and surplus economies.[49] Our objective now is to characterize the orderliness of that free-market setting.

First, in the entire history of the Euromarkets, no bank has failed solely or even mainly because of Eurobond underwriting.[50] The worst shock to hit the market was the failure in June 1974 of Bankhaus Herstatt, a relatively small German institution. The collapse of Herstatt was the result of imprudent foreign exchange activities. In terms of bond defaults, Mendelsohn[51] reports that in the period 1963–1977, $72 billion was raised through 2700 Eurobond issues. Losses to *investors* were 0.24% ($170 million) because of default by 10 small U.S. companies.[52]

The composition of leading Eurobond underwriters has changed considerably during the history of the market. The top 20 underwriting firms as of 1982 and their rankings since 1978 are given in Table 10.7. Among the top 10 firms in 1982, we find five American firms. Of the top 10 firms in 1978, only three (Crédit Suisse First Boston, Deutsche Bank, and Warburg) remained in the top 10 of 1982. Part of the shuffling of ranks is the result of exogenous events—DM weakness on the foreign exchange market prompted the German authorities to be cautious about allowing new DM issues (almost always led by German banks), continued dollar strength has increased demand for Eurodollar bonds (often managed by U.S. houses), and U.S.

Table 10.7 Top 20 Underwriting Firms in the Eurobond Market as of 1982 and Their Ranks in Earlier Years

Firm	1978 Rank	1978 %	1979 Rank	1979 %	1980 Rank	1980 %	1981 Rank	1981 %	1982 Rank	1982 %
Crédit Suisse First Boston	3	6.26	1	11.48	1	9.57	1	13.48	1	15.09
Deutsche Bank	1	23.31	2	8.71	2	8.56	4	5.91	2	10.44
Morgan Stanley	22	1.13	3	4.79	3	6.72	2	6.49	3	7.87
Morgan Guaranty	–	–	–	–	36	0.75	12	2.26	4	4.19
Salomon Brothers	NA	0.30	24	1.26	13	1.81	6	4.43	5	3.76
Merrill Lynch	17	1.41	30	0.88	30	0.96	5	4.68	6	3.64
Swiss Bank Corp.	29	0.82	33	0.85	22	1.46	16	2.06	7	3.63
S. G. Warburg	5	3.58	5	3.77	4	4.32	3	6.02	8	3.37
Goldman Sachs	NA	0.10	13	2.20	5	3.51	13	2.25	9	2.50
Société Générale	16	1.54	6	3.60	8	3.18	10	2.50	10	2.12
Union Bank of Switzerland	9	2.31	10	2.78	19	1.65	15	2.07	11	1.98
Dresdner Bank	4	5.55	7	3.40	7	3.26	–	–	12	1.60
Commerzbank	7	2.63	21	1.41	20	1.62	–	–	13	1.53
Nomura	12	1.92	16	1.93	24	1.19	7	2.85	14	1.53
Amsterdam-Rotterdam	16	2.76	26	1.07	16	1.74	30	0.81	15	1.49
Orion Royal Bank	14	1.63	12	2.28	11	2.22	8	2.72	16	1.42
Crédit Lyonnais	19	1.22	15	2.15	29	1.03	34	0.72	17	1.41
Citicorp	27	0.94	11	2.30	12	1.97	23	1.22	18	1.37
Manufacturers Hanover	–	–	14	2.15	–	–	25	1.01	19	1.30
West deutsche Landesbank	2	9.83	4	4.78	10	2.23	18	1.35	20	1.23

Source: Prepared by Clifford Austin Billinghurst for Morgan Guaranty Ltd., London.

Note: Eurobonds include Floating Rate Notes and bond issues in all currencies. Percentages are calculated by allocating the full amount of the issue to sole lead managers and equal amounts to joint lead managers.

borrowers have returned to the market in large numbers (generally choosing U.S. underwriters). In 1978 the situation was reversed, and German and Swiss banks dominated the list with only two U.S. houses in the top 20. Mendelsohn[53] notes that, going back 10 years further, U.S. houses again dominated the list as American companies, driven away from the U.S. market by OFDI requirements, were heavy borrowers in the Eurobond market. Only in the 1970s did "placing power" assume importance and cause the Swiss, German, and other European banks to enter into the top ranks of underwriters.

Concentration ratios for Eurobond underwriters are reported in Table 10.8. Percentage shares are calculated by awarding full credit to a lead manager and equal credit to joint lead managers. The data suggest a slight decline in concentration among the top 10 houses, but this may reflect the decline in the role of the DM after 1978. Comparable ratios for U.S. investment banking are shown in Table 10.9, which gives full credit to the lead manager. The market share of the largest firm is approximately the same in both the U.S. and Eurobond markets. However, the concentration ratios for the largest five through 25 firms is considerably smaller in the Eurobond market. The inference is that competitive forces are greater among Eurobond underwriters. (Note that affiliates of U.S. commercial banks listed in Table 10.7 include Morgan Guaranty, Citicorp, and Manufacturers Hanover.)

In their study of U.S. investment banking, Hayes et al.[54] argue that the stability of client relationships over time is a significant indicator of competition. Switching of relationships suggests the presence of competitive forces, whereas inertia in relationships may create a persistent state of market disequilibrium. The authors conclude that although relationships give the appearance of fluidity, the major apex firms have maintained a firm hold on the large and important clients in the U.S. domestic market. However, we may expect to observe some differences between "bought

Table 10.8   Concentration Ratios in Eurobond Underwriting, 1978–1982

	1978	1979	1980	1981	1982
Top 1	23%	11%	10%	13%	15%
Top 4	45	30	29	32	38
Top 5	49	34	33	37	41
Top 8	56	44	43	47	52
Top 10	61	49	47	52	57
Top 15	70	60	57	63	65
Top 25	82	76	72	76	77

Source: Prepared by Clifford Austin Billinghurst from *Investment Dealers' Digest.*

Note: Eurobonds include Floating Rate Notes and bond issues in all currencies. Percentages are calculated by allocating the full amount of the issue to sole lead managers and equal amounts to joint lead managers.

Table 10.9   U.S. Concentration Ratios in the Underwriting Business, 1975–1983

	1975	1976	1977	1978	1979	1980	1981	1982
Top 1	21%	23%	24%	23%	18%	18%	18%	18%
Top 4	55	59	57	57	55	50	56	60
Top 5	63	66	64	64	63	59	64	69
Top 8	79	79	78	80	79	79	78	83
Top 10	87	85	83	86	85	84	84	88
Top 15	97	92	93	94	94	93	92	95
Top 25	100	97	99	98	98	98	97	99

Source: Investment Dealers' Digest annual Directories of corporate finance for 1975 to 1982. Percentage of total dollar volume of underwritings using figures giving full credit to the manager handling the books.

deals'' and Rule 415 issues. The latter appear to be making the U.S. market more competitive.

Evidence from the Euromarket suggests a considerable degree of switching among management syndicates. Mendelsohn[55] notes that although a few major firms may dominate the rankings, ''one does not find the same group of managers united in an offering with monotonous regularity.'' An analysis by *Euromoney* of two top-ranking underwriters, Crédit Suisse and Deutsche Bank, drew similar conclusions.[56]

Finally we compiled data on the number of lead managers used by issuers with three or more Eurodollar bond issues outstanding (see Table 10.10). For the sample of 107 issuers, 75% had used the services of two or more lead managers. For the

Table 10.10   Number of Lead Managers for Agencies with Three or More Eurodollar Bond Issues[a]

		Number of Lead Managers							
		1	2	3	4	5	6–10	More than 10	Total
	3	12	8	7	NA	NA	NA	NA	27
	4	9	3	7	2	NA	NA	NA	21
Number	5	5	7	1	1	0	NA	NA	14
of	6–10	3	8	4	6	2	7	NA	30
Issues	11–15	1	1	0	1	1	2	0	6
	16–20	0	1	0	0	1	1	0	3
	More than 20	0	1	0	2	0	1	2	6
	Total	30[b]	29	19	12	4	11	2	107

Source: Based on information in *Weekly Eurobond Guide,* October 28, 1983.

Notes: [a]Reflects issues outstanding on October 28, 1983. Agencies include corporations, governmental bodies, and supranational agencies. Bond issues include straight bonds, zero coupon bonds and floating rate notes.

[b]Includes 5 banks who lead managed all of their own issues.

For all companies with three or more issues, percentage with two or more managers is 77/107 = 75%.

entire group, the average number of issues is about six and the average number of managers nearly three. This reflects both aggressive bidding for new business by underwriters and the willingness of issuers to switch lead manager affiliations.

PROBLEMS AND RISKS IN THE EUROBOND MARKET

The evidence in the two previous sections portrays the Eurobond market as a dynamic and highly competitive market. Our objective now is to describe some of the most serious criticisms concerning Eurobond market operations. Because the Eurobond market operates subject to a minimum of regulations, it is reasonable to ask whether the U.S. domestic securities market might develop similar "problems" if barriers restricting competition in securities underwriting were removed. It is important to keep in mind that the Euromarket began *de novo* only about 20 years ago, making it essential to distinguish temporary from permanent problems. We will also stress that what may be perceived as "problems" for individual firms (e.g., being forced out of the market) may simply reflect the natural operation of competitive forces that are desirable from a broader perspective.

Degree of Competition

Problems of excessive competition in the Eurobond market have been cited for the last 10 years. The alleged problem manifests itself in two ways: (1) too many houses competing for a position on tombstones and (2) mispricing caused by houses bidding too aggressively for new issues. Obviously, these are relative statements and are difficult to characterize as "problems." There may indeed be too many houses competing relative to the number that would allow existing houses to make fair underwriting profits. And new issues, priced *ex ante* with incomplete information, may appear mispriced relative to the price necessary to clear the market *ex post*, after the actual market demand has been revealed.

Regarding the first point, Mendelsohn[57] argues that "most banks are in the new issue market for prestige rather than money." With simple arithmetic, it is easily shown that underwriting returns are heavily skewed toward the managers, and the remainder of the selling group receives very little.[58] Gewirtz[59] maintains that rankings on the league table of active issuers may be important, but many houses see their presence in the Eurobond market as defensive. A house that cannot service a borrower offshore may lose the borrower's business onshore as well. Many houses are still small but expect to grow, covering current underwriting losses with secondary market trading profits.[60]

The first problem of many houses competing for business contributes to the second problem. If an oversupply of houses is vying for syndicate participations, lead managers will be encouraged to bid more aggressively for new issues. Gewirtz[61] concludes that "as long as underwriting syndicates are used to swallow mispriced deals, the problem will never go away." As long as competition does not destabilize the system, however, it is immaterial that some institutions lose money on some deals.

The excess competition problem is serious because it leads to other difficulties. Houses that accept allocations for prestige may have to dump their securities in the gray market. Houses without placing power may be easy targets for professional buyers seeking discounts. This leads to two-tier pricing and problems of syndicate discipline, although not necessarily problems related to institutional safety and soundness.

Although shortages or surpluses sometimes arise in a particular market, when competition exists these conditions are both temporary and self-correcting. In 1977, *Euromoney* commented that although ''Underwriters are given several opportunities to drop out of an issue . . . in the Euromarkets underwriters seldom drop out . . . not only because they would lose their underwriting fee, but they would lose face with the manager if they did so.''[62] Less than four years later, in an article focusing on the return of realistic pricing, *Euromoney* reported that as a consequence of past losses, ''banks increased the number of underwritings they refused. The refusal rate, it is thought, was running at 30% at the end of last year. This has almost certainly increased to over 50.%''[63] Continuing the trend, Engel noted ''sharply reduced willingness of banks to support mispriced issues.''[64] He argued that the development of a highly liquid gray market has permitted managers to observe prices firsthand. ''The mechanism (of the gray market) is so effective and so anonymous that some lead managers have ended up buying virtually the whole of an issue whose price they chose to defend.''[65]

Thus at present the problem of excess competition appears to have eased. Syndicate members have some scope for refusing mispriced deals, and lead managers have increased incentives for accurate pricing.

Secondary Market Liquidity

Closely related to primary market problems is the efficiency of secondary market transactions. Mendelsohn[66] indicates that the secondary market for Eurobonds used to be described ''accurately, if unkindly, as consisting of a broker telephoning himself.'' This is still the case for some among the 3600 Eurobond issues currently outstanding.[67] Liquidity was not an essential factor in the early days of the market, when bonds were held to maturity primarily by individual investors. Now that institutional buyers dominate the market, liquidity is an important factor. Engel[68] argues that it will cost borrowers more if the manager does not have a long-term commitment to the issue in the secondary market. Lead managers generally respond that their primary responsibility is to the issuers, not to other professional market makers. They participate in market making, but capital allocated to this activity must be balanced against other considerations.[69] By some measures—volume of new issues (Table 10.1) and secondary market trading (Table 10.5)—liquidity has grown substantially. However, formal tests of transaction costs and efficiency of the Eurobond market have not been reported.

''Excessive'' Spreads

Although transaction costs in the secondary market are not known, the breakdown of primary market gross spreads is widely publicized (see Table 10.6). As noted, spreads in the Eurobond market appear high relative to the U.S. domestic market, but moderate relative to foreign markets. The origin of these costs lies in the crucial role played by the Continental banks in placing a new issue. Initially, it was essential to have the cooperation of Continental banks in order to guarantee the success of a new issue. To get the full cooperation of distributors, it was necessary to provide compensation at least equal to what they earned on domestic issues. Because sales to individuals predominated, the large selling concessions may have been justified. After large institutional buyers entered the market, the generous spread "became an anachronism," and two-tiered pricing resulted.[70]

It is difficult to judge where matters stand at the present time. Mendelsohn[71] argues that Continental banks are still the marginal sellers of an issue and therefore set the price for services, even though their role in the market is smaller than it was initially. On the other hand, Engel[72] claims that "large-scale placing at about the same price level throughout the market" is characteristic of current practice. The issue of uniform primary market pricing is important because it affects our assessment of conflicts of interest, as discussed below.

The notion of "excessive" spreads might also be interpreted to mean excessive relative to the underwriting risks incurred. We have already noted the asymmetric structure of fees earned by syndicate members. Those in the selling group earn very little, but this seems commensurate with the risks involved. A member of the selling group holds no underwriting risk; the seller need request bonds only if he has a buyer. The seller might request more bonds than he knows he can sell (1) if he wants to appear as a larger force in the market and improve his image, or (2) if the manager is likely to allot him only a fraction of his request. In either case, the seller will have unsold bonds that can be dumped anonymously in the gray market. Managers, on the other hand, bear true underwriting risk, but Mendelsohn[73] argues that the risk is "significantly small," because "issues are largely circled before the underwriting agreements are signed, and . . . in most instances the circling commitment is honored." This observation seems consistent with the less-disciplined syndicate organization and the reluctance of managers to pursue syndicate members for excess underwriting costs. If profits were more scarce and less certain, organizational arrangements would change.

Managers feel (relatively) secure with their risks because new issues are largely circled. Issuers feel secure because they can compete among lead managers for the best terms and the best services. The members of the selling group generally feel secure with their positions because allocations can be sold forward in the gray market. This leaves only the buyers to protect their interests, and these as noted, are dominated by large players.

Conflicts of Interest

Conflicts of interest in the Eurobond market do not seem to pose serious problems even in the absence of external regulation.[74] The primary conflict of interest cited in the literature is for Continental banks, which simultaneously underwrite new issues and carry responsibility for individual investment funds. It is claimed that the placing power of many Continental banks comes precisely from their ability to sell new issues to relatively passive clients.[75] In addition to the question of whether the Continental banks can perform unbiased investment analysis for their investment accounts, is the issue of two-tier pricing. Continental banks with a vested interest in underwriting the new issue are presumed to buy for their clients at par (retail) rather than passing along any institutional discounts, or discounts that might be apparent from gray market prices prior to the formal issue date. The investment managers under such conditions hardly perform a "best-efforts" service on behalf of their clients.

Sales of this nature, from bank underwriting department to investment clients, are not allowed under U.S. regulations. And disclosure of transactions and gray market prices would allow individuals to monitor the performance of their portfolios.

Still, if owners of individual investment accounts are being "stuffed," why don't they move their accounts elsewhere? The answer is that individual trusts receive the tremendous tax advantage of bearer bonds and no taxes withheld on interest, which more than offsets the extra 1% or 2% they may have paid on issue, and the fact that a few bonds of questionable quality may have crept into the portfolio. It is a reasonable bargain for all the participants to have struck. The real problem is the limited extent of price competition in the supply of "secrecy services"—it appears that individual account holders must sacrifice some performance to obtain secrecy.[76]

The Gray Market

The gray market, or pre-market, was originally perceived as a threat to an orderly primary Eurobond market with uniform pricing. The gray market made it easier for members of the selling group to break ranks with the syndicate and dump their allocations early—actually, to sell them today for future delivery.

In the short run, it is not clear whether the gray market helped to fragment pricing further, or simply brought the extent of weakness in any new issue under public scrutiny. Over the longer run, it is clear that the second effect has dominated. The gray market is credited with helping to increase the liquidity of the primary market. It also offers new information to syndicate managers by indicating the market's response to a new issue. It provides a useful reference point with respect to pricing. By increasing liquidity and providing information, the gray market decreases the chance for issue mispricing and increases the chance for a successful offering. The gray market could also supply a reference point for individual investors to evaluate the performance of investment managers. As such, it potentially reduces the practice of "stuffing" individual investment accounts, as noted above.

Effectiveness of the Self-Regulatory Organization

Although the Eurobond market operates with minimal government regulation, participants in the market have found it in their interest to establish a self-regulatory body. The Association of International Bond Dealers (AIBD) fills this role. AIBD was founded in 1969 under Swiss law and is based in Zürich.[77] Membership is nearly 600, and includes all the major financial institutions active in either primary or secondary markets. The Board of AIBD has created several subcommittees to study general areas of concern, such as education, settlements, market practices, and so forth. The Association holds an annual meeting each April to consider specific proposals.

Mendelsohn[78] asserts that AIBD's major role has been in secondary market trading, and that the Association's authority concerning primary market practices is not accepted. Even though most Eurobonds are exchange-listed, most secondary market trading takes place over-the-counter through market-makers recognized by AIBD.[79] In the primary market, there is no way to recognize a bona fide member of the brokerage community entitled to selling reallowance (i.e., wholesale price reduction). Consequently, price cutting in the primary market depends on individual market power.

Complaints by underwriters concerning primary market practices have been a regular theme of trade publications.[80] Smaller firms complain of being stuck with mispriced issues, and being left out when quality paper comes to the market. The larger firms point out their discipline problems, and the difficulties of stabilizing a price when small underwriters dump in the gray market. Although the Association's Primary Market Committee has discussed the mispricing of new issues and related problems, the debate has never been raised in public at an annual meeting. As noted earlier, the refusal rate among underwriters has risen, and the spread of new issue prices has converged so that, to some extent, these primary market problems have been self-correcting.

For its part, AIBD prefers to deal with technical issues—Eurobond settlements, a specialized calculator for Eurobond dealers, a standardized form for all bonds—and it appears to be fairly successful in these pursuits.[81] It has left insoluble problems (such as trying to enforce a code or realistic new issue pricing) to be worked out by the market. AIBD does not possess any statutory powers, and so it must operate on consensus. The membership recognizes the need for self-regulation (to promote investor confidence and demand), but also realizes that freedom from regulatory constraints has contributed enormously to the growth and success of the market. Given this history, it seems that AIBD will seek market solutions to problems rather than attempting to impose rules of behavior.

Distinguishing Micro Problems from Macro Problems

In 1982, 780 new Eurobond issues were launched, raising over $50 billion. Secondary market trading volume surpassed $800 billion. Given these orders of magnitude and the volatility of exchange rates and interest rates, it seems unlikely that all transactions could have been executed without problems, or that there were no frictions among competing parties. However, it is important to differentiate between problems that affect a single issue, an individual firm, or a particular time period, and problems that are life-threatening to the Eurobond market as a whole and to its constituent institutions.

Trade publications delight in describing broken deals, perhaps more so than great successes.[82] The chance of launching an issue when interest rates or exchange rates change suddenly, or trying an innovative issuing approach (e.g., the zero-coupon Eurobond) that suddenly loses market favor is an integral part of the underwriting risk.[83] Naturally, mistakes of this sort (and underwriting losses) occur, but the market appears to learn quickly and to respond rationally. Activity ceases and maturities shorten in response to interest rate volatility. Firms seek other innovations (e.g., Floating Rate Notes), or return to traditional straight debt, depending on demand conditions in the market.[84]

To a great extent, then, micro problems (i.e., problems of individual issues, firms, or time periods) in the Eurobond market appear to have been self-correcting without threatening its overall integrity. Operating in the absence of statutory regulation is not a license for stupidity—it is almost the contrary. Underwriters who make mistakes must either learn from experience or leave the market. Problems of excess competition and mispricing appear to have been attenuated by members of selling groups learning to refuse bad deals, and by a gray market that sends an early warning to lead managers.

Large borrowers appear to be well treated in the Eurobond market. They have shown a propensity to switch lead managers and to shop for the best deal. Large investors and institutions also have the skill to spot mispriced deals and the power to extract fair pricing. Only the ''small'' investor whose funds are managed by some Continental banks appears to be at a perpetual disadvantage. This problem could be reduced if investment managers were required to perform in the best interests of their clients at arm's length from the same firm's underwriting activities. Considering the tax advantages captured by these ''small'' investors, their ''revealed preference'' to incur these costs for the benefit of secrecy may in fact suit their individual needs.

SCOPE FOR INCREASING COMPETITION IN U.S. INVESTMENT BANKING

The first four sections of this chapter analyzed the operations of the Eurobond market. Competition among managers and underwriters is virtually unrestrained in the U.S. dollar and Canadian dollar segment of this market. Proposals to increase competition in U.S. investment banking would repeal the Glass-Steagall Act and permit separately capitalized securities affiliates of U.S. commercial banks to perform the full range of investment banking services for corporations and municipalities.[85] This is currently the case in most of the world's major developed countries.

Our purpose in this section is first to review the experience with combined commercial and investment banking in the rest of the world, and to draw lessons concerning conflicts of interest, operational efficiency, and related issues. We then combine these findings with our analysis of the Eurobond market to assess the chances for a favorable transplant of competitive Eurobond underwriting practices into the U.S. domestic market.

Permissible Bank Activities Worldwide

An overview of permissible banking activities across countries is presented in Table 10.11. Among these countries, only Canada and Japan have regulations similar to

Table 10.11   International Comparison of Permissible Business Activities for deposit-taking Banks

1. United States	Commercial banks are not allowed to underwrite corporate securities or municipal revenue bonds. They may underwrite U.S. Government and general obligation bonds and arrange private placements. Restrictions on interstate banking and nonbank activities.
2. Belgium	Banks may hold equity shares in connection with their underwriting activity.
3. Canada	Insurance, fiduciary, and underwriting activities are not allowed. Banks cannot own more than 10% of shares in a nonbank company.
4. France	Underwriting allowed. Deposit banks may hold up to 20% of shares in a nonbank company. Investment banks may hold up to 100% of shares in a nonbank company, only financed by deposits greater than or equal to two years maturity.
5. Germany	Universal banking, banks engage in all financial activities. Banks hold a legal monopoly on all securities brokerage activities.
6. Hong Kong	Underwriting allowed. Banks cannot hold more than 25% of their capital in nonbank company shares.
7. Italy	Underwriting allowed. Banks cannot hold more than 2% of their capital in nonbank company shares.
8. Japan	American pattern. Underwriting prohibited except for public sector bonds and by bank overseas subsidiaries.
9. Luxembourg	No statutory restrictions.
10. Netherlands	Underwriting allowed. No direct restrictions on bank activities. Equity participations greater than 5% are subject to approval.
11. Singapore	No separation of commercial and investment banking. Banks cannot hold more than 25% of their capital in nonbank company shares.
12. Switzerland	Universal banking. No formal restrictions on banks.
13. United Kingdom	No specific controls. All activities allowed subject to capital adequacy constraints. By tradition, a separation between deposit-taking banks (i.e., accepting houses) and merchant banks (i.e. issuing houses).

Source: Richard Dale, ''Bank Supervision Around the World.'' New York: Group of 30, 1982.

the United States, which prohibit the combination of commercial banking and investment banking activities. Dale[86] notes that in Japan the U.S.-style separation of commercial and investment banking "is regarded as an historical accident rather than a prudential necessity." Table 10.11 suggests that banks outside the United States have the right to engage in a wider range of activities, including life insurance, equity participations in nonbanking firms, and security market transactions. An extreme example is in Germany, where the banking act grants a monopoly for all securities brokerage business to banks.[87]

The relationship between the nature of the banking system and the degree of competition or macroeconomic control is complex. Japan emulates the U.S. style of separation between commercial and investment banking, yet official guidance is used heavily to effect interest rates and credit allocation.[88] European countries, on the other hand, allow banks to compete with each other and to offer the widest possible variety of financial services. Yet, as Table 10.12 illustrates, the concentration of commercial banking activities is much higher in Europe than in the United States.[89]

Factors in the United States Favoring a Successful Adaptation of Competitive Eurobond Practices

We now turn to consider those factors in the U.S. economy that would either complement the positive features of the Eurobond market or offset the negative features described earlier. For the sake of this exercise, we assume that concentration (and returns) in the U.S. investment banking industry are currently high relative to a fully competitive industry (see Chapter 5). Regulation has prohibited one natural group of competitors (commercial banks) from entering the market. High economic costs have restricted new competition from the United States and abroad from entering the market and reducing concentration.

The Eurobond market is close to a textbook example of a purely competitive market.[90] As such, it is not difficult to enumerate the key features that contributed to the growth and stability of that market:[91]

1. Financial expertise: Skilled people to establish realistic offering prices, adjust for changing market conditions, innovate new products, and contain risks.
2. Techniques for risk management: Formation of large syndicates, well-known issuers, forward sales in the gray market, yield pricing.
3. Marketing expertise: Knowledge of borrower and investor preferences concerning issue costs, information disclosure, tax benefits, and so forth; access to an effective distribution system.
4. Communications technology: Reuters monitor; Euro-clear and Cedel for clearing transactions.
5. Liquid secondary markets: To promote primary market demand.
6. Financial capital: To absorb temporary losses.

We assert without formal proof that these features of the Eurobond market are also characteristic of U.S. financial markets and U.S. commercial banks. By analogy, if

Table 10.12   International Comparison of Market Shares of Major Banks, 1979

		Percentage of Liabilities of:		
		Commercial Banks	Deposit-taking Institutions	All Financial Institutions
Germany	big three banks[a]	51	13	11
France	big three banks	61	25	18
Italy	big five banks	43	23	19
Netherlands	big three banks[a]	80	35	15
Switzerland	big three banks	77	32	17
Sweden	big four banks	87	51	24
Japan	12 city banks	61	30	21
USA	176 money-center banks	43	27	15
UK	London clearing banks[a]	68	38	20

Source: "Wilson Report". Sir Harold Wilson, Chairman of the Committee to Review the Functioning of Financial Institutions, London: Her Majesty's Stationery Office, June 1980.

[a]Based on group figures.
The banks included are as follows:
Germany: Deutsche Bank, Dresdner Bank, Commerzbank
France: Banque Nationale de Paris, Credit Lyonnais, Societe Generale
Italy: Banca Nazionale del Lavoro, Banca Commerciale Italiana, Credito Italiano, Banco di Roma, Banco di Napoli
Netherlands: Algemene Bank Nederland, Amsterdam-Rotterdam Bank, Nederlandsche Middenstandsbank
Switzerland: Swiss Bank Corporation, Union Bank of Switzerland, Swiss Credit Bank
Sweden: PK Banken, Svenska Handelsbanken, Skandinaviska Enskilda Banken, Gotabanken

U.S. investment banking activities were left open to free competition, the level of financial expertise, risk management skills, and communications technology is such to encourage a stable supply of investment banking services at competitive rates.

Our review also noted several negative factors about the Eurobond market and the operation of commercial bank affiliates in that market. Might similar negative features also become part of a U.S. banking system if free competition in corporate financial services were permitted?

1. *Conflict of Interest.*   One potential conflict involves Continental banks and their roles as part of the underwriting group and as managers of investment funds. The suggestion in the literature is that excess underwriting fees or unrealistic prices have been passed along to unsuspecting, usually passive trust accounts. In contrast, "self-dealing" is now prohibited under U.S. regulations and applies to subsidiaries as well as affiliates.[92]

Another conflict arises between banks and corporate borrowers. European practice of combined commercial and investment banking has been associated with relatively close and exclusive ties between banks and nonfinancial corporations. One fear is that the banks might refuse to provide certain commercial banking services (e.g., loans, lines of credit, foreign exchange) to a corporation unless the bank also provides investment banking services. In the United States, such "tie-in" sales are in restraint of competition and prohibited by the Sherman Act.[93] A related fear is that closer bank/ corporate ties might reduce the bank's ability to prepare unbiased loan appraisals or increase the chances for unsound lending. This abuse is a theoretical possibility but rather remote, given that imprudent lending could be detected by astute bank examiners and subject the bank and its management to regulatory sanctions and civil liability.[94]

2. *Concentration in Banking.* The data suggest that banking concentration is substantially higher abroad than in the United States. Japan, however, which does have a U.S.-style separation of commercial and investment banking, also shows higher concentration. The United States currently has more than 14,000 commercial banks. Even if interstate banking is permitted and a wave of mergers follows, the Sherman Act could be used to preclude anticompetitive mergers in either commercial or investment banking activities.

3. *Macroeconomic Regulation.* We have pointed out that macroeconomic regulation in countries with combined commercial and investment banking often takes shape through controls on the amount and distribution of credit. These measures would be contrary to a free market for credit. We have argued that these macroeconomic policies are more characteristic of small, open economies with a tradition of strong central direction. It is highly unlikely that the United States would tend toward more centralized control over credit, even if it were easier to implement under a more integrated banking system.

Factors Favoring a Less-Successful Adaptation and/or Small Gains from Competitive Eurobond Practices

Markets may establish efficient pricing through competition from either the supply or the demand side. Traditionally, one thinks of competition among suppliers to provide services at the lowest possible prices to capture market share. The result is that all buyers, even those who are completely uninformed about the market, pay the same fair price for services. On the other hand, one can imagine competition from the demand side to pressure a group of oligopolistic suppliers. Well-informed buyers, who know the fair price for services, may withhold demand, seek close substitutes (bank loans, commercial paper, auction issues), and otherwise pressure suppliers to offer services at a fair price. Eventually, virtually any cartel will break and fair prices will result.

In the U.S. investment banking industry, the statistics on concentration do not reveal much variation. If anything, concentration has tended to increase in the 1970s. However, Hayes et al.[95] conclude that the concentration data are deceptive because the market is actually composed of distinct segments "within which substantial competition takes place but between which competition may be less robust."

On the demand side, market observers describe a kind of "in-house" competition that has developed in the last 20 years.[96] Historically, corporate financial officers relied heavily on their investment bankers for expertise. Over the years, the quality of financial staff resources of major U.S. corporations has improved substantially. Consequently, firms are more capable of distinguishing the value of alternative investment banking services, and to judge which are cost-effective. In some cases, clients have turned to alternatives that avoid the use of investment banking services altogether.[97] SEC Rule 415 on shelf registration should allow corporations additional time to shop for the best deal.

Large corporations can also turn to the Eurobond market for active competition if they feel that the domestic market conditions are not sufficiently competitive, as U.S. corporations are increasingly prepared to do.[98] The initial attraction is the lower cost of offshore funding, but corporations often enjoy secondary benefits in having their underwriting business sought by more competitors. Unfortunately, the Eurobond market alternative is available primarily to larger firms.[99]

There is reason to believe that the larger, well-informed U.S. corporations have already inspired a highly competitive atmosphere in U.S. investment banking. By actively comparing Eurobond and U.S. domestic bond issues, U.S. corporations may be "arbitraging" these differences and forcing the price of U.S. investment banking services to competitive levels. It is not clear whether small corporations, without access to the Eurobond market, also receive competitive prices for securities underwriting services. Accepting this argument, efficiency gains from allowing further competition in U.S. investment banking would be relatively small.

SUMMARY AND CONCLUSIONS

At the beginning of this chapter, we observed that the market for investment banking services in the United States is not freely competitive because the Glass-Stegall Act excludes one major group of competitors (securities affiliates of commercial banks) from the market. As a result, agents that provide both commercial and investment banking services have been severely constrained in the United States. The Eurobond market offers an opportunity to examine the operation of a market in which there are few official regulations and no restrictions on who may provide securities underwriting services. The behavior of foreign banks which combine commercial and investment banking was analyzed through their operations in the Eurobond market and in their onshore activities.

Data on the Eurobond market were presented to describe the dimensions and competitive efficiency of the market. By all standard measures—new issue volume, secondary market volume, default rate on bonds, underwriting concentration ratios—the Eurobond market must be labeled a success. Without official guidance or subsidy, it has grown to a size essentially equal to the U.S. domestic bond market. Adaptation and innovation—syndicate organization, the gray market, automated clearing, and so forth—have accompanied growth. To some extent, individual underwriting successes may have been the result of exogenous events (e.g., exchange rate changes that affected the supply of DM bonds always led by German banks) or the beneficial impact that financial secrecy may have on placing power (in the case of Swiss banks). Overall, however, competitive conditions appear to have stabilized the market, with the availability and terms for funds responsive to market conditions and the more efficient and innovative firms (including affiliates of U.S. commercial banks), capturing market share. Firms in the market have behaved prudently and did not use the absence of regulation as an opportunity for taking excessive risks.

In our review of European banking practices a number of areas for concern were highlighted, including conflict of interest between investment management and underwriting activities, excessive linkages between banks and corporations, and concentration in banking activities. We pointed out that U.S. regulations pertaining to disclosure, fiduciary responsibility, anticompetitive practices and the like would prevent similar developments in the U.S. market. The tendency for official guidance in many foreign credit markets, we argued, has little relationship to the combined commercial and investment banking in these countries.

The chapter has documented one case in which a largely unregulated financial market produced very favorable results. Existing U.S. regulations seem capable of dealing with known abuses and points of concern about the linkage of commercial and investment banking activities. The decision to abolish Glass-Steagall restrictions could be framed in terms of cost/benefit analysis. The costs are the increased risk to the banking system via bank/corporation, bank/trustee, and bank/depositor relations. From the Eurobond market experience, the risks appear small and manageable. The benefits result from increased competition in the supply of investment banking services. Given the power of large corporations and their access to a competitive Euromarket, the benefits of increased competition may be small for this group. However, allowing increased domestic competition would make these benefits more certain and expand their availability to all firms.

ACKNOWLEDGMENT

This chapter was written while the author was a visiting Fellow at Centre d'Enseignement Superieur des Affaires (Jouy-en-Josas, France) and the Australian Graduate School of Management (Sydney, Australia). The author is grateful to William Dudley, Sheppard Poor, Arthur Stonehill, and Ingo Walter for helpful comments on earlier drafts and to Fabian von Hofe and Tony Mayer for background discussions and data on the Euro-bond market. The author acknowledges responsibility for any errors that remain. The author is affiliated with the NBER's research program in International Studies and project Productivity (World Economy). Any opinions expressed are those of the author and not those of the National Bureau of Economic Research.

NOTES

[1] The distinction between the Eurobond market and foreign securities markets is discussed in the following section.

[2] Most OECD countries do not formally separate commercial and investment banking and, as we will describe, some countries permit banks to engage in essentially any activity (i.e., universal or multipurpose banking) including substantial equity positions in nonfinancial companies. The few exceptions—the United States, Canada, Japan, and perhaps the United Kingdom, where precedent separates commercial and investment banking—comprise the three largest financial markets in the world. In the United Kingdom, however, three of the "Big Four" clearing banks own investment banks, and two of these are fairly important. See Richard Dale, *Bank Supervision Around the World*. (New York: Group of Thirty, 1982).

[3]In some sense, the second question probes into the macroeconomic costs and benefits associated with eliminating the separation of commercial and investment banking. Our research design might propose to compare the macroeconomic performance of industrial countries in which commercial banking and investment banking are formally separated with those in which the activities are combined. Macroeconomic performance varies considerably across countries, and undoubtedly regulations affecting the financial sector and the institutional structure of banking play a role. However, macroeconomic performance is a function of many variables and without a highly detailed model it is impossible to determine how great that role is.

[4]M. S. Mendelsohn, "The Eurobond and Foreign Bond Markets," Section 5.1 in A. George and I. Giddy (eds.), *International Finance Handbook*. (New York: Wiley, 1983), makes the argument that the thrust of regulation in the United States is disclosure, whereas in Europe, regulation is directed toward resource allocation, national planning, and monetary control. Consequently, U.S. authorities for the most part impose no restrictions on issue volume as long as the appropriate disclosure is made. European authorities frequently establish a queue for new issues which is managed to prevent market "congestion" or to achieve interest rate or exchange rate targets. One could argue that these regulatory objectives play the dominant role in European capital markets rather than the coincidence of commercial and investment banking. For more on the regulation of security markets in Europe, see Wymeersch (Eddy Wymeersch, "Securities Markets Regulations in Europe," Section 6.2 in A. George and I. Giddy (eds.), *International Finance Handbook*. (New York: John Wiley, 1983).

[5]Throughout this chapter we assume that existing U.S. regulations concerning information disclosure, anticompetitive behavior and anticompetitive mergers would apply, even if the Glass-Steagall act were abolished.

[6]Although it would be interesting to document the innovations in the Eurobond market made by U.S. commercial bank affiliates, it is beyond the scope of this chapter to do so. Our purpose is to shed light on the behavior and characteristics of an unregulated financial market rather than specific individuals within that market.

[7]If existing restrictions on interstate branching were maintained, the ability of securities affiliates of U.S. commercial banks to place securities across state lines might be questioned. For our analysis, we assume that such restrictions would not apply to securities affiliates and that they would be permitted to compete on equal terms with existing investment banking houses.

[8]M. S. Mendelsohn, *Money on the Move*. (New York: McGraw-Hill, 1980), p. 137.

[9]Coussement ("When the Bonds Went Round Luxembourg in a Van," *Euromoney* [February 1981], pp. 81–83.) states that the first Eurobond issue was in 1961 for the Portuguese oil company SACOR in the amount of 5 million European Units of Account.

[10]*World Financial Markets,* Morgan Guaranty Trust Company, New York (November 1983). Total volume in the first 10 months of 1983 was down 7% from 1982. See Carl Gewirtz, "Declines in Eurobond Activity Tied to Drop in Dollar Issues," *International Herald Tribune* (November 29, 1983a), p. 9.

[11]See *Ibid.,* and *Weekly Eurobond Guide,* Datastream International Limited, London, various issues.

[12]These are gross new issues, without netting out security redemptions. See *Financial Statistics Monthly,* OECD (November 1983), p. 14.

[13]M. S. Mendelsohn, "The Eurobond and Foreign Bond Markets," Section 5.1 in A. George and I. Giddy (eds.), *International Finance Handbook*. (New York: Wiley, 1983), pp. 4–5.

[14]Mendelsohn, "The Eurobond Market," p. 10.

[15]After January 1, 1983, new federal regulations required U.S. citizens to hold Eurobonds in registered form. U.S. investors had to elect registered form as an option, even though the bulk of Eurobond issues remained in bearer form. See H. Read, "The Secondary Market Wrestles with TEFRA," for further details.

[16]M. S. Mendelsohn, "The Eurobond and Foreign Bond Markets," Section 5.1 in A. George and I. Giddy (eds.), *International Finance Handbook*. (New York: Wiley, 1983), p. 10; and Daniel Magraw, "Legal Aspects of International Bonds," Section 5.3 in A. George and I. Giddy (eds.), *International Finance Handbook*. (New York: Wiley, 1983), p. 3.

[17]Frederick G. Fisher, *International Bonds*. (London: Euromoney Publications, 1981), p. 95; and Mendelsohn, "Eurobond Markets," 1983, p. 7.

[18]In the United Kingdom, the Bank of England controls the queue: In West Germany the Federal Department of Commerce is in charge of domestic issues. In France, new issues must be cleared with the Treasury. And in Switzerland there is an official Issues Committee. See James E. Maycock. "United Kingdom: Banking, Money and Bond Markets," Section 4.3 in A. George and I. Giddy (eds.), *International Finance Handbook*. (New York: Wiley, 1983), p. 5; Gunter Dufey, and Krishnan, E., "West Germany: Banking, Money and Bond Markets," Section 4.4 in A. George and I. Giddy (eds.), *International Finance Handbook*. (New York: Wiley, 1983), p. 14; Florin Aftalion, and Bompaire, Frederick, "France: Banking, Money and Bond Markets," Section 4.5 in A. George and I. Giddy (eds.), *International Finance Handbook*. (New York: Wiley), 1983, p. 3; and Mario A. Corti, "Switzerland: Banking, Money and Bond Markets," Section 4.6 in A. George and I. Giddy (eds.), *International Finance Handbook*. (New York: Wiley, 1983).

[19]Antoine W. Van Agtmael, ("Issuance of Eurobonds: Syndication and Underwriting Techniques and Costs," Section 5.2 in A. George I. Giddy (eds.), *International Finance Handbook*. (New York: Wiley, 1983), p. 5) notes, we believe incorrectly, that no queuing exists in the Eurobond market. Compare Fisher, *International Bonds,* p. 20.

[20]See Mendelsohn, "Eurobond Markets," 1983 p. 10; Dufey and Krishnan, "West Germany," 1983, p. 15; Corti, "Switzerland," p. 3; and Eddy Wymeersch. "Securities Markets Regulations in Europe," Section 6.2 in A. George and I. Giddy (eds.), *International Finance Handbook*. (New York: Wiley), 1983.

[21]M. S. Mendelsohn, *Money on the Move*. (New York: McGraw-Hill, 1980), p. 139.

[22]A bought deal is a preunderwritten issue, offered to a borrower on a take-it-or-leave-it basis, which is valid for a specified short time period. Bought deals have been offered and closed out within 24 hours. See Fisher, *International Bonds,* p. 83; and David Shirreff, "The Warrior Style of CSFB's Rudloff," *Euromoney,* (December 1981), pp. 24–32, p. 31.

[23]For the view that Eurobond selling concessions are relatively high, see Fisher, *International Bonds,* p. 81, Mendelsohn, (*Money on the Move,* 1980, p. 184) and Mendelsohn "Eurobond Markets," 1983, pp. 13–19).

[24]The differential has reached 100 basis points or higher for some issuers. See Richard Karp, "How U.S. Companies Are Catching the Eurobond Habit," *Institutional Investor* (August 1982), pp. 127–135, and Mendelsohn ("Eurobond Markets," 1983).

[25]Mendelsohn (*Money on the Move,* 1980, p. 136) citing World Bank records.

[26]Fisher, *International Bonds,* p. 19.

[27]Mendelsohn, "Eurobond Markets," 1983, p. 5.

[28]*Ibid.*

[29]Fisher, *International Bonds* 1981, p. 19.

[30]Fisher, *International Bonds,* p. 19.

[31]Mendelsohn, "Eurobond Markets," 1983, p. 15. The purchase is made by the lead manager as agent for the underwriting syndicate in order to avoid double taxation.

[32]Fisher, *International Bonds,* p. 77, notes that underwriters are rarely mailed copies of the subscription agreement prior to closing, and so they must have trust in the management group. See also Mendelsohn, "Eurobond Markets," p. 16.

[33]Mendelsohn, *Money on the Move,* p. 183.

[34]Fisher, *International Bonds,* p. 80.

[35]This is the general view expressed by Fisher (1981, p. 80). In the Deutsche mark segment of the market, the major German issuing banks monitor early trading closely to identify banks that break ranks. (See Tim Anderson, "Germany's Exclusive Club," *Euromoney* [May 1983b], pp. 50–52.)

[36]Gray market prices first appeared on the Reuters Monitor in August 1982, although telephone prices were circulated earlier. (Tim Anderson, "Clearing the Grey Clouds," *Euromoney* [May 1983a], pp. 26–28, and private interviews.)

[37]See, for example, *AGEFI International Finance Review,* London: AGEFI Press Limited.

[38]Large institutions buying for trust accounts need not pass along these gains, a problem we explore in the section on "Problems and Risks in the Eurobond Market."

[39]In the Eurobond market, there is no rule compelling sellers to charge the same price to all buyers as there is in the U.S. market. See Mendelsohn, "Eurobond Markets," p. 16.

[40]Fisher, *International Bonds,* p. 38, notes that estimated ratings based on comparison with similar domestic securities are often reported.

[41]*Ibid.,* p. 60.

[42]*Ibid.,* p. 81.

[43]See Shirreff, "Warrior Style," 1984.

[44]See Fisher, *International Bonds,* pp. 83–86, and Fisher, "Imagination Wins Again," *Euromoney* (February 1981), pp. 125–128, for details.

[45]In 1980, the principal amount of dollar Floating Rate Notes totaled $4.0 billion or 31.5% of all Eurodollar issues, up from $1.1 billion and 12.7% in 1976. See Fisher, *International Bonds,* p. 103.

[46]At the end of 1980, Euro-clear had 123 shareholders and serviced 1080 member banks. Cedel had 94 shareholders with 1050 member banks. (Ibid., p. 182).

[47]Tim Anderson, "The Growing War Between Cedel and Euroclear," *Euromoney* (February 1981b), p. 35.

[48]Fisher, *International Bonds,* p. 182.

[49]Mendelsohn (*Money on the Move,* p. 61) displays a deep reverence for the Eurobond market exclaiming, "It saved the industrialized world from an even deeper recession (in the 1970s) than it actually suffered and allowed many industrial countries to maintain an almost unchecked economic expansion."

[50]Ibid., p. 47.

[51]M. S. Mendelsohn, *Money on the Move.* (New York: McGraw-Hill, 1980), p. 50.

[52]Mendelsohn ("Eurobond Markets," 1983, p. 11) cites Fisher *The Eurodollar Bond Market,* 1979) claiming that by mid-1976 there had been 19 defaults totaling more than $300 million. Moreover, a 1984 case alleges that a trader from Bear, Stearns (New York) and another from Union Bank of Switzerland engaged in fraudulent trading, defrauding both companies of $8.3 million. The case raises the issue of whether the incident reflects an isolated case resulting from poor internal controls, or whether the market's general lack of regulation is at fault. The resolution of this dispute, with its third-party implications, is an important challenge for the Association of International Bond Dealers's arbitration procedures. See "Bear-Faced Fraud," *The Economist,* July 14, 1984, pp. 72–73.

[53]M. S. Mendelsohn, *Money on the Move.* (New York: McGraw-Hill, 1980), p. 194.

[54]Samuel L. Hayes, A. Michael Spence and David Marks, *Competition in the Investment Banking Industry,* p. 55.

[55]M. S. Mendelsohn, "The Eurobond Markets," p. 12.

[56]See "Are the Eurobond Markets Incestuous?" *Euromoney* (November 1977), pp. 46–47.

[57]M. S. Mendelsohn, *Money on the Move.* (New York: McGraw-Hill, 1980), p. 185.

[58]Mendelsohn (*Money on the Move,* pp. 185–190) shows that in a typical Eurobond underwriting ($45 million for nine years with spread totaling 2.5%), the lead manager and co-managers (if any) will claim half of the fees. The underwriting group (about 90) would share about 38% of the fees, and the selling group (perhaps 100) would share about 12% of the fees. Mendelsohn draws the conclusion that most members of the syndicate do not expect profits from their activity. This, of course, presupposes that the entire issue is sold at the offering price—that is, that the full 2^{1}/$_{2}$% is earned—which may well not be true.

[59]Carl Gewirtz. "Decline in Eurobond Activity Linked to Drop in Dollar Issues," *International Herald Tribune,* November 29, 1983b.

[60]Peter Koenig, "Why Trading Is Fun Again," *Institutional Investor* (May 1983b), p. 174.

[61]Gewirtz, "Decline in Eurobond Activity," 1983b.

[62]"How the Citicorp issue Rocked the Euromarkets," *Euromoney,* (November 1977), p. 14.

[63]Tim Anderson, "Optimism Shyly Creeps Back to the Bond Markets," *Euromoney* (May 1981c), p. 46.

[64]Gerald Engel, "Underwriters Need to Know Where They Stand," *Euromoney* (May 1983), p. 24.

[65]*Ibid.*

[66]M. S. Mendelsohn, *Money on the Move.* (New York: McGraw-Hill, 1980), p. 195.

[67]Koenig, "Trading is Fun Again," May 1983b, p. 172.

[68]Gerard Engel, "Underwriters Need to Know Where They Stand," p. 24.

[69]Koenig, "The Great Liquidity Debate," pp. 158–159.

[70]Mendelsohn, "Eurobond Markets," 1983, p. 14.

[71]M.S. Mendelsohn, "The Eurobond Markets," (1983), p. 16.

[72]Gerard Engel, "Underwriters Need to Know Where They Stand," (1983), p. 24.

[73]M.S. Mendelsohn, "The Eurobond Markets," (1983), p. 15.

[74]In any market setting, one expects to observe agents taking steps to protect their interests—sellers limit their product claims, buyers search out product information, and so forth. As we have noted, participants in the Eurobond market have similarly developed effective mechanisms to protect themselves from loss.

[75]Mendelsohn, *Money on the Move,* 1980, p. 174; and Mendelsohn, "Eurobond Markets," 1983, p. 21.

[76]For more on secrecy in banking, see Ingo Walter, "Global Players in the Financial Secrecy Game," *NYU Business,* 3, No. 2 (Fall 1983/Winter 1984), pp. 10–17, and Ingo Walter, *Secret Money* (London: George Allen & Unwin, 1985).

[77]Fisher, *International Bonds,* pp. 183–184.

[78]"M. S. Mendelsohn, "The Eurobond Markets," p. 14.

[79]Mendelsohn, *Money on the Move,* 1980, p. 195. See the *Weekly Eurobond Guide* for a listing of AIBD secondary market makers.

[80]See for example, Tim Anderson, "Hambro, Hamburg and the Social Club," *Euromoney* (May 1981a), pp. 31–33; and Tim Anderson, "Optimism Shyly Creeps Back to the Bond Market," *Euromoney* (May 1981c), pp. 45–48.

[81]See Anderson, "Hambro, Hamburg and the Social Club," 1981a, p. 33. However, concerning recently alleged fraudulent trading (see footnote 52), *The Economist* (July 14, 1984, p. 72) has commented that "Self-regulation in such a market relies heavily on the probity and vigilance of its members, but when they fail a strong watchdog is needed. The AIBD is neither strong nor a watchdog."

[82]See for example, Sherreff and Martin, "Milestone Deals," *Euromoney* (Oct. 1981), pp. 269–275.

[83]See Karp, "U.S. Companies," 1982, pp. 134–135 for a discussion of how several major underwriting firms were caught in May 1982 when expectations of a lower U.S. budget deficit led them to believe that interest rates would drop.

[84]Floating Rate Notes in the Euromarket have proved to be a major success. Money managers have been drawn to these instruments because of yield (typically the six-month LIBOR rate + $1/4$%) and liquidity has improved so that the bid-ask spread is only 5 basis points (compared to 25 basis points on the most active fixed-coupon Eurobond). See Gewirtz, "Eurobonds," 1983a. During 1983, the overwhelming percentage of Eurodollar bonds were reported to be classic straight issues, without sweeteners of any sort. See Gewirtz, "Decline in Eurobond Activity," 1983b.

[85]*Universal banking* is the term generally used, but may be a poor choice because some readers will associate it primarily with German banks which are allowed to perform almost any financial service. For the moment, we ignore the important distinction as to whether the commercial and investment banking activities take place in legally separate subsidiaries of a bank holding company or simply in separate departments of a single bank.

[86]Richard Dale, *Bank Supervision Around the World.* (New York: Group of 30, 1982), p. 42.

[87]Wymeersch, "Securities Markets," 1983, p. 45.

[88]The extent of official guidance has been relaxed recently. See Deborah L. Allen, "Japan: Banking, Money, and Bond Markets," Section 4.7 in A. George and I. Giddy (eds.), *International Finance Handbook,* New York: Wiley, 1983. Mario A. Corti, "Switzerland: Banking, Money and Bond Markets," Section 4.6 in A. George and I. Giddy (eds.), *International Finance Handbook.* (New York: Wiley, 1983) and Eisuke Sakakibara, "The Japanese Financial System in Transition," in T. Agmon, R. Hawkins and R. Levich (eds.), *The Future of the International Monetary System.* (Lexington, Mass.: D.C. Heath, 1984).

[89]Concentration in the United States may be artificially low because of the ban on interstate banking. But note also that the concentration ratios in Europe represent three to five banks.

[90]The U.S. and Canadian dollar segments of the market are least subject to governmental regulations. See the discussion in the second section.

[91]The U.S. OFDI controls in the 1960s were a key feature that led to the Eurobond market, whereas the IET diverted foreign borrowers from the U.S. as well. However, because entry into the Eurobond market was never restricted, we expect to see the elimination of any excess profits that might have arisen from these distortions.

[92]See Chapter 8 on the conflict of interest question.

[93]See Chapter 5.

[94]This point is developed further in Chapter 7.

[95]Samuel L. Hayes, "The Transformation of Investment Banking," *Harvard Business Review,* January/ February 1979, p. 170.

[96]This term is used by Samuel L. Hayes Spence, A. Michael, and Marks, David Van Praag. *Competition in the Investment Banking Industry.* (Cambridge, Mass.: Harvard University Press, 1983).

[97]Hayes, ibid., p. 156 cites the Exxon "Dutch auctions," corporate dividend reinvestment plans and stock-for-stock corporate mergers as three examples.

[98]It appears that large U.S. corporations are monitoring very closely both U.S. and Eurobond market conditions. Exxon devised an issue which it was prepared to launch in either market. See Karp, "U.S. Companies," 1982, p. 135.

[99]On February 1, 1984, the Alaska Housing Finance Corporation became the first U.S. State agency to offer securities to the Euromarket. To complete the $100 million, 10-year issue, the agency was required to establish an overseas financing corporation in the Netherlands Antilles. See "Alaska to Offer First Eurobonds," *International Herald Tribune,* January 11, 1984.

REFERENCES

Aftalion, Florin, and Bompaire, Frederick. "France: Banking, Money and Bond Markets," Section 4.5 in A. George and I. Giddy (eds.), *International Finance Handbook.* New York: Wiley, 1983.

"Alaska to Offer First Eurobonds." *International Herald Tribune,* January 11, 1984.

Allen, Deborah L. "Japan: Banking, Money, and Bond Markets," Section 4.7 in A. George and I. Giddy (eds.), *International Finance Handbook,* New York: Wiley, 1983.

Anderson, Tim. "Hambro, Hamburg and the Social Club," *Euromoney* (May 1981a), pp. 31–33.

———. "The Growing War Between Cedel and Euro-clear," *Euromoney* (May 1981b), pp. 35–42.

———. "Optimism Shyly Creeps Back to the Bond Market," *Euromoney* (May 1981c), pp. 45–48.

———. "Clearing the Grey Clouds," *Euromoney* (May 1983a), pp. 26–27.

———. "Germany's Exclusive Club," *Euromoney* (May 1983b), pp. 50–52.

"Are the Eurobond Markets Incestuous?" *Euromoney* (November 1977), pp. 46–47.

"Bear-Faced Fraud," *The Economist* (July 14, 1984), pp. 72–73.

Corti, Mario A. "Switzerland: Banking, Money and Bond Markets," Section 4.6 in A. George and I. Giddy (eds.), *International Finance Handbook.* New York: Wiley, 1983.

Coussement, André. "When the Bonds Went Round Luxembourg in a Van," *Euromoney* (February 1981), pp. 81–83.

Dale, Richard. *Bank Supervision Around the World.* New York: Group of 30, 1982.

Dufey, Gunter, and Krishnan, E. "West Germany: Banking, Money and Bond Markets," Section 4.4 in A. George and I. Giddy (eds.), *International Finance Handbook.* New York: Wiley, 1983.

Engel, Gerard. "Underwriters Need to Know Where They Stand," *Euromoney* (May 1983), pp. 24–26.

Financial Statistics Monthly, Paris: Organization for Economic Cooperation and Development, various issues.

Fisher, Frederick G. *The Eurodollar Bond Market,* London: Euromoney Publications, 1979.

————. *International Bonds,* London: Euromoney Publications, 1981.

————. "Imagination Wins Again," *Euromoney,* February 1981, pp. 125–128.

Gewirtz, Carl. "Eurobonds," *International Herald Tribune,* October 31, 1983a.

————. "Decline in Eurobond Activity Linked to Drop in Dollar Issues," *International Herald Tribune,* November 29, 1983b.

Hayes, Samuel L. "The Transformation of Investment Banking," *Harvard Business Review* (January/ February 1979), pp. 153–170.

Hayes, Samuel L., Spence, A. Michael, and Marks, David Van Praag. *Competition in the Investment Banking Industry.* Cambridge, Mass.: Harvard University Press, 1983.

"How the Citicorp Issue Rocked the Euromarkets," *Euromoney* (November 1977), pp. 12–19.

Karp, Richard. "How U.S. Companies Are Catching the Eurobond Habit," *Institutional Investor* (August 1982), pp. 127–135.

Koenig, Peter. "The Great Liquidity Debate," *Institutional Investor,* (May 1983a), pp. 153–166.

————. "Why Trading Is Fun Again," *Institutional Investor* (May 1983b), pp. 171–174.

Magraw, Daniel, "Legal Aspects of International Bonds," Section 5.3 in A. George and I. Giddy (eds.), *International Finance Handbook.* New York: Wiley, 1983.

Maycock, James E. "United Kingdom: Banking, Money and Bond Markets," Section 4.3 in A. George and I. Giddy (eds.), *International Finance Handbook.* New York: Wiley, 1983.

Mendelsohn, M. S. *Money on the Move.* New York: McGraw-Hill, 1980.

————. "The Eurobond and Foreign Bond Markets," Section 5.1 in A. George and I. Giddy (eds.), *International Finance Handbook.* New York: Wiley, 1983.

Pugel, Thomas A., and Lawrence J. White. "An Analysis of the Competitive Effects of Allowing Commercial Banks to Underwrite Corporate Securities," in this volume.

Read, Hastings. "The Secondary Market Wrestles with TEFRA," *Euromoney* (August 1983), p. 54.

Sakakibara, Eisuke. "The Japanese Financial System in Transition," in T. Agmon, R. Hawkins and R. Levich (eds.), *The Future of the International Monetary System.* (Lexington, Mass.: D.C. Heath, 1984).

Saunders, Anthony. "Conflicts of Interest: The Case of Commercial Banks and Their Corporate Underwriting Affiliates," in this volume.

Shirreff, David. "The Warrior Style of CSFB's Rudloff," *Euromoney* (December 1981), pp. 24–32.

Shirreff, David, and Sarah Martin. "Milestone Deals in the Euromarkets," *Euromoney* (October 1981), pp. 269–275.

Van Agtmael, Antione W. "Issuance of Eurobonds: Syndication and Underwriting Techniques and Costs," Section 5.2 in A. George I. Giddy (eds.), *International Finance Handbook.* New York: Wiley, 1983.

Walter, Ingo. "Global Players in the Financial Secrecy Game," *NYU Business,* Vol. 3, No. 2 (Fall 1983/ Winter 1984), pp. 10–17.

————. *Secret Money.* London: George Allen & Unwin, 1985.

Weekly Eurobond Guide, London: Datastream International, various issues.

"Wilson Report." Sir Harold Wilson, Chairman of the Committee to Review the Functioning of Financial Institutions, London: Her Majesty's Stationery Office, June 1980.

World Financial Markets. New York: Morgan Guaranty Trust Company, various issues.

Wymeersch, Eddy. "Securities Markets Regulations in Europe," Section 6.2 in A. George and I. Giddy (eds.), *International Finance Handbook.* New York: Wiley, 1983.

11 Summary and Implications for Policy

INGO WALTER

This volume has attempted to lay out the various dimensions of deregulation in the provision of financial services to corporations in the United States. Given the enormous changes that have taken place in the American financial system and the economy as a whole, it is certainly appropriate, over a half-century after the Glass-Steagall Act came into force, to reexamine the separation of commercial and investment banking in light of the national interest with respect to financial efficiency, safety and stability, and contribution to sustained economic growth.

Taken together, the various chapters in this volume lead to the conclusion that the substantial separation of commercial and investment banking, as it has evolved in the United States, is an anachronism that the nation cannot easily afford in an era marked by growing competitive challenges in economic performance. They suggest, indeed, that deregulation in the area of corporate finance is fundamentally consistent with an appropriate, modern design for a financial system that is both efficient and stable.

TRACING THE ISSUE TO ITS SOURCE

The studies in this volume suggest that, in today's context, the Glass-Steagall prohibitions are neither a necessary nor a desirable component of the rules governing the American financial system—that the competitive distortions and erosion of financial efficiency involved are not outweighed by any associated gains in financial stability. From a social cost-benefit viewpoint, therefore, Glass-Steagall today appears to be a bad bargain. Why, then, was it instituted?

The separation of commercial banking from corporate securities underwriting and dealing was part of an effort by Congress to restore order to a severely strained financial system during a period unprecedented in its economic turbulence. Given the unquestioned abuses in U.S. capital markets that led to the financial panic of 1929, it is understandable that the lawmakers faced great pressures to try many remedies in their search for appropriate solutions. Of paramount importance were federal desposit insurance and carefully crafted securities regulation. By themselves, these measures contributed critical elements of stability that were badly needed under the circumstances. And they have proven themselves over the years. The Glass-Steagall legislation in hindsight appears as a policy aberration, an oddity triggered by fears that careful historical analysis shows were based largely on myths. According to chapters 3 and 4 in this volume by Mark Flannery and Edward Kelly, the activities of commercial banks in securities underwriting and dealing had little to do with the financial abuses that took place at the time, nor with triggering the Great Depression.

If the analyses contained in this volume are correct in their adverse cost-benefit assessment of the Glass-Steagall Act today—with significant efficiency gains predicted to come from deregulation, yet without material impairment of financial stability—it follows that the Glass-Steagall legislation must also have imposed economic costs on the United States during the past half-century. Although it is obviously impossible to predict with any certainty how the American financial system would have evolved differently in its absence, the presumptive evidence suggests that vigorous competition, market efficiency, financial innovation, and the overall contribution of the financial services industry to capital formation and sustained economic growth would have been enhanced. It may be significant, in this connection, that few other countries have found the separation of commercial and investment banking a necessary or desirable attribute of their own financial systems.

IDENTIFYING THE GAINS FROM DEREGULATION

If the economic cost of the Glass-Steagall Act to the American economic and financial system is to be documented, the focus must be on the competitive structure, conduct, and performance of the commercial and investment banking industries, as well as economies of scale and economies of scope in the financial services industry.

Thomas Pugel and Lawrence White suggest in this volume that competition in several segments of the investment banking industry today is not as vigorous as it might be, and that the incremental market participants that would be introduced by the securities affiliates of commercial banks would certainly enhance the degree of competition in corporate finance with lower fees, better service, broader access, improved secondary markets, and greater innovation. It seems probable that the entry of affiliates of investment banks into commercial banking would similarly enhance competition and dynamism in that industry, as has in a sense already been demonstrated by the innovation of cash management accounts (CMAs) by Merrill Lynch in the 1970s. Nevertheless, the fact that commercial banks have favored interpenetration of markets and open competition, whereas investment banks have fiercely resisted deregulation, suggests that the excess returns attributable to restricted competition fall mainly on the investment banking side.

If deregulation in investment banking is indeed justifiable in economic terms, that justification must come in large part through substantive change in competitive performance in the provision of corporate financial services. Substantial competition between investment banks and commercial banks exists for a wide variety of such services, as well as in the international capital market. In areas where there had been an absence of artificial barriers to competition, the degree of efficiency and innovativeness that characterize the various competing financial services firms has been very high indeed, with commensurate benefits accruing directly to the users of the services and more broadly to the economic and financial system as a whole.

It is only in domestic underwriting and dealing in corporate securities that entry has continued to be artificially restricted under the Glass-Steagall legislation. Economists generally work under the assumption that any such limitation of competitive opportunity will involve a reallocation among potential competitors of the gains from the economic activities involved, in favor of those who benefit from protection, as well as a reduction in the efficiency with which resources are allocated—the *static* "deadweight losses" associated with protected markets. There are also adverse *dynamic* consequences (such as accelerated financial innovation) that arise, which are likely to be substantially more important. Measuring the static and dynamic efficiency and redistributional effects of protection involves estimating what a number of key variables would look like in the *absence* of existing constraints on competition. Because there is no way to ascertain this alternative, this has to be done either by examining these variables "before and after" distortions have been imposed or removed, or by means of "cross-sectional" comparisons between distorted and undistorted markets. Both approaches involve serious empirical problems of research design, comparability, data availability, and interpretation of results.

In Chapter 5, on the competitive dimensions, Professors Pugel and White evaluate the implications of the Glass-Steagall competitive distortions on the structure, conduct, and performance of the securities industry with respect to corporate finance. Their conclusion, that more competition is better than less, comes as no great surprise either from the standpoint of efficiency or equity, and seems well justified in terms of the inferential evidence presented on concentration and competitive structure.

Other evidence on the size and stability of underwriting fees, the quality of service provided to small issuers, and the underpricing of new issues seems to follow the pattern one would expect to find in a protected market. Comparisons with the market for general obligation bonds of state and local governments appear to reinforce this evidence. So, despite the fact that no credible data are available on the actual returns to factors of production used in underwriting and dealing in corporate securities, the inferential evidence does suggest that protection involves costs, and that deregulation would indeed generate material benefits to the users of corporate financial services and to the economy at large. This is certainly an area in which substantial additional research needs to be done in the future.

IDENTIFYING THE COSTS OF FINANCIAL DEREGULATION

If there are potential benefits associated with the deregulation of corporate financial services in the United States, there are also potential costs. These have both economic and political dimensions, which focus on implications for the stability of the financial system and conflicts of interest within financial institutions undertaking commercial as well as investment banking activities.

The first question concerns the riskiness of corporate securities activities that might be undertaken by commercial bank affiliates. That these activities involve risks is clear. If there were no risks, such activities would produce far smaller gains, both to the direct participants and to society. Risk can be managed through astute evaluation, diversification, and exposure limits, as well as a growing array of hedging vehicles. But beyond this, there is the empirical question of how risky corporate securities activities have been in the United States.

The risks involved can produce either gains or losses for securities underwriters, and may be traced to specific developments affecting a given security issue to general developments in financial markets that occur during the underwriting process of (in the case of dealing) thereafter. Specifically of interest here are the potential downside risks associated with securities underwriting and dealing, their bearing on the safety and soundness of individual financial institutions and the system as a whole, and the nature of the risk/return tradeoffs in the market for corporate securities.

Once again, it is impossible to obtain direct data on securities industry profits and losses. One can presume, however, that such activities have been quite profitable over the years for those permitted to engage in them, a presumption reinforced by the vigor with which the investment banking industry argues its case for continued protection from increased competition. One can also glean some additional evidence from the movement of stock or bond prices during the underwriting process to ascertain possible gains or losses to securities firms during the period in which the securities could have been held.

In Chapter 6, Ian Giddy, undertakes an analysis of U.S. equity issues during 1976–1983, and finds that, on balance, the potential gains did indeed far outweigh the potential losses. Moreover, even ignoring the gains entirely, and focusing on the loss side under certain worst-case assumptions, there is nothing to indicate that such equity underwriting losses in any sense impaired the viability of the securities firms involved during this period. Corporate debt underwriting, which is generally held to be less risky than equity underwriting, appears to have exhibited an even more limited loss profile under worst-case assumptions during the same period of time, although the absence of adequate price data prevented empirical verification comparable to the analysis of equities. Again, this is an area in which additional research would yield valuable new insights.

The record on corporate securities underwriting suggests that affiliates of commercial banks engaged in such activities would not be exposed to inordinate risks, particularly given the increasing availability of hedging vehicles. To be sure, there is no guarantee that a given entity engaged in corporate securities underwriting and dealing will indeed succeed. But neither is there any evidence that bank affiliates would necessarily encounter greater rates of failure than other industry participants.

Moreover, by adding a range of financial-services activities—whose returns are not perfectly correlated with those of traditional banking activities—the ability to engage in corporate securities business promises to enhance the earnings stability of bank holding companies. It suggests that safety and stability in a modern and competitive financial-services environment (one that throws off significant efficiency and growth benefits for the economy as a whole), depend more on careful balance and breadth of scope of activities engaged in by firms in the industry than they do on traditional notions of narrow activity limitations and controls.

This is a conclusion of Chapter 7 by Professor Anthony Saunders on this subject. In discussing how corporate securities underwriting and dealing by affiliates fit into the general imperative of banking safety and soundness, he concludes that greater activity diversification may indeed contribute to greater institutional stability, and presents evidence in support of this view. The data complement his conceptual argumentation that the structure of economic incentives and disincentives driving the management of institutions combining commercial and investment banking tend to ensure effective insulation of securities activities from commercial banking, even in the absence of legal constraints. Given the latter, it is highly improbable that even rather serious underwriting or trading losses on the part of the securities affiliates of a bank holding company would impair the viability of the bank itself.

The 1984 Continental Illinois difficulties (clearly attributable to asset-related problems within the traditional definition of commercial banking) may have been seriously exacerbated by legal and regulatory impediments that effectively constrained management's search for returns to a relatively narrow set of activities, and thus limited its ability to diversify. On the liability side as well, the bank's funding alternatives were limited by state and federal (McFadden, Douglas) regulatory constraints, preventing the development of a broad and stable retail deposit base. Quite apart from management errors of judgment and control, had Continental Illinois enjoyed regulatory access to a substantially broader range of assets and liabilities, as well as related financial services, its stability profile might have been far more robust, and one of the least encouraging chapters of American financial history might never have been written. Thoughtful observers, therefore, ask whether the Continental Illinois case was not a signal to proceed with, rather than to halt, the process of financial deregulation.

In addition to questions relating to the potential impact of market interpenetration between commercial and investment banking on financial stability, there is also the nagging issue of potential conflicts of interest between the two types of activity housed in the same institution, as there is between both of these and fiduciary activities.

There are three potential conflict vectors: (1) Between fiduciary activities and commercial banking, (2) between fiduciary activities and investment banking, and (3) between investment banking and commercial banking. The first two have not presented a major problem in the United States. Trust and investment business has long been handled by a variety of financial services firms, including commercial and investment banks, that are engaged in many other lines of activity as well. Although there are indeed serious potential conflicts of interest related to efficiency and equity aspects of information access and dissemination, these have been contained quite effectively by a combination of institutional, behavioral, legal, and competitive constraints. Chinese walls exist, legal sanctions threaten, but ultimately competition and the discipline of the market limit the factual importance of conflicts of interest involving fiduciary activities. There are simply too many actual and potential competitors in the investment management business, and it is too easy to gauge comparative portfolio performance for management to deviate very far from serving the basic interests of their fiduciary clients. Moreover, the potential for conflict in this area may erode still further as information flows and the associated technologies continue to improve.

If potential conflicts can be effectively handled with respect to fiduciary business under the existing institutional framework, the addition of securities affiliates of bank holding companies should involve few incremental problems. Merrill Lynch and Shearson/Lehman American Express engage in both fiduciary and investment banking activities, whereas Bankers Trust and Morgan Guaranty cover both fiduciary and commercial banking activities. There is no reason that allowing the latter to engage in investment banking, or the former to engage in commercial banking, should result in conflicts involving fiduciary activities.

So the remaining question is whether there are serious potential conflicts of interest between investment and commercial banking activities undertaken by separately capitalized affiliates of the same institution. Again, one can point to the fact that commercial banks in the United States already engage in a broad range of investment banking business, with the notable exception of corporate securities—and even in corporate securities business outside the United States—without encountering significant conflicts of interest. Why the addition of domestic corporate securities underwriting and dealing should fundamentally alter this picture is not clear.

Anthony Saunders and Edward Kelly have explored this issue in considerable depth in Chapters 8 and 9 of this volume. Kelly traces the historical roots of the conflict of interest issue, and examines the institutional and legal safeguards that now exist to contain their exploitation. He concludes that these safeguards are more than adequate to cope with the deregulation of investment banking. Saunders assesses the economic and behavioral dimensions in terms of the structure of incentives and disincentives that underlie the exploitation of conflicts of interest. In his view, such exploitation is fundamentally inimical to the economic interests of the firm and its shareholders—the value of the enterprise as a going concern. The competitive nature of the markets for financial services provides sanctions against deviations from this standard that are both timely and painful. Moreover, institutional factors that influence the behavior of managers, such as the structure of bonus schemes, the use of profit centers, and the market for corporate control, tend to ensure that behavior which is at variance with fundamental corporate interests is not tolerated for long.

In an environment where performance information is readily available, consistent and profitable exploitation of conflicts of interest is thus impeded; (1) by market competition that aligns managerial behavior with the fundamental interests of the firm and its shareholders, and (2) by legal and institutional constraints that align the behavior of the firm with the fundamental interests of society.

INTERNATIONAL DIMENSIONS

Concepts of banking and finance that regard domestic financial systems in isolation have, over the years, become increasingly irrelevant as global economic integration and interdependence have progressed. The integration of world capital markets has at least two important implications for financial deregulation in the United States: (1) Its bearing on the global competitiveness of American financial institutions, and (2) its demonstration of the efficiency and stability characteristics of institutions operating in substantially unregulated offshore (Euro) capital markets—markets that permit the free interplay of competitive forces.

American commercial banks today are virtually alone among major international competitors in their inability to provide a full range of corporate financial services. Only in Japan, whose rather inefficient financial system was patterned after the American structure following World War II, is this also the case. Japan's stellar achievements in economic growth and competitiveness, it can be argued, have occurred despite—rather than because of—the structure of that country's financial system. If U.S. institutions are to compete successfully around the world, they must be able to offer a broad range of financial services in support of American clients as well as foreign-based corporations. An artificially segmented domestic market provides a poor foundation from which to project competitive performance in an industry where the United States should have a comparative advantage.

Also of relevance is the long-standing ability of American commercial bank affiliates to engage in corporate securities origination, underwriting, and dealing in domestic financial markets abroad, as well as in the offshore Eurobond market.

With respect to national financial markets overseas, foreign institutions are often restricted in their ability to compete with domestic institutions for corporate business. Indeed, the United States has made liberalization of international trade in services, including financial services, a priority matter for the next round of trade negotiations under the auspices of the General Agreement on Tariffs and Trade (GATT). Given this thrust, it is ironic that American banks remain restricted in the range of financial services they can offer at home, even as a number of foreign banks (those grandfathered under the International Banking Act of 1978) can in fact engage in investment and commercial banking in the United States itself. It seems evident that an open international competitive environment in financial services is consistent with financial deregulation at home.

Moreover, in Eurobond underwriting and dealing, U.S. commercial bank affiliates have shown no less stability over time than other market participants, nor have significant conflicts of interest surfaced. Richard Levich, in Chapter 10 of this volume, clearly demonstrates this. Indeed, American commercial banks have been among the innovators in Eurobond activities such as the development of floating-rate instruments (Bankers Trust), the creation of a pioneering Eurobond clearing system (Morgan Guaranty), and the application of interest-rate swaps to a broad array of international corporate client needs (Citibank). Levich's conclusions suggest that the beneficial effects of a commercial bank's presence in the Eurobond market, which has operated effectively in the absence of tight regulation and control, embodies a considerable degree of "transferability" to the U.S. domestic financial environment. Further, the potential effects on the domestic bond market and the Eurobond market of the elimination of U.S. withholding taxes on interest payable to foreign bondholders threatens to compromise additionally the competitive positioning of American commercial banks, by causing borrowers and investors to shift business into the domestic market, where commercial bank affiliates have been barred.

BALANCING COSTS AND BENEFITS: IMPLICATIONS FOR POLICY

Fundamentally, this book concerns one of the major issues affecting the design of an *appropriate* financial system to serve the United States well into the twenty-first century. Financial systems can be thought of as embodying a variety of specific functions. These include a viable payments mechanism, a safe network of repositories for savings and an effective means of channeling those savings into productive investments and meeting the fiscal needs of the public sector, and a consistent window on the foreign exchange and international financial markets. Each of these functions should be aimed at the objections of maximum efficiency, adaptability to changing circumstances, and stability. The specific institutions that emerge to carry out these functions are of secondary importance. Efficiency and adaptability require that competition among institutions be allowed maximum freedom within each of the functions that characterize the national financial system. Freedom of entry and exit, the right to succeed and to fail, must be safeguarded.

At the same time, it is clear that confidence in the system must be maintained as well. Collapse of financial structures in modern economies is, simply put, economically and politically unacceptable. Thus some form of deposit insurance and access to standby sources of liquidity are needed, which in turn permit far higher gearing than otherwise would be possible. This creates a "moral hazard" problem that has to be addressed through supervision, regulation, and control, as well as deposit insurance premiums explicitly linked to the risks involved. Possibly, significantly lower gearing ratios would have to be mandated for commercial banking as a matter of public policy.

So, carefully designed insurance, supervision, regulation, and control of the insitutions that perform critical financial functions in an economy is a fact of life, and will continue to be. The key is to design the regulatory systems in such a manner that their "opportunity cost" in terms of lost efficiency and dynamism is driven to a minimum. Greater stability and safety invariably involve such costs, yet systems of financial control can indeed be made cost-effective. In the case of the separation of commercial and investment banking, the absence of equality of competitive opportunity without clear-cut gains in financial stability suggests that cost-effectiveness of this continuing restriction remains substandard in the United States today.

If the empirical evidence on the characteristics of securities underwriting suggests that the risks are both limited and manageable, if activity diversification enhances the earnings stability of financial institutions, and if economic incentives and legal constraints provide effective insulation and safeguards against conflicts of interest, then the case for permitting bank affiliates to engage in the origination, underwriting, and dealing in corporate securities would appear to be very strong indeed. This is true even if the static and dynamic gains from more competitive financial institutions and markets were minimal; we have suggested they are not.

In any consideration of financial efficiency, institutional safety and soundness, and problems relating to potential conflicts of interest, it becomes clear that important policy tradeoffs exist.

First, we have seen that efforts to foster safety and soundness through separation, as Glass-Steagall has attempted to do, sacrifice the diversification (and hence stability) gains of bank involvement in corporate securities underwriting and dealing activities. Any stability benefits attributable to separation are thus partially or wholly offset by stability losses due to reduced diversification of earnings streams.

Second, we have also seen that financial regulation generates efficiency losses. At the level of the firm, regulation prevents management from optimally deploying the institution's capital and human resources, designing optimal financial and organizational structures, and developing optimal business strategies. At the level of society, regulation fosters misallocations of resources, stifles innovation, initiative and international competitiveness, and constrains the contribution of the financial system to economic growth.

Third, quite apart from safety and soundness concerns, regulation aimed at conflicts of interest may similarly cause inefficiencies. In financial services, perhaps more than in some other sectors, information plays a critical role. But the collection, organization, and dissemination of information by firms requires (often substantial) investments, on which a return must be earned. By creating institutional barriers to address the conflict of interest problem, regulation limits the expected return on investments in information, and thereby influences the nature, quantity, and quality of information that is assembled. Multiple units of the same firm (in the case of Chinese walls) or multiple corporate entities may invest in generating the same information. Or firms may underinvest in information because management knows it cannot be used throughout the enterprise. Either way, inefficiencies result.

One is led to the conclusion that repeal of Glass-Steagall should be seriously considered as a matter of public policy. The objective is to capture for society the efficiency gains from greater competition and market interpenetration between commercial and investment banking *without* at the same time compromising the safety and stability of the nation's financial system. What are the options?

We have assumed throughout this book that any deregulation would take the form of separately capitalized affiliates of bank holding companies, engaging in corporate securities underwriting and dealing—and investment banks operating separately capitalized commercial bank affiliates. This is a highly conservative assumption that seeks to minimize the risks inherent in repeal of Glass-Steagall. On the other hand, it does not maximize the potential efficiency gains inherent, for example, in the economies of scope or in the returns on investment in information.

Such a highly conservative arrangement, if aimed solely at safety and soundness of the banking system, would prohibit capital flows between the bank and the securities affiliate, but would permit information flows in both directions. If, on the other hand, such an arrangement were aimed *also* at creating impediments to conflicts of interest, it would additionally prohibit information flows in either direction. Both kinds of constraints involve sacrifices in terms of efficiency, costs, convenience, and marketing advantages (the latter more so than the former).

On the other hand, such an arrangement also retains the safety and anticonflict attributes of "insulation" of securities activities from commercial banking. From an efficiency point of view, it is clearly a second-best solution. But it may well be an appropriate solution in an area of public policy where the degree of risk-aversion is rather high. What is important here is that, even under such a conservative institutional assumption, the studies contained in this volume suggest that the potential benefits of repeal significantly outweigh the prospective costs.

There are, of course, a number of less conservative options available. One is simply to permit banks to do both traditional commercial banking business and securities business, as is now the case with trust and investment activities, and install any needed safeguards (perhaps including Chinese walls) within the organization itself. This may entail smaller efficiency losses and preserve economies of scope, eliminating one layer of bureaucracy and maintaining some (but not all) of the incentives to invest in the generation of information. But at the same time, it may make banks more vulnerable to a loss of confidence emanating from developments in the securities markets, because any potential for "insulation' of banking from securities activities is necessarily absent. The pros and cons of this form of deregulation depend largely on the assessed value of such insulation and of institutional impediments to conflicts of interest.

Another option is to use the pattern already set for U.S. commercial bank involvement in the Eurobond markets—an alternative that seems to work rather well despite the absence of U.S.-style securities regulation. Still another alternative is to consider the adoption of European-type universal banking, which could maximize economies of scale and of scope, but could ultimately raise problems of competition and concentration of economic power.

Precisely how the integration of commercial and investment banking ought to proceed, and the costs and benefits of each alternative approach, are certainly subjects for further research and policy discussion. The studies contained in this volume suggest that the gains from permitting equality of competitive opportunity in commercial and investment banking are indeed significant, and that the costs in terms of financial system stability are manageable. The nation may thus be getting short-changed by the existing, restrictive institutional arrangements, and policy change may well be overdue.

INDEX